WASSERSTROM

D0745035

THE SAMUEL AND ALTHEA STROUM

LECTURES IN JEWISH STUDIES

THE SAMUEL AND ALTHEA STROUM

The Yiddish Art Song, performed by Leon Lishner, basso,
and Lazar Weiner, piano (stereophonic record album)

The Holocaust in Historical Perspective
Yehuda Bauer

Zakhor: Jewish History and Jewish Memory
Yosef Hayim Yerushalmi

Jewish Mysticism and Jewish Ethics
Joseph Dan

The Invention of Hebrew Prose:
Modern Fiction and the Language of Realism
Robert Alter

Recent Archaeological Discoveries and Biblical Research
William G. Dever

Jewish Identity in the Modern World
Michael A. Meyer

I. L. Peretz and the Making of Modern Jewish Culture
Ruth R. Wisse

The Kiss of God: Spiritual and Mystical Death in Judaism
Michael Fishbane

LECTURES IN JEWISH STUDIES

THE JEWISH
LIFE CYCLE

Rites of Passage from
Biblical to Modern Times

IVAN G. MARCUS

UNIVERSITY OF WASHINGTON PRESS

Seattle and London

© 2004 by the University of Washington Press
Printed in the United States of America
Designed by Pamela Canell
12 11 10 09 08 07 06 05   5 4 3 2

All rights reserved. No part of this publication may be reproduced or
transmitted in any form or by any means, electronic or mechanical,
including photocopy, recording, or any information storage or retrieval
system, without permission in writing from the publisher.

University of Washington Press, PO Box 50096, Seattle, WA 98145
www.washington.edu/uwpress

Library of Congress Cataloging-in-Publication Data
Marcus, Ivan G.
The Jewish life cycle : rites of passage from biblical to
modern times / Ivan G. Marcus.
p. cm. (The Samuel and Althea Stroum lectures in Jewish studies)
Includes bibliographical references and index.
ISBN 0-295-98440-6 (cloth : alk. paper)
ISBN 0-295-98441-4 (pbk. : alk. paper)
1. Judaism—Customs and practices.   2. Life-cycle,
Human—Religious aspects—Judaism. I.   Title. II. Series.
BM700.M27 2004   296.4'4—dc22   2004053599

The paper used in this publication is acid-free and recycled from
20 percent post-consumer and at least 50 percent pre-consumer waste.
It meets the minimum requirements of American National Standard
for Information Sciences—Permanence of Paper for Printed
Library Materials, ANSI Z39.48-1984.♾ ♻

THE SAMUEL AND ALTHEA STROUM

LECTURES IN JEWISH STUDIES

Samuel Stroum, businessman, community leader, and philanthropist, by a major gift to the Jewish Federation of Greater Seattle, established the Samuel and Althea Stroum Philanthropic Fund.

In recognition of Mr. and Mrs. Stroum's deep interest in Jewish history and culture, the Board of Directors of the Jewish Federation of Greater Seattle, in cooperation with the Jewish Studies Program of the Henry M. Jackson School of International Studies at the University of Washington, established an annual lectureship at the University of Washington known as the Samuel and Althea Stroum Lectureship in Jewish Studies. This lectureship makes it possible to bring to the area outstanding scholars and interpreters of Jewish thought, thus promoting a deeper understanding of Jewish history, religion, and culture. Such understanding can lead to an enhanced appreciation of the Jewish contributions to the historical and cultural traditions that have shaped the American nation.

The terms of the gift also provide for the publication from time to time of the lectures or other appropriate materials resulting from or related to the lectures.

Contents

Preface and Acknowledgments

At the invitation of the University of Washington, I delivered the Samuel and Althea Stroum Lecture in April and May 1998. I want to thank Robert Stacey for the invitation, and my host, Naomi Sokoloff, and her colleagues for ten enjoyable and memorable days in Seattle, during which it uncharacteristically never rained.

Before going to Seattle, I spent several months researching and writing parts of this book in anticipation of the three public lectures. Several weeks before the scheduled trip, I realized that I did not want to read draft chapters from a book. And so, I made a set of outlines and quotations, as well as hundreds of slides, just for the lectures. I returned to the book from time to time, over the past four years, and completed it thanks to grants from the National Endowment for the Humanities, the John Simon Guggenheim Memorial Foundation, and a triennial leave from Yale University for which I am extremely grateful.

I have tried to keep the appearance of this book as accessible to general readers as possible, while not stinting in the notes and bibliography to show scholars the basis for my findings. For this reason, I ask my colleagues in Judaica to overlook the fact that I have avoided using diacritical marks in transliterating Hebrew and related languages. Except for most proper names, letters alef in the middle of a word and 'ayin, wherever it appears in a word, are represented by an apostrophe ('); heh and het are both *h;* samekh and sin, as *s;* tav and tet, by *t;* zayin and zadeh as *z;* kaf is *k* and quf is *q,* unless it is in an English spelling, such as Kaddish, or in a common spelling of a name, like Rabbi Akiva. Readers who know Hebrew will know the differences; I hope that those who do not will not mind the omission.

Hebrew and other foreign words that have become part of English are spelled in their English forms. Thus, a commandment is translated *mizvah,* but the English term "bar mitzvah" is spelled *tz,* not *z. The American Heritage Dictionary of the English Language* (4th ed.) has been my guide, and I have tried to be consistent, but there will be a few exceptions from time to time. Foreign terms are italicized the first time and romanized thereafter.

Among other rules that I have tried to follow: words I have added to quotations are in square brackets, but I supply the identification of biblical verses and translations of foreign terms in the text in parentheses. I have retained square brackets or parentheses as they appeared in the original quoted material. All references in the endnotes are found in short form throughout the book, even the first time, but they are all included in the comprehensive Bibliography, which is divided into Primary and Secondary Sources. The few abbreviations to rabbinic texts that I have used also appear there in their proper alphabetical location. For example, B. for Babylonian Talmud is in the Bibliography under Primary Sources, under B.

Among those colleagues and friends who have been especially helpful, I want to thank Elisheva Baumgarten, Robert Bonfil, Daniel Boyarin, Shaye J. D. Cohen, Yaakov Deutsch, Steven Fraade, Joseph Gutmann, Samuel Heilman, Elliott Horowitz, Gershon Hundert, Paula Hyman, Moshe Idel, Willis Johnson, David Kogen, David Kraemer, Vivian Mann, Michael Meyer, Carol Matzkin Orsborn, Julie Parker, Joel Rascoff, Benjamin Ravid, David Roskies, Shalom Sabar, Jonathan Sarna, Raymond P. Scheindlin, Menachem Schmelzer, Stuart Schoenfeld, Seth Schwartz, Mel Scult, Ephraim Shoham-Steiner, Don C. Skemer, Sol Steinmetz, Israel Ta-Shema, Roni Weinstein, and Chava Weissler.

It is also a pleasure to thank the staff of the Library of the Jewish Theological Seminary of America, its previous librarians, Dr. Menachem Schmelzer and Dr. Mayer Rabinowitz, and Sharon Liberman Mintz, Rabbi Jerry Schwarzbaum, Naomi Steinberger, and David Wachtel, all of whom make the collection accessible to a visiting scholar. My thanks as well to the helpful staffs of the Beinecke Rare Book and Manuscript Library and the Sterling Memorial Library of Yale University.

My appreciation to Naomi Pascal, Marilyn Trueblood, and Xavier Callahan of the University of Washington Press, for all of their help and encouragement in seeing this book through to publication.

Finally, it is a great joy to dedicate this book to my children and grandchildren: Yuval and Elizabeth Marcus, and grandchildren, Talia Phoebe, Nathaniel Ayal, and Caleb Samuel; Magen Marcus; Sasson and Beverly Marcus; and Ehud and Erica Marcus.

THE JEWISH
LIFE CYCLE

Introduction

This book is a comprehensive guide to Jewish rites of passage that mark off special days of the individual's life. Here I explore the many collective meanings that Jews assigned to these events throughout history. It is written for the general reader and for the scholar. In scope and design, it is meant to supersede the single best book written in English on the Jewish life cycle, Hayyim Schauss's *The Lifetime of a Jew* (1950). Though grounded in the entire history of all significant Jewish life cycle customs, this book also draws on American and Israeli life today, instead of the world of Eastern Europe in which Schauss grew up. It combines historical and anthropological perspectives and focuses less on modern Sefardic and Mediterranean examples than those parts of Harvey Goldberg's *Jewish Passages: Cycles of the Jewish Life* that treat the Jewish life cycle. The bibliography includes a broad range of sources and is meant to be a reference guide for those who want to study this important part of Jewish experience or to explore the design of new rituals today.

Rites of passage mark the ways Jews grew up over the years. I mean this in two senses. The rituals refer to how individual Jews celebrate the different stages of their own lives as they grow to maturity and reach old age and death. In another way, as members of a complex and dynamic religious culture, the Jews have developed and inno-vated a variety of celebrations that mark a collective historical jour-ney from biblical origins to today.

Throughout the course of ancient, medieval, and modern times, Jews lived as single families, in small or large communities, in which they were closely involved on a daily basis with members of other strong cultures that vastly outnumbered them. And yet, of all the communities living in the ancient Near East and the Greco-Roman world, Jews are the only recognizable surviving ancient religious ethnic culture. Today, there are no Sumerians, Akkadians, Egyptians, Canaanites, Greeks, or Romans who worship ancient gods. But Jews of all kinds exist and practice some form of biblical religion and ancient Judaism even though they live in Seattle and Tokyo, Bombay and Jerusalem, New York, Berlin, and Kiev.

The study of life cycle rites sheds light on the dynamic processes through which Judaism and Jews persisted as communities of a rec-ognizable religious culture. They did this in two stages. Jews first negotiated with majority cultures that were pagan or Christian, Mus-lim or secular, adapted some customs, and rejected others. Future gen-erations then regarded the product of those cultural interactions as part of Jewish tradition that they transmitted to the next generation. Then the twofold process of negotiation and transmission began again.[1]

I call this dynamic process "inward acculturation."[2] By selectively introducing into their own Jewish patterns of living many customs and practices that were widespread all around them, Jews remained Jews and usually did not think of themselves as also being Greeks, Christians, or Muslims.

Inward acculturation is what the Talmud meant when it interpreted the verse in Genesis about two of Noah's sons, "May God enlarge Japheth, and let him dwell in the tents of Shem" (Gen. 9:27), to mean, "let the chief beauty (*yafyut*) of Japheth [the culture of the gentiles] be in the tents of Shem [the Jews]."[3] Take it in, but make it part of

Judaism. From rites of birth through rituals of death and memory, Jews did precisely this in countless ways. Even if Jews did not avoid behavior that was indistinguishable from that of non-Jews, they continued to think of such behavior as Jewish, even when rabbis disapproved. If they succeeded in crossing over into another culture, they usually left their Judaism behind.

The main point of "inward acculturation" is to contrast it to the more familiar case of modern acculturation or assimilation, mainly in secular societies, or "outward acculturation." Jews traded in much of their traditional culture and appropriated an identity based primarily on modern national cultures, sometimes modified by the idea of being Jewish in private: Germans of the Mosaic persuasion, as the parade case has it.

Inward acculturation could take different forms of mapping relationships between Jewish and majority cultures in ancient as well as modern times:

Common ways of doing things. Sometimes, Jews and non-Jews lived in the same society and just did things the same way. This was the case for most of the people most of the time and may be referred to as Jews and non-Jews participating in common vernacular cultural traditions. Jews and Christians ate with spoons and knives in medieval Europe because nothing else was available; the table fork had not yet been invented.[4]

Adaptation by imitation and reinterpretation. It is impossible to work out in detail all customs in relation to their pagan, Christian, Muslim, or contemporary contexts. In some cases, there is direct evidence; in most, not. But by presenting a significant sample of customs and contexts, it becomes overwhelmingly clear that Jews were always open to reinterpreting earlier Jewish tradition and to adding to it by adapting customs from their environment that also were in flux.

Adaptation by polemic. Sometimes, these adaptations took the form of internalizing the company's elite symbolic vocabularies that Jews transformed into a Jewish idiom that challenged the truth claims of the majority culture. Not every adapted similarity was a polemic. On the other hand, some cases reveal a complex argument, expressed in gestures, against the majority's symbols and truth claims.[5]

Resisting by avoiding the other. Withdrawal can leave a negative imprint when Jews go out of their way to avoid the presence of members or symbols of another culture in various circumstances. This is relatively rare in Jewish history.

In its various forms, inward acculturation sometimes failed, as when Jews converted to the dominant culture, in effect adopting the other culture as their own, at least in theory. The history of conversion (from) and proselytism (into) Judaism has not been written, though there is a great deal of material from ancient times through modernity.

Another important exception, especially in antiquity, involves the notion of "hybridity." This refers to when Jews thought of themselves as belonging to two cultures. Jewish hybridity characterizes much of ancient Jewish history, such as the Israelite cultures of Judah and Israel, and those Hellenized Jews who refused to give up their Jewish identity and who opted for a combined Hellenized and Jewish way of life. Hybridity also characterized some Jews who lived under direct Roman administrative rule in Judea from the destruction of Jerusalem in 70 C.E. to the middle of the fourth Christian century.[6]

In contrast, medieval Jewish communities in Muslim and Christian lands down to early modern times do not betray anything of the kind, except for a tiny elite in Muslim society, the courtier class, who were culturally hybrid. The vast majority of Jews who lived in Muslim and Christian lands thought of themselves as Jews and belonged to Jewish communities. Even then, however, it was possible for some individuals to go hybrid on the edge of two cultures. In medieval Europe, for example, a Jew or a Christian who acted like both was thought to be insane.[7]

In early modern Europe, thousands of forced converts (*conversos,* or New Christians) in Aragon and Castile lived alongside Jewish communities from 1391 until the expulsion of 1492, and for hundreds of years pockets of so-called Marranos existed in European and New

World Jewish communities as examples of hybrid Jewish-Christian identity. Apart from these, there were a few Jewish individuals who were free thinkers and lived at the margins of Jewish and Christian society. Otherwise, Jewish communities that remained in Christian Europe, mainly in the German Empire and the Italian states, in the vast Ottoman Empire, and in North Africa, were strongly Jewish in structure and content.

And, of course, even in modern times, not only in eastern Europe but also in parts of western Europe and in the Americas, Jews were members of legal corporations much of the time before the option of individual citizenship presented itself along with a neutral or semi-secular space in which religious membership was not a disability. At that point, Jewish individuals could opt for membership in a voluntary community, be culturally hybrid, or assimilate into the culture of the majority.

Regardless of the era, the process of cultural innovation was so successful that Jews eventually forgot the foreign origins of various practices. Even those Jews who claim to be the most traditional and conservative and assume that they are following biblical or rabbinic or ancestral precedents in fact often observe rites that at one time were innovations. For example, among the many customs and rites that are not mentioned in either the Hebrew Bible or Talmud are the *ba'al brit,* or godfather, sometimes called the *sandeq,* as well as the invocation of the prophet Elijah and his chair at a ritual circumcision; cutting the hair for the first time of a three-year-old boy and then immediately teaching him Hebrew from an alphabet chart smeared with honey; bar mitzvah as a ceremony for boys age thirteen years and a day, as well as bat/bas mitzvah for girls, either at age twelve or thirteen and a day; the bride and groom fasting before the wedding, the bride wearing a white dress, and her circling the groom three or seven times; an officiating rabbi who recites blessings on two cups of wine, a four-posted wedding canopy, the betrothal ring, the text of the wedding contract, or *ketubbah,* and the groom's breaking a glass at the end of the wedding in memory of the destruction of

Jerusalem; reciting mourner's Kaddish, saying Yizkor memorial prayers four times a year, and lighting candles and marking in other ways the anniversary of the death of one's parents annually in the rite called Yahrzeit.

Each of these and many other life cycle practices are now common and traditional, but each one was an innovation at some point and many represent an adaptation into Judaism of non-Jewish practices. Even customs that are found in the Bible or Talmud,[8] the canon of Jewish rabbinic high culture, were themselves once adaptations of still earlier ancient Near Eastern or Greco-Roman practices. Later generations of Jews considered them to be Jewish because they got into the Hebrew Bible or Talmud or became widespread custom at least in a particular region. Once a life cycle rite appeared, it did not remain static but continued to develop and acquire new meanings and variations of gesture or performance that, in turn, then also became part of the growing tradition.

The extraordinary contribution of non-Jewish cultures to the innovation and development of Jewish life cycle events yields a paradoxical truth about the history of Jewish culture in general. Judaism often survived and flourished, not despite the influence of the great cultures of the ancient Near East, Greece, Rome, Christian and Muslim powers, or even modern western thought and political policies, but because of it.[9] With few exceptions, those cultures stimulated Jews to adapt aspects of the majority culture to existing institutions and patterns in Judaism. In large measure, the secret of Jewish creative persistence lies in mechanisms of cultural adaptation. One area of Jewish experience that illustrates in some detail how this happened is the history of Jewish rites in the life cycle.

Although the dynamic process of selecting some customs, adapting others, while rejecting still others, is not always clear, two key factors held true in almost all pre-modern Jewish societies. In combination, they produced ideal conditions for the Jewish cultural vitality that we see reflected in the history of life cycle rites. On the one hand, the leaders and thinkers of a non-Jewish culture usually wanted the Jews to be Jewish for reasons of their own. Persians, Greeks, Romans (before 70 C.E.), Christians, Muslims, and modern liberal states all offered a legitimate way for Jews as Jews to be a corporation of subjects or citizens within a larger non-Jewish society. It was rare for a persecution such as the physical elimination of Egyptian Jewry in the second century C.E., the defeats by Rome in 70 and 135 C.E., or the genocidal policies of the Nazi regime in the twentieth. Had persecution been the norm, Jews simply would not have survived. Complementing the non-Jewish positive role assigned to the Jews was the Jew's own positive religious self-image. Most Jews thought of their religious culture as embodying the only true covenant of a people with God or as a culture supported by a true ideology about history and the world.

When both positive factors converged, Jews successfully introduced elements of the majority culture into Judaism and still remained fiercely Jewish. If the combination of two positive factors broke down, either because of repressive measures taken by the majority power or on account of Jews' self-doubt, the result was a breakdown of Jewish solidarity that I have called "outward acculturation." This is primarily a modern phenomenon, when a Jew could form a new competing individual identity either in hybrid tension with or at the expense of the Jewish one, but it was also true of significant periods in ancient Jewish history as well.

In modern western countries, in particular, some Jews sought to merge their Jewish identity into a larger national one and lost a coherent sense of a collective and individual Jewish self. Sometimes, the process of outward acculturation resulted in the complete assimilation and disappearance of any trace of an individual's Jewish past. Before modern times, some Jews "became Greeks" or converted either to Christianity or to Islam and assimilated into the majority culture. Otherwise, they remained Jews and adapted aspects of majority culture for their own.

Jewish rites not only emerge and develop over time, but they also are diverse at any one point in time. Just as there is no single standard Jewish naming ceremony for a newborn boy or girl, or a wedding or funeral from earliest times to today, at any time along the way different Jewish communities throughout the world observe life cycle events in their own way. Although they share some features, each celebration is unique.

The underlying dynamic of constant innovation, development, and diversity means that Jewish communities continuously renew their celebration of life and death both as part of a specific historical community and, at the same time, as an extension of an ancient culture. Experimentation did not begin only in modern times, let alone in the twentieth century. Rather, the new rituals that continue to be formulated and instituted for women's or gays' experiences, for example, are just another extension of the age-old process of Jewish ritual innovation and inventiveness. The very process of constant ritual innovation is itself a characteristic feature of Jewish traditional practice, although various periods and places set different limits to what would change and what would not. The same is true today, even if the contexts are different. Ironically, the view held by some Orthodox circles today that innovation is forbidden is itself an innovation![10]

RITUALS AS PERFORMATIVE MIDRASH

Why study rituals? Although there is a bias in the West to privilege written words or texts that we are taught to read silently, without moving our lips, gestures are the stuff of religious celebration, and they contain and express multiple layers of meaning. Rituals include words to be read out loud, chanted, sung, and otherwise enacted or performed by moving the body. In rituals, gestures and words are inseparably joined as expressions of the inner being.[11]

Rituals embody the values of a culture. Rabbinic Jewish culture produced extensive written commentaries on sacred texts, especially the Hebrew Bible. The ancient rabbis called these elaborations of Scripture *midrash,* from the Hebrew root D-R-Sh, meaning to delve into, probe, and explore. They believed that Scripture is the infinite word of God and that the interpreter is obligated to tease out from Scripture the implicit and unstated meanings encoded in it. God's will consists of those meanings, as well as the obvious ones.

Rituals in Judaism are performative midrash. Like midrash delivered in a sermon or a study session, the rituals that develop around daily life, the Sabbath and festivals, the acts of waking up and going to sleep, and a host of other everyday activities, dramatize the beliefs and values that are attributed to the sacred texts of the Hebrew Bible, Talmuds, and prayer book. In addition, early texts are invoked as an authoritative basis for emulation and elaboration. Often as not, custom rules and learned men end up rationalizing the existing practices by searching for a peg in Scripture or Talmudic texts on which to hang that which has developed outside the academy.

THE "AGES OF MAN" AND THE STAGES OF LIFE

Rites of passage presuppose that a culture constructs a lifetime into a span of years that can be divided into different periods, each constituting a stage that is marked off from previous ones by a passage that must be crossed. We find a guide to a typical life in Psalm 90:10: "The span of our life is seventy years, or, given the strength, eighty years," this despite the age of Moses of a hundred and twenty and the Jewish custom of wishing each other "'ad me'ah ve-'esrim" (may you live to a hundred and twenty), based on Moses' age when he died (Deut. 34:7). Already we have a contradiction! There are many more to come.

How should a lifetime, whatever its length, be divided into meaningful occasions and stages?[12] In the biblical book of Ecclesiastes (Qohelet), composed in the second century B.C.E., the seasons of a life are defined as polar categories of joy or sadness:

A time for being born [literally, for giving birth][13] and a time
    for dying (3:2) . . .
A time for weeping and a time for laughing (3:4) . . .

A time for embracing and a time for shunning embraces (3:5b) . . .
A time for ripping and a time for sewing (3:7).

These lines already hint at stages in the life cycle—birth and death, times of joy and of mourning.

Formulations like those in Ecclesiastes became landmark statements in Judaism because the book is part of the Hebrew Bible and Jewish liturgy. Legal contexts can also generate life stages such as infancy, childhood, adulthood, and old age. For example, in biblical society, adults were called to serve in the army or contribute to the building of the Tabernacle from age twenty. The census to determine which male Israelites were available to bear arms also counted only men age twenty and older.[14] The Book of Exodus stipulates that the requirement to contribute to the building of the Tabernacle falls on each person age twenty, who was to contribute a half shekel (Exod. 30:11–16).[15] Twenty also continued in rabbinic times to be the minimal age for buying and selling real estate, even though thirteen years and a day for boys and twelve years and a day for girls was introduced as the age of majority for religious obligation.

At the end of the Book of Leviticus, we find a provision for Israelites to make offerings to support the Tabernacle, the equivalent of a synagogue's building fund today. In this passage, a person can vow—we would say pledge—to contribute metaphorically his weight or social value in silver. The text stipulates different amounts, according to a person's age and gender. Some of these ages persist into postbiblical Judaism as occasions that generated rites of passage.

When anyone explicitly vows to the Lord the equivalent for a human being, the following scale shall apply: if it is a male from twenty to sixty years of age, the equivalent is fifty shekels of silver by the sanctuary weight; if it is a female, the equivalent is thirty shekels. If the age is from five years to twenty years, the equivalent is twenty shekels for a male and ten shekels for a female. If the age is from one month to five years, the equivalent for a male is five shekels of silver, and the equivalent for a female is three shekels of silver. If the age is sixty years or over, the equivalent is fifteen shekels in the case of a male and ten shekels for a female (Lev. 27:2–7).

Apart from defining adulthood from the ages of twenty to sixty years, childhood here has two stages. The first is from thirty days to five years, and the second is from five to twenty years. Note that age thirteen does not appear at all. Moreover, the group we would today call "senior citizens" received a discount and contributed less from age sixty and over than those who were age twenty to sixty. Was this a progressive tax, imposing the most on those who could most afford to pay? Or, does this system reflect some assessment of the social or cash value of different segments of the population? While biblical criminal law disagrees with other codes of ancient Mesopotamian laws that gave a monetary value to a human life, and instead posited the infinite value of a person, created in the image of God, certain circumstances in everyday life required an assessment of different groups according to a monetary scheme.

Although rabbinic Judaism treats this life as a prelude to a future life to come, a time in the future often referred to as the "days of the Messiah," rabbinic sources, even more than the Hebrew Bible, teach about the life cycle from birth to death. Some four hundred years after the Book of Ecclesiastes, the *Tosefta,* from third-century Palestine, offers more specifics about these milestones:

> R. Lazar b. R. Zadoq said: This is what the voluntary associations (havurot) in Jerusalem used to do. Some went to the house of a feast; others to the house of a mourner; some to the feast of the betrothed; others, to the feast of the married; some to the seven-day [feast after] a son [is born]; others to collect the bones [of the dead].[16]

Contexts vary in which ages are mentioned. For example, the Mishnah, the first rabbinic document from early third-century Palestine, refers to different ages for bloodletting and says when one is young one may do it every thirty days; when one is in middle age, which Rashi of Troyes (d. 1105) defines as age forty, one should do it less frequently; and when one is at a more advanced age, which Rashi says means sixty, even less frequently.[17]

Or the Babylonian Talmud (ca. 200–650 C.E.) treats ages and maturity in yet other legal contexts:

> Rava said: There are three grades in a boy [under the age of thirteen]. [If being given a stone] he throws it away and given a nut he keeps it, he can take possession [of property] for himself but not for others. A [fatherless] girl of the same age can be betrothed so effectively as not to be released [on coming of age] without definitely repudiating the betrothal. "Peutot" [age six to eight or nine] can buy and sell movables with legal effect and a girl of the corresponding age [whose father dies] can be divorced from a betrothal contracted by her father. When they reach the age at which vows are tested [twelve for a boy, eleven for a girl], their vows and their sanctifications are effective and a girl of corresponding age performs halizah [if the brother of her betrothed dies without children]. The landed [property] of his [deceased] father, however, he cannot sell till he is twenty.[18]

And in *Masekhet Semahot* (Mourning), a collection of laws about burial and mourning from early medieval Palestine, the ages of man are stipulated in connection with funeral arrangements for (1) "a one-day-old infant"; (2) "an infant who died before he was thirty days old"; (3) "an infant of thirty days to twelve months"; (4) "an infant of twelve months to three years"; (5) a "three-year-old" or "four-year-old"; (6) a "six-year-old" or a "seven-year-old"; (7) "a child who knew how to manage his affairs"; (8) "from the age of twenty to thirty, the deceased is carried out as a bridegroom"; (9) "from the age of thirty to forty, he is carried out as a brother"; (10) "from the age of forty to fifty he is carried out as a father"; (11) "at the age of sixty, this is the death of which Scripture speaks, for it is said: 'You will come to the grave in ripe old age, as shocks of grain are taken away in their season'" (Job 5:26); (12) "at the age of seventy, this is the death of divine love, for it is said: 'The span of our life is seventy years'" (Ps. 90:10); (13) "at the age of eighty, this is the age of 'strength,' for it is said: 'Or, given the strength, eighty years'" (Ps. 90:10).[19]

More expansive than these legal texts is the midrash on Ecclesiastes. The exegetical problem of the word *hevel* (vanity) appearing seven times triggers a passage about the seven ages of man:

> Rabbi Samuel ben Isaac taught in the name of Rabbi Samuel ben Eleazar: The seven times the word vanity is mentioned in Ecclesiastes correspond to the seven worlds that a man beholds: [1] At age one, he is like a king, seated in a litter while all hug and kiss him; [2] at two and three, he is like a pig, sticking his hands in the gutters; [3] at ten he skips like a kid; [4] at twenty, he is like a neighing horse, adorning himself and seeking a wife; [5] having married, he is like an ass [that is, a beast of burden]; [6] when he has children he becomes brazen like a dog, in order to bring in bread and food; [7] he becomes aged, he is like a monkey. That is true of ordinary people, but among Torah scholars it is written, "King David was now old" (1 Kings 1:1) [meaning], even though he was old, he was [like] a king.[20]

By far the most popular ages-of-man scheme in rabbinic literature is the addition to the fifth chapter of the non-legal section of the Mishnah that serves as a summary of rabbinic values. Called "The Fathers" (*avot*), it is sometimes referred to as the "Ethics of the Fathers," and it is included in most prayer books. Consider the fourteen ages of man in Mishnah Avot 5:23:

> He used to say:
> At five years of age the study of Scripture;
> At ten, the study of Mishnah;
> At thirteen, subject to the commandments;

> At fifteen, the study of Talmud;
> At eighteen, marriage;
> At twenty, pursuit [of a livelihood];
> At thirty, the peak of strength;
> At forty, wisdom;
> At fifty, able to give counsel;
> At sixty, old age creeping on;
> At seventy, fullness of years;
> At eighty, the age of "strength";
> At ninety, body bent;
> At one hundred, as good as dead and gone
>   completely out of the world.[21]

The process of indicating different stages of a lifetime continued in the Middle Ages, as in this poem by the Spanish-Jewish poet Rabbi Abraham Ibn Ezra (twelfth century). After addressing ages five, ten, twenty, thirty, and forty, he deals with advancing age:

> His days of waste at fifty do encroach;
> He mourns for mourning does indeed approach;
> The splendour of this world's a mere reproach;
> He shan't be long alive.
> What is the fate of one who is three-score?
> And now his deeds to vanish evermore?
> His limbs are all too feeble and too sore
> To help him in his battle to survive.
> If three-score and ten he does attain,
> To listen to his speech will be a strain;
> The patience of his friends he'll surely drain;
> A burden he can't bear although he strive.
> At four-score his sons must bear the yoke.
> He has no eyes, no mind he can invoke.
> To all about he is a sorry joke;
> Of sustenance he's painfully deprived.[22]

Compare to the Jewish versions Shakespeare's "ages of man" speech in *As You Like It,* which begins, "All the world's a stage, and all the men and women merely players," in which he refers to "his acts being seven ages":

> At first the infant, mewling and puking in the nurse's arms. Then the whining schoolboy, with his satchel and shining morning face, creeping like snail unwillingly to school. And then the lover, sighing like furnace, with a woeful ballad made to his mistress' eyebrow. Then a soldier, full of strange oaths, and bearded like the pard, jealous in honor, sudden, and quick in quarrel, seeking the bubble reputation even in the cannon's mouth. And then the justice, in fair round belly with good capon lin'd, with eyes severe and beard of formal cut, full of wise saws and modern instances; And so he plays his part. The sixth age shifts into the lean and slipper'd pantaloon, with spectacles on nose and pouch on side, His youthful hose, well sav'd, a world too wide for his shrunk shank, and his big manly voice, turning again toward childish treble, pipes and whistles in his sound. Last scene of all, that ends this strange eventful history, is second childishness, and mere oblivion, sans teeth, sans eyes, sans taste, sans every thing.[23]

Unlike Shakespeare's seven acts, the Jewish texts focus on the domestic life, the infant, child, young suitor, the burdened and hard-working husband and father. There is no place in most Jewish ages-of-man lists for a soldier, although the great Jewish poet and rabbi Samuel Ha-Nagid led Muslim armies into battle in Granada in the eleventh century. Nor do Jewish lists feature a justice playing a political role in the larger society, although some Jews did serve as courtiers, as in Muslim and Christian Spain and in early modern Europe. These were unusual situations and even provoked opposition from other Jews.[24] Perhaps it is not an accident, then, that the midrash on Ecclesiastes compares the one-year-old child to a "king" who always gets his way. A Jewish adult, on the other hand, is like an "ass" because he is burdened with heavy family responsibilities. It is the family, not the public arena, that is the setting of the typical Jewish adult.

The text from Mishnah Avot combines the life of the advanced student with domestic living. This reflects the rabbinic class's ideal of a progression through different ages from elementary to more advanced studies. For the first time, the age of thirteen makes an appearance as a sign of maturity, instead of the biblical age of twenty. It is followed by the age for advanced study at fifteen and climaxes at age eighteen as the ideal age for male marriage.

Other rabbinic teachings are not so specific about which age is meant when a particular stage is reached. For example, the Babylonian Talmud says about a son's growth: "A father is responsible to circumcise him, to redeem him [if he is a firstborn], to teach him Torah, to teach him a craft, and to get him married. Some say: And to teach him how to swim."[25] The first two obligations are biblically prescribed events, at age eight and thirty days, respectively, but the ages when the other stages should take place are not clear.[26] There is much room for inventiveness and multiple interpretations. From the variety of biblical and rabbinic texts already examined, it is clear that many different views exist about how a lifetime should be divided into stages.

THE THREE PARTS OF RITES OF PASSAGE

The need for culturally constructed transitions through significant points of change in the life cycle was recognized in 1909 when Arnold van Gennep proposed a structure for rites of passage, a term he coined for the rituals one enacts upon reaching a new stage of life. In his pioneering investigation, van Gennep thought of these occasions as cultural, rather than biological, changes. The process that we moderns sometimes assume follows universal scientific rules of physiology and psychology, van Gennep argued, actually reflects a culture's interpretation of the very idea of a child and of an adult.[27]

Today, we would say that each culture interprets the markers of different stages of life and uses gestures, including words, foods, dress, and interruptions of routines, in order to represent these ideas dramatically and thereby enable the individual going through the particular passage or transition to experience with his or her family and community this change in all of their lives. Among the changes in the life cycle that van Gennep said are historically shaped in a particular culture are rites of birth, weaning, initiation into adulthood—either manhood or womanhood—apprenticeship into study or work, marriage, birthing, parenting, becoming an elder, and, finally, death and remembering a life after it is no longer here and now.

Each rite of passage, van Gennep argued, has a three-part structure. As the rite begins, there is a stage of "separation," in which the individual is removed or taken away from the group or identity in which he or she has been living up to this point. The person then is taken through some type of "transition" from the earlier stage of life to a new stage. This is sometimes called the "liminal" stage, from the Latin *limen,* meaning a boundary. Finally, the individual goes through the third stage of "incorporation" during which he or she is made part and parcel of the new stage of life. The individual, then, goes from something old, through something in-between, and into something new. His schema explains how at each stage of development a person stops being what he or she was, travels along a path of change, and then adjusts to living in a new pattern of living.

In addition to exhibiting the three-part structure of all rites of passage, Jewish life cycle rituals share a special awareness of being part of remembered Jewish past experience from Sinai to the present. Jews share the memory of a common past and, within traditional circles, share a common present and anticipate a common future. Regardless of their geographical and cultural circumstances, traditional Jews regard the Hebrew Bible, or Tanakh, as containing their sacred writings that describe Jewish origins in remote antiquity as a covenanted community that remembered the Israelites' Exodus from Egypt as its collective birthing event.[28] Similarly, all Jews of tradition mark each day, week, and year with synagogue or home rituals of some kind that contain required prayers, gestures, religious customs, and practices. And they look to and pray for a messianic future that will, in one way or another, bring about an era of world peace and Jewish unity and restoration to wholeness.

RE-RITING JUDAISM YESTERDAY AND TODAY

For centuries, Jewish and Christian authors summarized Judaism by describing the Jewish life cycle. Jews wrote legal codes and collections of customs that usually included festival as well as life cycle celebrations. Some of the custom books were compiled as early as the mid-twelfth century in northern Europe. Among them are versions of the liturgical compendium *Mahzor Vitry,* based on Babylonian traditions but compiled in northern France (twelfth century), and *Sefer ha-Roqeah* (Book of the Perfumer) by Rabbi Eleazar ben Judah of Worms (d. around 1230). A sub-genre of these are the decisions and customs of famous rabbis written by their students, such as *Sefer ha-Tashbez,* compiled by a student of Rabbi Meir ben Barukh of Rothenburg (d. 1293), the leading rabbinic figure in the German Empire in the second half of the thirteenth century. Readers learn not only Rabbi Meir's decisions about Jewish law, but also how he behaved. An even more influential example of this genre is *Minhagei Maharil,* a book of practices of Rabbi Jacob ben Moses Ha-Levi Molin, known by the acronym Maharil (d. 1427), also from Germany.

In addition to these and other rabbinic anthologies, Jews also produced a series of illustrated custom books (*sifrei minhagim*). One with woodcuts from the holiday and life cycles was Simon Levi Ginzburg's Yiddish *Minhagim* (Venice, 1593). An even older one was recently discovered. It is a Yiddish manuscript, from the late fifteenth century, that also contains illustrations of the life cycle.[29] Printed ones appeared with woodcuts that were used over and over again in Amsterdam and elsewhere.[30]

Christians also compiled such books, particularly in early modern Germany from the sixteenth through the eighteenth centuries. Many were illustrated with etchings and engravings of scenes of Jewish life. Some of the authors were converts from Judaism who sought to ridicule or belittle their former co-religionists and urge them to convert to Christianity.[31] Christian scholars of Judaism, known as Christian Hebraists, compiled others. They too were interested for conversionist reasons to learn about and propagate their knowledge of Judaism.[32] Ironically, many Jewish publications today reproduce these illustrations without realizing that their source was intended not for Jewish edification but for Jewish conversion to Christianity.

Although there are exceptions, many traditional Jewish life cycle compilations often start with the laws of betrothal and marriage, followed by childbirth and circumcision of male offspring, and only then proceed to the customs of death, of the parents. Many Christian representations of Jewish customs in early modern times begin with the birth of a Jewish baby and then follow that life through circumcision, redemption of the firstborn, marriage, and finally death.

These different sequences suggest culturally determined ways of thinking about a religious lifetime. The Jewish sequence is determined by the first two commandments in the Torah. The first is to be fruitful and multiply, addressed to young adults who marry and become parents (Gen. 1:28); the second is the commandment to the father to circumcise his eight-day-old son (Gen. 17:12). In contrast, the Christian sequence of a Jewish life follows, not Jewish law, but the life of Jesus, as portrayed in the Gospels of Luke and Matthew. They track Jesus' birth, then his career, and finally his death.[33]

Christian presentations of Jewish life are sometimes referred to as "ethnographies of the Jews." Some scholars have correctly objected to the term as muting the polemic and tendentious assumptions of selection and presentation their authors bring to the task. To be sure, no ethnographic account can be totally free of bias and pre-conceptions, but the expanded phrase "Christian ethnography of Jews" for these accounts serves to warn the reader that these are not academic treatments but are written by deeply engaged Christian interpreters. They tell us as much if not more about various Christian perspectives than about the Jewish world they present. In reality, of course, they do both.[34]

Among the most important Christian presentations of Judaism, itself following earlier ones that appeared in the sixteenth century, was *Juden Schül* (German, 1603; Latin, *Synagoga Judaica*), by the Basel Christian Hebraist Johann Buxtorf the Elder (1564–1629).[35] Its negative depiction of Jewish religious life apparently prompted Venetian rabbi Leon Modena to write his Italian *Historia de' riti hebraici* (Venice, 1638), one of the few systematic Jewish books of this kind, at the request of the English ambassador in Venice for James I. It was translated into English as *The Rites of the Jews*. Neither version was systematically illustrated.[36]

In addition to a few individual depictions of Jewish rites in Holland,[37] Bernard Picart (1673–1733), a Protestant French artist who settled in the Netherlands, produced sketches and engravings of many ceremonies from Sefardic Jewish life there in the first volume of his *Cérémonies et coutumes religieuses de tous les peuples du monde.* (Amsterdam, 1723). These influenced many others to do the same.[38]

Though Picart was the first to produce a systematic set of etchings about Jewish ceremonial life, German Christian writers became especially active in this genre in the eighteenth century. Of special importance is the Jewish convert to Christianity Paul Christian Kirchner, who first published *Ceremoniale Judaicum* (Erfurt, 1717), which Christian Hebraist Sebastian Jungendres expanded and revised as *Jüdisches Ceremoniel* (Nuremberg, 1724). In addition to making many substantive changes in the text, he ordered a set of copperplate etchings about Jewish life, including several on life cycle events.[39]

Two other very important contributions to the visualization of Jewish life cycle events in German lands were by the Orientalist Johann Jacob Schudt (1664–1722), *Jüdische Merkwürdigkeiten* (4 vols.; Frankfurt-Leipzig, 1714–17/18), and the German Protestant theologian and Hebraist Johann Christoph Georg Bodenschatz (1717–97), *Kirchlicher Verfassung der heutigen Juden,* also published with many engravings, in four volumes (Erlangen and Coburg, 1748–49), and in a second edition as *Aufrichtig teutsch redender Hebräer* (Frankfurt am Main, 1756). This clustering of Christian presentations of Judaism, many in the first half of the eighteenth century, reflects the re-emergence of Jews in German cities around the turn of the eighteenth century, the building of synagogues there, and Christian curiosity about their newly prominent ways of behaving.[40]

Among nineteenth-century Jewish depictions, Moritz Oppenheim's paintings have received special recognition for their artistic merit and ethnographic value, but others are also waiting for their researchers. To date, we have no comprehensive visual database about Jewish practices. Some depictions of how Christians imagined Jewish life can be gleaned from the Index of Christian Art at Princeton University, and there is a growing Index of Jewish Art in Jerusalem, but as yet we do not have a well-indexed database of images and passages on Jewish life, let alone on the life cycle.

The importance today of Jewish life cycle events is reflected in the growing bibliography on the subject. Until the 1970s the only comprehensive books were Leopold Löw's still-basic study *Die Lebensalter in der jüdischen Literatur,* published in Hungary in 1875, and Hayyim Schauss's more popular and better-organized *The Lifetime of a Jew,* published under American Reform auspices in 1950 and reprinted since. In addition, scholars of Jewish cultural history made important contributions to the ways Jews lived and paid some attention to the comparative framework of Jewish life cycle and other practices. Among these are the seminal Moritz Güdemann and, more recently, Jacob Lauterbach, Joseph Gutmann, Daniel Sperber, and Israel Ta-Shema.[41]

The Jewish Catalogue[42] was a Jewish response to *The Whole Earth Catalogue,* which expressed the anti-establishment youth cultural revolution of the late 1960s. Viewed as a Jewish hippie's *Shulhan 'Arukh* (Prepared Table), the standard code of Jewish law dating from the sixteenth century, the first *Jewish Catalogue* included rites of passage for adults, but not for children, who appear belatedly only in later editions.

Over the past thirty years, a focus on the individual has been complemented by members of various groups, each seeking a place in the Jewish sun: feminists, converts, adults returning to Judaism, gays and lesbians, intermarried couples. Each has generated new rites, and Jewish books have been published that treat aspects of these subjects as guides for contemporary Jewish living, rather than as subjects of study. In addition, feminist Orthodox groups such as JOFA (Jewish Orthodox Feminist Alliance) have begun to publish discussions and essays that advocate the legitimacy of Orthodox women celebrating rites that formerly had been thought to be part of the male domain.

It should not be a surprise that there are hundreds of books and articles on life cycle passages today. The gender revolution, the same-sex revolution, the intermarriage revolution, all are reflected in the abundance of rereadings and "re-ritings" going on in Judaism over the past generation.

Since Schauss's book, other general surveys have appeared. Filled with comparative notes, and focused on "origins" rather than development, is Theodor H. Gaster's *The Holy and the Profane: Evolution of Jewish Folkways* (William Morrow, 1955, 1980). One that focuses briefly on traditional sources of the Jewish life cycle is Abraham P. Bloch's *The Biblical and Historical Background of Jewish Customs and Ceremonies* (KTAV, 1980). A good comparative essay prefacing an important collection of visual items is art historian Joseph Gutmann's *The Jewish Life Cycle* (E. J. Brill, 1987). Concerned with progressive approaches and contemporary times is Ronald H. Isaacs's *Rites of Passage: A Guide to the Jewish Life Cycle* (KTAV, 1992). Jacob Neusner's *The Enchantments of Judaism: Rites of Transformation from Birth through Death* (Basic Books, 1987) is about many things including some life cycle events. Rela M. Geffen's collaborative collection of essays, *Celebration and Renewal: Rites of Passage in Judaism* (JPS, 1993), is part of the trend that also included specialized books like Maurice Lamm's, written from a modern Orthodox perspective, on Jewish marriage, *The Jewish Way in Love and Marriage* (Jonathan David, 1980, 1991), and death, *The Jewish Way in Death and Mourning* (Jonathan David, 1969), and Anita Diamant's several books on the life cycle today, including *The*

New Jewish Baby Book (Summit Books, 1985), *The New Jewish Wedding* (Simon and Schuster, 1985), and *Saying Kaddish: How to Comfort the Dying, Bury the Dead and Mourn as a Jew* (Schocken Books, 1998).[43]

A new genre about marking the year of mourning for a parent includes E. M. Broner's pioneering *Mornings and Mourning: A Kaddish Journal* (HarperCollins, 1994), a journey described in unique ways by the part memoir and part research book of Leon Wieseltier, *Kaddish* (Knopf, 1998), and of ethnographer and sociologist Samuel C. Heilman's *When a Jew Dies: Ethnography of a Bereaved Son* (University of California Press, 2001). Ari Goldman's *Living a Year of Kaddish: A Memoir* (Schocken, 2003) is a recent addition to this growing library of personal accounts.

Rabbi Debra Orenstein, in *Lifecycles,* volume 1: *Jewish Women on Life Passages and Personal Milestones* (Jewish Lights, 1994), summarizes many years of innovative writing by Jewish feminists who have often discussed new practices in magazines such as *Moment, Response,* or *Lilith* since the 1970s. New books continue to appear every year.

Comparing Löw, Schauss, Neusner, and Geffen, on the one hand, and the *Jewish Catalogue* (1–3) and books like Orenstein's *Lifecycles* (volume 1), and pamphlets published by JOFA, on Jewish women's life cycles, on the other, it seems that the desire to understand the background of existing rites has been overwhelmed by a need to create new rites of passage.

The tendency to innovate is nothing new in Jewish rites of passage. When we look back over the course of Jewish historical experience, we see that every age has contributed to the creation of new ones, such as bar mitzvah, in early modern Germany, or the first haircutting, in sixteenth-century Palestine. These rites and many others were invented at a specific time, in a particular Jewish community, and then were either preserved locally or adopted by other Jews and disseminated so that they became widely practiced customs. Rites of passage are of the people, not just the rabbis or ancient sages. And the people speak in each generation by acting out and re-riting Judaism.

A NEW JEWISH LIFE CYCLE

In *Rituals of Childhood,* I presented an analysis of one particular celebration, the initiation ceremony of a Jewish boy into schooling in medieval Germany and France. This custom came into existence at a particular point in time. It built on earlier elements that were appropriated, in part at least, by stimulation from contemporary Christian symbols. The combination of the earlier Jewish elements into one new ceremony seemed to be directly responsive to Christian rites and patterns of behavior.

This book, in contrast, is a broad study of many rites, over the time span of recorded Israelite and Jewish practice, from Hebrew biblical times to the latest cyber-fad for celebrating a bar mitzvah. From the history of these rites, I indicate some of the ways Jews negotiated with their majority cultures to express Jewish life cycle moments and give meaning to their lives as members of a tiny minority. The evidence demonstrates that Jews were active participants in the society in which they lived and never were isolated in ghettos from their surroundings, even when they lived in legal ghettos in the early modern or Nazi periods. The product of those interactions became Judaism for the next generation. Process became product; interaction became tradition.

This book is not a history of childhood, marriage, and death in Judaism. Others have begun to write those stories, and this book only touches on certain aspects of those larger historical investigations.[44] Instead, I focus on the history of the rites that Jews have created to demarcate the transitions between periods of life experience. These are not constant but constantly change over time.

My interpretive survey is comprehensive and includes the major examples of how Jews have celebrated life cycle events from biblical times to today. Instead of adopting a strictly historical approach that looks first at all rites in antiquity, then in the Middle Ages and modernity, I have divided the book into chapters about the experiences of the life cycle, from birth to childhood, from maturation to marriage, from adulthood to death and memory. But unlike Schauss, who also divides his book into stages of the life cycle but then includes in each chapter discussions of *the whole rite* in biblical, ancient, medieval, and modern times, I trace the historical and ethnographic development of the *elements of various key rites* from ancient times to today within each stage of a lifetime. This approach enables the reader to see clearly how particular features of each life cycle rite underwent development in various times and places. In each chapter, I also include one or more narratives of the entire rite of passage being discussed. Whereas Schauss drew on his ethnographic vignettes from his own experience in east Europe at the beginning of the twentieth century, I construct a brit or a bar mitzvah or a wedding or a funeral from my own experiences in the United States or Israel mainly in the second half of that century and beyond.

Unlike most books written over the last five hundred years about Jewish ceremonies, this one is neither a set of essays directed at non-Jews to explain how Jews behave, nor is it a how-to guide intended to encourage Jews to do something. Instead, I seek to point out for all readers when many different features of Jewish life cycle rites emerged, how they acquired new meanings over the centuries, and to explore the many ways the history of different life cycle rites sheds light on the dynamics of Jewish inward acculturation. The story shows how Jews continued to live as a religious minority in larger social and cultural environments by being selectively open to them. It also demonstrates the intense localism of Jewish culture. Rarely was anybody in charge of even one local community, and even then variety was the norm.

There will be some surprises along the way. Jews sometimes assume that, at least until the modern era, there was a single Jewish traditional approach to everything and that it is preserved today in the religious behavior of Jews who call themselves "Orthodox" or "haredi" (Ultra-Orthodox) or "Hasidic," such as the Lubovitcher Hasidim.

Although different Orthodox groups today may agree with the above statement, it is not an accurate portrait of how Jews for the last two thousand years or so have actually behaved.

First of all, Jews did not do everything that the rabbinic documents said they should, and, conversely, they did some things that are not mentioned in rabbinic texts and others that the rabbis explicitly opposed but had no power to stop. From the beginning, there is a difference between Jewish culture, the behavior of the vast majority of Jewish men, women, and children, and the norms of rabbis.

Moreover, major Jewish sub-cultures existed at any one time, and rabbis in each also differed among themselves and with rabbis in other sub-groups. For example, Jews from Franco-German lands of Christian Europe had different customs from those in Muslim Iraq, North Africa, and Spain. Even before the Iberian expulsion in 1492, members of each main sub-group already had begun to immigrate and influence the others. Still, major differences between the two cultural domains persisted despite the mixing of populations that characterizes Jewish life in early modern times.

Even Ultra-Orthodox Jews innovate "traditions" by selectively taking earlier customs and combining them into totally new configurations. Ultra-Orthodoxy not only has a history, in the sense that it came into being only in modern times as a religious movement aware of modernity, influenced by it even when seeking to oppose it, but Ultra-Orthodoxy also invents traditions.[45] Far from being living remnants of ancient or medieval Jewish life, the Ultra-Orthodox world is really a neo-traditionalist, modern form of Judaism. It is as impossible today to find pre-modern, traditional Jews untouched by modernity as it is for a cultural anthropologist to locate an aboriginal tribe in the heart of Africa or the Australian outback.

For practical purposes, European traditional Jewish life ended in the nineteenth century, and to the degree that it persisted in Poland or Lithuania or other parts of Christian Europe it was already reacting to modernity and was mainly destroyed in World War II during the Shoah. Some traditional Jewish communities persisted into the second half of the twentieth century, displaced to the United States or Palestine/Israel or the Muslim world, though modulated by European values influenced, as in Morocco, by the Alliance Israélite Universelle schools. Soviet Communism secularized much of the east European traditional Jewish life that survived World War II. Even the remote Jewish community of Yemen, most of which migrated to Israel in the 1950s, came under modernizing influences there. Only a tiny group has remained in Yemen and in some other parts of the Muslim world.

By focusing on the development of traditional Jewish practices and innovations, I show that the wide range of improvisations being made today are but the latest examples of a continuously innovative process of ritual invention that is evident from biblical times to the present. Objections today that tradition always was the way it is now are simply misinformed. Every generation has negotiated between earlier practices and norms and the needs of the day.

I begin with the beginning of life itself—birth.

1

Birth,

"Bris,"

Schooling

In the Hebrew Bible, fertility is a blessing, and barrenness a problem that requires divine assistance. In the Code of Hammurabi and rabbinic Judaism, barrenness was a justification for a man to divorce his wife and take another.[1] In narratives such as the birth of Isaac to Sarah and Abraham, the narrator stresses that God remembers those to whom he promised his blessing and covenant. The motif is adopted in the Gospel of Luke, regarding the birth of John the Baptist, and in the apocryphal New Testament Gospel of James, about the birth of Mary, mother of Jesus.

Despite the significance in biblical narratives about the births of many important figures often following initial barrenness, few rituals accompany the act of birthing.[2] Perhaps this testifies to the biblical authors' strong faith in God's protection, which might be compromised were anyone, as many later would, resort to protective measures. Did everyday Israelites make use of amulets, incantations, and other techniques to make the experience safer? Most likely they did, but this is not mentioned in the narratives.

In late antiquity and medieval times, many customs are attested that were thought to protect the mother and the unborn child. A pregnant woman might wear around her neck special stones or a gold coin, part of a rabbit, or an inscription meant to protect against miscarriage. Others would wear a belt on which women had woven or written phrases to protect the mother from miscarriage, hang amulets on the walls of her room to protect her from Lilith, or place a symbolic iron knife under her pillow, all customs that persisted into modern times either in Europe or in the Mediterranean Jewish communities. Christian churches owned relics such as belts for expectant mothers, to protect them during pregnancy.[3]

BIRTH RITES

The birth itself is described briefly and is portrayed in illuminations from later times as a form of sitting. The account of a woman in labor in Egypt seems to indicate that she sat on two stones placed a small distance apart: "'When you deliver the Hebrew women, look at the birthstool'" (*avnayim*) (Exod. 1:16), a local Egyptian practice. The meaning of the term "avnayim" is not clear but may refer to birthing stones, as in a magical inscription from an Egyptian papyrus that includes the phrase, "from on the two brick stones of the birth."[4] There are suggestive drawings of a god making human forms on a potter's wheel that may have developed into the stones on which women, in imitation of the god, delivered a baby.[5] Birthing stools are well known even in modern Europe.[6]

A baby could also be delivered while the mother sat on someone's knees.[7] This is the procedure when barren Rachel asks Jacob to sire a child with her maid Bilhah, who eventually will "'bear on my knees'" while giving birth (Gen. 30:3). We also see this when Joseph's descendants are born: "the children of Machir son of Menasseh were . . . born upon Joseph's knees" (Gen. 50:23). Using the knees as a platform or table area will be retained in Jewish traditions, not for birthing, but for holding a baby boy steady during his circumcision. Elsewhere, the birthing position is described as kneeling. For example, if a distraught mother in labor takes an oath not to have sex with her husband again, an act of impiety for which she must make a sacrifice after her days of impurity (Lev. 12), the phrase used is, "when she kneels in bearing, she swears impetuously."[8]

Whatever the mother's position, we do not know if anything was said to greet the birth—certainly not "Mazel tov!" From a chance remark by the prophet Jeremiah, we see that the father was usually not present at the birth itself. Someone else had to bring him the news: "Accursed be the man who brought my father the news and said, 'A boy is born to you'" (Jer. 20:15). The presence of fathers in delivery rooms, now common, was still being resisted in the late 1960s in New York City. And since men were not present at birth, they did not write down what usually happened.

In this all-female experience, midwives play an important role in the Hebrew Bible's descriptions of birthing, especially of a child to an important woman. Called *meyaledet* (literally, birther) in biblical Hebrew—*hakhamah* (skilled woman) or *hayyah* (life-bringer) in the Talmud[9]—a midwife appears in several biblical accounts of important births. For example, during the difficult breach delivery of twins to Tamar, the daughter-in-law of Jacob's son Judah, we find: "While she was in labor, one of them put out his hand, and the midwife tied a crimson thread on that hand, to signify: This one came out first" (Gen. 38:28). A midwife assisted Jacob's wife Rachel in delivering her youngest, Benjamin, a birth that ended in Rachel's death (Gen. 35:17–19). Similarly, the unnamed daughter-in-law of Eli, the priest of Shiloh, died in childbirth, although assisted by women who are referred to as "ha-nizzavot 'alehah" (those standing over her) (1 Sam. 4:19–22).

Midwives also played a central role in the introduction to the momentous story of Moses' birth. They foiled Pharaoh's plan to have all Israelite male newborns killed. The narrative suggests that the use of a midwife was the usual practice for Egyptian women, but that some Israelite women were able to give birth without one:

The king of Egypt spoke to the Hebrew midwives, one of whom was named Shiphrah and the other Puah, saying, "When you deliver the

Hebrew women, look at the birthstool (ha-avnayim): if it is a boy, kill him; if it is a girl, let her live." The midwives, fearing God, did not do as the king of Egypt had told them; they let the boys live. So the king of Egypt summoned the midwives and said to them, "Why have you done this thing, letting the boys live?" The midwives said to Pharaoh, "Because the Hebrew women are not like the Egyptian women: they are vigorous. Before the midwife can come to them, they have given birth" (Exod. 1:15–19).

This observation reflects the divine assistance that the narrative wants to ascribe to the Israelite women. It also may mean that the biblical narrator thought that use of a midwife was more common among Egyptian women and less frequent among Israelites. The presence of a midwife was no guarantee that a birth would be safe, and the deaths of the mother or of the infant posed constant dangers until very recent times. It was because birth was so dangerous that the rabbis of the Mishnah, by early second-century Palestine, declared that "one may help a woman give birth on the Sabbath and call a midwife (hakhamah) for her even from far away, and one may desecrate the Sabbath over her."[10]

Fear of facing this real danger generated rituals, as we learn from Ezekiel, the prophet who was with the exiles from Judah in sixth-century B.C.E. Babylonia. He compares Jerusalem to a newborn: "As for your birth, when you were born your navel cord was not cut, and you were not bathed in water to smooth you; you were not rubbed with salt, nor were you swaddled" (Ezek. 16:4)—all of which presumably was done for normal births. Some apparently abandoned their newborns, for Ezekiel continues: "On the day you were born, you were left lying, rejected, in the open field" (Ezek. 16:5).[11]

Everything in this passage seems familiar except salting the infant. This practice has a history, often in combination with applying oil, not mentioned in the Hebrew Bible, and it is done today among some Arabs, for example. Greek medical writers like Galen (130–200 C.E.) mention it as being medicinal, but salt is also thought to have the magical power of checking evil.[12] We are familiar with the related custom of throwing some spilled salt over the left shoulder.[13] Compare, too, the popular Talmudic expression that compares salt to the God-given soul: "Shake off the salt and cast the flesh to the dog."[14] Applying salt to the newborn, then, may have held both symbolic and magical meanings of enhancing or preserving the life of the newborn at the dangerous time of birth. Medieval Christians and Jews continued this practice, and salt was also inserted into the newborn's mouth during infant baptism.[15]

Swaddling or wrapping the infant also had a long history, and in medieval illuminated manuscripts newborns are represented as tightly wrapped cocoons.[16] By rabbinic times at least, a baby could be placed in a cradle (*'arisah*).[17] In medieval Ashkenaz, a special ceremony is described after birth in which a Pentateuch is placed under the baby's head in the cradle.[18]

Although today we may regard certain practices as magical and primitive or as superstitions, there is little objective basis for distinguishing what some call "magic" from "religion." The actual practices or actions that are performed are all acts carried out by humans who feel so helpless before overwhelming forces that they seek somehow to control either psychologically or physically, or both. (Fig. 1)

In ancient Palestine and Babylonia, where most Jews lived from the first through the seventh centuries, the sources of rabbinic literature, ancient pagan authors, inscriptions, and other archeological findings offer us a variety of incantations, amulets, and rituals, some of which accompanied the birthing process. Many practices were derived and adopted from the cultures of Egypt or Mesopotamia; others may have been produced by local Jews themselves and were borrowed and adopted by Greek-speaking pagans living in the cities of Palestine. In some cases, these were popular practices that the rabbis opposed; in others, the rabbis themselves promoted the practices. Jews who did them made them part of Jewish culture, regardless of their origin. They are part and parcel of lived Judaism no less than the most complicated tracts of Talmud or commentary.[19]

1. *Amulet for childbirth.* Sefer Raziel, *Amsterdam, 1701, fol. 43b. Courtesy of the Library of the Jewish Theological Seminary.*

We should remember that the religious behavior of Jews was not identical with the wishes of the rabbis. After the Muslim conquest in the seventh century C.E., the sway of rabbinic norms increased, but at the same time, some popular practices of non-rabbinic Jews infiltrated the rabbinic norms and changed them. We should also remember that rabbis, including those in the Talmud itself, were practitioners of what we call magical acts and that part of the power the rabbis claimed derived from their charismatic powers.[20]

This was true among later rabbis who were kabbalists as well, including such figures as Rabbi Israel Ba'al Shem Tov, the founder of Hasidism,[21] and it is an error to ascribe magical acts just to the world of either popular culture or outside influences, as though they were not frequently integral parts of Jewish culture at all levels. They were. Several of these practices survived in Jewish communities for hundreds of years, attesting to the belief that they were effective protections against the terrifying experience of childbirth.[22]

35

Birth Day Party

No festive meal or other rite at the time of birth is mentioned in the Hebrew Bible, and Josephus (first century) observes that the Torah "does not allow the birth of our children to be made occasions for festivity."[23] The Talmud refers to a custom that marked the event in Palestine, where parents planted a cedar tree for a newborn boy and a pine tree for a newborn girl.[24] Although this source is often read to mean that the tree was later used to form the child's wedding canopy, the Aramaic *genana* being equivalent to the Hebrew *huppah,* in antiquity huppah meant wedding chamber, not canopy. The four-poled wedding canopy was an innovation in early modern Germany (see Chapter 3).

There also are obscure Talmudic references to a celebration after the birth of a son called *shevu'a ha-ben* (week of the son) and *yeshu'a ha-ben* (salvation of the son). In northern France, Rashi interpreted the former to mean the circumcision and the feast that the father made at the end of the week, as though the term meant a time that marked one week after the birth of a son.[25] Rashi took the latter term to refer to the redemption of the firstborn (*pidyon ha-ben*). His grandson, Rabbi Jacob ben Meir (d. 1171), the great Talmudic commentator from northern France and known as Rabbeinu Tam, disagreed.[26] He wrote that the word yeshu'a cannot strictly refer to redemption but means "salvation." The term refers to a party made right after a son is born, when he was "saved" from his mother's womb.[27]

That a link between shevu'a ha-ben and circumcision is secondary, and not its original meaning, is proven by medieval texts that refer back to early rabbinic times to a parallel celebration called *shevu'a ha-bat* for the birth of a daughter.[28] As the term itself suggests, shevu'a ha-ben possibly referred to a Jewish equivalent of the Greco-Roman feast that took place *for seven days* after the birth of a son. Originally, it meant "the son's birth week" of continual feasting, not just the circumcision feast after the child was a week old, but this practice disappeared even in late antiquity.[29]

A seven-day feast after the birth of a child is also an early Arab custom and may underlie the term in rabbinic texts, even though the original practice was forgotten by Talmudic times. Muslim women cook and bring things over to the mother and visit her, and the father invites his friends over to celebrate, too. Parallel customs of weeklong feasting developed to celebrate a Jewish wedding (see Chapter 3). Cooking for Jewish mourners is mentioned in the Talmud (see Chapter 4), and there are customs about friends eating with the mourners for seven days of the shiva (literally, *shiv'ah*=seven), including reciting a special Grace after Meals. Weeklong communal eating is still done after the marriage feast and for the seven days of special meals after a death, but is not done following a birth. The number seven is a lucky number in many cultures.

The interpretation of shevu'a ha-ben as a circumcision party, rather than a weeklong celebration after a birth, was insisted on in several early medieval Palestinian texts, such as *Pirqei de-Rabbi Eliezer, Midrash Tehillim,* and *Midrash Tanya Rabbati,* for example. The midrash observes that Abraham immediately obeyed God whenever he was commanded to do something. When God specifically commanded Abraham to circumcise his son when eight days old (Gen. 17:12), he did so immediately: "And Abraham circumcised his son Isaac when he was eight days old" (Gen. 21:4).

"Hence," the midrash continues, "you may learn that everyone who brings his son for circumcision is like a high priest bringing his meal offering and his drink offering upon the top of the altar. From this, the rabbis said: A man is bound to make festivities and a banquet on that day when he has the merit of having his son circumcised, like Abraham our father, who circumcised his son, as it is said, 'And Abraham made a great feast on the day *he circumcised Isaac*'" (Gen. 21:8, italics added). And, in fact, we know that fathers in late antiquity and in the Middle Ages did make festive parties on the occasion of a son's *brit milah* (ritual circumcision, known more commonly as a *bris*).[30]

The midrash, however, has invented a proof text and the italicized words are not in the Bible. The verse actually says that Abraham made a great feast "be-higgamel et yizhaq" (on the day Isaac was weaned), not when he was circumcised. By a clever rereading of the Hebrew, this verse now became the scriptural basis of a different religious custom. The midrash in *Pirqei de-Rabbi Eliezer,* as we have it, does not explain the linguistic basis of the reinterpretation of that phrase, but Rabbi Jacob ben Meir, Rabbeinu Tam, quotes a version of the passage that does. The midrash reads the verse as though the verb for weaning (*higgamel*) is reduced to two letters that have the numerical value of eight [h=5 and g=3], plus two letters that contain the root of the verb, "he circumcised" [ml]. The resulting interpretation is: "And Abraham made a great feast at the circumcision of Isaac, like the sum of [the numerical values of the Hebrew letters] h[eh] g[imel], [which is eight]."[31]

These early medieval Palestinian midrash texts were defending the custom of celebrating a boy's circumcision for a week as biblically based, even though it was derived from a deft slight of hand. Perhaps this forced exegesis to justify understanding shevu'a ha-ben as a circumcision party is a Jewish response, following the Muslim conquest of Palestine in the seventh century, to the newly felt presence of the competing Arab practice of celebrating a birth for a whole week.

By fourteenth- and fifteenth-century Germany, Rabbi Israel ben Petahiah Isserlein (1390–1460) mentions the custom of holding a party in the home on the Friday evening after a birth. This custom was reinforced in sixteenth-century Poland, though no name is given for it in either source. Perhaps the term *ben zakhar* developed in Germany, based on a phrase from Jeremiah's comment about his own birth: "Accursed be the man who brought my father the news and said, 'A boy (ben zakhar) is born to you'" (Jer. 20:15). A different custom there, of having a party on Shabbat afternoon, was sometimes called *shalom zakhar,* an allusion to a Talmudic teaching, "When a boy (zakhar) is born, peace (shalom) comes too."[32]

This festive gathering on the Sabbath after the birth of a boy or a girl still takes place today. In Ashkenazic communities, a shalom zakhar (welcoming/wishing well the boy) takes place the first Friday evening after the boy is born. A celebration for a girl is called *shalom bat* (welcoming/wishing well a daughter) and it also takes place on the first Sabbath, but not necessarily Friday evening. For the Ashkenazic celebration, friends gather after Friday night Sabbath dinner at the home of the new parents, and someone offers a *devar torah* (Torah lesson) that links the weekly Torah reading to the arrival of the new child. To be sure, there are huge gaps of time between mention of the Talmudic custom, the late medieval Ashkenazic one, and more recent practice, and we do not know if this custom was practiced continuously or reinvented from time to time.

Sefardic Jews from various places of origin refer to the party for a newborn girl as *zeved ha-bat* (the gift of a daughter). This party may resemble the Ashkenazic one, but it is distinct in that the girl is named at this celebration, if it takes place in the home, as is the case for Moroccan and Judeo-Spanish Jews, or in the synagogue, as among Syrian and some Spanish and Portuguese Jews. Some biblical and other texts are recited as well as the wish that the girl may grow up to have many sons.[33]

Annual Birthday Parties

Not only were Jews no longer celebrating a birth for seven days in late antiquity; they hardly celebrated birthdays annually until modern times.[34] Birthday parties each year were also far less common among Christians in medieval Europe than today. Another sign of the relative insignificance of birthdays in Jewish life is the omission of the date of birth on tombstone inscriptions, again, before modern times. On the other hand, elegies for children often mention the child's age, as in the case of Rabbi Eleazar of Worms, whose daughters he saw killed at ages thirteen and six, and Asher ben Turiel, who died at fifteen just after being married.[35]

There are rare exceptions that prove the rule. One is a reference in the Talmud to a sage who celebrated his sixtieth birthday. The reason offered is a special one. He was happy that he had lived that long and not been taken by God earlier, which might have been interpreted as being due to his sinfulness, since the usual interpretation of the rabbinic punishment called *karet* (literally, cutting off) was to die before the age of sixty, or around fifty-five.[36] Rabbi Israel Isserlein also marked this occasion of his sixtieth birthday in fifteenth-century central Europe, and there is mention by Rabbi Ya'ir Bacharach (1638–1702) that some have a party when they turn seventy, perhaps a custom in one or more places where he lived in Germany.[37]

From the fifteenth century on, Jews in northern Europe began to note the dates of their children's births in family Bibles. This is about the same time Christians were doing the same thing in Europe for the first time.[38] Before this, we have a medieval gloss on the biblical phrase that refers to Pharaoh's birthday ("yom huledet et par'o") (Gen. 40:20), on which a feast was made. The rabbinic comment might be taken to imply that the writer himself was aware of annual birthday celebrations among Jews in twelfth-century Italy, but a closer reading suggests that the comment is probably referring to the biblical protagonist and the Egyptians who made a party for Pharaoh, not to the author's own time and place.[39] The bar/bat mitzvah rite, which I discuss in detail in Chapter 2, is another exception to the rule and developed only gradually in Germany in the Middle Ages and early modern times until it reached a recognizable shape no earlier than the sixteenth century, and even then, only in central Europe. It apparently did not reach Italian Jewish communities until the eighteenth century and was not important in eastern Europe into modern times. Jews sometimes did remember their birth date, but annual celebrations were not commonplace until modern times.[40]

Recently, a Jewish variation of the birthday party developed in the Israeli kindergarten birthday celebration. Children form a circle and sing special songs to the birthday boy or girl, who is seated in the middle wearing a wreath of flowers. Each child takes a turn going up to his or her classmate to wish him or her a special blessing, such as "May you grow up to be a strong soldier," or "May you enter first grade."[41]

There might have been a negative reinforcement for Jews to celebrate their birthdays regularly in late antiquity, since Greeks and Romans did so, and the practice was associated with paganism. This continued in Christian Europe, where Christian children were often named after the saint on whose "birthday" they were born. The "dies natalis" of a saint, however, refers to the day they died and went up to heaven, exceptions being the traditional birthdays of John the Baptist, Mary, and Jesus. This was a Christian adaptation of the pagan Roman custom to celebrate the "deus natalis," the birthday of the god on whose day someone was born.

It is still the custom in Catholic countries, such as Poland, for example, for people to celebrate their birthday on their "Name Day," that is, the date of the "birthday" of the saint for which they were named. I am told that on September 8, the traditional birthday of Mary, after whom so many Catholic girls are named, "half the population" in Poland celebrates their birthday.[42]

Given the negative religious associations Jews attached to the pagan gods and Christian saints that lie at the heart of this custom, perhaps Jews were inhibited from imitating it, especially since there was no good Talmudic precedent to do so, other than for celebrating at age sixty. Moreover, the only biblical reference to an adult celebrating a birthday is Pharaoh, a traditional enemy of the Jews (Gen. 40:20–21). There is even some evidence that Egyptians were the first culture to celebrate annual birthdays, and Israelites apparently resisted this practice already in very ancient times.[43]

We have even less information about private birthday anniversaries mentioned in the thousands of documents preserved in the Cairo Geniza about Jews who lived in Muslim lands. The exact date was noted and sometimes a horoscope was prepared. S. D. Goitein thinks that the date was not celebrated because of "the belief that numbers were ominous, attracting the evil eye."[44]

Apart from the exceptions noted, birthday parties were not part of a traditional Jewish way of life. How and when this changed in modern times is still unclear and worth investigation.

Caring for the mother and child was the responsibility of women for at least a week after the child was born. In eleventh- through thirteenth-century Europe, there are signs that the mother got up from her bed a week after giving birth, and in the fifteenth century, only after a month of recuperation. I will return to the mother's coming out of seclusion in connection with the naming of a baby girl and the re-entry of the parturient mother into Jewish society.[45]

BRIS OR *BRIT MILAH*
(COVENANT OF CIRCUMCISION)

Circumcision is the practice of cutting and removing the foreskin and is practiced in many cultures, including Islam.[46] In Israelite religion and Judaism, the rite takes place on the eighth day after birth (Gen. 17:12; Lev. 12:3), unless the baby is weak for some medical reason such as being premature or jaundiced. Then it is postponed until the child is well. As time went on, various participants, additional texts, gestures, and ritual objects were added; implements used to effect the medical operation changed, and containers were designed to hold them and varied in material and design in accordance with local medical and artistic styles and standards.

In contrast to birth, when a female usually supports the mother from behind, and the female midwife crouches in front to bring forth life from the mother who sits in between them, in the brit, it is usually a man, called either "sandeq" or "ba'al brit," who holds the baby on his lap, and the person performing the operation, again usually male crouches facing them and produces something new. Moreover, as is the case in many cultures, East and West, the "second, or initiatory, birth" is more ritualized than the "first, or biological," birth.[47]

In a significant way, the act of a female giving birth was symbolically transformed in pagan Rome, ancient Christianity, and medieval Judaism into a male act of cultural begetting and rebirth. In Rome, at a ceremony presided over by the goddess Levana, the still-red newborn was placed at the father's feet. If he recognized the child as his own, he lifted him up from the ground, a gesture especially associated with infant boys.[48] As the baptismal font became a second womb from whose waters the child receives eternal life of the spirit, the godparent received the child after being immersed in the water or held the child as the person in charge poured water over the child's forehead.[49] Still later in Judaism, the sandeq/ba'al brit, like the Christian godparent in infant baptism, held the child during the initiation rite, though on the knees.

Despite the similarities, a significant difference exists between Christian sponsors and the sandeq. Christians selected unrelated persons sometimes of higher status as a way of enhancing the family with whom the godfather/mother would have an ongoing relationship. The Jewish parents selected a relative as sandeq, often a grandparent, and the honor was limited to the ceremony itself and had no social or other ongoing consequences for the family.[50]

Circumcision recalls the account in Genesis of God's commandment to Abraham that the family and community remember, while physically re-membering the child's sexual "member." At that very moment, he also becomes a member of the Jewish people. The plays on words in English reflect the layers of meaning in the Jewish rite. The Hebrew root Z-KH-R, for both "memory" and "male," suggests that there is an authentic Jewish/Hebrew basis for this interpretation as well.

Accounts in Exodus 4:25 and Joshua 5:2–3 refer to use of a flint knife, a sign of the custom's antiquity, prior to the Bronze Age. In the Hebrew Bible the father is to perform the rite, as when Abraham circumcised Isaac (Gen. 21:4) when he was eight days old. Sometimes the mother does it, as when Moses' wife Zipporah circumcises their son Gershom, who had been brought up in Egyptian culture (Exod. 4:25). By the time of the Maccabees, in the second century B.C.E., nonfamily specialists apparently did it too (1 Mac. 1:59). The Hebrew term in the familiar Hebrew form *mohel* is post-Talmudic;[51] only the Aramaic form *mahola* or the title *ha-gozer* (the surgeon) appears in the Talmud.[52] In the early modern codes of Jewish law, the opinion is mentioned that where a qualified man is not available, an expert woman may perform the rite.[53] Unless the father himself performed the rite, as sometimes happened,[54] the person does so according to traditional Jewish law, as the father's surrogate.

In many cultures, the practice of circumcision is associated with a rite of passage preceding marriage as a puberty rite, not infancy. In the Bible, Abraham's son Ishmael, the prototype of the Arab peoples, is circumcised at thirteen years, around the age of puberty. This tradition may reflect the widely attested association between male circumcision and readiness for marriage. Various Muslim traditions found not in the Qur'an but in Hadith traditions about the Prophet, require circumcision of a boy anywhere from the seventh day to the thirteenth year, as with Ishmael (Gen. 17:25).[55]

Although Jewish tradition has followed the biblical practice of circumcision on the eighth day, there are hints in the Hebrew Bible that it might once have had an association with puberty in early Israelite culture as in Islam. Thus, in Hebrew the terms for bridegroom (*hatan*), son-in-law (also *hatan*), and father-in-law (*hoten*), as well as the biblical term for wedding (*hatunah;* Songs 3:11), are all derived from the three-letter Hebrew root H-T-N, which has an Arabic cognate (*hatana*) that means both "to cut" or "to circumcise" and "wedding."[56] When Zipporah circumcises her son Gershom, she refers to him with the obscure expression, "'You are truly a bridegroom of blood to me!'" (Hebrew: "'hatan damim'"—Exod. 4:25). The text also includes a gesture that seems to be a sexual allusion: "So Zipporah took a flint and cut off her son's foreskin, and touched his legs with it" (Exod. 4:25). The text continues to explain this oddity to the biblical reader as well as to us: "And when He [God] let him alone, she added, 'A bridegroom of blood because of the circumcision'" (Exod. 4:26). Is this to say, Gershom is not a real bridegroom— obviously, since he is Zipporah's son—but the echo is still there from ancient times when an Israelite was circumcised prior to his marriage? It appears that the Israelites did not differ from the Canaanites in this regard.[57]

In Judaism, as in other cultures, certain rites of passage are achieved by symbolic acts of subtraction; others, by acts of addition.[58] In the case of the male Jew, circumcision is an act of subtraction that Judaism views as an addition, a move from a natural and imperfect state to the higher status of entering the community or cultures of Israel, becoming a civilized human being in God's special community of Israel. Compare the first haircut of a little Jewish boy at which a father said to his son, "'In a few minutes you will be a nice little Jew; you'll have your *peyos* (earlocks).'"[59]

The act of circumcision may be interpreted as the infant's passage from a state of "nature" to one of Jewish "culture." A midrash makes this point when it says that several biblical figures were born already circumcised, such as Jacob, who was called *tam* (perfect) (Gen. 25:27). He got that tag because he was born circumcised.[60]

The Greeks and Romans never understood it. To them, Jewish male circumcision was an act of mutilation that bordered on castration; the male form at birth was already perfect. Early Christian writers understood Jewish circumcision very well as a sign of the covenant but rejected it. Today, heated disagreements take place not only over male circumcision but also about a practice that never took effect among Jews, the excising of part of a young girl's genitals. Today this practice takes place in parts of Africa, for example, and in many Muslim communities. In the modern West, this act is thought of as barbaric. Ancient Greeks and Romans thought of Jewish male circumcision in much the same way.[61]

The association between cutting something and making a covenant or an agreement has deep cultural roots in the ancient Near East. In the biblical account of God's initial covenant with Abram (Gen. 15), before he tells Abram to circumcise himself (Gen. 17), God first tells Abram, who still had no son, "'Look toward heaven and count the stars, if you art able to count them.'" And he added, "'So shall your offspring be'" (Gen. 15:5). Abram asks God how he can know that he and his future generations will possess the Land of Israel. God tells him to get a heifer, a she-goat, a ram, a turtledove, and a young bird.

Abram "cut them in two, placing each half opposite the other" (Gen. 15:10), and "when the sun set and it was very dark, there appeared a smoking oven, and a flaming torch which passed between those pieces" (Gen. 15:17). The next verse explains what the strange act means: "On that day the Lord made a covenant with Abram, saying, 'To your offspring I assign this land'" (Gen. 15:18).

An act of sacrifice involving the cutting of animals to seal a bargain or covenant was an ancient Near Eastern practice. When the narrative says that God's presence in the form of fire passed between the two halves of the animals, it meant it was an oath in which God says, as it were, "May this happen to me if I break my word." We still refer to making an agreement as "cutting a contract," or "cutting a deal," and the word "decision" comes from the Latin "decidere," which means "to cut off."

Symbolic of God's promise that Abram will have many offspring, though he has none at present, God changes his name to Abraham and explains the new name to mean "father of a multitude of nations" (Gen. 17:5), and "such shall be the covenant between Me and you and your offspring to follow which you shall keep: every male among you shall be circumcised. You shall circumcise the flesh of your foreskin, and that shall be the sign of the covenant between Me and you" (Gen. 17:10–11). Moreover, God continues, "if any male who is uncircumcised fails to circumcise the flesh of his foreskin, that person shall be cut off from his kin; he has broken My covenant" (Gen. 17:14).

Very little of the now traditional circumcision ceremony is found in the Bible or the Talmuds. One searches there in vain for the Hebrew term mohel (circumciser), the presence of a sandeq or ba'al brit (godfather), the chair of Elijah; the cup of blessing and those who are to taste from it (father, child, mother, mohel); most of the texts of the blessings and prayers recited; the text in which the boy is named; the requirement of a male quorum of ten; the requirement to have a festive meal; and the custom to have a bowl of earth or water placed under the act itself. Aside from a small part of the liturgy, all of the other elements in the traditional rite of brit milah today developed in medieval and early modern times in rabbinic or popular circles as practices that were taken into Judaism.[62]

The Night before the Brit — the Wachnacht

For example, Jewish customs developed to ward off the danger that was believed to accompany the procedure. This demarcation of the night before the brit resembles and owes some of its coloring to Christian customs that marked the night before a newborn child's baptism. From the *Mahzor Vitry* in northern France (twelfth century), we know of a festive meal that was arranged the night before the brit and sponsored by the person who was to be honored as the ba'al brit, or godfather, the next day. This meal was different from the celebratory one that the boy's father made the evening after the circumcision, and it served as protection against perceived dangers that lurked around the baby and mother.[63]

In medieval Germany the eve before the brit was known as the "night watch," or *wachnacht,* a term that appears only in the sixteenth century. It consisted of a meal that took place in the parents' house in the presence of the mother.[64] This tradition was a Jewish adaptation of the German Christian custom, by the same name, the night before baptism. A further sign of the derivation of aspects of this Jewish custom from the local environs is the prescription that special cakes be prepared. Christians baked similar cakes to appease a demon known as Frau Holle and thus protect the Christian child prior to his or her baptism.[65]

Some time after the custom was adopted, Jews tried to anchor it in Jewish sources by pointing back to a phrase in God's charge to Abraham about the religious commandment of circumcision: "'You and your offspring to come throughout the ages shall keep (*tishmor*) My covenant'" (Gen. 17:9). The verb "tishmor" can also be translated "You shall watch" and be harmonized with the German *wachen* as an authentic hint of the later custom derived from non-Jewish custom.[66]

Part of the power of the Christian and Jewish practice of eating on the night before an important rite of passage was the shared belief that food would placate any evil spirits that lurked around at a time of danger. Another measure taken to do this was to hang signs that appealed to good supernatural forces to ward off the danger that might come from less benign ones. Among the latter was Lilith, an ancient Near Eastern figure, originally imagined as a bird or owl, lurking and waiting to harm a newborn child.[67]

One way to prevent Lilith from doing any harm was for the mother to put a symbolic knife around her neck or under her pillow. Wall hangings inscribed with special invocations were designed to protect the baby and the mother from such forces. In early modern times, some of these Lilith hangings were made out of papercut designs. In more recent times, a baby bonnet might be knitted on which were embroidered the special supernatural names whose power was invoked to protect the baby: SHADDAI SANVI, SANSANVI, SAMANGELAF, ADAM VE-HAVAH HUZ LILITH.[68]

The first name, Shaddai (Almighty), is also associated with the protective power of the *mezuzah* (Hebrew: doorpost), the amulet or ritual container that encloses biblical passages. Jews have traditionally placed one on their doorposts outside and within their house. In most such *mezuzot,* the letter "shin," the first letter of the Hebrew word Shaddai, is visible or represented in the shape of the container itself.

The next to the last phrase invokes "Adam and Eve," the first parents of humankind. Lilith is then told to be removed, "HUZ LILITH," from the room. But they are to be aided by the other names, "Sanvi, Sansanvi, Samangelaf," angelic beings whose names have no special semantic meaning but have become traditionally associated with the task of protecting the newborn. Many amulets in silver and other materials contain this phrase. Recently, in Columbia Presbyterian Hospital in New York City, Ultra-Orthodox parents of a baby boy who required extensive medical care prior to his postponed circumcision hung photocopied paper "amulets" on the four walls of the hospital room to ward off Lilith and other agents of harm.[69]

Circumcision Becomes a Sacred Rite

The rabbis of late antiquity sacralized the rite of circumcision, as they did so many others, by prescribing the recitation of words in the form of blessings that invoked God's commanding the performance of the act in the Bible. The formulas of three texts are presented in the *Tosefta,* a Palestinian legal collection from the third century C.E., and the Talmud. The person carrying out the operation, just before doing it, recites the first blessing: "Blessed are You, O Lord our God, King of the Universe who has commanded us about circumcision ('al ha-milah)." The father of the boy then says: "Blessed are You, O Lord our God . . . who has commanded us to initiate him [literally, enter him] into the covenant of Abraham our father (le-hakhniso bi-verito shel avraham avinu)."

On the passage in the Babylonian Talmud, a twelfth-century Talmud glossator, or Tosafist, observed that the father's blessing, which comes second in the Talmud, should come first, before the blessing said by the person performing the operation. He reasoned that the language of the father's blessing, "who has commanded us to initiate him," implies the future tense, that the child is to be entered into the covenant, in the future. Since the person who performs the circumcision recites his blessing and then immediately performs the rite, the future language of the father's blessing seems out of place, since he says it *after* the rite has already been performed.

The great Talmudic authority, Rabbi Jacob ben Meir, Rabbeinu Tam, rejected his colleague's reasoning and the liturgical innovation he had instituted. Rabbeinu Tam reasoned that the order of the blessings in the Talmud is attested in all the manuscripts. The one who performs the rite says his blessing first, completes the circumcision, and then the father recites his blessing, despite its language. The formulation of the father's blessing did not bother Rabbeinu Tam. In effect, he decided that written authorities trump innovative custom, and the sequence of the two blessings has remained as it appears in the Talmud to the present.

In the Talmud, after the two blessings, those assembled link the week-old child's first initiation to three later stages in a Jewish male's life and say to the father: "As you have entered him into the covenant, so may you enter him into the Torah, the huppah and a life of good deeds." That is the text according to the *Tosefta,* and this reading is in the manuscripts of the Babylonian Talmud as well as in most medieval rabbinical authorities. Rabbi Amram Gaon, in ninth-century Iraq, codified this version in the first Jewish prayer book.

Although the formulation addressed to the father ("as you have entered him") is widely attested in late antiquity and the Middle Ages, the formula changed in early modern times from active to passive and to refer not to the father's action but to the baby's change of status. The reading in the late printed editions of the Talmud and in prayer books in use today has the assembled say: "As he [the baby] has entered the covenant, so may he enter the Torah, the wedding chamber, and good deeds" (keshem she-nikhnas la-brit, ken yikkanes la-torah, la-huppah, u-le-ma'asim tovim). It is not clear what this change means. The emphasis places the focus on the child and his future life cycle events of "entering the Torah," marriage, and a life of following God's commandment, not on the father.[70]

In addition to the rabbinic additions of three formulas that made the occasion a sacred one and linked it to a lifetime of the child's future religious living, a partner to the parents was added in the form of a godfather, a person honored by holding the infant during the ceremony. As with the newer language in the community's response, which shifts attention from the father to the baby, and the introduction of the professional mohel, who also puts the father in the background, the addition of the godfather as the assistant to the mohel broadens the occasion to include another family or community member.

The term generally in use today of sandeq reflects the late Greek term for godfather at an Orthodox Christian child's baptism or christening, "syndiknos," although Hebrew sources especially in medieval Europe also refer to this person as the "ba'al brit" (partner to the covenant). The term sandeq is already found in the early medieval

Midrash Tehillim and is in competition with the Hebrew term ba'al brit in medieval Christian Europe, until the original Greek term replaced the Hebrew one in early modern times.[71]

Two further additions broadened the social and symbolic meaning of the circumcision ceremony and raised it to a cosmic level. The first was the association of the prophet Elijah's presence at the ceremony. Adding the messianic figure of Elijah, a biblical prophet whose appearance the rabbis and later mystics associated with the days of the Messiah and national redemption, meant that the circumcision of one child now had collective Jewish meaning.

The biblical underpinnings for the presence of Elijah at every Jewish boy's brit was a verse, as interpreted in the early medieval midrash *Pirqei de-Rabbi Eliezer,* in which chapter 29 is devoted to lore about circumcision. The text says that "the Rabbis instituted [the custom] that there should be a seat of honor for the 'messenger of the covenant' [also: angel of the covenant]; for Elijah, may he be remembered for good, is called the 'messenger of the covenant,' as it is said, 'And the messenger of the covenant, whom you delight in, behold, he comes'" (Mal. 3:1).[72]

The passage is a rationalization of an existing custom probably in Palestine or southern Italy. The association of Elijah and the Messiah is biblical, and in the New Testament John the Baptist is interpreted as Elijah, the foreteller of the Messiah. In Jewish interpretation, Elijah is invoked when Jews think of national deliverance, as at every Seder meal on Passover and at every Jewish boy's brit. The introduction of Elijah, then, may be viewed as an anti-Christian polemic that reaffirms Elijah as a Jewish protector, despite the Christian associations that sought to co-opt him as a Christian icon.

At the Seder meal, a special fifth cup of wine is poured and left full for the prophet. It is known as the cup of Elijah, and the door is opened for him. At the brit, a special chair came to be set aside for the prophet Elijah. In some communities, twin chairs were built especially for circumcision ceremonies. Before the child was placed on the lap of the godfather who sat on the sandeq's chair, someone else had the honor of placing the baby for a moment on the chair of Elijah, which remained empty, or occupied, as one believed it to be, during the rest of the ceremony. In some Mediterranean and Asian Jewish communities today a miniature chair for Elijah is elevated on one wall of the synagogue; in other communities, a double chair is created, one for Elijah and the other for the sandeq/ba'al brit.[73]

Another custom that is mentioned in *Pirqei de-Rabbi Eliezer* for the first time and has been practiced from early medieval Palestine to the present is the practice of burying the foreskin in a pot of earth. In Babylonian communities, and later Sefardic ones that follow the medieval Iraqi rite, the practice was to hold a bowl of water under the circumcision and catch drops of blood in the water.[74] Today, after the ceremony, an Ashkenazic mohel may discreetly plant the foreskin in a flowerpot.

Unlike the birth ceremony, which is intimate and mainly female, the brit is male-centered, with a few exceptions.[75] It is communal as well as familial, and it is not surprising that elements of Christian baptism were taken over into the brit ceremony, since baptism itself replaced circumcision in early Christian practice. In Yiddish-speaking Europe, the terms for godparents followed the terms of Christian godparents, called *Gevatter* and *Gevatterin* in German, of newly baptized Christian children.[76]

Those terms were added to the ceremony in late medieval Europe, increasing considerably the cast of characters at a brit: the baby; the father, whose religious obligation is to circumcise his own son; the mohel as the father's agent; perhaps a rabbi or other functionary in the community; the ba'al brit or sandeq, on whose lap the baby is circumcised; and the godparents, called *kefatter* and *kefatterin* in Yiddish, who are also honored; and the rest of the assembled minyan and members of the family and community.

There was another important way the Jewish practice of the brit came to resemble the dramatis personae at a Christian baptism. By the twelfth century, in the Christian practice in medieval Europe, the sex of the child determined the number of godparents: for a boy,

2. Circumcision ceremony in vol. 1 of Cérémonies et coutumes religieuses de tous les peuples du monde *by Bernard Picart, Amsterdam, 1723. Courtesy of the Library of the Jewish Theological Seminary. Photo credit: Suzanne Kaufman*

two men and one woman served as sponsors; for a girl, the opposite number. In Judaism, where a ba'al brit was involved, the same ratio prevailed: in addition to a man generally serving as ba'al brit or sandeq, an additional two adults were added, the male kefatter and female kefatterin, adding up, as in the Christian rite of baptism, to two men and one woman for the boy's retinue. (Fig. 2)

The presence of Christians at Jewish rites included circumcisions. For example, in 1498, the Jewish scholar and professional scribe Abraham Farissol of Ferrara performed a circumcision on a Jewish boy in the home of a Christian acquaintance whom he was instructing in Jewish lore.[77] One of the most thorough premodern accounts of the detailed elements of a Jewish circumcision is preserved by French essayist Michel de Montaigne, who was present at a brit in sixteenth-century Italy (1580) in a Jewish home:

> The godfather sits on a table, placing a cushion on his knees: the godmother brings him the child, and then withdraws. The child is all swaddled, according to our custom; the godfather holds him out with his legs hanging down, and then the assistants, and the one who is to perform the operation, begin to chant, and the chant accompanies everything they do, though the whole thing lasts less than a quarter of an hour. The minister may also be someone who is not a rabbi, anyone there among them, anyone who wishes to be called to this task, since they consider it a great blessing to be frequently involved in it; they even pay to be invited, one offering an article of clothing, another something else useful for the child, and they believe that a man who has circumcised up to a certain number known to them, has the privilege that when he dies the parts of his mouth will never be eaten by the worms. On the table where the godfather sits, all the instruments used in the performance of the operation are laid out in order. Besides this, a man holds in his hands a carafe full of wine and a glass. There is also a brazier on the ground, at which the minister first warms his hands, then, seeing the child safely held in place by the godfather, with his head towards the latter, he takes hold of the child's member and with one hand he pulls on the skin at the tip, while with the other he pushes in the glans and the member. At the inner extremity of the skin which he holds still away from the glans, he places a silver instrument which holds the skin in place and ensures that in cutting it no harm is done to the glans or to the member. After which, with a knife he cuts the skin, which is immediately buried in the earth gathered in a basin which is among the other objects which form the panoply of this mystery. The minister then proceeds to use his fingernails to take hold of a certain membrane which covers the glans and to tear it off forcibly, pushing it back behind the glans. It appears that this involves a considerable effort and some pain. Nonetheless,

they do not consider it in the least dangerous and the wound invariably heals in four or five days. The crying of the child is the same as one of our children held at baptism. As the glans is thus uncovered, wine is quickly offered to the minister, who takes a little in his mouth and then proceeds to suck the bleeding glans of the child, then he spits out the blood, repeating the operation as many as three times. This completed, he is handed a screw of paper containing a red powder that they call dragon's blood, and with it he powders the wound. Then he wraps the child's member with specially prepared bandages. Having done this, he is handed a glassful of wine, which, on account of certain prayers that he recites, is said to be of benediction. He takes a sip, then he dips his finger in it and makes the child suck it three times. The same glass, exactly as it is, is then sent to the mother and the other women who are waiting in another room so they can drink what is left of the wine. Then a third personage takes a round object riddled with holes, like one of our civet boxes, and holds it first to the minister's nose, then to the child's, and lastly to the godfather's: they believe in fact that scents fortify and clear the mind making it more suited to devotion.[78]

Although these elements have remained part and parcel of the brit in most communities today, one custom accompanying the brit in northern France did not survive. In some respects, this practice resembles the custom of placing something under the head of a newborn to protect it from harmful spirits; in other ways, the custom is a northern European anticipation of the boy's initiation into schooling ceremony:

A custom after circumcision, soon thereafter, a quorum of ten [men] is gathered. A Pentateuch (humash) is taken. The baby is in the cradle (ba-'arisah) and is dressed up festively, as on the day of his circumcision. The book is placed on him and they say: "May this one fulfill that which is written in this." And someone says, "May God give you" (Gen. 27:28) and all the [other] verses [that are] blessings [in the Bible] up to "only then will you be successful" (Josh. 1:8). An inkwell and pen are placed in [the baby's] hand so that he will become "a skilled scribe in the Torah of the Lord" [based on Ezra 7:6].[79]

Although Jews did not practice any form of female excision or circumcision, some Jewish feminist writers have advocated a ceremony that would make a rite equivalent to male circumcision. Writing in *Response* magazine in 1974, Mary Gendler proposed "a ritual rupturing of the hymen soon after birth. The ritual should be performed by a woman. A special blessing and perhaps celebration (if the girl wishes it) upon the occasion of her first menstruation." Although the rupturing of a newborn's hymen has not been accepted, liturgies for other female infant rites of passage have followers today. Such celebrations are sometimes called "brit banot" (daughters' covenant) or "simhat bat" (joy of a daughter), among other terms, and need not be held after the first week.[80]

One innovative ritual is described by the Israeli (American-born) Orthodox feminist Haviva Ner-David:

> When our first daughter, Michal, was born, Jacob and I wanted her to start her life as a Jew who felt like an equal member of the Jewish people. . . . and we wanted to perform a ritual that would symbolize her participation in this brit with God. We wanted it to be something physical, something she would experience through her body, something akin to *brit milah,* but nothing that would leave a mark on her perfect miniature body or make her experience pain.
>
> On the seventh day after her birth we held a carefully crafted ceremony welcoming Michal into the brit, complete with songs, blessings, and rituals garnered from traditional sources, a variety of birth ceremonies others had done for their newborn daughters, and some of our own innovation and heartfelt creative outpouring at this emotional time. Most of the ceremonies we drew from were from families who are not Orthodox, although we did base a part of our ceremony on the *Zeved HaBat,* a traditional Sephardi ceremony for welcoming

a baby girl. When I was born, parties were common, but ceremonies were unheard of. Today, it is becoming more and more acceptable even for Orthodox Jews to have some kind of formal ceremony for newborn girls. For Michal's *brit ha-bat* (covenant of the daughter), as we called it, Jacob and I chose the seventh day rather than the eight, which is when boys have their *brit milah,* to follow the example of bat mitzvah, which occurs one year earlier for a girl than does bar mitzvah for a boy. . . . One of the rituals we performed at both of our daughters' ceremonies was dipping their hands into mikveh water.[81]

A Modern Orthodox/Traditional Brit Milah

A healthy baby boy is born. Among the first things the new parents want to arrange is the time and place of the brit and who will be the mohel. Family and friends are consulted. A mohel is contacted and booked. The place needs to be decided upon. It could be in the home. This brit will be in the local synagogue. It takes place right after the morning services, on the *bimah* (dais) on the large chairs where the rabbi and cantor usually sit. As it is customary to have a festive breakfast afterwards, those arrangements need to be made as well. One of the parents will order the juice, bagels, fish, cakes, and coffee and remember to bring the special prayer booklets so that the guests can all recite the Grace after Meals in honor of a brit.

There is much to do. Even before the brit, the parents will host a Shalom Zakhar in their home the coming Friday evening. As the day of the brit arrives, little else need be done except to think of the all-important name. An announcement about when the brit will take place is made locally and by phone to relatives and friends, but no invitations are sent out. Traditionally, if one is invited to a brit, there is an obligation to come. And so, usually, one makes an announcement and people are free to come or not.

The brit is on a weekday. The family and guests arrive at the synagogue for morning services. Immediately afterwards, the various honorees are reminded of their assignments. There are usually a kefatterin (godmother), who will help bring in the baby; the kefatter (godfather); and the sandeq (special godfather), who will hold the baby on his knees. Perhaps another female relative, a grandmother or a great-grandmother, will be asked to hand the baby to the kefatterin, making a kind of extra initial ceremony of transmission from generation to generation.

All is in readiness. Everyone awaits the arrival of the baby, sometimes brought to the synagogue by his mother and doting grandmothers. The mohel takes out his medical instruments and prepares for the ceremony, dressing in a gown, gloves, and a mask. A special cup of wine is prepared for the prayer in which the baby will be named. The scene combines an operating room with a festive celebration in home or synagogue.

The cast of characters in the drama is ready. Just outside the entrance to the synagogue, the women who are being honored line up and the baby is passed from one to the other. The last woman hands the baby to the kefatter, who hands him to the mohel. The baby is dressed in a special gown and cap and is sometimes carried on a satin- or silk-covered pillow.

When the baby arrives, the mohel greets him with the phrase "barukh ha-ba" (welcome). It is the same greeting the groom hears when he arrives at the huppah. Some explain that the words refer not to the baby but to the prophet Elijah, who is present. The mohel takes the child and places him on one of the special chairs that has been designated the Chair for Elijah (*kisei eliyahu*), and he recites a short passage that begins, "This is the Chair of Elijah, may he be remembered for good."

He then lifts the child and places him on a special wrapped pad that the sandeq is holding securely on his knees. He is seated in a second special chair, feet placed on a box or stool under them, so that his knees are elevated. The sandeq is instructed to hold the baby's legs and arms firmly so that he cannot move during the operation. The mohel asks the boy's father if he appoints him his agent to perform the rite. The father consents. The mohel undresses the infant and just before he begins, he recites the blessing to perform the circumcision.

The mohel then performs the rite. As he concludes, the father recites a blessing acknowledging that God has commanded him to "enter him into the covenant of our father Abraham." Those assembled reply to his words: "As he has entered the covenant, so may he enter the Torah, the wedding chamber, and a life of good deeds."

That is the first part of the ceremony. Immediately following, the mohel or the rabbi takes a full cup of wine and recites the blessing over wine and the prayer that includes the naming of the child. At the conclusion of the ceremony, the baby is dressed and handed back to the women who are there. Everybody then goes into the room where the breakfast has been set up. At the meal, the parents or others may make a brief devar Torah or talk about the significance of the name and the event, alluding to family members after whom the child has been named and other associations that are considered important. Following the meal, the Grace after Meals is recited and a special set of prayers thanking God are read, each beginning with the word "harahaman" (the Merciful) and each recited by a different guest. The baby is then brought home and people rush off to work.

NAMING BOYS AND GIRLS

Although naming a boy at circumcision became a standard practice in ancient Judaism, in the Hebrew Bible, a child was named right after he or she was born.[82] Either mother or father could name the child, as when Leah and Rachel named Jacob's sons and his daughter Dinah (Gen. 29:31–30:24). Jacob's youngest son, Benjamin, receives one name from his mother, Rachel, and another from his father, Jacob (Gen. 35:18). Hannah names her son Samuel (1 Sam. 1:20). On the other hand, Abram named Hagar's son Ishmael (Gen. 16:15), and God tells Abraham that Abraham will name Sarah's son Isaac (Gen. 17:19); Moses names his son Gershom (Exod. 2:22).

In the biblical narratives, the names parents give their children often seem to be Hebrew puns or glosses that are meant to express the special circumstance of the person's birth. They are not named after relatives, such as parents or grandparents. The plays on words are a kind of linguistic midrash or tag to be attached to the essence of that person for life. They emphasize the unique importance of each birth. For example, when Pharaoh's daughter finds Moses and names him, the text has the Egyptian queen supposedly making a Hebrew pun: "She named him Moses, explaining, 'I drew him out of the water'" (Exod. 2:10). This kind of naming story probably reflects the ancient practice of naming a child after circumstances that accompanied the birth.

The sound of the Hebrew for "I drew him" (*meshitihu*) sounds like Moses (*moshe*), but the name actually is derived from the Egyptian for "born of man," and other names of Israelites associated with the tribe of Levi are as well, such as Aaron, Moses' brother, and Hophni and Phinehas, Eli's sons.[83] This should not be surprising, considering the biblical account of Moses and his family in Egypt. Note that the names with special derivations are not found again in the Bible. There is only one Abraham, Isaac, Ishmael, Jacob, Esau, Moses, Aaron, and so on.

In the Bible children are sometimes given names alluding to elements of God's name, like "ya" or "yahu," or names of animals, plants, or trees. The earliest sign we have of the custom of naming a Jewish child after a grandfather, including a living relative, is from the Aramaic papyri that have survived from the Jewish military garrison at Elephantine, in upper Egypt, from the fifth century B.C.E., in late biblical times. This was a widespread practice in the ancient Near East, including among Egyptians, Phoenicians, Babylonians, and Persians, and Jews adopted it.[84] In rabbinic times, it is rare but is found, for example, in the ruling patriarchal family in ancient Palestine.[85]

This practice becomes very common in the medieval Muslim and Christian worlds. In the case of European Jews, it was customary in the eleventh century in Germany to name a child after a living grandfather, but this yielded to the custom, still prevalent among Ashkenazic Jews, to name a child only after a relative who is deceased. Spanish Jews still name newborns after living relatives.[86] Some American Jews name their sons after themselves, such as Samuel Goldwyn Jr.

An early example of the assumption that a Jewish boy could be named after his living relative occurs in the New Testament Gospel of Luke, which is also the first reference we have to a Jewish boy being named at the time of his circumcision, not right after he is born. This does not mean the custom was Christian, and then taken over by Jews, but only that the account in Luke reflects a Jewish practice in Judea from the second half of the first century, and perhaps earlier.[87]

In the Greco-Roman world, male circumcision could be a significant marker of Jews in contrast to gentiles, at least in some places, and the shift to naming a boy during that rite, instead of at birth, indicates circumcision's cultural significance in Judaism in late antiquity.[88] Some Jews tried to hide their circumcision by undergoing a painful operation to undo it.[89] Occasionally they had themselves recircumcised.[90] All of this suggests that the phenomenon was a cultural marker of significance.

In the narrative in Luke about the birth of John the Baptist, we see a combination of the Jewish practice from the Hebrew Bible of either the father or mother naming the child but delayed from birth to eight days later: "On the eighth day they came to circumcise the child, and they were going to name him Zechariah, after his father. But his mother said, 'No; he is to be called John.' They said to her, 'None of your relatives has this name.' Then they began motioning to his father to find out what name he wanted to give him. He asked for a writing tablet and wrote, 'His name is John.' And all of them were amazed" (Luke 1:59–63).

The custom of naming a Jewish boy at the circumcision rite is also mentioned in Luke's account of the birth of Jesus: "After eight days had passed, it was time to circumcise the child; and he was called Jesus, the name given by the angel before he was conceived in the womb" (Luke 2:21). Naming the boy during the circumcision rite is also mentioned in the Talmud[91] and in the medieval midrash *Pirqei de-Rabbi Eliezer,* which describes the naming of Moses at his circumcision,[92] not true to the biblical custom of naming him at birth, one more indication that the practice from at least first-century Palestine continued. It is also found in the earliest liturgies for the brit in the prayer books of Rabbi 'Amram Gaon (ninth century) and of Rabbi Saadia Gaon (tenth century),[93] and naming a Jewish boy at the time of circumcision persists to this day.

Hebrew or Jewish names accompany a child through most life cycle rites. In pre-egalitarian times, the main significance of the boy's Hebrew name was especially for the occasions in the synagogue when boys were called to read from the Torah or to recite the blessings. In egalitarian circles today, this applies to girls and boys. In addition, the Hebrew names of a bride and groom appear on the marriage documents, like the *ketubbah,* and they also are inscribed on the gravestone.

Although women have public uses for such a name, the need for men to be called up to read the Torah in the synagogue led to men having Hebraic names. To be sure, over the centuries, many men as well as women had Greek, Latin, German, Arabic, and other names as we find in thousands of inscriptions. Still, because of their restricted role in the synagogue, Jewish women were more likely than men to have only a vernacular name, not one also derived from Hebrew or Aramaic. In the Middle Ages, a girl's name was announced in the synagogue a month after she was born, the same time when boys received a vernacular name. More recently, a girl is named in the synagogue on the first Sabbath after she is born, the time a son is named if, for medical reasons, he cannot have a brit on the eighth day.

In the Bible, no parties are given when a child is born; nor is there one on his circumcision. Abraham and Sarah gave a party only when Isaac was weaned (Gen. 21:8), perhaps as much as two years after he was born, a practice that has been revived only recently in some circles. The *Mahzor Vitry* mentions a new custom that the ba'al brit provides a meal in the home the evening before the brit and then mentions the earlier custom that the father makes a party the night after the brit. The proof text is adduced from Gen. 21:8, which refers to the feast Abraham gave when Isaac was weaned.[94] The early medieval midrash now seems to refer as well to the newer custom of the evening before the feast and shows how eager the author was to justify a newly borrowed custom. Linking it to an irrelevant biblical precedent only served to reveal his anxiety about the custom's non-Jewish pedigree.

Boys are given their Hebrew or Jewish public name at the circumcision, So-and-So, the son of (name of the father). Even this formula has recently changed to include the name of the child's mother and father. Before egalitarian forms of Judaism developed in the twentieth century, a person was referred to in the synagogue by his or her mother's name, as today in traditional circles, only when a prayer was said for the recovery of his or her health. This practice was based on the ancient assumption that a person's maternity was certain.

In premodern times, girls were given their name, whether a Jewish one or not, on the fourth week after the birth, the same time the mother came out of seclusion and rejoined the community by going to the synagogue for the naming ceremony. The basis of the period of maternal seclusion and re-emergence is the biblical stipulation that after a mother gives birth to a boy she is ritually impure like a menstruant (*niddah*) for seven days and remains "in a state of blood purification" for thirty-three more days—forty all told; for a girl, however, a mother is unclean like a menstruant for fourteen days and is "in a state of blood purification" for sixty-six more days, or a total of eighty. Sexual relations could resume after either seven or fourteen days, but the mother was separated from the community for either forty or eighty days. In Second Temple times, the mother had a sacrifice offered and was thereby purified.[95] The sacrifice after childbirth continued until the destruction of the Temple in 70 C.E.[96]

In the Christian West, the biblical requirement was interpreted as the practice of "churching," when a newly parturient Christian mother went to church for the first time. Like it, the Jewish tradition varied from time to time and place to place. In early Christianity, Mary's presumed behavior became the norm. Since she gave birth to Jesus, a boy, Christian writers assumed that she returned to the synagogue after forty days.[97] Jews from late antiquity followed the Christian practice of sequestering the parturient mother for forty days, regardless of the sex of the child. The Talmud gives as the reason for the separation that during labor pains the mother vows never to have sex again with her husband.[98] In the fifteenth century, the custom is attested for the mother to come to the synagogue on the fourth week after the birth of either a boy or a girl, when the father received an 'aliyah and the girl's name was publicly announced. This custom is also mentioned in Italy (Modena) in the seventeenth century and in eastern Europe.[99]

In medieval Germany, when the mother came out of the house after four weeks, a Jewish girl had a double naming ceremony and a Jewish boy a second, secular naming rite. This occurred at home in the peculiar custom known as the Hollekreisch. Rabbi Moses ben Isaac Mintz, in fifteenth-century Mainz, already knew the term Hollekreisch from his father. In a responsum in which he deals with the problem of how to write a bill of divorce (*get*) for a woman who has the Hebrew name Hannah and the German name Hanalein—he answers that Hannah is the way to write it—he mentions the secular naming ceremony. He says his father taught him that "Hollekreisch" comes from two Hebrew words: "qeriyas" (calling out) and "hol" (the secular [name]), and so it means "calling out the secular name," that is, for the first time.[100]

This etymology is forced. The name of the rite contains one word, not two, and the Hebrew etymology reverses the syllables of the actual word: hol kreisch, not qeriyas hol. As is often the case with secondary forced etymologies, the effort indicates that a non-Jewish term and custom have been taken over and made Jewish. In this case, a German or central European custom connected to intimidating a demon known as Frau Holle has become part of a Jewish naming ceremony for boys and girls.

It took place after the Shabbat meal. If the child is a boy, boys age seven to nine would lift the baby's crib three times and cry out: "Hollekreisch, Hollekreisch wie soll das Kindschen heissen?" (what shall the little child be called?). A girl celebrated the Hollekreisch on the same Sabbath on which she received her Jewish name in the synagogue; it took place on the Sabbath afternoon in the home, and young girls lifted the cradle three times.[101]

An additional early modern German-Jewish custom (sixteenth century on) connected the boy's religious naming ceremony at circumcision with the day his mother went to synagogue for the first time, four weeks after his birth. At that time, the father received an 'aliyah and gave the synagogue the embroidered cloth in which the boy was swaddled during his brit, known as the "wimpel." The child's Hebrew name was written on it, along with other decorative motifs echoing the refrain at the brit, "as he has entered the covenant, so may he enter the Torah, the wedding canopy, and a life of good deeds." Baptism cloths were likewise returned to the church when a Christian mother was "churched," or returned to the religious community.[102]

The practice of Hollekreisch has basically disappeared for boys and girls. Today, a girl is usually named in the synagogue on the first Sabbath following her birth. The father (or both parents, in egalitarian synagogues) is called to the Torah, the name is announced, and the child is given a special blessing. A boy is given a Hebrew name at the brit. No second ceremony exists to bestow a secular name on boys or girls. In the United States, for example, the baby's legal name is simply entered on the birth certificate and word spreads as to the child's "English" name. Nor is there, in the vast majority of Jewish communities, a special rite today to mark the emergence of a parturient mother, though rituals continue to evolve.

The wimpel also disappeared as a general practice, though it remained a peculiarity of Jewish life in early modern and modern Germany. It became a record of a new male member of the community. In some communities, the wimpel was stored in the synagogue and used during the boy's bar mitzvah ceremony as a Torah binder and again during his wedding.

Pidyon ha-Ben *(Redemption of the Firstborn)*

The redemption of the firstborn is not a common occurrence. Although it has a biblical mandate, few Jews actually are required to perform it. The commandment is derived from verses in the books of Exodus and Numbers: "The Lord spoke further to Moses, saying: 'Consecrate to Me every first-born; man and beast, the first issue of every womb among the Israelites is Mine'" (Exod. 13:1–2); "'and you must redeem every first-born male among your children'" (Exod. 13:13 and 34:20); "'You shall give Me the first-born among your sons'" (Exod. 22:28).

The connection of the rite with sparing the Israelites' firstborn in Egypt is made explicit:

> The Lord spoke to Moses, saying: I hereby take the Levites from among the Israelites in place of all the first-born, the first issue of the womb among the Israelites: the Levites shall be Mine. For every first-born is Mine: at the time that I smote every first-born in the land of Egypt, I consecrated every first-born in Israel, man and beast, to Myself, to be Mine, the Lord's (Num. 3:11–13 and Num. 8:16–18).[103]

The time of the commandment is stipulated as well as the amount: "And the Lord spoke further to Aaron [ancestors of the Kohanim]: . . . Take as their redemption price for the age of one month up, the money equivalent of five shekels" (Num. 18:8, 16). The New Testament offers early evidence that it was done in the Temple with sacrifices for Jesus, according to Luke 2:22–24.

The statistical rarity of the event is clear from the biblical texts alone. First of all, the child must be male. That eliminates fifty percent of all births. In addition, the boy must be the firstborn, which means to the exclusion of any miscarriage or stillbirth. Moreover, the child must be born naturally; caesarian birth is excluded by the phrase, "the first-born, the first issue of the womb among the Israelites" (Num. 3:12). This is taken to be restricted to those firstborn who are also "the first issue of the womb" and not the stomach. Finally, the mother and father may not be descended from the tribe of Levi. That excludes fathers who are a Kohen or Levite and mothers who are a firstborn of those groups.

Consequently, unlike a brit, which depends only on a fifty-fifty chance of a child's being a male, a pidyon does not occur in more than five to twenty percent of first births, depending on how many Jews who live in a particular community claim descent from the tribe of Levi. If one takes into account all subsequent births that are not eligible by definition, the odds that any birth will require the ceremony drops dramatically, depending on the family size of a particular community. The biblical thirty days is observed, and the amount of the redeeming was stipulated in the Talmud as "five coins" that are given to the Kohen who officiates as the representative of the priestly class.[104] As in most of the rites, the rabbis sanctified the act itself by stipulating blessings over the event. In this case, the father says two over the redemption of the firstborn son: "Blessed are You, O Lord our God, King of the Universe, Who has sanctified us by His commandments and commanded us on the redemption of the firstborn ('al pidyon ha-ben)."

The second is the blessing that is recited the first time one reaches a particular stage of life or season of the year. In it one thanks God for "having kept us alive, preserved us, and enabled us to reach this season" (*sheheheyanu*).[105] In post-Talmudic times, a dialogue was composed between the father and the Kohen. One elaborate version is found in that great compilation of Ashkenazic rites attributed to the Maharil. In recent years, a new rite has been crafted for firstborn daughters, called "Pidyon ha-Bat" (Redemption of a Daughter).[106]

A ceremony that did not outlive biblical times is the celebration of a child's weaning, as mentioned earlier. From biblical times to today, then, the only rites of infancy that have persisted are circumcision and the redemption of the firstborn, both male rituals. In each case, the rabbis sanctified the ceremony and Jews internalized commonly practiced customs from the non-Jewish surroundings and made them part of the Jewish rite. This pattern of openness to the larger culture is also clearly seen in two additional rites of passage that developed for the first time in Christian Europe: the initiation of the Jewish boy into Hebrew learning and the first haircut.

A JEWISH BOY'S INITIATION INTO TORAH

Because of the unlikelihood that any child might be eligible for being redeemed as a firstborn, the liturgical refrain at the end of the brit omits any mention of it and goes on to wish that the child next "enter the Torah," then "enter the huppa," and then live a life of "good deeds." The phrase "enter the Torah" is ambiguous. Even as ambiguity in a text can generate midrash commentary, so ambiguity in a rite can generate different ritual interpretations in the form of new rites. This is what happened to the enigmatic phrase, "to enter the Torah."

It first came to mean to enter or to be initiated into the study of the Torah as a small child. That meaning is ascribed to it when a newly fashioned Torah initiation ceremony emerges in the Rhineland and northern France sometime in the late twelfth and thirteen centuries. We do not know what the phrase meant before then, but by the sixteenth century in Germany, as most of the ceremony began to disappear, "to enter the Torah" came to mean the time when a boy of thirteen years and a day performed a rite when he began to perform all the commandments of the Torah as an adult male for the first time. That rite of passage came to be called "bar mitzvah" (literally, obligated), a newly elaborate ceremony of a different kind of cultural initiation that developed around a slim ancient and medieval core but came to full expression for the first time only in early modern central Europe. It did not become widely practiced until modern times, and it is now universal among Jews around the world.

By the time Franz Kafka used the phrase it meant neither rite, but had been transformed into a secularized literary metaphor. In his novel *The Trial,* Kafka begins his parable "Before the Law": "Before the law stands a doorkeeper. To this doorkeeper there comes an ordinary man and requests *entry into the Law.* But the doorkeeper says that he cannot grant him entry now."[107]

The medieval details of the small Jewish boy's school initiation ceremony into Torah learning have been revived recently among Ultra-Orthodox Jews, even though it did not exist in biblical, rabbinic, or early medieval times under Islam. It appears for the first time in medieval Christian Europe as a special ceremony that takes place, at least in Germany, on the late spring festival of Shavuot (Pentecost), the time rabbinic Judaism taught that God gave the Torah to Moses on Mount Sinai.

Although the new rite combines variations of elements found in Talmudic mnemonics and early medieval magical traditions for increasing and retaining one's learning, this ceremony emerged when Jews in medieval northern France and Germany took these early elements and their awareness of contemporary Christian images and rituals all around them and fashioned this ritual as a polemical response to them. It dramatically denied the efficacy of Christian liturgical rites by instead affirming the truths of Jewish learning of the Torah, expressed through food symbols and their associations with the Torah as God's word. (Fig. 3)

The special ritual initiation ceremony is preserved in six extensive written versions, in one illuminated manuscript, and in a few fragmentary manuscript allusions.[108] Early on the morning of the late spring festival of Shavuot (Pentecost), someone wraps the boy in a coat or *tallit* (prayer shawl) and carries him from his house to the teacher. The boy is then seated on the teacher's lap, and the teacher shows him a tablet on which the Hebrew alphabet has been written. The teacher reads the letters first forwards, then backwards, and finally in symmetrically paired combinations, and he encourages the boy to repeat each sequence aloud. The teacher smears honey over the letters on the tablet and tells the child to lick it off.

Cakes on which biblical verses have been written are brought in. They must be baked by virgins from flour, honey, oil, and milk. Next

3. *The school initiation scene.* Leipzig Mahzor, *Leipzig, Universitätsbibliothek, Hebrew Manuscript, Vollers Catalogue 1102, vol. 1, fol. 131a. Reprinted with permission. Photo credit: Suzanne Kaufman*

come shelled hard-boiled eggs on which more verses have been inscribed. The teacher reads the words written on the cakes and eggs, and the boy imitates what he hears and then eats them both.

The teacher next asks the child to recite an incantation adjuring POTAH, the prince of forgetfulness (*sar ha-shikhehah*), to go far away and not block the boy's heart (*lev;* i.e., mind). The teacher also instructs the boy to sway back and forth when studying and to sing his lessons out loud.

As a reward, the child gets to eat fruit, nuts, and other delicacies. At the conclusion of the rite, the teacher leads the boy down to the river bank and tells him that his future study of Torah, like the rushing water in the river, will never end. Doing all of these acts, we are told, will "expand the [child's] heart."

The child's schooling initiation rite was a new way of concretely acting out the biblical vision of the prophet Ezekiel, who pictures himself literally eating God's words in the form of a scroll:

He said to me, "Mortal, eat what is offered you; eat this scroll, and go speak to the House of Israel." So I opened my mouth, and He gave me this scroll to eat, as He said to me, "Mortal, feed your stomach and fill your belly with this scroll that I give you." I ate it, and it tasted as sweet as honey to me (Ezek. 3:1–3).

In the child's initiation ceremony, the Jewish boy actually licks honey off of the written Hebrew alphabet and proceeds to eat honey cakes and hard-boiled eggs on which Hebrew letters of biblical verses and other texts have been written. Honey is mentioned, for example, in the first century by Philo of Alexandria as a source of learning and exemplifies the idea of the ritualization of metaphor.[109]

In the transition from adult Torah learning rites from antiquity into the medieval initiation for young Jewish boys, some elements were mixed together, while others were omitted in the ceremony as we have it. Although claiming that the ceremony was "a custom of our ancestors," the authors cite only biblical texts, such as the passage from Ezekiel, but no Talmudic or post-Talmudic literary sources as proof texts for their claim.[110] Appearing for the first time in late twelfth- and early thirteenth-century Germany and France, the initiation rite places special emphasis on eating symbolic foods at a time when Christian culture was newly focused on the central significance of the eucharistic sacrifice in the form of specially sweetened wafers and wine.[111]

Jews certainly knew about the eucharistic sacrifice and its requirements, since they sold Christians everything they needed to enact it.[112] We also have an interesting complaint by Rigord, King Philip Augustus's court biographer, around 1200, about Jewish behavior in northern France that he regards as blasphemous mocking of the Eucharist, and it overlaps at least in part with elements of the children's initiation ceremony:

Certain ecclesiastical vessels consecrated to God—the chalices and crosses of gold and silver bearing the image of our Lord Jesus Christ

crucified—had been pledged to the Jews by way of security when the
need of the churches was pressing. These they used so vilely, in their
impiety and scorn of the Christian religion, that from the cups in which
the body and blood of our Lord Jesus Christ was consecrated they gave
their children cakes soaked in wine.[113]

Although the Jewish children's initiation ceremony does not
make use of wine, Rigord's report from the same time and place as
some of the Hebrew accounts makes it plausible to interpret the cakes
as part of a mock Eucharist. Of related interest are Hebrew manuscript references from early fourteenth-century Ashkenaz to a Jewish magical ceremony designed to enhance someone's memory, one
of the purposes mentioned for the cake ceremony. Jewish adults are
to eat small honey cakes inscribed with the Hebrew alphabet and some
of the same verses used in the children's ceremony. In this case, since
the ceremony is to be performed on the eve of a festival, the celebrant
is also to drink a cup of wine over which special formulas are to be
recited. Here, then, we have wine and honey cakes together![114]

The overlap among the various references to cake and wine ceremonies suggests that the boy's initiation ceremony, Rigord's accusation, and the Jewish magical memory rite share a ritual vocabulary
that makes use of the symbols of the Christian Mass. Those elements
are directed toward Jewish purposes, and some of the time they also
serve as a mock Eucharist in a polemical confrontation with Christian sanctities.

One might also compare the cakes to be eaten on Shavuot to a Christian Pentecost custom: "Before the vigil service starts . . . blessing is
bestowed on a bowl of cooked wheat cereal mixed with ground nuts,
spices, and honey. Cakes and breads of wheat flour, which the people
bring are also blessed. These foods are called Kollyba (fine pastry), a
symbol of resurrection of the body (John 12:24). They are offered by
the faithful."[115]

A short related rite, preserved in two manuscripts, reports that a
child who learns the Hebrew alphabet is to recite the letters in groups

of four-letter combinations but is to recite twice as a word only the last four letters of the Hebrew alphabet. Doing so results in a sound that resembles "Christe, Christe!" The medieval author Rabbi Leontin says that the reason that only these four letters are doubled and pronounced is that they alone appear twice in the biblical verse, "When Moses charged us with the Torah as the heritage of the congregation of Jacob" (Deut. 33:4). This is one of the verses written on the tablet during the initiation ceremony. Those letters are in fact found twice in that verse, but so are other letters, such as *lamed* and *heh*. It is a forced interpretation designed to rationalize a custom that was borrowed from Christian practice. It Judaizes the import into Jewish ritual of words that are derived from the name Christ itself.[116]

The Ceremony Breaks Up

What became of the medieval initiation ceremony? Elements of it persisted in schools, but not in most localities. If anyone continued to eat letters baked on cakes or written on eggs on Shavuot, it was adults, as reflected in magical formularies, not children beginning schooling. And yet, we occasionally catch a trace of selected elements of the complex medieval initiation rite that somehow survived into modern times.

For example, in Hebrew alphabet wall charts from seventeenth- and eighteenth-century Italy, influenced by customs from northern Europe, we find quoted the phrase first found in the northern French liturgical compilation *Mahzor Vitry:* "first we entice him, and then it is the strap on his back." On these charts we also find a woodcut or engraving that illustrates the two parts of this saying. Angels hover over the schoolboys and drop coins or candies to illustrate the enticement part of the proverb, and in a second scene, a teacher raises a whip to a terrified child.

The illustration of the angel recalls not only the Hebrew saying but a ritual in Christian practice. In western Germany, on the feast of the Annunciation, March 25, "a boy dressed as an angel and suspended on a rope from the Holy Ghost Hole would slowly descend inside the church and hanging in midair would address 'Mary' with the words of Gabriel [Luke 1:26ff.]. While the children stared up at the approaching "angel" their mothers put cookies and candy on the pew benches making their little ones believe that Gabriel's invisible companion angels had brought them these presents from Heaven."[117]

The angels dropping rewards from heaven were also made into a ritual in eastern Europe and brought to America. As portrayed in the American Jewish film *Hester Street,* about New York Jewish immigrant life on the Lower East Side in the early twentieth century, the teacher stands behind the schoolboy who is poring over his studies. He drops candies onto the book and says, in Yiddish, "Look what an angel has dropped from heaven." The rite is a ritualization of the Italian wall-chart image of an angel dropping something on the child in the form of a blessing.

The Zionist and educator Shmarya Levin (1867–1935) relates in his memoir, *Childhood in Exile,* that when he began his elementary Jewish education in Poland a party was held at the house at which the teacher (*melamed*) and family and guests all went to his house for a big celebration:

> To me was handed a prayer-book. Two of the pages had been smeared with honey, and I was told to lick the honey off. And when I bent my head to obey, a rain of copper and silver coins descended about me. They had been thrown down, so my grandfather told me, by the angels. . . . When the ceremony was over, my father lifted me up, wrapped me from head to foot in a silken Talith, or praying shawl, and carried me in his arms all the way to the cheder. My mother could not come along—this was man's business. Such was the custom among us. The child was carried in the arms of the father all the way to the cheder. It was as if some dark idea stirred in their minds that this child was a sacrifice, delivered over to the cheder—and a sacrifice must be carried all the way.[118]

In this passage from the late nineteenth century, elements of the medieval written ceremony have become abbreviated or eliminated. Those that remain have been transformed into something related to but different from the earlier written versions. The core experience is licking honey from a Hebrew book. Here it is the prayer book, not an alphabet chart. There is no mention of inscribed eggs or cakes, no invocation to POTAH, demon of forgetfulness. Note, too, that the honey ceremony takes place in the home with the family, not in the school with the teacher.

The other element found in Levin's memoir that is also in the original texts from medieval Germany and France is the gesture of the father wrapping the child in a tallit, or prayer shawl, and taking him that way to the teacher. But the sequence is now reversed. In the medieval texts, the parent or a wise person wraps the child and takes him to the teacher, who presides over the alphabet ceremony. In Levin's memory, the honey ceremony is a family custom and is followed by the trip to the teacher. Nothing else in the written versions survived.

Apart from such fragmentary traces of the medieval ceremony, Jewish children tended to enter school, as in ancient rabbinic times, whenever they were ready, not just on Shavuot. Adults, rather than children, continued to associate special foods with the holidays. The incantation against POTAH, the prince of forgetfulness, as part of a school initiation, like its namesake, was forgotten.

Another element from the medieval initiation ceremony persisted down to modern times but migrated to a different time of the year. The custom of giving schoolchildren honey cakes is no longer associated with the Shavuot holiday in the spring but now comes at Rosh Hashanah, the Jewish New Year, in the fall. This custom is a merging of two separate sets of food symbols. Since in Jewish tradition the New Year is thought to be the anniversary of the day the world was created, marking it by eating honey was understood to represent that the entire cosmos was a divine gift. But honey need not be given to children in the form of a sweetened cake. In northern Europe, adults customarily ate red apples and honey and still do. The honey cake is a faint trace of the medieval school initiation rite. And since children begin their studies now in September, the association of honey with school and with the Jewish New Year have been merged—a contemporary equation of honey cakes and Torah.

A New Combined Rite by Ultra-Orthodox Jews and Others

Recently, part of the honeyed-alphabet custom has been revived in Ultra-Orthodox Jewish circles (*haredim*) in Israel and America with the unprecedented twist of combining it with the first cutting of a boy's hair at age three. This practice never had any historic connection with the Hebrew alphabet initiation ceremony. The custom of cutting a Jewish boy's hair for the first time at a specific age or date in the calendar is unknown to biblical and Talmudic culture. It is not mentioned in many medieval sources either. It originated, in fact, as an Arab custom in which parents cut a newborn boy's hair and offer a sacrifice of thanksgiving. In Islam, there are several rites associated with the child on the seventh day after birth. These often include three parts: sacrifice of a sheep, shaving the child's hair, and a festive meal.

Some viewed removing the hair as a way of eliminating the influence of evil spirits. It was the custom to weigh the hair and take the weight in metal and give it to the poor. The poor and others also partook of the sacrificial sheep. The meal was an opportunity to express joy at the birth of a new member of the Muslim community.[119] Jews in Palestine borrowed part of this custom from the Arabs and adapted it to a Jewish context. Haircutting in Jewish ritual is characterized by moving the ceremony to age three, based on the analogy of a three-year-old boy to fruit trees that may not be eaten until the fourth year.[120] The custom of weighing the hair and giving an equivalent amount to charity was part of the Jewish ceremony in eastern Europe and is still practiced elsewhere today.[121]

It started in Palestine. For centuries, a month after Passover, on the so-called Second Passover (*pesah sheni*), in the middle of the late spring Hebrew month of Iyyar, Jews made pilgrimages to holy graves in the town of Meron in Galilee, especially those of the first-century Palestinian sages, Hillel and Shammai. Their graves were located in a cave whose waters were thought to have healing powers. When Jews from Spain began to arrive in Ottoman Palestine, they shifted the focus of pilgrimage to the gravesite there of Rabbi Shimon bar Yohai, the traditional author of the Spanish-Jewish mystical classic *Zohar*. Important Iberian Jewish scholars, such as Rabbi Joseph Karo and Rabbi Solomon Ha-Levi Alkabetz, who lived in cities of the Ottoman Empire, such as Adrianopole, moved to Safed, in Palestine, and would visit the grave of Rabbi Shimon on the Jewish festivals, because they thought special spiritual powers remained from the days when Rabbi Shimon had taught Zoharic traditions there.

The important Safed mystic Rabbi Isaac Luria, also known as ha-ARI (ha-Ashkenazi Rabbi Isaac), started going to the grave of Rabbi Shimon bar Yohai especially on the eighteenth of the month of Iyyar. This date is also known by the Hebrew name *lag ba-'omer*, the thirty-third day between the second day of Passover, when the first sheaf (*'omer*) of the barley harvest was first offered in the ancient Temple, and Shavuot. Jews count off the days between the festivals and refer to it as "counting the Omer" (*sefirat ha-'omer*). (The word *lag* is an acronym for thirty-three {l = 30; g = 3}). According to medieval tradition, Lag ba-Omer was an interruption of a plague that killed thousands of Rabbi Akiva's students between Passover and Shavuot in second-century Palestine. Activities otherwise forbidden during the counting of the Omer period, such as marriage and cutting one's hair, were permitted on Lag ba-Omer.[122]

According to one of his students, when he first visited the grave of Rabbi Shimon bar Yohai, Rabbi Shlomo Luria cut his son Moshe's hair for the first time. The festivities on this day were also linked to a phrase in the *Zohar*, the festival of Rabbi Shimon bar Yohai ("hilula de-rabbi shimon bar yohai"). Jews lit great bonfires, echoing the Arab custom to make fires for the sacrifice of sheep after a child was born, and special songs were sung in the ancient rabbi's honor. Even though the holy graves in Meron had been visited as pilgrimage sites for centuries, Rabbi Shlomo Luria's custom set in motion the practice of cutting a son's hair for the first time in Meron on Lag ba-Omer, and it has continued to the present there.

In addition, the great sanctity Jews ascribed to the mystical teachings of Rabbi Shlomo Luria led other Jews who studied the *Zohar* to follow this custom. Soon Jews who were not mystical scholars began to treat Lag ba-Omer as the time to make a pilgrimage to Meron, where they would sing and dance, cut the hair of their small sons for the first time, engage in various mystical exercises, and visit the graveside of Rabbi Shimon bar Yohai. By the seventeenth century, the additional tradition developed that Rabbi Shimon bar Yohai had died on Lag ba-Omer. This added to the day the sanctity of remembering the anniversary of the death of a great sage. (See Chapter 4, on anniversaries of one's parents' death, or Yahrzeit.) On Lag ba-Omer today, Israelis customarily light bonfires and have cookouts throughout the country, a secularized form of the original celebration in Meron.

Sometime in the late eighteenth or early nineteenth century, many liturgical and other customs begun by the mystical circles of Rabbi Shlomo Luria in Safed spread to eastern Europe among the growing communities of the Hasidim or Jewish pietists. They adopted the Friday evening service of "Welcoming the Sabbath Bride" (*qabbalat shabbat*), recited by all traditional Jews of the Ashkenazic or northern European rite today. Safed mystics also wrote cycles of Sabbath songs to accompany the Friday evening and Sabbath noon meals, and they are still sung today by most traditional Jews.

Another part of the Safed legacy to Hasidic and later traditional Jewish piety was the haircutting ceremony. In eastern Europe, the Hasidim celebrated it on the child's third birthday, not on Lag ba-Omer. Although the Hasidic Jews refer to this haircutting rite as "upsherenish," Yiddish for "haircut," Israeli Hasidim today call it "halaqa," which is Arabic for "haircut," thereby preserving its Arab origins even in Yiddish!

The haircutting practice continued in Palestine and eastern Europe through the nineteenth century and down to the 1940s (in Europe) and to today in Palestine/Israel without making any connection to the nearly forgotten honeyed alphabet initiation rite until just a few years ago.[123] In the 1990s, books describing a combined rite—a first haircut followed by the honeyed alphabet ceremony—were published in Israel in Hebrew and in the United States, in English and Yiddish, as how-to books for parents to show their children. They explain that on the boy's third birthday, he receives his first pair of long pants and his first ritual undergarment, a kind of mini prayer shawl worn under the shirt. He also gets his first haircut. Note that by doing this, he goes from being a little wild thing to becoming a little hasid, since now his earlocks are left uncut and flow down the sides of his face. Like the transition from birth to brit, when the Jewish boy first is transformed from an imperfect natural creature into a little Jewish boy by being circumcised, the three-year-old is further civilized now by growing up ritually.

The cutting away of his hair, again an act of removal viewed as a positive change culturally, leaves the hair that is significant, the earlocks, or "pe'os," which by Jewish law are forbidden to be cut off. He also puts on two garments that add to his Jewish life: first, ritual fringes (*zizit*), which are to remind him of the commandments he begins to follow, and, second, long pants, which are a further sign that he is becoming a little man. An indication of the link between the first haircut and maturity, is a special gold-colored round sticker to be placed on little boys when they are three. It pictures a boy wearing a big black skullcap and long side curls, smiling in his new *arba' kanfot* (child's tallit), which he wears over his dress white shirt and on which is written "Mazel Tov." Written in a band, encircling the boy, are the Yiddish words "I am three years old!" and pairs of scissors cutting hair are pictured at the bottom of the circular band. The sticker is dated 1994. Some modern Italian boys used to receive their first pair of long pants when they were confirmed as teenagers.[124]

Following the haircut, the boy is taught the Hebrew alphabet on a special chart smeared with honey, which he licks up, a link to the medieval initiation ceremony. He now ingests Torah and honey, God's gifts to the Jews. He will start learning his aleph bets, or ABCs. In combination, these two independent ceremonies are an innovation, a new compound rite that Ultra-Orthodox Jews have invented in the late twentieth century. Three books for children and parents were published only in the early 1990s.

The alphabet ceremony is not part of an ongoing European tradition. In reality, most of the *heder* initiation rite faded away in late medieval times. Only small parts persisted and then in newly fashioned forms, such as the parent or teacher throwing coins or candy on the book and saying that an angel had thrown it from heaven. Other Jews have already adopted and adapted the idea, and it has spread to other sectors of the Jewish world. For example, Jonathan and Gail Schorsch created their own combined ceremony in Berkeley, California, for their son Emanuel.[125] Some Orthodox Jews introduce three-year-old girls to Friday night and festival candle lighting as a female equivalent to a first haircut for boys.

The pattern of reinventing the ceremony from one of the earliest medieval sources, Rabbi Eleazar ben Judah of Worms's *Sefer ha-Roqeah,* exemplifies the recent form of Jewish fundamentalism and neo-traditionalism that is a late twentieth-century phenomenon.[126]

This liturgical and ritual inventiveness is also characteristic of the late 1960s and the return-to-Judaism movement of progressive, egalitarian varieties. They have in common a break from any organic, historical tradition from parent to child and replace it with a book, either a venerable one, as in the case of the Ultra-Orthodox taking up *Sefer ha-Roqeah* from early-thirteenth-century Germany, or the *Jewish Catalogues,* in the progressive community.

It should also be noted that the very process of ritual inventiveness is itself a persisting pattern of traditional Jewish culture. The alphabet ceremony itself was an innovation in the twelfth and thirteenth centuries; its revival as part of the haircutting rite, then, is new but also a continuation of that pattern of Jewish ritual experimentation and self-discovery that is a constant. That pattern is also demonstrated in the gradual emergence of the bar mitzvah ceremony as marking the coming of age of a Jewish boy and the modern rites of bat mitzvah and confirmation.

2

Bar Mitzvah, Bat Mitzvah, Confirmation

Twenty, not thirteen, marks a biblical Israelite male's time of maturity, responsibility, and adulthood.[1] Even after the rabbis introduced age thirteen for the first time, along with signs of physical maturity, twenty continued to be significant as the minimum age for buying and selling real estate, for example. What is the meaning, then, of "at age thirteen, subject to the commandments" (Pseudo-M. Avot 5:23)?[2] It is not clear when the significance of age thirteen first emerged; nor do we know what it implied about how a boy could act religiously before he reached thirteen.[3]

The Mishnah and Talmud make it clear that a Jewish father is required to train his son to perform many commandments, not when he reaches a certain age, but when he is able to do them properly, at an indeterminate age, which the rabbis spent time trying to define. The rabbis developed categories such as "she-eino zarikh le-imo" (when he no longer needs his mother)[4] or "ke-she-hegi'a le-hinukh" (when he reaches the age of training)[5] or "qatan ha-yodei'a" (when a minor knows [how to take care of something]), as, for example, in the Mishnah, "A minor who knows how to shake the lulav is subject to the obligation of lulav" (Mishnah Sukkah 3:15). The Talmud adds:

Our Rabbis taught: A minor who knows how to shake [the lulav] is subject to the obligation of the lulav. [If he knows how] to wrap himself [with the tallit] he is subject to the obligation of zizit; [if he knows how] to look after tefillin, his father must acquire tefillin for him; if he is able to speak, his father must teach him Torah and the reading of the Shema.[6]

Although the phrase "at age thirteen, subject to the commandments" refers to the age when a boy is obligated to do all of the commandments, like an adult male Jew, several ritual commandments are to be done by a young boy who is capable of doing so earlier. Among these are putting on tefillin and being called to read the Torah in public with the blessings before and after the reading itself.[7] These two commandments would later be associated in particular only with a boy who reached the age of thirteen years and a day. But being thirteen was not required for a Jewish boy to do either of these public acts either in Talmudic or early medieval times.[8]

In some Muslim-Jewish communities, long after certain commandments had been restricted in parts of Christian Europe only to thirteen-year-old boys, Jews continued to teach their sons to perform them when ready. In Yemen, for example, the customs of bar mitzvah did not develop at all. With little difference between religious minority and majority, there was no need for a rite when a boy became thirteen.[9]

Before the late Middle Ages, it was also possible for a boy under age thirteen to be part of a religious quorum of ten men (*minyan*) or the threesome needed to recite the public version of the Grace after Meals (*zimmun*). About Rabbi Isaac ben Judah, head of the Mainz academy in the eleventh century, there was a tradition that "At the time of a fire in his city, he had to organize a minyan so he could pray and could find only nine who were over thirteen (*benei mizvah*) and he included a young boy (*na'ar*) holding a Pentateuch to pray with [a quorum of] ten."[10] This was vigorously debated in the Middle Ages, an indication that the practice was persistent. Rabbeinu Tam, for example, wrote that this was a stupid custom (*minhag shtut*), since it obviously was the boy alone who constituted the tenth, not the book![11]

At some point, it was precisely such religious acts that were reserved only for the moment a boy reached age thirteen years and a day, not before. It was then, as part of his initiation rite of becoming "bar mitzvah," or obligated *for the first time,* and not before, that he was required for the first time to do them. And when that change began to occur, the moment of transition from religious childhood to adulthood was made into an increasingly more elaborate rite of passage. A boy of age thirteen years and a day eventually came to be called a "bar mitzvah," meaning a newly responsible religious Jewish male. Exactly how the restrictions on the religious behavior of pre-thirteen-year-olds developed, and in their wake eventually emerged a compound rite of passage between a newly carved out religious minority and adulthood, is difficult to say in more than a sketchy way.[12]

BAR MITZVAH

To trace the history of the bar mitzvah rite, we first need to clarify what it means. A boy reaches age thirteen years and a day. For the first time, the boy is now no longer prohibited and is also obligated— both are needed—to perform certain religious acts that adult males are required to do, such as put on tefillin, get called to the Torah for an 'aliyah, be counted in a prayer quorum. On the day that this happens, his father gets up in public and blesses God that now he is not responsible for his son's sins. The boy gives a specially prepared Torah discourse at a festive meal that marks the occasion. Finally, it is the practice of the community where this takes place not to expect boys younger than thirteen to do any of the commandments that are part of the bar mitzvah rite. When all of these elements are in place, we can speak of the bar mitzvah being part of a community's religious experience. There will be some places where boys will start to put on tefillin a month or longer before their bar mitzvah, but it is the bar mitzvah that matters. These elements appear together for the first time in the German Empire no earlier than the sixteenth century, and it is still not clear how long it took to develop and become popular elsewhere.[13]

The history of the rite of bar mitzvah did not have a linear development, and it is not possible to correlate its development at each point with a trend to restrict certain religious obligations only to thirteen-year-olds. The complete rite did not exist as such in late antiquity or even in medieval times. As we will see, one or more elements of a ceremony marking a boy at age thirteen crop up from time to time, usually in connection with one particular rabbi, almost always in the German Empire from the eleventh century on. There is no evidence to support the idea that each dot on the graph represents anything more than an isolated case.

This means that when we find a source that refers to a practice that later was incorporated into a complex bar mitzvah rite, we can refer to it as a bar mitzvah rite, but we should not confuse that isolated practice with what developed much later. Moreover, even the appearance at a certain time of the compound rite does not mean it was practiced in more than one region. The history of the diffusion or, less likely, independent development of the complex rite needs to be studied systematically, but the indications are that we are talking about modern times—nineteenth and twentieth centuries—for most Jewish communities outside of the German Empire and eastern Europe.

We will also see that the same pattern occurred with the beginnings of bat mitzvah: though the earliest occurrences found thus far of any recognition of a Jewish girl reaching her twelfth birthday are no earlier than the nineteenth century. Here too we have to define what we mean and examine carefully any practice that marked off a girl's twelfth or thirteenth birthday with a special act. Again, we will see that there was no linear development and that one early rite in the United States was connected with the family of a particular rabbi. Moreover, it was decades later before what we have come to know as an egalitarian bat mitzvah emerged, let alone became widespread.[14]

S. D. Goitein already sensed the multi-stranded history of the bar mitzvah rite. He pointed out the absence of any celebration of bar mitzvah in the Mediterranean communities documented in the Cairo Geniza and added: "Long ago it was observed that the term 'bar mitzvah' for a ceremony appeared only in the Late Middle Ages in Central Europe." But he continued, "A kind of ceremony seems to have been older . . . A recent study by Arnoldo Momigliano . . . makes it likely that some such ceremony was in vogue in Germany around 1100, that is, in Geniza times."[15] I agree that *the* bar mitzvah ceremony appears first as a central European rite of passage, though even later than Goitein thought, but its absence in even later Italian and eastern Europe memoirs raises many questions about its universal emergence in modern times.

Several such misunderstandings have led to dating "bar mitzvah" to rabbinic or gaonic (early Muslim) times. For example, in light of the well-known ages-of-man post-mishnaic text that is now attached to Mishnah Avot, one author writes, "The bar mitzvah . . . ritual can be traced back to the second century C.E.,"[16] that is, the time of the Mishnah. Apart from not being part of the Mishnah, that oft-quoted text does not actually refer to any ritual at all. Nor does it use the term "bar mitzvah." Moreover, as we have seen, age thirteen years and a day meant for the rabbis in late antiquity the age by which a Jewish boy was required to take on the obligations of an adult man. He was required do so earlier for certain ritual commandments, if ready, but all were obligated to do so no later than that age. The age of thirteen years and a day, then, did exist by the early third century, but there was no rite attached to the day because it was not yet a sharp time of transition into religious adulthood.

Others have pointed to a passage in *Masekhet Soferim,* an early medieval Palestinian legal source on liturgical practice, that "there was a good custom in Jerusalem to train the minor sons and daughters for a fast day: an eleven year old a half day, and a twelve year old a full day. Afterwards, [the father] carried him [not her?] to each elder to bless him and encourage him by praying that he derive merit from doing the commandments and good deeds."[17] This translation is based on a corrupt version of the text that actually refers to a child of the age of one or two, not eleven or twelve.[18]

An innovative feature of the bar mitzvah rite is that age thirteen years and a day became the age every Jewish boy is first required to take on adult male religious obligations. Before that age, he is increasingly being discouraged or even prohibited from doing so, even if he is capable and ready. Indeed, the term "bar mitzvah" changes its meaning to reflect this. In rabbinic times, bar mitzvah means "being obligated," as in the case of a Jewish male *of any age* after thirteen years and a day. It was a synonym for *bar 'oneshin,* meaning "culpable or responsible for one's actions" as an adult Jewish male. In the Middle Ages, the term begins to shift its meaning and is associated with a child's rite of passage, the age when he must act like a Jewish male *for the first time,* at age thirteen years and a day, when "he becomes bar mitzvah."

In addition to the ancient rabbinic idea of thirteen years and a day as the age when religious obligation takes effect for all males,[19] only one of the other elements is even rabbinic in origin. The earliest hint of an action of any kind associated with a boy who reaches age thirteen is from late antique Palestine in *Midrash Bereishit (Genesis) Rabbah,* compiled perhaps by the fifth century C.E. There we are told, "whoever has a son who has reached the age of thirteen years should say the blessing: 'Blessed [is the One] who has exempted me from [responsibility for] this one's punishment.'" The midrash refers to the age of thirteen, at which the boy, not the father, is legally responsible for his own religious acts. That age, we recall, did not coincide in antiquity with the earliest time he was allowed to perform some adult male religious obligations, but after he reached it, he was responsible for all of them on his own.[20]

The boy does nothing when the father makes his declaration. We do not even know if they are together when the father recites it. Nor do we know where the father is. For all we know, he could say it privately at home on the day in question. Although the passage might refer to something liturgical, we are not told if any ceremony marked the occasion. The fact that medieval European and modern Jews came to link the father's declaration with a rite of passage for the son does not mean that it meant that in ancient Palestine. All the other features of bar mitzvah rites are post-Talmudic customs that developed at different times and seem to crop up earlier in medieval Germany than anywhere else.[21]

We do not hear about a boy's rite at age thirteen until many centuries later. Two medieval European texts refer back to an eleventh-century German rabbi as observing a rite that connects a boy's reaching the age of thirteen years and a day, when he gets his first 'aliyah to read from the Torah in the synagogue, with his father's reciting the blessing that is mentioned in the ancient midrash. There is a gap from the fifth to the eleventh centuries here and a geographical leap from ancient Palestine to the Rhineland.

The first text is from Rabbi Aaron ben Jacob Ha-Kohen of Lunel, a rabbi writing in southern France in the fourteenth century. He seems to refer to an element in a rite that dates back to the Geonim, the centralized rabbis of Baghdad from the early Middle Ages. If this were true, it would be an exception to Goitein's observation that there is no hint of a bar mitzvah rite in Muslim lands in the Middle Ages. As we will see, the authority only seems to be one of those Geonim and, in fact, refers to a German rabbi.

In his compilation *Orhot Hayyim* (Paths of Life), Rabbi Aaron quotes the passage from *Midrash Bereishit Rabbah* about a father who recites a blessing when his son reaches the age of thirteen, and continues:

> [A] There are those who say it the first time their son goes up ('oleh) to read the Torah.
> [B] And the Gaon Rabbi Yehudai, of blessed memory, stood up in the synagogue and recited this blessing the first time his son read from the Torah.[22]

Notice that Rabbi Aaron does not actually say that the son goes up to read the Torah for the first time when he is age thirteen. This is implied in the second clause [B] and is not stated in the first [A]. But even if we assume that this is what he means, Rabbi Aaron tells us that even in fourteenth-century Provence there is no regular linkage between the father's recitation of the blessing of release from parental responsibility for his son's sins after he reaches age thirteen and the son's getting called to the Torah at that age. He only says, "there are those who say it" on that occasion, which implies that it is a relatively new custom, at least in southern France, and was not universally practiced there. He does not tell us where or when it was done or how old such a practice is. Moreover, his comment implies only that the combination of the father's reciting the formula and the son getting called to read the Torah for the first time is new.

He then supports this newly combined practice by citing a precedent that "the Gaon Rabbi Yehudai, of blessed memory," did it. At first glance, Rabbi Aaron seems to be speaking about the great Iraqi Gaon, Rabbi Yehudai ben Nahman (mid-eighth century), the head of the academy of Sura (southern Iraq) and compiler of the code of Jewish law known as *Halakhot Pesuqot* (Decided Laws). But the reference is not to that great sage. If it had been, we would expect this custom to be incorporated into the earliest liturgical books that were created in Sura in the ninth and tenth centuries, the basis of all subsequent Jewish prayer books.[23]

Rather, Rabbi Aaron of Lunel is alluding to a medieval German rabbi. Although the title *gaon* is often linked to the sages of Iraq, it was also applied to distinguished rabbis of medieval Europe, and that is the case here. Rabbi Aaron is referring to Rabbi Judah ben Barukh, who is sometimes quoted with the title *ha-gaon*.[24] He apparently was a student of Rabbi Gershom ben Judah of Mainz (d. 1028) and a teacher of Rashi of Troyes (d. 1105). This locates his custom in the German Empire around the second third of the eleventh century.

This becomes clear from a second medieval text that contains an explicit written tradition about Rabbi Judah ben Barukh on this practice. It is part of a collection of thirteenth-century rabbinic decisions from northern Europe and transmitted by later German authorities:

[A] Whoever has a son age thirteen, the first time he gets up in public to read the Torah, the father must bless [as follows]: Blessed are You Who redeemed (!) me from the punishment of this one.[25]

[B] And the Gaon Rabbi Judah ben Barukh got up in the synagogue and said this blessing when his son got up and read for the first time from the Torah, and this blessing is an obligation (hovah hi).[26]

The thirteenth-century compiler/author takes for granted that sons will get called up to the Torah for the first time at age thirteen. From the emphasis on the father's blessing being "an obligation" it apparently had not been the practice for some fathers to do so. Sons were getting called to the Torah without the father's participation. This text is found among a series of short traditions compiled by Rabbi Yehiel of Paris (mid-thirteenth century), many of which are German-Jewish sources.

To make an impression on his readers, the author points to the precedent of the Gaon, Rabbi Judah ben Barukh, who "got up in the synagogue and said this blessing when his son got up and read for the first time from the Torah." Even if Rabbi Judah ben Barukh did recite the midrashic blessing when his son went up to read the Torah for the first time when he reached the age of thirteen, an innovation not attested earlier, there is no indication of how widespread that custom was. This practice is found in a single source and may have been this rabbi's family custom. There is no reason to assume that it was practiced in other circles. We may just as well think that younger boys continued to be called to the Torah earlier and that some fathers either did or did not follow the custom in *Midrash Bereishit Rabbah* of saying a blessing when a son reached age thirteen, even if the boy himself did not go up to the Torah then for the first time.

Besides these two late medieval references to the innovation of Rabbi Judah ben Barukh in eleventh-century Germany, there is another to what seems to be a bar mitzvah practice in early fifteenth-century Germany. It is in the compilation of Rabbi Jacob ben Moses

Ha-Levi Molin, known as Maharil. Although the report is cited in the name of Rabbi Mordecai ben Hillel Ha-Kohen (1240?–98), also of Germany, the passage has not been found in his writings.

> When MaHaRI SeGaL [=Maharil]'s son became bar mitzvah and he read the Torah, he would bless him: "Blessed Are You, O Lord, our God, King of the universe, who exempted (petarani) me from this one's punishment." And this blessing is also found in *Mordekhai ha-Gadol* with the name of God and His Kingship [="O Lord, our God, King of the universe"].[27]

This passage is sometimes cited as the first case of a bar mitzvah ceremony, but this is not at all clear. From the way the text is written, we do not know if Maharil's son did anything when he "became bar mitzvah," that is, reached the age of thirteen years and a day. The subject of "he read" could be the father who read the Torah, rather than the son. Nor does this text say that "he" read the Torah for the first time. The text may simply reiterate the midrash in *Midrash Bereishit Rabbah* and add that the father said his blessing in the synagogue when he or his son had an 'aliyah when the son reached age thirteen. This text, unlike the one about Rabbi Judah ben Barukh, does not say that the boy got an 'aliyah—if it was the boy and not his father who got called to the Torah—*for the first time* when he "became bar mitzvah," that is, age thirteen years and a day. Even if it was the son who read the Torah for the first time, again, not stipulated here, it would only be another instance of what we found in the case of Rabbi Judah ben Barukh, not a first.

The other new information is that Maharil's blessing used the complete formula of a rabbinic blessing and not an abbreviated form, which later rabbis would insist on as proper, since this blessing does not have the authority of one prescribed in the Talmud, but is based only on a midrashic compilation.

In any event, there is no proof of any continuity of this new practice from the days of Rabbi Judah ben Barukh. We do not know how often age thirteen was the occasion for a boy to read from the Torah for the first time. Clearly, some fathers did not recite the blessing on the occasion a son got called to the Torah for the first time at age thirteen. This seems to have been a relatively isolated practice of some German rabbis, and the anonymous author of the tradition wants it to be "an obligation." Rabbi Aaron wants to enforce the custom that fathers in southern France do so, too. Clearly, some did not do it there either.

An underlying factor that may account for the relatively rare documentation of a father blessing God that he is no longer responsible for the religious behavior of his son as he turns thirteen is a debate on that very subject that is hinted at in medieval German sources, the very place the earliest instances of some kind of rite of passage at age thirteen appears. When the Talmudic authorities concluded that a boy who "knew" or "who was ready" was supposed to put on tefillin or eat in a *sukkah,* and so on, the question arose about who was responsible if he failed to do so properly. Was the father responsible or the son, even though he was still a minor?

In point of fact, the rabbis still considered the boy's father responsible for the boy's failure to carry out some of the commandments that he had begun to do before he turned thirteen. The boy did commit a sin when he did not do what his father had taught him, but it was the sin of not obeying his father's instructions. The father, on the other hand, deserved punishment when the son failed to carry out one of the special commandments, because he was responsible for teaching him properly and he did not do so.[28]

Perhaps the custom developed in late antiquity for a father to recite a blessing that he was no longer responsible for his son's punishment because there were others in ancient Palestine who thought the son should be punished like an adult for not doing the commandment even though he was still a minor. The emergence of the father's blessing may be contextualized by proposing that a debate was already underway about this. Those who argued that minors were not responsible directly to God, but only to their fathers, created a public gesture to indicate their point of view. And so, when a man's son reached the age of thirteen, the father acknowledged that he, the father, not the son, had been responsible before, but now the son, not the father, was. The blessing does not place the emphasis on the boy: it does not say that the boy now will be able to earn greater reward from God because he is now responsible for his own religious conduct. Rather, it emphasizes the consequences of the boy's sinning for the father, specifically that the father's responsibility is over.

Although we do not have contemporary texts that indicate such a debate was going on in the circles in ancient Palestine where *Midrash Bereishit Rabbah* was edited, there are later signs in Germany of such a difference of opinion. Methodologically, this leap is not as far-fetched as it might at first appear, since there is good evidence that some German rabbis in the late twelfth and early thirteenth centuries, known as Pietists (*hasidim*), were aware of many ancient Palestinian customs and traditions. The debate over parental responsibility of minors may in fact be yet another example of this cultural stream of transmission from Palestine to Germany.[29]

In the early thirteen century, the author of *Sefer Hasidim* comments that a boy is responsible for his sins even though he is a minor:

Someone came before a Sage and said to him, "I remember that when I was a child (qatan), I used to rob people and commit other sins. Perhaps I do not require atonement since when I committed the sins I was not yet thirteen years and a day old? Since I was a minor, why should I need atonement and to make restitution?" The Sage said to him: "[For] the sins you remember [you need atonement] and everything you stole you have to repay." But if other people tell him, "You were very young when you stole," he does not have to make restitution now that he is an adult, since he does not remember doing so himself.[30]

About a century later, Rabbi Asher ben Yehiel, also originally from Germany, wrote, "it is a law derived from Moses at Sinai" that only a thirteen year old is responsible for his sins, not someone younger, an indication that the issue was still not settled.[31]

The debate over religious responsibility and its meaning may be connected with the scattershot appearance of the ancient blessing a father is to recite when his son becomes thirteen. It may well be that many Jews were accustomed to thinking that the boy was responsible, even as a minor, and only a few rabbis considered the age of thirteen the time when the son was on his own. Both Palestinian traditions reached medieval German Jewry, the blessing recited by those who thought only thirteen-year-olds and older were responsible, as in the view of Rabbi Asher ben Yehiel, and the other tradition that surfaced in *Sefer Hasidim* that minors were responsible for their own sins.

From the late twelfth century, and especially at the end of the thirteenth in Germany, restrictions on minors to perform even ritual commandments permitted them in the Talmud were more frequently expressed. A trend to limit religious activities to children of the age of discretion was also a feature of contemporary Christian institutions that stressed the importance of a person's awareness of his or her acts and of requiring sufficient age to assure taking conscious responsibility for them. Although by itself this restriction does not explain the emergence of the fully formed bar mitzvah rite centuries later, it does suggest the beginnings of a gap being created between religious minority and the age of responsibility of thirteen years and a day.

An indication of the same pattern is the criticism mounted by the Cistercian Order against the ancient and venerable practice of parents donating their small children to a life of monastic service. Infant oblation, as it was called, was strongly discouraged from the twelfth century on, even though it continued in many places. The trend by the twelfth century was to defer religious obligation to the age of fourteen for boys and twelve for girls.[32]

The Talmud seems to recommend a similar criterion when it refers to a Jewish boy's readiness to perform a commandment as the requirement for doing so, even if he is not yet thirteen years old. One might have expected that Christian insistence on maturity as a prerequisite for anyone to participate in adult rites, as in the Talmud, would positively reinforce the ancient Jewish practice of permitting children who were aware and capable to perform adult Jewish rites. But the very opposite seems to have happened.

Christians determined that the measure of a child's maturity was the age of fourteen, for boys, and twelve, for girls, an ancient Roman standard, not some indeterminate time based on a vague concept such as readiness (higi'a le-hinukh). The principle of stipulating a specific age seems to have overridden the more subjectively determined yardstick of the child's readiness. Observing older Christian children participating in rites that had formerly been open to younger children may have driven this change home for Jews. The shift in Christian practice, in other words, may have led Jews to apply more broadly than before the Talmudic age of majority of thirteen years and a day for boys and twelve years and a day for girls. By the late twelfth and thirteenth centuries, some rabbis began to assume that the age of thirteen, not readiness, was required for adult male religious participation.

A sign of the restrictive trend occurred in the late twelfth century. Rabbi Isaac ben Abba Mari of Marseilles (ca. 1120–90), the author of *Sefer ha-'Ittur,* objected in Provence to a boy's putting on tefillin before age thirteen and interpreted the Talmudic text that seems to permit it to refer to a Jewish male who is over thirteen.[33] At first, northern French and German authorities did not accept the implications of this view. Rashi's grandson, Rabbeinu Tam, continued to enforce the plain meaning of the Talmud that permits even young boys who know how to take care of tefillin to put them on. He was followed by such German-Jewish authorities as Rabbi Mordecai ben Hillel Ha-Kohen.[34]

Even as late as the sixteenth century, Rabbi Joseph Karo (1488–1575), the great Sefardic codifier of Jewish law, also upheld this generally accepted sense of the Talmud, but his Ashkenazic glossator,

Rabbi Moses Isserles (1525/30–72), disagreed. Isserles reaffirmed the implications of Rabbi Isaac ben Abba Mari's view: "The practice (*min-hag*) is in accord with the author of the *'Ittur*: minors *should not* put on tefillin until bar mitzvah, that is, thirteen years and a day."[35]

Note that Isserles also has to explain the meaning of the term "bar mitzvah" to refer not to any Jewish male thirteen and over who is "obligated" to perform the commandments of Judaism, as in the Talmud,[36] but to a boy when he becomes thirteen years and a day, who then becomes obligated *for the first time at that age*. In Isserles's comment, the term is acquiring a new meaning that reflects the prohibition of young boys acting like adult men with regard to performing certain ritual commandments. The term "bar mitzvah" was beginning to mean the *earliest* time a boy must do the religious acts he formerly had been encouraged to do earlier.

Elsewhere, Isserles cites Maharil to support restricting another religious duty to boys only of that minimum age. In places that do not already permit it, one may not let a boy lead the synagogue services as cantor Saturday nights unless he is of the minimum age of obligation (bar mitzvah) on the Sabbath in question. This ruling is issued despite the *Shulhan 'Arukh* explicitly permitting minors to do this.[37]

Yet another custom was being modified in the sixteenth century based on the minimum age of thirteen years and a day. Rabbi Mordecai ben Hillel and Maharil would recite the blessing when "a boy becomes bar mitzvah" introduced by the regular formula that mentions the name of God, "Blessed are You, O Lord our God, King of the universe."[38] This refers to the ancient Palestinian and medieval German custom of the father reciting a blessing when his son reaches this age, the earliest rite that became in time part of the bar mitzvah ceremony. Isserles insisted that the blessing should be recited without mention of God's name and kingship, in a truncated form, since this blessing is not found in the Talmud but is merely a custom.

Although we have seen that there was a custom for at least one boy in Germany in the eleventh century, and maybe later as well, to read the Torah for the first time when he reached age thirteen, other

Jews apparently continued to permit minors to do this for centuries. Rabbi Isaac ben Moses of Vienna (ca. 1180–1250) observed that young boys could get called to the Torah in Germany, but the northern French rabbis had limited them to reading it once a year on the festival of Simhat Torah, a custom that continues today. In effect, a boy's religious minority was being newly defined in practice, and an exception was permitted on that holiday, instead of all year round.[39]

Of special influence in this matter was Rabbi Meir ben Barukh of Rothenburg (d. 1293), the most important rabbinical authority in the second half of the thirteenth century in the German Empire. As Elisheva Baumgarten has shown, Rabbi Meir reversed centuries of custom that permitted Jewish women to participate in synagogue rituals such as serving as a *ba'alat brit* who held the baby on her lap during the circumcision ceremony.[40] Rabbi Meir ben Barukh of Rothenburg also opposed a custom involving minors. He argued that a minor should not be counted as the tenth man in a male quorum (minyan): "To put it bluntly, I tell to you that when they add a minor to make up the ten, you should walk out of the synagogue and no harm will come of it!"[41]

Further confirmation of the German origin of some kind of rite of bar mitzvah—not counting the ancient Palestinian blessing—meaning a boy who reaches the age of thirteen and obligation and reads the Torah for the first time, is from the major Polish rabbinical figure, Rabbi Shlomo ben Yehiel Luria (Maharshal, 1510?–74). He observed that when a boy reaches age thirteen, "the German Jews make a bar mitzvah feast" and "there is no greater obligatory religious feast than this. . . . One offers praise and gratitude to God that the young boy (na'ar) has been able to become bar mitzvah (lihiyot bar mitzvah) . . . and that the father has been able to raise him until now and initiate him into the covenant of the complete Torah (le-hakhnisho bi-verit ha-Torah bi-khelala)."[42]

Rabbi Shlomo's words allude to the phrase from the circumcision ceremony of "entering the Torah," which he glosses "covenant of the complete Torah" and takes to mean not learning the Hebrew alphabet at the beginning of schooling but entering the life of observing the commandments for the first time at age thirteen years and a day. The phrase "becoming bar mitzvah" was becoming associated mainly with the threshold ritual of a boy's new obligation at age thirteen. By the seventeenth century, Yuspa Shamash of Worms can say, "a boy who is thirteen years and a day old is called 'bar mitzvah.'"[43] From there, the term would eventually come to refer to the boy himself as "the bar mitzvah boy."

The bar mitzvah feast, Rabbi Shlomo continues, should be considered an obligatory religious meal (*se'udat mizvah*), "when the boy is trained to offer a Torah exposition appropriate to the occasion."[44] This is the first reference to a bar mitzvah speech involving Torah exposition and demonstration of Jewish learning in association with the compound rite that we have come to think of as bar mitzvah. It is documented, then, no earlier than the middle of the sixteenth century, only about Jews living in (or from?) German lands, and remarked upon by someone living in Poland as something German Jews do.[45]

Although some have pointed to hints at a feast for Jewish boys at age thirteen perhaps as far back as twelfth-century Germany as well as in thirteenth-century Spain, no rite is clearly attested then, only literary allusions, and Rabbi Shlomo was surprised to hear about such a bar mitzvah feast even in the sixteenth century. In his Latin account of his conversion to Christianity, the former Jew, Judah the Levite, writes, under his new Christian name Hermannus, that when he was thirteen he had a dream. He was at a feast and received presents and made a speech of thanks. This report is part of the symbolic language of the dream that Hermannus constructed in order to drive home his argument that Christianity is more attractive than Judaism. But it is also possible a feast at age thirteen was a Jewish practice already in twelfth-century Germany. This possibility led Arnoldo Momigliano to propose that the report may reflect the practice in Judah's life of a celebration of his reaching the age of thirteen.[46]

To reinforce further that central Europe is the source of rites related to the marking of a boy's thirteenth birthday, we have a partially preserved reference from the thirteenth-century rabbinic scholar Rabbi Avigdor Ha-Zarfati, a colleague from Vienna of Rabbi Isaac ben Moses of Vienna. Rabbi Avigdor refers to the custom of preparing a meal when a boy reaches his thirteenth birthday. This German custom found its way, as did many scores of other German-Jewish customs, into the *Zohar,* the great compilation of Spanish mystical and legal traditions that appears in the end of the thirteenth century in Castile.[47]

The surprise Rabbi Shlomo expresses in his comment reflects his concern that this new custom may not actually be a religious meal that entails certain consequences. That is why he mentions the learned Torah talk as part of the occasion, the first evidence we have of this part of a bar mitzvah celebration. It would give the meal the function of a ceremony of celebration accompanying study of Torah. From the way he describes it, it seems that even this was not yet firmly established even in Germany.

Nor did the literary tradition in the *Zohar* spawn a Spanish-Jewish ritual meal there; in Poland, it was associated with German Jews (Ashkenazim). Again, as with other features of the bar mitzvah rite, we do not know if the meal was practiced continuously from the twelfth century (if, in fact, it was even done then), or from the thirteenth century, when the *Zohar* was written down for the first time, or even from the sixteenth century, even in Germany. Once again, we see the regional character of the sources that are part of a bar mitzvah rite throughout the Middle Ages and well into early modern times. It was a gradually developing German-Jewish custom, sporadic, idiosyncratic, nearly trivial, and only extended beyond Germany in some limited respects, either to Spain (*Zohar*) or Provence (Rabbi Aaron ben Jacob Ha-Kohen).

The bar mitzvah speech has been captured by the nineteenth-century German-Jewish painter Moritz Oppenheim, but today the typical visual symbol of the bar mitzvah, outside of learned traditionalist communities, is the child reading from an open Torah scroll or at least reciting the blessings over it. The open Torah scroll and the learned Torah discourse as bar mitzvah symbols again echo the phrase from the ancient circumcision refrain "to enter the Torah."

Since early Polish rabbinic authorities point to Germany as the place where some kind of innovation attached to "becoming bar mitzvah" began and grew, it is not surprising to see it attested there, at least sporadically, from early modern times. For example, the Worms synagogue sexton (*shamash*) Yuspa left memoirs that include a comment about his own bar mitzvah in 1617:

> The following incident occurred when I reached the age of thirteen on Sabbath, *Parshat Tezaveh,* 13 Adar I, 5733 [February 18, 1617]. I was taught to chant the Torah portion, but when the Rabbi was informed of the situation, he did not permit me to read *Parshat Tezaveh.* Rather, he required me to read *Ki Tavo* on the following Sabbath, for they decreed that the one who chants the Torah portion must have reached the age of thirteen years and one day. The incident occurred in the community of Fulda.[48]

How widespread was it? We need a comprehensive study of this question, but the evidence suggests it was not that common except in some parts of central Europe well into modern times. For example, in sixteenth-century Ferrara, Daniel ben Samuel Rosina could describe his son's growing up and not mention it because it was not needed. The boy could still do the religious rites when younger, as in the days of the Talmud:

> At three Joseph encountered his Creator [in other words came into contact with the world of religion]. He began studying the first day of the month of Iyar 5320 [=1560]. At four and a half he read the Haftorah in the synagogue, on the occasion of the wedding of Messer Baruch of Arles. . . . At five and a half he learned to write. At six he started wearing the Phylacteries [tefillin]. At eight and a half . . . he was studying the Alfasi [a famous medieval Talmudical compendium].

At twelve and a half he began reading the Torah in the synagogue . . . and the same year he learned ritual slaughtering. . . . During the feast of Simchat Torah in the year 5322 [=1571] he recited the morning liturgical service in the synagogue.[49]

There is no bar mitzvah ceremony because there is no gap that the ceremony helps the child cross over. Memoirs from modern times do not make much of the event at all. Leon Modena, the first Jew to write an extensive autobiography, refers in the seventeenth century to births, circumcisions, weddings, and deaths, especially of children, but does not mention a rite of bar mitzvah in his own life or that of his sons. Indeed, in his book about Jewish rites, which was a response to descriptions of Jewish life in Christian Hebraist Johann Buxtorf's *Juden Schül* (1603; English trans. 1663), Modena describes no rite at all but only the enhanced status of a Jewish boy who reaches religious responsibility at thirteen years and a day:

> When a Son is now come to be Thirteen years, and a day old, he is then accounted a Man, and becomes bound to the Observation of all the Precepts of the Law and therefore is now called Bar mitzvah, that is to say filius mandati, a Son of the Commandment, although some call him Bar de minian, that is to say, one that is of age to do any businesse, and may make One, in the number of the Ten, that are required to be present at any of their Public Acts of Devotion. And whatever contracts he makes, they are of force; and if he were formerly under, he is now Freed from their Jurisdiction over him: and, in a word, both in Spirituall, and Temporal Affaires, he is Absolute Lord and Master of Himself.[50]

Even Buxtorf's description is no more than the father reciting a blessing that God "had delivered and unburdened him of the punishment due unto his son for his sin." Beyond that Buxtorf says that the boy has now "learned the manner and custom of the *Zizim* and *Tephillin* [tallit and tefillin]." There is no description of the boy's being called to the Torah or a festive meal at which the boy delivers a special Torah lesson.[51]

The bar mitzvah rite does not come up in the extensive memoir that Glueckl of Hameln wrote about her life and that of her family in the late seventeenth and early eighteen centuries in Germany. She dwells at great length on the various attempts to arrange marriages for her daughters, but there is no hint that any of her sons had a bar mitzvah ceremony or that it was important. The Jewish Kantian philosopher Solomon Maimon does not mention it in his autobiography either.

Among the many presentations of Jewish life and ritual that Christian Hebraists and converts to Christianity wrote from the sixteenth through eighteenth centuries, hardly any of the dozens of accounts ever refer to the rite of bar mitzvah and the few that do are from the late seventeenth century.[52] One of these is reported from Venice in the second part of the extensive polemical tract written by the former Jew, now turned Christian, Giulio Morosini. On the Sabbath, the boy of thirteen comes to the synagogue, where everyone greets him. After the morning service, the boy is called to read the Torah, "which he was not permitted to do before." The boy then recites a special blessing, "thanking God that he has become bar mitzvah," and he announces gifts of different amounts of charity contributions in honor of the occasion to the functionaries in the synagogue. When the boy finishes, he is blessed again and kisses the hands of his father and his teacher.[53]

But even such ceremonies apparently were rare until the eighteenth century or even the nineteenth century. In a striking way, the development of the history of bar mitzvah in Europe may illustrate the famous thesis proposed over forty years ago by the amateur historian Philippe Ariès. Although medievalists and Judaica scholars have criticized his claims that children before the eighteenth century were treated only as small adults and that parents did not have a strong affective bond with their children, one wonders if the newly fashioned notion of childhood to which he pointed from the eighteenth century on might in fact be reflected in the history of the diffusion of the rite of bar mitzvah.[54]

In the Muslim world, S. D. Goitein noted not only that the bar mitzvah ceremony "left no trace whatsoever in the Geniza" among Jews living in Mediterranean societies in the Middle Ages, but also that the Jews of Yemen never developed much of a bar mitzvah ceremony until they became acculturated to Israeli Jewish life:

> The situation was probably similar to one observed in the traditional Yemenite community about fifty years ago. Since those Yemenites gave their children a strictly religious education starting at the age of four or so, there was no marked passage from childhood to adulthood worthy of an elaborate celebration. When a father noted that his boy was ready and eager to comport himself religiously like an adult, he adorned him with the prayer trappings described in the Bible (Deuteronomy 6:8) even before he reached the obligatory age of thirteen.[55]

One comes across references from eastern Europe much later, of course, but how the pattern of celebrating it developed in different parts of the Jewish world is still not clear. The brief references from eastern Europe stress the learned speech more than anything else. For example, Shmarya Levin mentions that several months before he became thirteen, "My Rebbe began to teach me the Shulchan Aruch." "The Synagogue ceremonies," he continues, "held no terrors for me. At the age of seven I had already been called up to the pulpit for the reading of the week's section of the Prophets." Presumably, he got called up to read from the Torah for the first time and his father recited the blessing of becoming exempt, but Levin does not describe this. His emphasis is placed on the learned discourse he delivered at a banquet to which nearly the whole town was invited. The description reads less like a bar mitzvah speech than a defense of a doctoral dissertation:

4. Bar Mitzvah photograph taken of Charles S. Lefkowitz in 1922 in New York City. Courtesy of Dr. Ruth S. Lefkowitz

My Bar mitzvah address was a complicated and involved treatise on a Talmudic point. I went through it without an error. At the close of it the four Rabbis questioned me closely on the subject matter, and I answered them on that day with unusual ease and skill. When the examination was over, they congratulated my father.[56]

So, then, how old is the bar mitzvah ceremony with which we are familiar today? When the father blesses his son at age thirteen years and a day and the boy becomes obligated (bar mitzvah) to fulfill all the commandments? Or, when he is allowed to read from the Torah in public for the first time at age thirteen years and a day (one rabbinical family in eleventh-century Germany)? Or when a festive meal is prepared for the boy who reaches age thirteen years and a day (Hermannus, Rabbi Avigdor Ha-Zarfati, *Zohar*)? We do not know. (Fig. 4)

The evidence discussed thus far points to the German Empire as the place where bar mitzvah rites developed well into early modern times and from there spread to eastern Europe. They moved with German Jews into northern Italy as well, but we do not know how long it took to become common in Italy, or in the Netherlands, with its mixed Sefardic and Ashkenazic populations, or into the parts of Europe to which Jews were readmitted, such as England and France. Nor do we know when the rite is taken for granted in the New World and in different Jewish communities in Muslim lands, where it was not all that important before. At some point, apparently no earlier than the eighteenth or maybe even the nineteenth century, or even later, modern Jews adapted an elaborate bar mitzvah rite in nearly all of these places. After considering the beginnings of bat mitzvah rites, I will turn to some of the modern permutations bar and bat mitzvah underwent.[57]

BAT MITZVAH

One of the most radical innovations in the United States was the introduction of a bat mitzvah ceremony ritually equivalent to bar mitzvah. There were occasional attempts to recognize a girl's coming of age in eastern Europe in the nineteenth and early twentieth centuries, the former in Warsaw (1843) and the latter in Lemberg (1902). The occasion was marked by a party without any ritual in the synagogue. More formal was the "entrance into the minyan" ceremony for boys and girls ages thirteen and twelve, respectively, in which several girls and boys were blessed by the rabbi and recited a blessing, documented in different Italian-Jewish communities from the mid-nineteenth century.[58] One recent Baghdadi authority, Rabbi Joseph Hayyim ben Elijah al-Hakam (1833/35–1909), also refers to a modest family occasion, without a festive meal, when the girl wears her Sabbath finest or, if her family can afford it, a new dress and recites the blessing of gratitude, known as "Sheheheyanu," thanking God "who has kept us alive" to mark the occasion of her coming of religious age.[59] None of these occasions to mark the coming of age of a Jewish girl of twelve years and a day is what we today would think of as a bat mitzvah, though they are rites to mark the occasion in different traditional Jewish communities.

The true history of the bat mitzvah, it is often said, begins with "the first bat mitzvah," that of Judith Kaplan, the daughter of Rabbi Mordecai Kaplan, founder of the Reconstructionist Movement of American Judaism.[60] Given the egalitarian nature of the American bat mitzvah today in non-Orthodox congregations, the claim suggests that Rabbi Kaplan created a ceremony analogous to the egalitarian service that is familiar today as an American bat mitzvah, when a young girl of thirteen reads part of the Torah and recites the haftarah and all blessings before and after each reading and possibly delivers a short devar Torah to the congregation during the services.

Something very different took place at Judith Kaplan's bat mitzvah, and it was not until the 1940s that the now familiar egalitarian ceremony first appeared anywhere, and it didn't spread until the 1980s, as part of the movement for Jewish women to participate in leading services and in being called to the Torah. The congregation where Judith Kaplan's bat mitzvah rite took place, the newly founded Society for the Advancement of Judaism (S.A.J.), still had separate seating for men and women in March 1922, only three months after Kaplan became Leader. He did not use the title Rabbi for several years. Judith reports: "The first part of my own ordeal was to sit in that front room among the men, away from the cozy protection of mother and sisters."[61] Kaplan introduced family pews in the synagogue only in the fall of that year for the High Holiday services.[62]

Moreover, Judith was not thirteen but "midway between my twelve and thirteenth year."[63] Her twelfth birthday had been on September 10, 1921, when her father was still the rabbi of the Jewish Center, an Orthodox synagogue. Kaplan began to conduct services at the newly founded S.A.J. only in January 27, 1922.[64] The oldest of his four daughters, Judith was the first to be of bat mitzvah age when he was in a position to create a ceremony for a young girl in the new synagogue. The rite took place on March 18, 1922, when she was still twelve, the traditional age for a girl to reach religious majority. As Judith herself remembered, the day had been planned and invitations sent to family and friends, but the ceremony itself was rather hastily improvised the evening before.[65]

She did not read from the Torah scroll but from her Humash (Pentateuch):

> Father was called up for the honor of reading the Maftir. When he finished the Haftarah I was signaled to step forward to a place below the bimah at a very respectable distance from the Scroll of the Torah, which had already been rolled up and garbed in its mantle. I pronounced the first blessing, and from my own Chumash read the selection that Father had chosen for me, continued with the reading of the English translation, and concluded with the closing berachah. That was it.[66]

Finally, although Judith later recalled that the occasion took place on "a sunny day, early in May of 1922,"[67] and that the reading of the week was "the magnificent Holiness Code,"[68] that is, Kedoshim, Leviticus 19–20, Kaplan's journal clearly records, at the time, that the event took place on March 18, when the portion of the Pentateuch read in synagogue was Ki Tissa (Exod. 30:11–34:35).

He wrote on March 28, 1922:

Last Sabbath a week ago (Mch. 18) I inaugurated the ceremony of the [in Hebrew characters:] *bat mitzvah* at the S.A.J. [Society for the Advancement of Judaism] Meeting House (41 W. 86th St.)—about which more details later. My daughter Judith was the first one to have her [in Hebrew:] *bat mitzvah* celebrated there.

Unfortunately, Kaplan added no further details in the journal about the ceremony.[69]

The section from Leviticus includes the great teaching of the Golden Rule (Lev. 19:18); the portion from Exodus deals with the sin of the Golden Calf! Later on, Judith Kaplan Eisenstein would recall that she had read a selection from Leviticus, and she says in her memoir that her daughters "each, in turn, read, on Shabbat Kedoshim, not only the highly ethical code of behavior in the Torah, but the poetic words of the final chapter of the book of Amos."[70]

There is a discrepancy between the date Kaplan wrote in his journal (March 18) and the date Judith herself remembered as the date when her bat mitzvah took place (early May). Kaplan clearly wrote the entry in his journal just ten days after the event, on March 28, and there is no reason to think he wrote it later and backdated it.[71]

Although Judith correctly remembered that she read from Leviticus that day, she did not realize years later that Kedoshim had not been the regularly scheduled portion of the week that the men had just read before she got up to speak. In fact, the men read Ki Tissa on March 18, but Kaplan had selected for her a passage from Kedoshim the night before, probably including the Golden Rule, because of its spiritual content. Years later, when each of her two daughters had her egalitarian bat mitzvah, she scheduled it on the Sabbath when Kedoshim was read. At some point, Judith either asked her father or looked up when Kedoshim had been read as the weekly reading in the synagogue in the spring of 1922, learned that it had been in early May, and inferred, incorrectly, that that was when she herself had celebrated her "bat mitzvah."[72]

Judith Kaplan's bat mitzvah rite, then, was sui generis. It was a ceremony one rabbi invented for his own daughter, and it was by no means the beginning of a new trend. As Judith Kaplan Eisenstein herself wrote, "It was many years before the full privilege of being called to the Torah was granted to a girl, even in the Society for the Advancement of Judaism."[73]

That it did not catch on for some time, is also clear from Kaplan's own comment, written in his journal Wednesday, May 31, 1933:

> The institution of the Bas Mizvah which I introduced into the SAJ not long after the Society was organized had fallen into desuetude of late. There has not been a single Bas Mizvah celebration during the last two years. This morning Shirley Lubell, the daughter of Sam and Jennie Lubell, celebrated her Bas Mizvah. I hope that from now on that institution will be kept up regularly.[74]

May 31, 1933, was the festival of Shavuot, but it is not clear from Kaplan's remarks if her ceremony was any different from his daughter Judith's. Since women being called to recite the blessings over the Torah did not begin there until the 1940s, and not on a regular basis until 1951, though well ahead of most American non-Orthodox congregations, the rite of bat mitzvah remained out of synch with women participating in the adult services for nearly thirty years.[75]

As the bat mitzvah developed in Conservative and Reform synagogues, the ceremony was usually relegated to the Friday night service, when the bat mitzvah girl, age thirteen, recited the haftarah scheduled to be recited by a man the next day. In the past, even young boys had been permitted to read the haftarah in traditional synagogues. In the seventeenth century, Leon Modena relates in his autobiography that he had done so, showoff that he was, when he was only two and a half years old! So it was not very threatening for a girl of thirteen to do so Friday night. In some Conservative congregations, a bat mitzvah ceremony took place at the Havdalah ritual that marks the transition from the Sabbath to the workweek.[76]

Although the rise of a bat mitzvah rite contributed to Jewish liturgical equality for women, it was only with the arrival of the women's movement in America and the concomitant American Jewish women's efforts to enable women to assume positions of liturgical leadership in progressive American synagogues that the *egalitarian* bat mitzvah developed on Saturday morning and involved the reading of the Torah. Girls of thirteen, like boys, were now called up to read from the Torah, recite the blessings, as well as read the haftarah and make a brief speech from the podium during the Sabbath morning services, no different from boys at their bar mitzvah rite. The process to reach this stage of bat mitzvah was a long one and only in hindsight can one say, with some degree of accuracy, that Judith Kaplan's bat mitzvah was a first. In reality, it was a straw in the wind, an indication of her father's egalitarian views that would sweep the American Jewish scene more than a half century later.

Viewed from the perspective of what was to develop, Judith Kaplan's bat mitzvah rite resembles some of the instances of a boy's bar mitzvah rite from the eleventh century on at age thirteen. Like the early medieval cases of bar mitzvah, Judith's was also a rabbinic family. Like theirs, her rite was an innovation that one particular rabbi introduced. And like those cases, there is no reason to assume that there was continuity afterwards before we encounter the next instance of another rabbi innovating another feature of the rite much later. Neither event was the beginning of a trend or tradition. In Judith Kaplan's case, it is not clear what prompted her father to make the innovation in the form he did, and he did not comment further on the rite itself.

One thing is clear. Kaplan was not influenced by a ceremony that Italian Jews had created to mark the entrance of Jewish girls and boys, ages twelve and thirteen, respectively, "into the minyan" and religious adulthood. He learned of that ceremony firsthand, but only months after he had created his daughter's rite in New York. The Italian-Jewish practice resembled Catholic confirmation, in that a group of teenagers were given a special religious blessing by a clergyman.

In the Catholic Church, confirmation is a sacrament, conducted by a bishop, and in which the Holy Spirit strengthens a baptized child in his or her faith and Christian identity. Several boys and girls of the same age are confirmed at the same time, though each individually approaches the bishop, who anoints each with oil "to mark their reception of the seal of the Holy Spirit." Each child also takes on an additional name at confirmation.[77]

Though in antiquity the three rites of baptism, First Communion, and confirmation were performed at the time of baptism, and the parent or godparent took the place of the child's confession by answering the bishop for the child, in medieval Europe, it was difficult to find a bishop and the rite of confirmation was often deferred to early childhood. From the late Middle Ages on, Catholic confirmation, together with First Communion, took place at age seven for centuries but in more recent times, especially since the Second Vatican Council in the 1960s, it is often celebrated between the ages of thirteen and sixteen, with the aim of extending a child's Catholic religious education, much like the rationale in Jewish Reform and Conservative synagogues. First Communion, however, has remained a childhood rite for boys and girls in the second grade (age seven or so), when girls dress up in white like little brides.

Italian-Jewish memoirs from the twentieth century record a Jewish rite that resembled Catholic confirmation in that a group of girls or boys and girls went through a ceremony that involved a clergyman's blessing them. For example, Dan Vittorio Segre pointed out, in his own memoir, that his mother had been taught "some vague notions in preparation for her bat mitzvah, celebrated in the style of a Christian girl's confirmation." About himself, he reports, "We children had all made our entry into *da-minyan,* a corrupted Jewish expression indicating our coming of age. Jews of thirteen years of age enter into a minyan. . . . To prepare for this they used to send us to Talmud Torah, courses of Judaism."[78]

The type of rite Kaplan saw in Rome, patterned on Catholic confirmation, was sometimes held on Shavuot (Pentecost), which is when teenage Jewish confirmation often takes place today. Edda Servi Machlin describes such a moment as a bat mitzvah in her memoir about Jewish life in the Tuscan village of Pitigliano:

> Toward the end of my sixth grade, on Shavuot 5698 (June 5, 1938), I celebrated my Bat Mitzva—a sumptuous ceremony in which I performed the role of the Rabbi. Roses of all kinds filled the temple and a carpet of rose petals covered its beautiful marble floor. The children's chorus sang Baruch Abba, the song sung on festive occasions, while my father escorted me to the Echal, the steps in front of the Ark, where the Torah scrolls are kept.[79]

Mordecai Kaplan himself wrote in some detail about an Italian ceremony that he witnessed in Rome, while on an extensive European trip, several months *after* he had independently created a bat mitzvah ceremony for his daughter Judith in New York. He did not connect what he saw in Rome to his daughter's ceremony in New York a few months earlier. Writing about it on the return sea journey aboard the S.S. *Arabic* on August 22, 1922, Kaplan recalled:

> I was very much pleased to see that they had the custom of taking cognizance of a girl's becoming Bas Mizvah. They call it entering "Minyan" at the age of twelve. The ceremony consists of having the father called up to the Torah on the Sabbath that the girl becomes Bas Mizvah. She accompanies him to the Almemar [Cantor's platform], and when he is through with his part she recites the benediction of [Hebrew letters:] sheheheyyanu ["Who has kept us alive," a blessing giving thanks to God for reaching a milestone]. Before Musaph [the additional service on the Sabbath], the Rabbi addresses her on the significance of her entering minyan. On the Sabbath I was at the synagogue there were three girls and one boy who entered Minyan. The assistant Rabbi who was supposed to address them read something to them out of a book in a very mechanical fashion. The fathers of the girls acted as if they were rather infrequent visitors at the synagogue.[80]

MODERNITY, BAR MITZVAH, CONFIRMATION, AND BAT MITZVAH

Although features of Catholic confirmation are reflected in the "minyan" ceremony for boys and girls among traditional Italian Jews, Protestant confirmation influenced leaders of the Jewish Reform Movement in Germany. An effort was made in early nineteenth-century Germany to replace the traditional bar mitzvah with a new Jewish ceremony for boys and girls age fifteen or sixteen. The emphasis in the Protestant rite was on religious education and study, not sacramental change by means of a clergyman's gestures. It apparently was first instituted in Dessau, in 1803, and was then taken up in Wolfenbüttel, where the future Judaica scholar Leopold Zunz was confirmed in 1807, and then in other communities.

The experiment with confirmation focused on introducing boys and girls to the principal teachings of Judaism in the form of questions and answers, an attempt to fashion a Jewish catechism. This educational technique had already been used in the late sixteenth century, in Abraham Yagel's *Leqah Tov* (Venice, 1595), based on a Catholic manual, but the Reform effort was an independent initiative. Not surprisingly, there was opposition to this, and combinations of bar mitzvah and confirmation persisted in different communities in Germany and beyond.[81]

Jewish teenage confirmation was introduced in France in the 1840s, with girls wearing the white dresses Catholic children wore when they celebrated their First Communion at a much younger age. And in England, also in the 1840s, the West London synagogue annually held a confirmation ceremony on the Jewish New Year, after the blowing of the ram's horn, in which boys and girls, age thirteen, participated. Even an eastern European community observed the Reform institution.[82]

In the United States, some American Reform congregations also replaced bar mitzvah with the egalitarian and education-oriented ceremony of confirmation. It was instituted in Temple Emanu-El, in

New York City, in 1847.[83] Other Reform leaders insisted that bar mitzvah should be retained where it was already customary. Opponents of bar mitzvah pointed to its exclusion of girls and to the fact that Reform men did not need to have liturgical skills since they did not participate as leaders in the synagogue service. The notion of an equally obsolete role for girls in the form of a bat mitzvah did not come up for obvious reasons.

Conservative congregations added a confirmation ceremony to bar mitzvah to mark the graduation of those children who continued their Jewish schooling in supplementary Jewish high school programs. These ceremonies usually were held on Shavuot and the girls wore white dresses, an echo of their Christian origin. Congregation by congregation also discussed introducing some kind of bat mitzvah ceremony to mark a girl's coming of age at thirteen and to set a goal for a girl's religious education in the supplementary synagogue school.[84] Although, as already noted, Conservative synagogues adopted a bat mitzvah ceremony when the girl read the haftarah at the end of the Friday night service, as the egalitarian movement grew in the United States in the 1970s and 1980s, the egalitarian bat mitzvah service on Shabbat morning became more common.[85]

Ironically, but for different reasons, most boys and girls who had a bar/bat mitzvah ceremony regarded it as a last rite in their Judaism. Before egalitarian times, the bat mitzvah was a unique, onetime event for girls. They could not repeat the rite in the synagogue service, where women were not able to participate. In reality, it was also the case that most bar mitzvah boys in Conservative and Reform synagogues considered the bar mitzvah the culmination of their Jewish education and would not repeat their rite in the synagogue either. The difference, of course, was that boys theoretically could do so, and some did over their lifetimes; girls, before egalitarian Judaism, could not.

The same can be said about bar mitzvah for secular Israelis today. Secular Israelis often have their sons prepare some of the liturgical readings in the traditional Orthodox synagogue nearby. They do not just have a party but move into the synagogue for the rite and its extensive preparation. To be sure, an Israeli boy whose native or acquired language is modern Hebrew does not have as difficult a time learning to chant the prophetic reading (haftarah) as does a typical American Jewish boy who may or may not know much of the language, but there is something new to learn even for a secular Israeli. What is interesting is that there is a sense of Jewish cultural identity at this moment of life cycle transition. Unlike marriage in Israel, which is controlled by the Orthodox rabbinical establishment, no law forces an Israel family to have a bar mitzvah in a traditional setting in the synagogue. Yet many do even if they never step foot into a synagogue again.

In the United States, egalitarian Jewish groups mark a girl's bat mitzvah at age thirteen and enable her, like a bar mitzvah boy, also to get an 'aliyah, read from the Torah, recite the haftarah, deliver a Torah speech, and do exactly what a boy does in the synagogue service.

One of the most recent chapters in the development of bat mitzvah is the emergence of rites for a girl at age twelve in modern Orthodox synagogues. There is much discussion, pro and con, of how this should be implemented or even if it should. Some rabbis raise objections precisely on the grounds that any rite is innovative, which it is, and per se unacceptable. Women in the Jewish Orthodox Feminist Alliance (JOFA), for example, have proposed various ways a girl can mark the occasion without violating accepted Orthodox rabbinic norms about women and girls not participating in the synagogue.[86]

The impact of the feminist movement on American Orthodox Jewish life has made the bat mitzvah more important than before, even though all ritual egalitarianism has until recently been rejected in mixed services. One option is to conduct all-women's services. Another recent development is for groups of Orthodox Jews to meet apart from the regular synagogue service and to permit women to receive 'aliyot. Some Orthodox rabbinic opinion has cautiously supported this option. Either way, there now are options for Orthodox women to read the Torah, receive 'aliyot, and serve as cantors. As a by-product, girls who reach age twelve can do the same, for the first time, in such services.[87]

Another possibility in modern Orthodox communities is for girls age twelve years and a day to address the congregation with a devar Torah after the services and celebrate the bat mitzvah at a festive kiddish reception in her honor.[88]

BAR MITZVAHS ARE LIKE WEDDINGS?

Sometimes rites that traditionally belonged to weddings were transferred to bar mitzvah celebrations. For example, in some communities a boy acquires a tallit to be used not only during the ceremony but also as part of his permanent religious equipment, complementary to phylacteries (tefillin), which he begins to wear at this age.[89]

In traditional Jewish communities in Europe and the Muslim East, tefillin is a rite associated with bar mitzvah, but a tallit is not, except when the boy leads the services as a cantor or receives an 'aliyah or other liturgical honor. Normally, Jewish men do not wear a large tallit over their clothes until they are married. Instead, boys and unmarried men wear an undergarment known as *arba' kanfot* (literally, "four corners"), to which are attached ritual fringes that are worn hanging outside the shirt as a visible reminder of the commandments.

Traditionally, Jews gave a groom an adult tallit, which he wore during the ceremony or which might serve as a canopy over his head (see Chapter 3), and which he continues to wear as a congregant, not just when he is a prayer leader. But modern Jews in the Mediterranean, Europe, and the United States have transferred this adult garment to the adolescent boy. Consequently, bar mitzvah boys in non-Orthodox synagogues will often wear a tallit as though they were married adults. In egalitarian groups, girls may too, even if they do not put on tefillin, which is a boundary marker between some Reform, Reconstructionist, and Conservative communities (and their officiating rabbis) and others who refer to themselves as Orthodox.

One of the ritual objects that is a distinctive bar mitzvah gift is the embroidered tallit and tefillin bag, the artwork of which reflects the styles of each larger culture. In the East, they tend to be embroidered

5. *Bar Mitzvah at Masada, Israel, 1968. Courtesy of the Israel Government Press Office, Jerusalem, Israel. Photo credit: M. Milner*

with silver and gold filigree designs, in Arabesque-like patterns; in Europe and related communities, the bags often are zippered velvet pouches and marked by the boy's name on the outside or with a decorative design on the outside to tell them apart from the others. Today matching sets are available, one for each ritual object. (Fig. 5)

An extension of the linking of the wedding prayer shawl to the bar mitzvah boy and rite is the wedding canopy topped by a prayer-shawl covering. Weddings, as we will soon see, reinterpreted the Hebrew term "huppah" over the course of thousands of years until it came to its present meaning, a four-poled covering under which the bride and groom undergo the wedding ceremony. In recent times, in Israel, trips have been organized for bar mitzvah families to celebrate the rite either at the Western Wall in Jerusalem or sometimes on the Herodian mountain fortress of Masada, to the west of the Dead Sea. When the rite takes place at such places, it is sometimes conducted under what can only be described as a wedding canopy, made of four poles attached to the corners of a large tallit. This is yet another example of the extension of wedding celebrations to bar mitzvah.

As the prayer shawl has been extended to the bar mitzvah from weddings, so have other elements, sometimes with surprising mixtures of Jewish and Christian influences. It is customary in many cultures for people to throw grain at a couple about to be or just married as a fertility wish to them to have many children. Just before a Jewish wedding in eastern Europe, the groom would be honored in the synagogue on the Sabbath, and, after he received his 'aliyah and perhaps also read the haftarah, the women in the gallery above would throw candies on him and the men below as a sign of congratulations (see Chapter 3). Throwing candy in the synagogue has been extended to the bar mitzvah boy after he receives his first 'aliyah and reads the haftarah even though it seems to be a custom that derives from throwing grain on a married couple. We recall that something similar came into existence in Europe in connection with the schoolboy receiving candies or coins thrown down from behind onto his alphabet chart.

Yet another feature that has been extended to the bar mitzvah celebration from Jewish weddings is the chairing of the bride and groom during the wedding feast. In Jewish celebrations, it became customary for the bride and groom to be lifted on separate chairs and danced around the room while each holds one end of a handkerchief or cloth napkin so that they do not touch each other. It has become common to see a bar or bat mitzvah boy or girl lifted on a chair and danced around the floor as though he or she were a groom or bride.

THE PARTY AND THE
CANDLE-LIGHTING CEREMONY

The party became a very important part of the bar mitzvah even in the nineteenth and early twentieth centuries. Lavish balls were planned and elegant invitations printed. Rabbis scowled that it was contrary to Jewish custom and practice. Already in Germany, parties included printed menus and invitations. In 1887, Rabbi Moses Weinberger lamented that the bar mitzvah was "the greatest of holidays among our Jewish brethren"[90] and went on to decry the boys in New York City who "by the hundred celebrate every year their benei mizvah, amid enormous splendor and great show." In the United States in the 1950s, for example, the caterer who was responsible for the event also printed color-coordinated napkins with the first name of the honoree, matchbooks with the first name, and possibly a menu of the meal with elaborate tassels holding two double pages together that might include a cameo photograph of the bar mitzvah boy on the cover. The matches complemented glasses filled with pastel-colored cigarettes that also were provided, often with the child's name printed on them, custom ordered from such specialist tobacconists as Nat Sherman in New York City.[91]

And then there is the cake and candle ceremony in the American bar/bat mitzvah, which can be read as a combination of a Torah 'aliyah ceremony combined with an American birthday cake celebration and a little of a wedding cake thrown in for good measure. Apparently, caterers concocted this ceremony.[92]

At the party for the bar or bat mitzvah, the master of ceremonies stops the proceedings and announces that the candle lighting ceremony will begin. The honoree holds a large lighted candle behind a white cake, usually a sheet cake on which a Torah scroll has been designed in icing or one in the shape of an open book or scroll. The bar or bat mitzvah may read a short tribute for each of a series of relatives, grandparents, uncles and aunts, cousins, siblings, and then parents, and each in turn is honored with "the first candle," "the second candle," and so on through thirteen. As each comes up to light a candle, the photographer shoots a still photo and the video continues to record each episode.

The special cake is of course reminiscent of the wedding cake combined with a child's birthday party cake to which the special candle ceremony has been added. Sometimes a little plastic figure of a bar mitzvah boy is placed on the cake, even as plastic figures of a bride and groom are seated atop wedding cakes. But in another way, the calling up to the cake, often baked in the shape or covered by a Torah, imitates the calling up, or 'aliyot, in the synagogue, when adult men or women are called to the real Torah and recite the blessings over it. Here the bar/bat mitzvah blesses each of the honorees instead of their blessing the Torah.

To be sure, if the party is being held on the Sabbath, right after services, as mine was, lighting candles may not take place, but if Sabbath observance is not customary, the candles will be lighted. In any case, the lighting of the candles, instead of reciting blessings, comes in the context of each relative blessing the child. In symbolic terms, the child and the Torah-as-cake have been assimilated to one another, reminiscent of the children's initiation ceremony into Torah learning when the boys eat honey cakes on which the alphabet and verses from the Bible have been written. The relatives bless the child-as-Torah in public, while at the same time marking his or her age with a number of candles. It becomes a Jewish child's last birthday party; he or she no longer is a child. (Compare the kindergarten birthday ceremony in the Israeli kindergarten when each classmate comes up to the child and blesses him or her with the wish that he or she be a good soldier, go up to grade one, etc.)

Although Jews have not traditionally celebrated birthdays at all, let alone with birthday cakes and candles, here we have a special adaptation of the non-Jewish birthday cake, and wedding cake, assimilated into the American bar and bat mitzvah parties. Of course, on regular birthday cakes one lights a candle for each year and an extra one for "good luck." The lighting of the candles on the cake seems to be an adaptation of the conventional birthday cake extended to honoring the child's relatives who have helped him or her reach this milestone of the bar or bat mitzvah. It is an American innovation, correlated with the special role birthday parties play in American children's lives in general. And of course a bar or bat mitzvah is celebrating a birthday and receives presents accordingly.

ADULT BAR/BAT MITZVAH

The efforts of the American Jewish community to renew itself have resulted in how-to books by the dozens for all aspects of Jewish life, including many on the life cycle, in general, and on bar mitzvah, in particular. Such information is also available on the Internet, not only in the local bookstore. One of the features of this renewal is the rite of adult Jewish men and women who "were never bar mitzvahed" having one at a more mature or even advanced age.[93] (Fig. 6)

From a traditional point of view, the rite in the synagogue, let alone the party, is not "the bar mitzvah" at all. That transition occurs by itself when the child reaches the age of thirteen years and a day (or twelve and a day for traditional girls) and not because of any rite. Indeed, the very idea of thinking of the bar mitzvah as a kind of sacrament, administered by a rabbi, in a synagogue ritual around the sacred Torah scroll, is an internalization of widespread Christian practice. If some Catholics today want to change the teenage rite of confirmation back to age seven so that it will not appear to be a Catholic bar or bat mitzvah, the circle of mutual awareness would be completed. Even more striking is the new Protestant Rite 13 that has been introduced in many American churches expressly to provide Protestant youth with a meaningful ceremony that compares to Catholic confirmation and Jewish bar and bat mitzvah.[94]

In a bar mitzvah rite, the boy is permitted to perform the acts he does, such as get an 'aliyah or put on tefillin, because he has "become bar mitzvah," already, reached the right age. This means, of course, that all of the adults who now seek to "be bar mitzvahed" already are, since they are well beyond the requisite age when they "became bar mitzvah."

Nevertheless, it speaks to the importance of the rites that have developed over the last hundred years that the commitment to Jewish living that we see in some adults is marked by having a public ceremony that consists of one or more parts of the rite as celebrated by young Jewish adolescents at the time they reach the required age.

6. *Mass Bat Mitzvah Service at Hadassah National Convention, Jerusalem, Israel, August 6, 2001. © 2001 Hadassah, The Women's Zionist Organization of America, Inc. Reprinted with permission. Photo credit: Avi Hayun*

Others who have done this include Russian Jews who were unable to have a public celebration when they lived as refusniks in the Soviet Union, adult Jews who became "returnees to Judaism" (*ba'alei teshuvah*) and who did not have one when they were secular and assimilated but now want one as a sign of their dedication to a form of traditional Jewish living.

BAR/BAT MITZVAH AS GRADUATION

Why have so many features of one Jewish life cycle event, Jewish weddings, been shifted to the bar mitzvah? We will also see that even more mourning customs were shifted to traditional Jewish weddings. Today in American Jewish life, at least, there is a culmination in the bar mitzvah as well as a celebration of youth. It often is the end of a Jewish child's formal Jewish schooling, his or her graduation. Most will not go on to high school Jewish studies and "be confirmed." Perhaps half may not have a Jewish wedding of any kind and it may not take place for decades, as the age of marriage is delayed. In some sense, then, one sees a shifting downward of rites that combine both the Jewish wedding and the earlier traditional elements of the child's bar mitzvah.[95]

In recent times, as Jews sought to mark the life cycle in ritual ways even in lives not otherwise filled with Torah observance, the bar mitzvah emerged as a rite of passage from Jewish childhood into adolescence and acculturation into the larger secular world, especially in American or Israeli life. In contrast, some Hasidic communities and other Ultra-Orthodox (haredi) Jews, for example, downplay the bar mitzvah rituals in the synagogue and have a festive meal at which friends and family celebrate and give the child presents, often as not, religious books for a lifetime of learning.[96]

In some ways, even as it is an initiation into Jewish identity for some older adults, it can be seen as a finishing rite for many young Jewish adolescents. It moves the child from Judaism into the larger world possibly without any additional traditional Jewish rites until death, if then. But, of course, there may be other chances to practice Jewish rites. With adolescence and puberty there is an awareness of the opposite sex. Many Jews marry or intermarry by enacting some kind of Jewish wedding ceremony. The next phrase in the circumcision refrain, "to enter the huppah," also has had a long and fascinating history, and its contemporary variations reflect, even more than the bar mitzvah ceremony, the complexities of Jewish life today.

3

Engagement,
Betrothal,
Marriage

When we consider a wedding today, we usually think of a public ceremony as a transition when a man and woman leave their childhood homes or singles pads and join together to form a new family unit, first as a couple, and later as parents. More realistically, a couple that has been living together for some time decides to formalize the relationship in public before having children or for some other reason.

Even more than childhood customs, the laws and customs attached to rites of courtship and marriage are closely related to those of neighboring civilizations. This dynamic process of inward acculturation is especially pronounced in the rites surrounding the Jewish wedding: in the biblical age, the culture especially of Mesopotamia; in antiquity, Greco-Roman civilization; in pre-modern times, the various Christian and Muslim cultures in Europe, Asia, and North Africa; in modern times, the mores of Christians or Muslims combining religious and secular societies. In each case, some text or custom from earlier Jewish practice is somehow linked to what actually is an appropriation of an outside practice turned into a Jewish one.

In the Hebrew Bible, there is no wedding ceremony at all, but several narratives were later invoked as justifications for practices that developed. It is clear that the marriage of sons and daughters in the

Bible, as in much of later Jewish history, is largely in the hands of the father or some equivalent male relative such as an uncle. This applies to the prospective groom as well as to the bride. Although aspects of what we today call romantic love between man and woman are found in the Bible, especially in the Song of Songs, a collection of sensuous poems between two smitten lovers, the matchmaking of young people was a typical parental responsibility, from biblical days well into the twentieth century, and love might sometimes come after, as with Rebekah (Gen. 24), or at other times before a marriage, as with Michal, Saul's younger daughter, for David (1 Sam. 18:28) and Samson for Delilah (Jud. 16:4).[1]

Although Deuteronomy stipulates for a divorce that the husband must write something referred to as "sefer keritut" (a writ of separation) (Deut. 24:1–3; Jer. 3:8), no comparable wedding rite is mentioned in the Hebrew Bible. Perhaps this tells us what we already know: it is easier to get married than to get divorced.

Still, key episodes, such as the unions of Rebekah and Isaac, Jacob with Leah and Rachel, Samson and Delilah, and David and Michal, as well as the metaphoric references to God and Israel's covenantal bond as a monogamous marriage of man and wife, in prophets such as Hosea and Jeremiah, give us more information about what seem to be commonly accepted norms for ancient Israelite society. A union of two families, not individuals, was uppermost on everyone's mind. Considerations of alliances, aggrandizement of family wealth, good social or political connections, ethnic and religious compatibility, all figure in the Bible and afterwards in Jewish traditional life down to the present.

We may think of Adam and Eve as the first arranged marriage, with God serving as their "parents" and matchmaker combined. This theme is made clear in the midrash. "A Roman noblewoman, interrogating Rabbi Yose ben Halafta, asked: In how many days did the Holy One, blessed be He, create His world? Rabbi Yose replied: In six days. She asked: And what has He been doing since? R. Yose replied: . . . He has been busy making matches—the daughter of Such-and-Such to So-and-So."[2]

In late antiquity, the rabbis read the narrative of the first parents, where no wedding ceremony is even hinted at, as the model of the first arranged marriage and declared that physical consummation was one of three means by which a betrothal could be completed, the other two being a written document of intent (not the same as the ketubbah or prenuptial contract) or the transfer of some personal property of minimal value from the groom to the bride. A form of each of these three modes of creating a betrothal became part of the rites of marriage, though not necessarily as a means by which the groom can betroth a bride.[3]

The biblical narrative sets up a series of expectations about what would become Jewish married life, including monogamy as a model union, even though there are exceptions, apart from concubines, in the patriarchal age, notably, Jacob, who marries two sisters.[4] The concluding section of the Book of Proverbs, known from the first phrase, "eshet hayil" (a woman of valor), is about an ideal wife, a woman who works and also tends to her family (Prov. 31:10–31).

The first of two accounts of the creation of humankind enigmatically begins: "And God created man in His image, in the image of God He created him; male and female He created them. God blessed them and God said to them, 'Be fertile and increase, fill the earth and master it; and rule the fish of the sea, the birds of the sky, and all the living things that creep on earth'" (Gen. 1:27–28).[5]

In this version, God creates humanity. We are immediately told that this refers to man and woman together. God then commands them to procreate and be dominant over the rest of the creation that is described in the first part of the narrative of the six days of creation. The narrative of human procreative generation seems to be an imitation of God, with a difference. God is depicted as creating the world and all living beings by verbal fiat, not mythic sexual acts. This willed creation culminates in human beings. Man and woman, created in the image of God, are to be like God in that they too create more life and are placed above the rest of animate, vegetative, and material parts of the world.

The second version of the creation of humans in Genesis describes the garden and continues, in Gen. 2:15, with man alone and demonstrates man's power over woman by actually naming her along with naming other creatures:

> The Lord God said, "It is not good for man to be alone; I will make a fitting helper for him." And the Lord God formed out of the earth all the wild beasts and all the birds of the sky, and brought them to the man to see what he would call them; and whatever the man called each living creature, that would be its name. And the man gave names to all the cattle and to the birds of the sky and to all the wild beasts; but for Adam no fitting helper was found. So the Lord God cast a deep sleep upon the man; and, while he slept, He took one of his ribs and closed up the flesh at that spot. And the Lord fashioned the rib that he had taken from the man into a woman; and He brought her to the man. Then the man said, "This one at last is bone of my bones and flesh of my flesh. This one shall be called Woman, for from man was she taken." Hence a man leaves his father and mother and clings to his wife, so that they become one flesh (Gen. 2:18–24).

Shortly we find them cohabiting: "Now the man knew his wife Eve, and she conceived and bore Cain" (Gen. 4:1), the first reference to the verb "to know" in what has come to be known as the "biblical sense," that is, meaning sexual intimacy. No other gesture or ceremony on Adam or Eve's part signals that they are man and wife, not just man and woman.

One expression that appears soon in the Bible for the act of becoming a married couple is the verb "taking," as in a man takes a wife. For example, "Lamekh took to himself two wives" (Gen. 4:19); or, "When men began to increase on earth and daughters were born to them, the divine beings saw how beautiful the daughters of men were and took wives from among those that pleased them" (Gen. 6:1–2). This expression is found again in connection with Abra(ha)m: "Abram and Nahor took to themselves wives" (Gen. 11:29).

Although the word *laqah* (took) may be similar to a purchase of an object, the act does not mean that the groom's father buys the woman for his son. In no biblical or rabbinic text, for that matter, can a husband sell his wife, as he can his cattle, for example. This distinction is also made clear in the ancient Near Eastern codes.[6] The future husband acquires the father's permission to begin the transfer of authority over the young woman from her father to her future husband and his family.

Adam's sexual union, described as "knowing," might seem to foreshadow what was involved in the act of "taking," that is, a sexual consummation. In fact, the most elaborate biblical courtship narrative suggests otherwise and provides a model for how a man takes a bride. The narrative does not begin with the two young people at all but instead with the groom's father, Abraham, who wants to marry off his son Isaac properly, which means to a relative back in "the old country," not to a local Canaanite woman.

According to Genesis, Abraham makes his servant swear that he will not "'take a wife (tiqah ishah) for my son from the daughters of the Canaanites among whom I dwell, but will go to the land of my birth and get a wife (ve-laqahta ishah) for my son Isaac'" (24:4). The servant asks what he should do "'if the woman does not consent to follow me to this land?'" (24:5). Should he bring Isaac there? Absolutely not, says Abraham: "'On no account must you take my son back there!'" (24:6). Trusting God, Abraham insists that "'you will get a wife for my son from there. And if the woman does not consent to follow you,'" he continues, "you shall then be clear of this oath to me" (24:7–8).

The servant goes off towards Aram (Syria), where Abraham's family had lived for many years, en route from Mesopotamia to Canaan. Immediately, the trusted servant encounters Rebekah at the well or stream. Although he asks her for water for himself, she offers water not only to him, but also to his camels, a prearranged sign he had worked out earlier to indicate that she is the one divinely chosen for Isaac. Of course, the woman is "very beautiful, a virgin whom no man had known" (v. 16). Before he even meets the family, Abraham's servant gives her "a gold nose-ring weighing a half-shekel, and two gold bands for her arms, ten shekels in weight" (v. 22).

Key elements of later rites appear here. The woman's consent is indicated as a prerequisite to the union, and this is required in later Jewish wedding arrangements. A second element adumbrated is that the groom's family present gifts to the bride. More of this will get illustrated in various combinations as the story progresses. The reference to a ring, however, should not be confused with the use of a ring in the Jewish betrothal ceremony, which dates to no earlier than Muslim times.

It turns out that Rebekah is Abraham's niece, Isaac's first cousin once removed: the daughter of Bethuel, who is the son of Abraham's brother Nahor and sister-in-law Milcah. Her immediate reaction is to tell "all this to her mother's household" (v. 28), to her mother, not her father, an indication that in the original story her father, Bethuel, is dead. Her brother Laban runs out to see what all the commotion is about. As soon as he sees his sister's new nose-ring and bracelets, his eyes light up and he immediately wants to know all about the visitor.

"'I am Abraham's servant,'" the stranger begins. "'The Lord has greatly blessed my master, and he has become rich: He has given him sheep and cattle, silver and gold, male and female slaves, camels and asses'" (vv. 34–35).

At the news, Laban and Bethuel, Rebekah's father, who makes a sudden cameo appearance, in an addition to the original narrative, both declare, "'The matter was decreed by the Lord'" (v. 50). Their reaction is predictable: "'Here is Rebekah before you; take her and go, and let her be a wife to your master's son, as the Lord has spoken'" (v. 51).

But first, "The servant brought out objects of silver and gold, and garments, and gave them to Rebekah; and he gave presents to her brother and her mother" (v. 53). The former are gifts from the groom's family for the bride; the latter are a kind of dowry or bride price that the groom's family contributes to the family of the future bride to secure permission from her family.[7] After some words about when she should leave, her family asks her, "'Will you go with this man?'" She replies, "'I will'" (v. 58). Again, note the consent as well as the etiquette of the groom's family smoothing things with gifts.

As "Rebekah and her nurse along with Abraham's servant and his men" (v. 59) are about to leave, her family "blessed Rebekah and said to her, 'O sister! May you grow into thousands of myriads; may your offspring seize the gates of their foes'" (v. 60). This formula will reappear as part of the ceremony in traditional Jewish weddings, just before the betrothal rites.

With that, the bride and her entourage head off toward Isaac and his family. The narrative emphasizes once again that Rebekah consents to the match: "'I will,'" a theme that complements the gift giving as part of the protocol arranging the match between senior members of one family and the agent of another. She is not portrayed as passive, though clearly the men are doing the arranging.

The scene now shifts to Canaan where "Isaac went out walking in the field toward evening and, looking up, he saw camels approaching. Raising her eyes, Rebekah saw Isaac. She alighted from the camel" (vv. 63–64) and asked who the man is walking in the field. "'That is my master,'" the servant tells her. "So she took her veil and covered herself" (v. 65).

The servant tells Isaac everything that took place, and "Isaac then brought her into the tent of his mother Sarah, and he took Rebekah as his wife." Only then does the narrative continue, "Isaac loved her, and thus found comfort after his mother's death" (v. 66–67). First an arranged match and her agreement, then a consummated union, followed by the possibility of love, at least theoretically, in that order, is the model in Rebekah's wedding to Isaac. Because the wedding took place as soon as the arrangements were made and the bride went to the groom's family and consummated the marriage, there are no stages of betrothal and marriage. What later would become three distinct stages of arrangement, betrothal, and marriage are collapsed into two.

This narrative is one of the most elaborate arranged marriages described in the Hebrew Bible, and it is no wonder that later customs were connected to it. As is typical in ancient marriages, the courtship is often not between the young man and woman, though this is possible,[8] but between related families who arrange a suitable match. Indeed, there are signs in the Hebrew Bible and the even more detailed story of a Jewish wedding found in the apocryphal Book of Tobit, a Jewish book written some time before the second century B.C.E. but not included in the Hebrew Bible, that a relative, especially a cousin, had a prior claim over anyone else.[9]

At the opposite extreme from marrying a relative are biblical marriages with non-Israelites. The biblical law codes frowned on the practice (Exod. 34:15–16; Deut. 7:3–4), so that Israelites would not follow other gods. But there is abundant evidence that it occurred, supporting the generalization, "they [Israelite men] took their [Canaanite] daughters to wife and gave their own daughters to their sons, and they worshiped their gods" (Judg. 3:6). Thus, Esau took two Hittite women (Gen. 26:34); Joseph, an Egyptian (Gen. 41:45); Moses, a Midianite (Exod. 2:21).

The royals outdid the commoners. David counted among his wives a Calebite and an Aramean (2 Sam. 3:3), and Solomon's many wives included "Pharaoh's daughter [and] Moabite, Ammonite, Edomite, Phoenician, and Hittite women" (1 Kings 11:1). Among well-known Israelite women who married foreigners was Bathsheba, who married a Hittite (2 Sam. 11:3). This pattern continued after the return of some Jews from Babylonia, and it is decried by the later prophets (Mal. 2:11–12) and legislated against by Ezra and Nehemiah in the fifth century B.C.E. as totally unacceptable.[10]

The story of Rebekah and Isaac dramatizes the central movement in a Jewish marriage of the bride going from her family to the groom and his family. This shift in the bride's life is also the central motif of the different parts of what became the Jewish betrothal and wedding ceremonies. Although the account in Genesis about Adam and Eve advises that a man and woman leave their parents to become one flesh, the union of two people usually meant that the bride left her parents' house and moved closer to the groom's family, even when the couple lived in separate quarters.

Other signs of becoming a new couple are found in the Bible, only some of which enjoyed continuity. There are many biblical references to the procession of the bride coming toward the groom's house. The groom wears a crown,[11] and as the bride approaches with her retinue, the groom comes out "with his friends and relatives to meet them, with drums and musicians" (1 Macc. 9:37–39). In medieval Europe, brides sometimes wore a crown, or were depicted in illuminations as wearing one, an influence at the time of depictions of the Virgin Mary.[12]

The bride wears a veil (Songs 4:1, 3; 6:7) and is bejeweled (Isa. 61:10; Ps. 45:14). As the Psalmist says in Psalm 45, a wedding song, "her dress [is] embroidered with gold mountings" (v. 14). As she is led inside to her groom (v. 16), the bride is told to "forget your people and your father's house" (v. 11). She is accompanied there by "maidens in her train, her companions" (v. 15).

In the Bible there are other examples or echoes of love songs sung to the bride and groom, including the transformation of Jeremiah's dire prophecy, repeated three times, to the Israelites just before the exile—"I am going to silence/banish from this place . . . the sound of mirth and gladness, the voice of bridegroom and bride" (Jer. 7:34; 16:9; 25:10)—into his expression of confidence in the restoration of the people and the land—"Thus said the Lord: Again there shall be heard in this place—in the towns of Judah and the streets of Jerusalem that are desolate, without man, without inhabitants, without beast—the sound of mirth and gladness, the voice of bridegroom and bride" (Jer. 33:10–11).

Part of this verse will be incorporated into the longest of the seven blessings recited at the wedding, under the wedding canopy, and again at the end of the wedding feast for each of seven days, and the words are also sung at most traditional weddings today. Medieval and early modern Hebrew poems, written in honor of the groom and bride are recited today in traditional weddings, when each arrives at the huppah, and the groom and his friends sing together at the reception a special melody for the entire text in Proverbs 31 about the ideal woman.

Rebekah's arranged marriage also left its mark on the subsequent custom of blessing the bride before the wedding ceremony. In eastern Europe it came to be called the "bedeken," or veiling of the bride, a motif attached to Gen. 24:65. The bridegroom covers his bride's face with a veil after he checks to see her face and verify that she is his intended. As Laban and Bethuel blessed Rebekah, so now the bride's father or the officiating rabbi or another relative addresses the bride: "O sister! May you grow into thousands of myriads; (may your offspring seize the gates of their foes)" (Gen. 24:60). "So she took her veil and covered herself" (24:65).

ARRANGEMENTS

When the families reach an agreement, they exchange gifts. Some are given when the match is agreed to; others are deferred to the time of the actual marriage. Frequently in the Bible, it is the groom's father who agreed to pay to the family of the bride what is sometimes called the *mohar*.[13] At the time of the wedding, the groom's family brings more gifts for the family of the bride and for the bride herself. Such gifts, are referred to as *matan* (Gen. 34:12) and seem to be distinguished in the Dinah-Shekhem story from the bride-price (mohar). In some cases, the mohar can be discharged by service to the bride's family, as when Jacob works off his obligation to his uncle Laban for fourteen years, the first seven for Leah, whom Laban tricked Jacob to marry, and seven more, after he married Rachel, the younger sister whom he wanted from the beginning.

Rebekah's consent to the match is indicated only after the arrangement is effected, when she agrees to go to Isaac's land and family sight unseen (vv. 57–58). In doing so she emulates trusting Abraham who left his paternal home to go to a land the Lord would show him (Gen.

12). Generally, the parents arrange their children's marriages, although there are cases of choice being expressed by young men, and even by a young woman. For example, regarding his daughters, Merab and Michal, Saul first tells David, "'Here is my older daughter, Merab; I will give her to you in marriage'" (1 Sam. 18:17). David protests he is unworthy to be "'Your majesty's son-in-law'" (v. 18), and mysteriously Saul gives Merab to another. At this point we learn that Saul's younger daughter, Michal, "had fallen in love with David" (1 Sam. 18:20). Even so, it is up to the girl's father to arrange the union. He stipulates the bride-price that David succeeded to pay (vv. 21–27). As a result, "Saul then gave him his daughter Michal in marriage" (v. 27).

There were consequences if the woman's father broke off the arranged marriage. According to the Code of Hammurabi, if the father receives gifts and then says, "I will not give my daughter to you," ". . . he shall pay back double the full amount that was brought to him."[14]

The civil arrangement that typifies the biblical notion of marriage began to change under the rabbis, as they first tried to make a marriage a public event and later on a sacred union. They called making arrangements "shiddukhin," a term that still reverberates in the Yiddish term *shiddekh,* or match, and the complementary term *shadkhan,* or matchmaker. The arrangement preceded any acts involving the couple, although they might be followed immediately by betrothal.[15]

In Palestine and some parts of Babylonia, a contract was written right before the betrothal, as it still is today (tena'im).[16] This document consisted of a set of conditions that stipulated monetary penalties if the proposed marriage was called off at the last minute. It is a promise of marriage arranged between the families. Breaking the agreement would have monetary consequences—something like breach of promise of marriage in modern civil law—but the young woman did not need a religious divorce. It did not change her personal status.

In third-century Babylonia, casual marriages carried out through sexual union were frowned upon: "Rab punished any man who betrothed [a woman] in a market place, or by intercourse, or without [previous] shiddukhin."[17] The rabbis tried to enforce these arrangements, but they obviously did not always succeed. There also is some evidence that some of the rabbis themselves were not above this temporary marriage practice.[18]

A genuine betrothal was the goal, such that the lack of the preliminary arrangements was not decisive. The rabbis' goal was to insist on arrangements in order to minimize casual sexual liaisons or marriages of convenience, and they tried to do this by making the relationship public, with monetary consequences for walking away after a brief fling. In the Jerusalem Talmud, it is stated: "Whoever betroths a woman without preliminary arrangements between the families (shiddukhin) is punished but the betrothal is valid."[19]

The assumption in rabbinic regulations was that one should maximize the social ties between two people that would lead to a serious relationship of marriage and minimize casual sexual partnering. In effect, the legal system served as an agency of matchmaking, and an inhibitor of promiscuity, which was no doubt real. Otherwise, so many rules would not have preoccupied the rabbis with methods of reducing it. Once the families got together and stipulated terms of a pre-nuptial agreement, signed by witnesses, there was a concrete incentive for the families to nurture the relationship and bring it to completion.

In some ways, the timing of the rabbinic shiddukhin was analogous to a modern engagement. At the engagement, the couple "go public" as a couple for the first time, and newspapers may even carry the announcement. The difference between engagement and arrangement is that the decision today usually rests with the couple, not the parents. Nearly all Jews today who have a Jewish wedding, except for Ultra-Orthodox Jews, get engaged in ways that are not much different from the way non-Jews do. The couple decide they want to get married; the two families meet; the man gives his bride-to-be a gift, often a diamond ring, thanks to the efforts of European royalty and the modern diamond cartel; friends and family throw a party or bridal shower; and a date is set for the wedding. Only at that time are all the rites of betrothal and marriage enacted.

Today, the document stipulating the arrangements as well as the wedding contract proper, or ketubbah, are both signed just before the ceremony. Nevertheless, the Talmud indicates that some people became betrothed privately, that is, without any of the above public ritual. They were customs, not requirements.[20]

The favored days for a wedding in the Talmud were Wednesdays for first-time brides (virgins) and Thursdays for widows.[21] In eastern Europe, weddings were sometimes held on Fridays (virgins) and Thursdays (widows), respectively, so that people could stay over the Sabbath. More recently, traditional Jews have overridden these traditions in favor of Tuesday weddings, based, it is said, on Genesis, where it says twice that God's creation was good on the third day (Gen. 1:10; 1:12). It is not clear how far back this contemporary practice goes.

Jewish wedding rites in the Muslim world were revealed in the thousands of documents discovered over a hundred years ago in the Cairo Geniza. Mainly from the tenth- through thirteenth-century Mediterranean communities, they disclose that weddings were not held in the synagogue. Nor were Muslim or early Christian marriages held in mosques or churches. It was still "predominantly a secular affair," as it had been in the Bible.[22]

As was the case with Abraham's decision for Isaac, Isaac's for Jacob, Samson's parents' for him, and Tobit's for his son, so Jews in the Geniza world favored marriage with a relative. A Jew writes a letter to a member of the family near Cairo about a young girl: "We have saved the girl for Abu l-'Ala [a relative] . . . P. S. She is well off."[23] In the small medieval communities in northern Europe, it may have been difficult to find marriage partners who were not cousins. Remember that Judaism, unlike Christianity, permits even first cousins to marry. Nevertheless, others married their daughters off far away in order to build a welcome family alliance.

Sometimes migration led to new unions, as in the case of Maimonides (1138–1204), who was born in Spain and married well in his new home of Fustat, Egypt, to the sister of a prominent scribe who married Maimonides' sister.[24] Memoirs throughout early and modern times stress the importance to parents and widowed mothers of finding a good match for daughters and sons.

The occasion of parents coming to terms or agreeing to arrangements generated rituals in Mediterranean and European communities, each bearing some resemblance to Muslim or Christian customs and practices, respectively. For example, Persian (and Kurdish) Jews have a special custom that marks the meeting of the two families for the first time and the engagement of the couple to be married.

It is called "eating the sweets" (shirini khuri). On the appointed day, the groom's parents invite the honored members of the community as well as the chief rabbi to their home. They take several sugar cones about eighteen inches high and go to the house of the bride's parents and tell them why they are there. If the bride's parents consent, the rabbi breaks two cones by hitting them together and says, "May your match succeed," and he concludes with Ps. 121:1: "A song for ascents. I turn my eyes to the mountains; from where will my help come?"

He offers the first piece of sugar to the bride's father and the next one to the groom's father. The two of them then exchange their pieces of sugar and say, "be-mazel tov u-ve-siman tov" (accompanied by a favorable star and a good sign), and they distribute the other pieces of sugar to everyone there.

In another room a table is laden with all kinds of delicacies. They eat and drink wine. The groom's father takes the piece of sugar that he received from the bride's father and gives it to his son, who has stayed at home, and says to him: "You have a bride and her name is so-and-so. Mazel tov!" The bride's parents give the bride a piece of sugar and say: "You have a groom. Mazel Tov!" It is still practiced, for example, among Iranian Jews in Great Neck, New York.

In Ashkenaz, the document of tena'im stipulates a financial settlement if the wedding were not to take place, even though every-

7. *Signing the Tena'im (Conditions of Engagement) just before a wedding at Nevei Ilan, Israel, June 2003. Photo credit: Judith R. Marcus.*

one has already gathered where the wedding will take place in a few minutes. The parties sign the document and it is witnessed. The two mothers, and sometimes others assembled, break a pot or plate as a sign that the bargain was sealed. In Germany, this rite was called Knasmahl (Penalty Meal). The idea was that if the engagement were broken, there would be penalties. The broken pottery was meant to ward off demons or bad luck. The rite is described in seventeenth-century customs books such as that of Yuspa Shamash of Worms. It is also illustrated in an etching in Johann Bodenschatz's eighteenth-century compilation of Jewish ceremonies. This rite functioned as a combined formal engagement and promise of marriage. The family of the groom usually paid for the party at the engagement.[25]

The making of conditions is also described, without the German addition of breaking the pottery, in Leon Modena's autobiography, as in the description of his own first engagement to the ill-fated Esther, who died a year afterwards, before they could be married, and he also includes this rite in his *History of the Rites*. He indicates in both accounts that, besides drawing up the written terms and making the traditional gesture of acquiring the document, bride and groom shake hands as a sign of the union.[26] (Fig. 7)

In many traditional weddings today, just before the witnesses sign the wedding contract, or ketubbah, the couple or their fathers and witnesses sign the tena'im, and the mothers of the bride and of the groom take a plate, usually wrapped in a cloth napkin, and smash it on the back of a chair. This symbolic act is now carried out moments before the complete wedding ceremony takes place, not months or even a year in advance, as in earlier times.[27]

BETROTHAL OR MARRIAGE?

The laws in Deuteronomy clearly refer to a woman who is betrothed (*arusah*) but not yet married. A man who is betrothed but not yet married does not have to go off to war, so that no other man sleeps with his fiancée (Deut. 20:7). And if a man who is not a betrothed woman's fiancé, sleeps with a betrothed young woman who had never been married before ("na'arah betulah me'orasah") (Deut. 22:23-27), the penalty is death, the same penalty as for a man who commits adultery by sleeping with a married woman (Lev. 20:10; Deut. 22:22).

At the moment of arrangement and betrothal, the groom's family gives the bride-price, or mohar, to the family of the bride and other gifts to the bride herself, as we see with Rebekah. When Saul promises his older daughter, Merab, to David, he uses the formula, "I will give her to you in marriage." They are not yet married.

In contrast, in the Book of Tobit, Tobias, Tobit's son, marries Sarah right after the parents reach an agreement, skipping betrothal altogether (Tob. 7:9–16). Aside from the narrative about Rebekah and

Isaac, Tobit's wedding is the most elaborate and takes for granted, as does Isaac's marriage to Rebekah, that a relative is preferable to a stranger. As described there, the bride's father "called in his daughter Sarah, and he took her by the hand and gave her to Tobias to be his wife, and said, 'Here, take her according to the law of Moses, and take her back to your father'" (Tob. 7:13).

This procedure adopts the biblical verb "take," and the expression, "according to the law of Moses," was later adopted and expanded as the rabbinic formula to solemnify the betrothal, not the arrangement/engagement stage prior to actual betrothal and marriage. The rabbis also stipulated that it is the groom, not the bride's father, who says it to the bride.

Sarah's father, Raguel, then blesses them: "He took a scroll and wrote an agreement, and they put their seals to it. And they began to eat" (Tob. 7:14). This ceremony illustrates an agreement using formulaic language by the bride's father, the use of some kind of arrangement or wedding contract, and a festive meal. We have no idea what the document contained, and there is no basis for referring to it as a ketubbah, the contract that came into Judaism as a means of protecting a wife in the case of divorce or becoming a widow. Finally, Sarah's parents take her into the bed chamber and prepare her. "When they finished supper, they took Tobias in to her" (Tob. 8:1).

Although Tobit compresses arrangement, betrothal, and marriage into one rite, the rabbis separated them from one another mainly because it was more common for a new bride and her family to require at least a year to gather what was needed to build a new household.

A separate betrothal rite was common for much of ancient and early medieval Jewish history, and its ritualization was undertaken first by the rabbis in late antiquity. The woman who is betrothed is in an in-between state. She still lives in her parents' house, but once she is betrothed, she is available only to her future husband, even though she is not yet living with him. Being betrothed also means that the woman or her family could still break things off.[28] One way of establishing the woman's changed status was to announce the betrothal. As today, in antiquity it was a public event: "Ulla said: torches are seen burning and couches spread and people entering and leaving, and then they said, So-and-so is being betrothed today."[29]

For the rabbis, the rite of betrothal itself was sometimes known as eirusin, from the biblical root A-R-S,[30] or it was called *qiddushin* (sanctification), a rabbinic term from the root Q-D-Sh, to sanctify, meaning set apart in some way. We recall the Adam and Eve narrative in which even as God creates the first couple in his image he commands Adam to procreate and, implicitly at least, be God-like. All of these associations are included in the term "qiddushin" for betrothal, though it is not clear why the term came into vogue only in rabbinic times. There is a hint, when Jews are referred to as the "holy seed" (zera' ha-qodesh) (Ezra 9:2), that marriage between Jews is sacred, each is to be set apart only for another Jew, and not to be profaned through intermarriage.[31]

Like the biblical arusah, the betrothed woman in rabbinic Judaism was not allowed to live with her fiancé, but if she had sexual relations with another man, it was viewed as adultery. She required a bill of divorce (*get*) to break the relationship, even though the couple did not sleep together. At first, betrothal might be separated from the actual marriage by as much time as one or more years. At different times, betrothal preceded marriage by years or months or minutes, as today.

In late antiquity, usually twelve months were stipulated, in an agreement, as to the time separating the qiddushin/eirusin from the actual consummation of the marriage and the woman's moving from her parents' domain to the family of her husband. After twelve months the man had to support the woman;[32] before that she was totally dependent on her family. Compare Esther, who goes to King Ahasuarus "at the end of the twelve months' treatment prescribed for women (for that was the period spent on beautifying them: six months with oil of myrrh and six months with perfumes and women's cosmetics")(Esther 2:12).

The Mishnah also assumes that a previously unmarried woman needs twelve months to get her trousseau together; for a widow, only thirty days were thought necessary, since she already owned much of it.[33] In the Talmud, some rabbis wanted the period of betrothal to be shortened to one month.[34] A trousseau could be elaborate and expensive. From twelfth-century Cairo, we have a list one collected for an upper-middle-class Jewish woman:

a pair of wristbands
a pair of earrings
one finger ring of gold and three of silver . . .
a greenish festive robe
a translucent veil . . .
a Sicilian robe
a snow-white slip and wimple
a wrap
two white robes and a veil
two red robes, a cloak and two wimples
a Rumi bathrobe and a piece of red *ladh* silk
a kerchief for the face
a gown of *khazz* silk a pink slip
a linen [prayer] mantle
a Sicilian robe
four kerchiefs and a bathrobe
a Baghdadi bucket and wash basin
a basin and a ewer
a chandelier and an [oil] lamp
a Damascene pot . . .
a Tabari sofa and pad
a brocade bed cover
a Buziyon sofa
a quilt coverlet and six pillows . . .[35]

By the twelfth century in Christian Europe, the two ceremonies were usually combined, as they are today, into a single compound rite of two distinct parts.

In the Mishnah, the acts stipulated to create the biblical status of betrothal still lacked any religious words and represented private acts of intention by the man and woman. There are no blessings yet, no cups of wine. The basic requirement was one of three minimal acts on the part of the man.

According to the Mishnah, the three ways a woman can become a man's betrothed are by means of a transfer to her of a minimal sum of money or property with the intention of betrothing her, by means of a written document drawn up for the purpose of betrothal, or by means of sexual relations with that intention. Only one of the three is required. This makes the matter less than precise and open to elaboration. Each act had to be accompanied by the man's verbal declaration that it was undertaken with the express intention on the man's part to betroth the woman. In each case, the act must be carried out with the purpose of making the woman the man's wife.[36]

The mode of acquiring by means of transferring property became widespread and is still in use today; by means of cohabitation alone was ruled out in the third century.[37] Today when a groom transfers property to the bride, usually a ring, the husband must say something to the woman; he must give the woman something; and there must be two witnesses.

Groom's Betrothal Formula

In the betrothal ceremony, what does the groom say? There are variations. The formula listed first among others in the Palestinian collection called the *Tosefta* was accepted and later elaborated: "See now, you are sanctified to me" (harei at mequdeshet li).[38] There are other formulas in the Talmud: "See now you are my wife" (harei at ishti), "See now you are my betrothed" (harei at arusati), "See now you are acquired for me" (harei at qenuyah li), or "See now, you are mine" (harei at sheli).[39]

When the groom recites the betrothal formula, he must say exactly what is required accompanied by the intent to marry the bride.

For example, if a man tried to betroth a woman by using an agent, which was permitted, the agent had to be very careful not to say, "See now, you are betrothed to *me*," but rather, "betrothed to so-and-so," the man who had sent him. There were cases in which an agent did say, "to me," and the woman had to be given a bill of divorce from the agent before she could marry her intended!

More important than using specific words to express the groom's intent to betroth the bride, he had to give her something of minimal value, observed by two proper witnesses. Proper meant that they were not relatives of the principals. No investigation into their worthiness was required, as is done in the case of witnesses about money matters. No written confirmation was needed of their oral statement. In short, the entire minimal act from a legal and institutional standpoint was very vague and fragile, subject to false claims and misrepresentations. This meant that it was not only easy to get married but also easy to be doubtful as to whether someone was married or not.[40]

The woman in the betrothal is relatively passive: the man says something to her, gives something to her, and she is observed not to object. She does not have to say anything, only not protest, and her silence is construed as consent, since the rabbis held that a woman is betrothed only with her consent.[41]

As with other life cycle events, the rabbis instituted specific blessings as part of a religious ceremony of betrothal, and they were designed to sanctify it. In this way, the betrothal, which had been purely a secular matter of a transfer of rights over the woman from father to husband, began to acquire a religious character in ritual. The rabbis formulated a special blessing of betrothal to be recited in the home of the bride:

> Blessed are You, Lord God, King of the universe, who has sanctified us by His commandments and has commanded us concerning the forbidden relations ('arayot) and has forbidden to us the betrothed [of others] and has allowed to us married [women] by means of the wedding chamber and sanctification. Blessed are You who sanctifies

Israel by means of the wedding chamber (huppah) and betrothal (ve-qiddushin)[42] [or] who sanctifies Israel.[43]

As it is written in the Talmud, the text contains two anomalies that begged for modification. The blessing forbids a Jewish man from having relations with a Jewish woman who is betrothed to another man but then seems to permit him to have relations with Jewish women who are already married to someone else! This is an absurdity, since it seems to permit what is obviously forbidden. To prevent this misunderstanding, rabbis changed the Talmudic formula by adding the phrase "to us" (lanu) to modify the word "married." This addition follows Rashi's comment to the passage in the Talmud and was legislated by his grandson, Rabbi Jacob ben Meir (Rabbeinu Tam).[44] The blessing now reads: "and has allowed to us the [women who are] married *to us* (lanu)," and this is the way the blessing is recited today at the betrothal stage of a traditional wedding ceremony.

A second problem is the order of the two elements that complete a marriage that are mentioned in the end of the blessing: "by means of huppah and qiddushin." Huppah, which eventually came to mean the wedding canopy, actually refers to the marriage chamber to which the couple go to consummate the marriage; qiddushin means betrothal, the first stage. Why is the proper order reversed? Although the blessing was emended already by the eighth century so that it reads in the logical order, "by means of qiddushin and huppah,"[45] most medieval authorities did not change the original sequence, but reinterpreted it, and the "wrong order" has remained ever since. Perhaps the phrase was originally understood to be a *hendiadys,* meaning sanctified consummation, in which the second term, ve-qiddushin, modifies the first, huppah.[46]

Ring as Means of Betrothal

A number of other enduring new features of the wedding ceremony developed in post-Talmudic times in the Mediterranean communities that were governed by the central rabbis of Baghdad, the Geonim, and in the various local communities of medieval Ashkenaz in northern Christian Europe.

In Muslim lands, Jews began to use a ring instead of a coin, or other object of minimal value, to enact betrothal, even though the practice was widely attested much earlier in Roman wedding ceremonies. It is not found in the Bible or Talmud. Even if the groom gives a gift of jewelry including a ring, the ring is not the means of betrothal. We know when it became part of the Jewish betrothal rite, but not why.[47]

Whatever the immediate source of this change, betrothal rings became important in some Muslim and European Jewish communities. Jewish law requires the ring to be a simple unornamented band, worth at least "a penny," and that it must be the property of the groom. A significant number of unusual rings have been preserved from medieval times in Christian Europe. They are anything but simple and were usually the property of a particular Jewish community before museums and private collectors acquired them. Yet, despite these two significant departures from the requirements of a Jewish betrothal ring, some scholars and collectors have continued to claim that these rings are Jewish wedding rings.[48]

One of the places where we see rings depicted in a Jewish ceremony is in Renaissance Italy. From fifteenth-century Pesaro, for example, we find portrayed, though not supported in written sources, an officiant holding the hand of the bride and groom together, a gesture that is standard in Christian marriage ceremonies. The bride also wears a ring. It is not clear if Italian Jews did this or if the portraiture is simply a Christian artistic convention that was used to depict Jewish as well as Christian wedding ceremonies.[49]

Note, though, that Leon Modena says about the arrangement or engagement ceremony, "then doth the Man take the Woman by the Hand, and acknowledgeth Her for his Spouse." He continues, "In some places they use, at this time, to put a Ring upon her finger, and so betroath her: but in Italy and in Germany they do not use this

Ceremony for the most part, when they are Contracted only."[50] Is it possible that Italian Renaissance illustrations that have previously been thought to refer to a Jewish betrothal ceremony (qiddushin), with joined hands and a ring, are actually portrayals of the engagement ceremony (shiddukhin)?[51]

In recent times, Yemenite goldsmiths, such as the Hizmi family in New York, have met the demand for gold wedding rings on which the Hebrew letters of biblical phrases have been engraved or cut out. Although these rings are decorated, they still conform to the requirements if the letters are inset or produced a distance away from the outer edges of the continuous band. Among the phrases that are popular for modern Hebrew wedding rings are "Ani le-dodi ve-dodi li" (I am my beloved's and my beloved is mine) (Song 6:3) and "Ahavat olam ahavtikh" (I will love you forever) (Jer. 31:3).

Other Innovations in Medieval Times

Another innovation, perhaps as early as the Gaon Rabbi Aha bar Shabha of Sura, the eighth-century author of the book of sermons known as the *She'iltot,* requires a quorum of ten for the blessing of betrothal, although the Talmud required this only for the blessing of the marriage (nesu'in).[52] Even if Rabbi Aha himself did not introduce this practice, Rabbi Samuel Ibn Naghrela, in eleventh-century Muslim Spain, reports that his copy of the *She'iltot* included the requirement, and it became generally accepted. As the two ceremonies of betrothal and marriage were celebrated together with increasing frequency, there was no problem having a quorum for the first as well as the second ceremony, although it is not clear what the relationship is between the demand for a second quorum and the joining of the two parts of the ceremony together.

In Muslim lands, the Geonim expanded the ceremony of betrothal to include reciting a blessing on a cup of wine and over such things as myrtle (*hadas*) prior to the blessing of betrothal, perhaps in imitation of the blessing on the wine as the first of seven blessings for the second, or nesu'in, ceremony (see later discussion). Preliminary blessings over wine and spices appear for the first time in the prayer book of Rabbi Saadia Gaon (d. 942). The blessing over the wine has remained; the one over spices dropped out.

Before the ring became widespread as the act of "acquisition," the coin that constituted the symbolic token of transfer of the bride to the groom was dropped into the cup, and in Babylonia there developed the formula of betrothal: "You are betrothed and sanctified to me, So and So, the daughter of So and So, to me, So and So, son of So and So, by means of this cup and what is in it," meaning the coin.[53] This custom, too, did not last, and betrothal by means of the groom's ring persisted as the means of symbolic transfer of the woman's status from herself (or her father, if she was a minor) to her husband.

Customs prior to the Wedding Ceremony

In antiquity, processions marched through the town with lighted torches and a litter bearing the bride to announce to all that a wedding was taking place. Already the prophet Jeremiah associates "the voice of the bridegroom and bride . . . and the light of the lamp" (Jer. 25:10). In the second century B.C.E. in Palestine, we see a description of people accompanying the bride from her father's house to the house of the groom.[54] The gesture was clear: the bride was escorted to the place where she would become part of a new family.[55]

Another early indication of the persistence of some of the festivities that are mentioned in the Bible and later in the Talmud appear in a Jewish narrative from early first-century B.C.E. Egypt known as the Third Book of Maccabees. While recounting a plot to kill the Jews of Alexandria, the author refers to Jewish brides and grooms and indicates common customs associated with newly married couples:

> Young women who had but lately entered their *bridal chamber* for sharing wedded life, . . . their *myrrh-drenched locks* sullied with dust, were driven unveiled, and with one accord chanted a dirge instead of a *mar-*

148

riage hymn. . . . Their husbands too, in the flower of their youth, wore halters about their necks instead of *garlands,* and instead of *feasting* and youthful ease they spent the remaining day of their nuptials in dirges.[56]

Each of the signs of disaster implies its opposite. When Jewish men and women married in times of peace and joy, the bride's hair was spiced, the groom wore a garland of flowers, the bride was veiled, and the couple was greeted with marriage hymns to accompany their celebration of feasting in the bridal chamber, where they consummated the marriage.

After betrothal and wedding rites were combined into a single compound ceremony, various new preliminary customs developed in Muslim and Christian lands. Following Muslim practice, it became customary for the bride's (sometimes the groom's) hands and face to be painted with henna, a reddish dye. Some brides from Mediterranean family backgrounds still do this. Jews borrowed distinctive henna patterns from Arab wedding practices or created them in different Jewish communities.[57]

In Christian Europe, several pre-nuptial practices developed related to fertility. A passage in the Talmud already attests to an ancient fertility custom, but we do not know if it was practiced continually: "By means of a cock and a hen Tur Malka was destroyed. How? It was the custom that when a bride and bridegroom were being escorted, a cock and a hen were carried before them, as if to say, Be fertile and increase like fowls."[58]

We do not hear again of this custom until medieval Germany in the thirteenth century and, after another gap, once again in the fifteenth. The first text adds throwing wheat as well as the groom carrying the bride over the threshold:

People would lead a chicken and rooster before the bride and groom, based on the verse, "Be fertile and increase" (Gen. 1:28), and they threw wheat on them because there is no peace in a house without food. . . . When the bride enters the house for the first time, she is accompanied by torches and lighted candles on Friday morning, and the groom lifts her up when she enters the house, as it is written in the Book of Chronicles, "Jehoiada *lifted* (=*took*) (va-yissa) two wives for him, by whom he had sons and daughters" (2 Chron. 24:3) "and they married Moabite women" (va-yissu lahem nashim) (Ruth 1:4). Now something one finds is acquired by lifting it up, and [about a woman, it is written], "He who finds a wife has found happiness" (Prov. 18:22). And on Friday, the students return to their studies. A woman is married on Wednesday, for if she becomes pregnant on a Wednesday, Thursday or Friday, she will not give birth on the Sabbath and people will not desecrate the Sabbath on her account.[59]

The customs of escorting the bride after the wedding with torches to the new house and of carrying her over the threshold have ancient Roman roots that ultimately go back to the belief that it was bad luck for the bride to touch the threshold. Roman girlfriends of the bride, not the groom, would carry her into the marriage house to protect her. The Jewish customs, however, are mentioned only at this time and only in this place, and it is not clear why we do not see them emerge earlier.[60]

The distribution of roasted heads of wheat was one of several indications in the Mishnah that a wedding was taking place for a previously unmarried woman or virgin,[61] and in the *Tosefta,* it is noted that fragrant or old wine may be passed through tubes before the brides and grooms. A passage in the Babylonian Talmud includes the addition that roasted heads of wheat and nuts may be thrown in front of a bride and groom, so long as the food is not ruined.[62]

In medieval European sources, Jews added that they should throw grains of wheat or other kinds of particles on the bride and groom. For example, Rabbi Eleazar ben Judah of Worms wrote in his compendium of laws and customs, *Sefer ha-Roqeah:* "It is the custom to throw wheat on the groom and bride when they are escorted early

Friday morning [to their wedding] based on [the verse], 'He satisfies you with choice wheat'" (Ps. 147:14).[63]

In the *Sefer Maharil,* from fifteenth-century Mainz, we have a more stylized version of this idea that is reinforced from contemporary medieval German Christian customs, and it is justified as a way of promoting the bride's and groom's fertility. It is related to May Day customs involving courtship and fertility, and some remnants of these practices exist today. May gave its name to the Jewish adaptation, called "Maien."[64]

> On Friday morning at dawn, the sexton calls everyone to come to the synagogue and at the same time, called them to go to the "Maien." The rabbi brings the groom before him . . . and the rest behind with torches and musicians to the courtyard of the synagogue. They go back and get the bride and her friends, also with torches and musical instruments. When the bride gets to the entrance of the courtyard, the rabbi and the other notables get the groom and bring him towards her. With hands clasped, the people shower them with grains of wheat and say three times, "Be fruitful and multiply."[65]

Today, Christian wedding guests throw rice on the heads of the bride and groom as they leave the church. Traditional Jews once threw grain before the wedding but no longer do so. Nor do they tie tin cans to a wedding limousine, on which "just married" has been written. On the other hand, a typical Israeli wedding car to and from the wedding is festooned with streamers and other eye-catching decorations.

Instead, traditional Jews throw candy at the groom the Sabbath before the wedding. In ancient Palestine, this Sabbath was a special time of celebration and was known as the "Sabbath before the wedding" or, in a mixture of Hebrew and Greek, *shabbat shel protogamia.*[66] In medieval Germany, this Sabbath was called *spinholtz,* an obscure name, sometimes tied to the female symbol of the "distaff" (German: *Spindel*) or used as a corruption of *sponsalia,* the Roman term for both betrothal and betrothal party. Both etymologies are forced derivations that work only if you ignore the second syllable.[67] The term appears only in early modern Germany, when it refers to two pre-nuptial Sabbaths. The first is called the "little spinholtz," two weeks before the wedding; the second, the "great spinholtz," the Sabbath prior to the wedding.[68]

At some point, the Sabbath before the wedding was also called the *aufruf* (calling up), based on the honor the community paid the groom in the synagogue by calling him to the Torah on that Sabbath. As in many traditional bar mitzvahs nowadays, bags of candy are thrown on the groom when he completes the blessings in the synagogue. One could consider this a kind of transferred fertility symbol, especially since as soon as the candy is thrown, little children run up and grab the bags for themselves. In effect, the rite anticipates the groom fathering children by provoking little children to appear when he is honored.

In modern Germany and eastern Europe, the festive Sabbath of the aufruf was a time of parties and celebrations sponsored by the family of the bride, not, as today, of the groom. This is because modern Jews have completely shifted their understanding of who is responsible for hosting and paying for the wedding. In traditional Jewish weddings, the betrothal party, when separated from the wedding by a significant amount of time, was held in the home of the bride, whereas the family of the groom paid for the wedding that took place in his family's home. When the ceremonies of betrothal and marriage were combined into one rite, the event usually took place in the groom's home and his family paid for the entire event. As a result, the family of the bride sponsored the preliminary celebration, such as the aufruf.

In recent times, in the United States, for example, Jews have assimilated the ancient Roman and traditional Christian traditions that the family of the bride is at least theoretically responsible for planning and paying for the wedding. The wedding today often takes place where the bride lives and is officiated by her family rabbi, with an assist perhaps from the groom's. This practice, however, is based on the Roman-Christian notion that the bride's father gives her away. Today, if Jewish parents are the ones who make the wedding with/for their children, responsibilities are often shared between the two families. But, as a result of the theoretical shift of the wedding from the domain of the groom to that of the bride, the aufruf became a preliminary party given by the family of the groom.

Sefardic, Mediterranean, and Asian Jewish communities tended to celebrate on the Sabbath after the wedding, sometimes called *shabbat hatan* (the Groom's Sabbath), as part of the seven days of celebration and feasting that take place after the wedding. This is also a common practice among modern Orthodox Jews in Israel today, regardless of their place of origin.

MOURNING RITES AT A WEDDING

Clusters of customs from one rite in the life cycle are sometimes transferred to another. We saw this in modern bar mitzvah celebrations, in which some wedding customs appear, especially during the festive party. Already in antiquity, a significant number of mourning customs were transferred, strange as it may be to modern sensibilities, to Jewish weddings. Recently an entire book has been compiled with these parallel customs.[69]

Some are rarely seen today. For example, Jews eat eggs in a house of mourning right after the mourners return from the cemetery, but in some Muslim lands, Jews and Muslims have a custom for the groom to throw an egg in the direction of the bride, to ward off demons. The Muslim Berbers in North Africa did this. Lancelot Addison, who wrote about the customs of the Jews there in the seventeenth century, mentions that "the [Jewish] Bridegroom takes a raw Egg which he casts at the Bride."[70]

In parts of Yemen, the mother of the bride took eggs when she accompanied the bride to the ritual bath for the first time, prior to the wedding. The mother held an egg over the bride's head, made with it a circular motion, and said that the eggs should be "an atonement for you." This gesture is a specialized application of the custom of *kapparot,* in which Jews take a living chicken and swing it over their heads, just before the Day of Atonement, as a way of transferring human sins to the animal, which is then killed. Jews from some Muslim communities sometimes "make kapparot" when eggs, for example, fall to the ground and break, a sign of bad luck, which is neutralized by immediately saying, "may this be atonement (kapparot) for my sins."[71]

Another symbolic reminder of death or of the destruction of Jerusalem that appears at Jewish weddings is the groom's wearing a white outer garment, known in Yiddish as a *kittel,* also called *sarganit/ sarganes,* and traditionally worn on the Jewish New Year and Day of Atonement and at certain other times of the liturgical year when a state of purity and atonement is important. The groom's special honored guests put it on him before the ceremony begins. This garment also alludes to the white color of the burial shrouds and the way others put the shrouds on the body. The sarganit/sarganes became associated especially with brides. When bride and groom wore the white garment, they were to be mindful of death and humbled.[72] Thus, long before brides wore elegant white wedding dresses, Jewish brides in northern Europe wore this special white outer garment.

Other mourning customs were incorporated into weddings. Among these are the custom of the bride and groom fasting on the day of the wedding, as on the day of a close relative's death or funeral; lighting candles at weddings as well as funerals and memorial days; using a tallit to bury a man and placing one overhead as the top of the wedding canopy or on the bride's and groom's heads instead of a wedding canopy; breaking a vessel made of clay at a funeral and the mothers of the bride and groom breaking a dish at the signing of the tena'im; the seven days of mourning after the funeral and the seven days of wedding feasts after the wedding; burial society members circling the open grave seven times and the bride circling the groom seven times.

The primary historical reason for these transfers is to fool demons that might jinx the wedding joy. By posing as mourners, Jews acted to deceive the demons and elude harm. Other reasons were adduced, all of which became part of Jewish wedding lore: humility, remembering death, and remembering Jerusalem, a motif that was first associated with the wearing of ashes on the groom's (and/or the bride's) forehead and also with the groom breaking a glass by throwing it against a stone wall in the synagogue courtyard or underfoot in the synagogue, as today.[73]

Placing burnt ashes on the head of the bridegroom, or sometimes the bride, as a reminder of the destruction of Jerusalem and the ancient Temple, was an early Babylonian custom. In the Babylonian Talmud, this relatively rare practice among some rabbis is justified by literally interpreting the word *rosh* (head) in the verse about not forgetting Jerusalem: "If I forget you, O Jerusalem, let my right hand wither; . . . if I do not keep Jerusalem in memory even at my 'head' joy" (Ps. 137:5). The question is raised in the Talmud exactly where on the head the ashes are to be placed. The answer is that they should go on the forehead, on the spot where Jews are to wear the phylactery (tefillah), or leather box in which are enclosed special parchment strips.[74] An early medieval midrash on Psalms indicates that in Palestine the bride or groom might wear ashes.[75]

Though the custom for the groom to wear ashes on his forehead is mentioned among some rabbis in ancient Babylonia, it was not common in southern Europe in the late Middle Ages for the simple reason that most Jewish men there did not put on tefillin. Instead, they placed a black or white cloth over the heads of the bride and groom as a way of remembering the destruction of Jerusalem. This act was also sometimes considered a form of canopy or head covering for other purposes as well.[76] In late medieval Ashkenaz, the ancient Babylonian custom of wearing ashes prevailed.[77] In Sefardic communities, some put wreaths of olive leaves on the bride's and groom's heads, the bitter taste of which served as yet another reminder of the loss of Jerusalem.[78]

By the sixteenth century, Rabbi Joseph Karo ruled that the groom should place ashes on the spot where the head phylactery (*tefillah shel rosh*) goes; Rabbi Moses Isserles, representing the customs of Polish Jewry, wrote that Jews could remember Jerusalem by breaking a glass or by covering the bride and groom with black cloth or placing some other sign of mourning on the groom's head.[79]

Related to the power of demons and the need to gain protection over them is the custom of the bride circling the groom either three or seven times just before the qiddushin rite begins. There are many customs in cultures involving either circles or the number seven or, together, making a circuit seven times. The Jewish wedding custom is not noted earlier than the fifteenth century and appears first in east Austria (Vienna, Neustadt) and then in eastern European communities. It is based on a Polish Christian practice, apparently taken into Jewish rites, in order to protect the groom from demons who are jealous that he is about to marry and beget children.[80]

The custom spread from there to other Jewish regions and is mentioned by Lancelot Addison in the late seventeenth century, supposedly about the Jews of Morocco, but possibly reflecting, as is often the case with him, German practice: "At the Wives first meeting of her Husband she walks thrice about him."[81]

NESU'IN (COMPLETION OF MARRIAGE)

Following arrangements and betrothal, the third stage of a Jewish marriage is called nesu'in. This is when the groom symbolically "takes" the bride and "enters the huppah," or wedding chamber, to consummate the marriage. The central gesture of the wedding ceremony is the movement of the bride from her house to the groom's.

In antiquity, the Jewish community knew that a young bride went out of her father's house accompanied by music (be-hinuma),[82] her hair hanging down to her shoulders.[83] For, as the baraita (third century) in the Talmud puts it, "The blessing of the bridegroom [for marriage] is recited in the house of the bridegroom." Another version states the contrast between it and the earlier betrothal blessing: "The blessing of the bridegroom is said in the house of the bridegroom and the blessing of betrothal in the house of betrothal."[84]

The blessing of the bridegroom is said in the presence of ten all seven days.[85] This quorum is required in Talmudic times for this final stage of the ceremony, a requirement not imposed on the betrothal stage that needed only two witnesses until Geonic times when it too came to require a minyan.

The ceremony known as "the seven blessings" (sheva berakhot) actually consists of six, ascribed to third-century authorities, and they are prescribed in the Talmud and called "birkat hatanim."[86] These blessings were recited at the time of the wedding, following which the groom led the bride into the huppah, or bridal chamber, to consummate the wedding sexually. This act of completion is also sometimes referred to in rabbinic language as when the woman "enters the bridal chamber" (tikkanes la-huppah),[87] that is, moved into the fiancé's bed and life in her husband's family's home or neighborhood.

Following the text of the blessing of betrothal, quoted earlier, the Talmud proceeds to provide the blessing for the bridegroom:

What does one say? Rav Judah said: Blessed are you, Lord God, King of the universe [1] who has created everything to his glory; and [2] creator of man; and [3] who has created man in his image, in the image and the likeness of his form, and has prepared unto himself out of himself a building for ever. Blessed are You, Lord, Creator of man; [4] May the barren greatly rejoice and exult when her children will be gathered in her midst in joy. Blessed are You, O Lord, who makes Zion joyful through her children; [5] May You make the loved companions greatly to rejoice, even as of old You did gladden your creature in the Garden of Eden. Blessed are You, O Lord, who makes bridegroom and bride rejoice; [6] Blessed are You, Lord God, King of the universe, who has created joy and gladness, bridegroom and bride, rejoicing, song, mirth, delight, love, brotherhood, peace, and friendship. Speedily, Lord our God, may be heard in the cities of Judah,

and in the streets of Jerusalem, the voice of joy and the voice of gladness, the voice of the bridegroom and the voice of the bride, the voice
of the singing of bridegrooms from their marriage chambers and of
youths from the feasts of song. Blessed are You, O Lord, who makes
the bridegroom to rejoice with the bride.[88]

It is not clear how old these formulas are, but one may note that there
is a similarity between the second, "Who creates man," and a phrase
in Tobias's blessing at his marriage, "Blessed are You. . . . You made
Adam [man]" (Tob. 8:5–6).[89]

From the Talmudic enumeration it is clear that we are dealing with
six, not seven, blessings. Yet, today the seven blessings are recited as
the liturgy of the marriage, or nesu'in, ceremony, and they are known
as "sheva berakhot." Actually, in the Talmud itself, opinions are
expressed that there are either six or five, since the second and third
seem to be about the same thing, the creation of man. But no one
refers yet to "seven blessings," which came a little later, after the
Geonim added a first to the six wedding blessings formulated in the
Talmud, making seven. That first blessing recited under the wedding canopy today is the blessing over wine, not mentioned among
the Talmud's six.[90]

In "The Differences between the Jews of Babylonia and Palestine,"
a list of competing customs practiced by Jews who live either in Christian Byzantine Palestine or in Muslim Iraq, there is a post-Talmudic
tradition that "the people of the East [Iraq] bless the groom with
seven blessings; the Jews of Palestine, with three."[91] The Palestinian
practice disappeared, and we do not even know what these blessings
were.

The practice of seven continues, and we find it in the first prayer
book, *Seder Rav 'Amram Gaon.*[92] Perhaps the early eastern Christian
practice of celebrating weddings over a cup of wine drunk by the bride
and groom, practiced near the Geonim in southern Iraq, suggested
the custom of adding a blessing over a cup of wine.[93]

Ketubbah

Although there are allusions in the Bible to marriage and a religious covenant,[94] we have no sign of a written contract in the Hebrew Bible itself. Nothing there matches the stipulation for a "book of severance" (*sefer keritut*) that is mentioned in connection with a divorce.

An important feature of Jewish marriage and the wedding rite is the ketubbah (a term used in the Mishnah), the document that includes the groom's commitment to provide financially for his wife in the case of her becoming a widow or divorcée. Though the term is rabbinic, the institution, with several variations from what developed into a fairly standard rite, is attested from nearly twenty-five hundred years ago in the ancient Persian Empire.

The ketubbah is a fascinating institution. In the Bible, a Jewish husband may divorce his wife without her consent. This situation changed only in the early eleventh-century ordinance of Rabbi Gershom ben Judah of Mainz (d. 1028).[95]

The ketubbah is the subject of an entire section of the Talmud. While this subject is an important one, it bears on the rituals of marriage at two points: the language used, along with its being signed by two proper witnesses usually before the ceremony begins and the presentation of the text from the groom to the bride during the ceremony.

Even earlier than the time the Book of Tobit (Tob. 7:13) was written, we have evidence from Aramaic papyri dated in the fifth century B.C.E. of a unique type of contract written by a bride's father, not the husband, on the occasion of a wedding. These documents come from the Jewish military colony of Elephantine, located on an island in the Nile on the border between southern Egypt and Nubia (northern Ethiopia), on the southern frontier of the extreme western part of the Persian Empire. The beginning of the Book of Esther introduces the reader to the vast size of King Ahasuarus's domain, by saying that he "reigned over a hundred and twenty-seven provinces from

India to Nubia" (Esther 1:1). The southwest border of the empire was at Elephantine.

A number of Jews served the distant Persian government there as a military colony responsible for collecting customs due on imports and exports across the imperial border. One of the most valuable objects traded was elephant ivory, which gave the name to the island, "elephantine" in Greek or "Svein" in Aramaic, which became the Arabic Asuan. When the Asuan High Dam was built in the 1960s, much of Nubia was flooded, including the former colony. Among the many papyrus documents written in Aramaic from Elephantine, we find the earliest preserved Jewish marriage contracts.[96]

Take the case of Mibtahiah bat (daughter of) Mahseiah, whose several legal transactions have been preserved in a personal archive from Elephantine.[97] It includes texts of various kinds that are related to her three marriages. The first is a legal contract that her father issued her in 459 B.C.E. in which he deeds her a house on the occasion of her marriage. It is not a marriage contract. "One Mahseiah b. Yedoniah, a Jew of Elephantine, of the detachment of Haumadata, said to Jezaniah b. Uriah of the said detachment as follows: There is the site of one house belonging to me, west of the house belonging to you, which I have given to your wife, my daughter Mibtahiah, and in respect of which I have written her a deed. . . . But you may not sell that house or give it as a present to others; only your children by my daughter Mibtahiah shall have power over it after you two."[98]

We see here that Mibtahiah's father might have arranged the match between his daughter and a neighbor. The document also indicates that the future groom belonged to the same military unit as the girl's father, and this gave him additional opportunity to know him well.[99] After Mibtahiah's first marriage ended with her husband's death, she married "Pia b. Pahi, the builder," an Egyptian. Although there were strong pressures in fifth-century Judah/Yuhud for Jews not to intermarry, this was not considered the norm in Elephantine, and we have a good deal of evidence of intermarriage there. No marriage contract for this union survived either.

By now Mibtahiah was a woman of means, and when her second marriage ended in divorce, her ex-husband challenged the title to some of her property, including "silver, grain, clothing, bronze and iron [vessels]; all goods, possessions and the marriage contract."[100] She was required to take an oath that the property was all hers, and when she did, Pia withdrew any claim to it. She swore her oath by an Egyptian god, and Egyptian witnesses signed the document of settlement.[101]

Then, around 440, some twenty years after her first marriage—she is probably in her late thirties now—we finally have a marriage contract. In it, one Ashor b. Seho—Egyptian names, apparently indicating that her new husband also was an Egyptian—records an ancient formula, not to Mibtahiah herself, but in archaic and formulaic language to Mibtahiah's father: "I have come to your house that you might give me your daughter Mibtahiah in marriage. She is my wife and I am her husband from this day forever. I have given you as the bride price of your daughter Mibtahiah [a sum of] five shekels, royal weight."[102]

This contract further stipulates that should Ashor die first without any heir from Mibtahiah, she inherits the house and all property belonging to her husband. Despite the differences between this document and the later rabbinic marriage contract, or ketubbah, the amount here stipulated for a widow or divorcee is half of what was required in Elephantine marriage contracts for first-time brides, the same 1:2 ratio found in the later Jewish ketubbah.[103]

Unlike the rite in the Book of Tobit, in which the bride's father, Raguel, issues the formula, in the marriage contracts of Elephantine it is the husband who states: "She is my wife and I am her husband, from this day for ever."[104] This formula did not survive to become part of the Jewish wedding rite. Part of the formula in the Book of Tobit did survive. But it is the groom, not the bride's father, who recites the phrase, "according to the law of Moses." Different elements from each period persisted; others disappeared or were transformed.

As will be the case in the rabbinic ketubbah, the point of the Jewish marriage contract is to protect the wife should the marriage end by her husband's death or by divorce. It is a kind of pre-nuptial agreement that creates a deferred lien against the husband's estate that had to be paid to the widow or divorcée unless she was judged at fault for the dissolution of the marriage. In that case, she would forfeit the payment stipulated in the ketubbah. Should the husband be judged at fault, he would have to divorce her and pay the ketubbah. This served both to protect the young bride from being abandoned and as a double incentive to both partners to protect the marriage bond. Fragments of other marriage contracts from the first two centuries found in the Judean Desert and in caves near the Dead Sea are often quite different from what was being promoted by early rabbinic circles.[105]

In addition to the traditional roles the ketubbah has played in the wedding rite, two other features should be noted. One consequence of combining the ceremonies of betrothal and marriage was the new custom of reading the ketubbah out loud, between the two parts of the ancient separate rites. This is attested for the first time in the twelfth century in northern France.[106] The practice of combining the two ceremonies became common in northern Europe, spread to Spain, and immigrants from Germany and Spain introduced it and the reading of the ketubbah out loud at the ceremony to Italy. By the seventeenth century, it was taken for granted there, too.[107]

Since early modern times, especially in Italy, Jews became intoxicated with lavishly illuminated ketubbot, and these are a special genre of Jewish art history and material culture.[108] Today, professional calligraphers are able to make a ketubbah by hand, and ketubbot of varying sizes and types are available as well.[109]

Huppah as Canopy

The word "huppah" appears in the Bible but only in certain contexts and does not mean a canopy under which the wedding ceremony took place, as today. The root H-P-H means to cover, especially overhead, as in the phrase "everyone covered his head" (2 Sam. 15:30), or in

Isaiah's image of a cloud or pillar of smoke forming a "canopy" over God's shrine (Isa. 4:5).

The groom or the bride in the Bible spends time in the huppah before the marriage, like in a bride's room or a greenroom today. The Psalmist compares the sun to a groom and says, "He placed a tent [in the heavens] for the sun, who is like a groom coming forth from his chamber (mei-hupato) like a hero, eager to run his course (Ps. 19:5–6). The groom came out, as the prophet Joel says, "of his chamber" (mei-hedro), and the bride, from "her chamber" (mei-hupatah) (Joel 2:16).

By late antiquity, the huppah has become the wedding chamber, to which the couple repairs after they are married. This is one of several customs enumerated in the *Tosefta* about the wedding chamber that existed in different parts of the Land of Israel and at various times.[110] In post-rabbinic times, huppah develops an interesting set of meanings and gestures as it is transformed from a wedding chamber to some other kind of head covering for the bride or the bride and groom, a kind of veil over both, then into a tallit over both. Any and all of these can be a huppah.

Thus, in medieval Ashkenaz, huppah was understood to mean that the bride and groom needed a head covering during the ceremony. Rabbi Eleazar ben Judah of Worms (d. ca. 1230) refers to placing a tallit over the heads of the bride, groom, and assembled. Two hundred years later, Rabbi Jacob ben Moses Ha-Levi Molin (Maharil) refers to draping the long hood (tzippel=Zipfel=end) of the groom's special poncho-like outer garment (*mitaron*) over the heads of the bride and groom "to be their huppah."[111]

From the writings of Rabbi Moses Isserles in sixteenth-century Poland, we see that the wedding canopy was an innovation. In his note to part of the *Shulhan 'Arukh* he comments on a statement made by Rabbi Joseph Karo on what constitutes a completed marriage ceremony. Karo writes that a husband may not sleep with his bride so long as she is only betrothed and still living in her father's house. It is necessary "that he bring her into his house and be alone with her (ve-yityahed imah), and set her apart for himself alone. This intimacy (yihud) is what is called entering the huppah and it is called nesu'in everywhere. . . . One should recite the wedding blessings (birkat hatanim) in the house of the groom before the nesu'in." For Karo, then, the term huppah means marriage in its last stage. To "enter the huppah" means one has undergone all of the rites of betrothal and marriage and now the couple may be alone together in his house, and it is this situation of intimacy or being alone (yihud), according to Karo, that is the definition of "to enter the huppah." On this meaning of the word huppah, Isserles comments:

> There are those who say that huppah does not refer to yihud but rather to whenever a groom brings his bride to his house for the purpose of marriage; others say that huppah means one spreads out a cloth on her head during the time of the blessing. . . . The custom today is widespread to call huppah a place where one places a sheet over poles and we bring the groom and bride under it in public (be-rabim). He betroths her there and the betrothal and wedding blessings are recited. Afterwards, one escorts them to their house where they eat together in a secluded place. This is [the meaning of] huppah as practiced today.[112]

For him, the term huppah now refers to the ceremony under a canopy followed by privacy (yihud). It still does not mean just the wedding canopy. (Fig. 8)

And yet, huppah has shifted significantly from its earlier meaning of being just the wedding chamber where the wedding is consummated, as in the Talmud, to being the canopy where the ceremony takes place and the completion of the rite is private. Whereas in the Talmud, the trees that some Jews planted on the birth of a child were used when they were married to build the wedding chamber, in eastern Europe, they were used to construct a wedding canopy.[113]

A little later, Rabbi Benjamin Aaron ben Abraham Slonik (d. ca. 1617) writes in Poland:

8. Marriage scene in Johann Christoph Georg Bodenschatz, Kirchliche Verfassung der heutigen Juden, *Part 4, p. 127c, Plate XI. Frankfurt am Main and Leipzig, 1748–49. Courtesy of the Library of the Jewish Theological Seminary.*

The custom of huppa has changed, however. The huppa used to be an elaborate tent with decorated curtains into which the bride and groom were ceremoniously led [after the ceremony; in contrast] . . . our practice is to spread a prayer shawl on four poles beneath which the bride and groom are led [for the ceremony].[114]

Sometimes the wedding canopy consisted of the groom's tallit that was tied to the four poles; at other times, a tallit or other cloth was draped over the couple, even though they were standing under a wedding canopy. All are variations on the common theme of huppah as a covering overhead and are related to the final stage of the ceremony of marriage, which ends in the groom bringing the bride into his chamber to consummate the marriage.

The term huppah today can be a four-poled canopy erected in the synagogue or in a banquet hall or outdoors. It is usually decorated with greens and floral arrangements. When modern synagogues install a skylight above the altar so that weddings can be held underneath, this is a compromise between the custom of placing a wedding chamber in the courtyard and holding a wedding inside a synagogue. The skylight has acquired additional meaning as a reminder of offspring as many as the stars in Abraham's covenant (Gen. 15) and the biblical commandment to "be fertile and increase" (Gen. 1:28).

Concluding Custom: Breaking a Glass

Both early modern Christian representations of a Jewish wedding and Hollywood depictions have immortalized the breaking of a glass as the culmination of a Jewish wedding. A passage in the Talmud connects this act, not to remembering the destruction of Jerusalem, as today, but to being serious even at a time of great joy: "Mar the son of Ravina made a wedding feast for his son. He saw that the rabbis were growing very merry and so he took a precious cup worth four hundred zuz and broke it before them. Then they became very serious." A similar story is told, with variations, about Rav Ashi, who broke a glass of white crystal for the same reason.[115]

As we have seen, the custom mentioned in the Talmud for the groom to wear ashes at the time of the wedding is motivated by a desire to remember the destruction of Jerusalem at even the most joyous occasion.[116] By the twelfth century in northern France, the gesture of breaking a glass is mentioned, but its motivation still seems attached to the Talmudic reason of creating a moment of solemnity at a time of great joy, not remembering Jerusalem. The Tosafist glossator comments on the passage about breaking "a glass of white crystal" at a wedding feast: "This is the basis for breaking glass (zekhukhit) at weddings."[117] Presumably, the "this" refers to both the Talmudic precedent and the motivation in the story.

The *Mahzor Vitry,* also from northern France at about the same time, points out that the glass to be broken was used during the ceremony for the seven wedding blessings, after which the wine is spilled out and, adding here a new element to the gesture, "he [the groom] throws the glass vessel at the wall and breaks it."[118] The verses that justify the act are still related to creating a mood of seriousness, not to remembering Jerusalem: "As it is written, 'From all sadness ('ezev) there is some gain' (Prov. 14:23) and 'Serve the Lord in awe; rejoice with trembling' (Ps. 2:11). [The last phrase means] where there is joy, there should be trembling," as in the Talmud. A few lines later, the same author connects putting ashes on the groom's head with remembering Jerusalem (Ps. 137:5), as in the Talmud, not breaking a glass.[119]

Writing in early twelfth-century Mainz, Rabbi Eliezer ben Natan points to important details not mentioned before, but there still is no connection with Jerusalem's destruction. He says that the cup the groom breaks is one that was used before, during one of the blessings over wine, and is worth only a penny. Rabbi Eliezer then questions how sad one can be by breaking a cup worth so little. He also questions the propriety of acting disrespectfully toward a cup of wine over which a blessing had just been recited earlier. From these reservations, it would seem that Rabbi Eliezer discouraged the custom. It continued in Germany anyway, as breaking a glass at a wedding is also mentioned by the German-Jewish authority Rabbi Eleazar of Worms with the same rationale as in the Talmud, decreased joy.[120]

The earliest reference to breaking a glass as a way to remember Jerusalem is as a substitute for the Talmudic custom that the groom is to put ashes on his forehead. A substitute custom was needed where most Jewish men were not in the habit of wearing phylacteries. This point is made by Rabbi Aaron ben Jacob ha-Kohen of Lunel in his *Sefer Orhot Hayyim* and is repeated with minor variations in the anonymous compilation known as the *Kol Bo,* both from fourteenth-century southern France: "A person must remember to mourn for Jerusalem at all his joyous occasions, as it says, 'If I forget you, O Jerusalem' (Ps. 137:5) and so on. . . . But in places where the Jews are not presumed to put on tefillin, it became the custom to perform a different act of memorialization instead, such as putting a black cloth over the head of the bride and groom. In addition, it became widespread to break the cup after the seven blessings."[121] This is the earliest reference that connects Jerusalem with breaking the glass after the wedding.

The indications are, then, that the custom we follow today of the groom's breaking a glass at the end of the marriage ceremony as a reminder of the destruction of Jerusalem was an innovation not much earlier than the fourteenth century in southern France. It was a substitute for the Talmudic act of the groom wearing ashes on the forehead where his head tefillin are placed, since, we are told, most Jews in southern France did not put on tefillin. Only very pious Jews did it there.

Over the next two hundred years, the custom and explanation spread north into Germany and Poland, but not every reference to the rite is explicit about its meaning. For example, in the early fifteenth century, in his long description of a wedding in Mainz, Rabbi Jacob ben Moses (Maharil) says that "the rabbi holds the cup and afterwards gives it to the groom who turns around, faces north, and throws the cup against the wall so that it breaks." He does not mention Jerusalem.[122] By the late fifteenth century, when Rabbi Moses ben Isaac Mintz describes this custom, he says that the groom throws the cup used for the betrothal (not, as earlier, the marriage) at the wall in memory of the destruction of Jerusalem (zekher la-hurban).[123] By that point, at least, the gesture was associated also in Germany with the destruction of Jerusalem.

Rabbi Joseph Karo repeats the Talmudic custom that the groom puts ashes on his forehead where he wears the tefillin, but Rabbi Moses Isserles, relying on the *Kol Bo,* says there are places where Jews were accustomed to break a cup at the time of a wedding or to put a black cloth or other sign of mourning on the groom's head.[124] Although he does not mention the reason, Rabbi David ben Samuel Halevi (1586–1667), the author of *Turei Zahav,* also writing in Poland, adds to Karo's comment that one should remember Jerusalem: "I have seen places where the shamash (beadle) says the verse (Ps. 137:5) and the groom repeats it, word for word, and it is proper to do so."[125] Elsewhere, Isserles adds that "it is the custom in these lands to break the cup after the seven blessings, and the groom breaks the cup over which the betrothal blessing was recited."[126] Thus, by the sixteenth century, variations of the custom were established in Poland as well as Germany.

Among early modern illustrations from Germany of Jewish life cycle rites, one depicts the groom throwing a glass at a special stone inserted in a wall. Such a stone, known as a *Traustein* (betrothal stone), has survived from Bingen (Germany) and is presently in the Israel Museum.[127] Another variation, in Sefardic practice, was to place a special plate on the floor and have the groom throw a glass against the plate. This is illustrated in Picart's illustration of a Portuguese wedding.[128]

Although most descriptions of Jewish weddings place the breaking of the glass at the end of the marriage ceremony, Hayyim Schauss recalled weddings in eastern Europe, in which the groom breaks the glass right after the betrothal blessing over the first cup, followed by reading the ketubbah, and then reciting the seven marriage blessings.[129] This actually makes sense if it was still customary in the early twentieth century there to break the betrothal cup in memory of Jerusalem, even though Isserles himself wrote that that cup is not broken until the end of the whole marriage rite.

The custom today of placing the glass, wrapped in a cloth, under the groom's foot, then, is relatively recent. It should be noted that most weddings today use metal cups for each of the two ceremonies of betrothal and marriage, not breakable ones, as earlier. Craftsmen made special matching two-cup sets for wedding ceremonies out of silver, for example.[130] The glass that is now broken is a third one, used in neither ceremony, and all of this is an innovation, no earlier, apparently, than the eighteenth century.[131]

In the first half of the twentieth century, when photographers, who tend to be ever present in wedding events, used removable flash bulbs, the groom sometimes crushed one of these bulbs wrapped in a napkin. As attached flashguns and strobes replaced bulbs, an actual wine glass came to be used. Some companies today take the broken pieces of the glass and mount them in Lucite as a momento of the act, a new memory of the destruction ("zekher la-hurban").

Wedding Feasts for Seven Days

In the Bible, the wedding feast is usually portrayed as taking place in the home of the groom. There are exceptions, as in the cases of Jacob, Samson, and Tobit, but it usually lasts seven days, as when Jacob "waited out the bridal week of [Leah] and then [Laban] gave [Jacob] his daughter Rachel as wife" (Gen. 29:28) or with Samson, who formulated a riddle and bet the locals they could not figure it out "'during the seven days of the feast'" (Jud. 14:12).

In the Book of Tobit, Tobias's in-laws gave him and Sarah a feast for two weeks (Tob. 8:20; 10:7). It will soon become seven days in most places. The power of the number seven is seen in all Jewish life cycle events from antiquity: the seven-day celebration after a birth (shevu'a ha-ben), the wedding feast, and the seven days of mourning right after burial of the dead (shiva).

EARLY MODERN MEMOIRS
AND WEDDING RITES

Although we found descriptions of various practices associated with a Jewish wedding in Rabbi Jacob ben Moses (Maharil)'s book of customs, it is relatively rare to find actual descriptions before early modern times. Autobiographical memoirs of Leon Modena (1571–1648), Glueckl of Hameln (1646–1724), and Solomon Maimon (ca. 1753–1800) are unusually rich examples from this period and indicate how important arranging matches was, especially for Glueckl, who was widowed at an early age.

One of the first Jewish autobiographies is Leon Modena's *Hayyei Yehudah* (Life of Judah) in which this seventeenth-century Venetian rabbi relates his own arranged marriage some time in 1589 at age 18. His mother kept after him to marry her niece, his cousin, "Esther—the daughter of my mother's sister Gioja."[132]

Despite the fact that the young Leon had a dream in which he sees his cousin Esther and inexplicably sees her replaced by another, they go ahead with plans for the match. While in Venice, her sister's residence, Leon's mother and aunt discuss the match and an agreement is reached. In late summer 1589, "we completed the marriage agreement, shook hands, and made the symbolic acquisition with great rejoicing."[133]

The wedding date was to be June 1590, and after arriving in Venice he found the bride confined to her bed. Just before she died, she reached out to Leon, despite the impropriety, and he reports that "she summoned me and embraced and kissed me. She said, 'I know that this is bold behavior, but God knows that during the one year of our engagement we did not touch each other even with our little fingers. Now, at the time of death, the rights of the dying are mine. I was not allowed to become your wife, but what can I do, for thus it is decreed in heaven. May God's will be done.'"[134]

In an uncanny twist recalling Jacob's courtship, Leon goes on to relate that after his betrothed had died that June 22 and was buried, "all the relatives set upon me and my mother saying, 'Behold her younger sister is as good as she. Why forfeit the opportunity to perpetuate the kinship and to give comfort to the mother and father of the young woman?' They entreated me to the point of embarrassment to take her sister Rachel to wife." Leon writes that he consulted his father, who replied, "'Do as you like, for the choice is yours.'" He agreed to marry the younger sister "to please my mother and the dead girl, who had hinted at it in her words. . . . Immediately we wrote up the agreement and were married on Friday the 5th of Tammuz 5350 [July 6, 1590], under a favorable star" less than a month after the ill-fated girl's funeral.[135]

The combination of matchmaking and individual choice, fatalism and cunning, revealed here are also reflected in other firsthand accounts that bring us into modern times. Glueckl of Hameln, for example, relates her family history in great detail.[136] At the time of her sister's engagement "to the son of the learned Reb Gumpel of Cleves, she received 1,800 Reichsthalers as her dowry, in those days a handsome sum."[137]

Glueckl says she herself was "betrothed when I was a girl of barely twelve, and less than two years later I married." She describes in detail the trip of her "parents together with about twenty wedding guests" from Hamburg to Hameln, her groom's small town, where the wedding was to take place. After the wedding, she continues, "my parents returned home and left me—I was a child of scarcely fourteen—alone with strangers in a strange world." Fortunately for Glueckl, her in-laws were warm and kind to her.[138]

She was to have fourteen children of her own, and she relates many details about their arranged weddings and marriages to which both families contributed dowries when possible. For example, when Zipporah, her oldest daughter, was almost twelve, a marriage broker in Amsterdam proposed a match to a son of a very wealthy man, Elias Cleve, "worth at least 100,000 Reichsthalers."[139] Her husband, still young and not as well established as her daughter's future in-laws, proposed a dowry of 2,200 Reichsthalers and set the wedding for a year and a half later in Cleves, the home of the groom.[140] The bride's family arrived fourteen days before the wedding and were lavishly hosted. Several nobles were in Cleves, including the future king, and father Cleve invited them all to the wedding. Their presence added to the importance of the match but also to the unusually busy preparations.

There was such commotion, in fact, that several unusual things happened, which Glueckl luckily notes for us. The ceremony itself almost went awry. "As the bridal pair were led beneath the chuppah [here, a canopy] out it came that in the confusion we had forgotten to write the marriage contract! What was to be done? Nobility and princes were already at hand and they were all agog to see the ceremony. Whereat Rabbi Meir declared that the groom should appoint a bondsman to write out the contract immediately after the wedding. Then the rabbi read a set-contract from a book. And so the couple were joined."[141]

Nor were the agreed-upon dowries from both families handled properly in all the rush. "On the marriage day, immediately after the wedding, there was spread a lavish collation of all kinds of sweetmeats and fine imported wines and fruits. . . . You can readily picture the bustle and excitement. . . . There was not even time to deliver and count over the dowries, as is customary. So we placed our own dowry in a pouch and sealed it, and Elias Cleve did likewise, that we might tally the sum after the wedding was over."[142]

We also hear that after the feast was cleared, "then appeared masked performers who bowed prettily and played all manner of entertaining pranks. They concluded their performance," she writes most revealingly and unexpectedly, "with a truly splendid Dance of Death."[143]

That match was a good one, but one even better did not come off. A marriage broker tried to arrange a marriage for Glueckl's son Nathan, about age thirteen,[144] to the daughter of one of the wealthiest and most influential Court Jews of the time, Samuel Oppenheimer. Both families were to send dowries to her brother-in-law in Frankfurt, and "we deposited with him precious stones worth several thousands, and Samuel Oppenheimer likewise sent on his dowry."[145]

But unfortunately floods delayed the arrival of the great man's dowry for his daughter, and under pressure from the marriage broker and Glueckl's brother-in-law's doubts that Oppenheimer might have changed his mind, Glueckel and her husband agreed to the newly proposed arrangement with another young girl whose father had died. The girl's mother agreed to a dowry of 4,400 Reichsthalers plus wedding expenses, and Glueckel and her husband agreed to 2,400, and "thereupon the betrothal stood fast."[146]

But "eight days later came a letter from my brother in law Isaac; the money had arrived, and my husband should without delay send on the authorization to conclude the match." But it was too late. The brother-in-law was furious when he learned about the new match, but Glueckl was philosophical about the outcome: "Without questioning His ways, we ignorant mortals must in all things thank our Creator."[147]

The betrothal took place with the bride's family, and, "upon his betrothal, we brought my son Nathan back home, that he make his gift to the bride," the occasion for more festivities. How much later the actual marriage was to be we do not know.[148]

Prior to Fielding's *Tom Jones,* it is hard to find a more remarkable set of near-marital adventures than those related in the autobiography of the Jewish philosopher Solomon Maimon (1754–1800), a Lithuanian Jew who came under the influence of the Berlin Enlightenment (Haskalah) of Moses Mendelssohn. Just to enumerate the many efforts made by fathers and mothers of young women of various shapes and demeanors to nab this catch is to overhear for a moment some of the vagaries of courtship in eighteenth-century central Europe.

All of the following occurred to the same young man named Solomon Maimon. First came a match at the initiative of a wealthy neighbor, with whom the Maimons always were quarreling, and who had three daughters. The oldest was already married; the second, Pessel, was about Solomon's age, and the town gossips had it that they were likely to marry. Moreover, Solomon tells us that he and this Pessel "formed a mutual affection."[149]

Unfortunately for her and for Solomon, the youngest daughter, Rachel, fell and broke her leg. The leg mended badly, leaving it crooked. The rich neighbor wanted Solomon for a son-in-law but only for the crooked-legged youngest daughter, Rachel, not for straight-legged Pessel, whom the father intended to marry into a wealthy family. Although the rich neighbor offered Solomon's father a great deal of money to tempt him, he refused to make the arrangement, and the families continued to quarrel without any match to mend fences.

Solomon's reputation had spread so far that a total stranger from another town wrote to Solomon's father seeking to arrange a match between him and the man's only daughter. Solomon's father paid the man a visit, met the daughter, and agreed to draw up a contract. It included fifty thalers paid to him on the spot as well as the traditional small gifts for the groom, such as "a cap of black velvet trimmed with gold lace, a Bible bound in green velvet with silver clasps, etc."[150] The groom to be was also to prepare a learned sermon for the wedding, two months ahead. Solomon's mother also got busy and started baking wedding cakes and perishable preserves that she planned to take to the wedding.

But just as Solomon was starting to work in earnest on his wedding speech, he learned that his bride had contracted smallpox and died. The groom and father did not have to return any of the presents or money and got used to the bad news. Solomon figured he could use his wedding speech another time. But his mother was inconsolable over the cakes and preserves that now would go to waste.

The Maimons' financial situation deteriorated even further. Solomon accompanied his father to the town of Nesvij, where they opened a private school, the father as teacher, the son as his assistant. In the same town it happened that there was a shrewish widow named Madame Rissia, who owned an inn located on the edge of town. Solomon relates: "She had a daughter who yielded to her in none of the above-mentioned qualities, and who was indispensable to her in the management of the house."[151]

Madame Rissia decided that her daughter Sarah should marry Solomon, the Talmudic prodigy, and she sent letters to his father. But Maimon did not think it was such a good match.

Once when Solomon and his father went to the widow's house to wait for transportation out of town, Solomon and his father were suddenly put upon by a half-drunk party of rabbis who had just been to a circumcision at someone else's house. Madame Rissia knew where they had been and had sent her son to bring them to her house in order to create a fait accompli. The rabbis assumed that a match had already been struck and began to write out the terms of the engagement. Solomon's father protested that he had agreed to nothing of the kind. But the rabbis proceeded to argue the case for Madame Rissia by pointing out that the bride's family had the pedigree of three generations of rabbis.

Hearing this, Solomon's father actually did agree and the engagement contract was made out.[152] The Maimons were to get Madame Rissia's boardinghouse, the couple was to be boarded there for six years, and the groom would receive a new set of Talmud worth, he says, "two or three hundred thalers," as well as other gifts. His father had no dowry obligations and moreover was to get fifty thalers that he stipulated were to be handed over to him in cash before the betrothal.[153]

The groom and his father went home and waited for the gifts to arrive. Nothing happened for several weeks. Maimon's father began to wonder if the widow had not been duplicitous with him. Perhaps she did not intend to make good on the conditions of the engagement after all. He began to look for a way out of the agreement.

A rich Jew who used to sell spirits in the widow's town of Unsaved would spend the night en route in the Maimons' town. He had an only daughter and was determined to get Solomon for her. Seeing that Solomon's father was poor but stubborn, he determined to get him into debt and then leverage the debt into an engagement contract in which the debt would be forgiven. And so he offered Solomon's father some barrels of liquor on credit. The date of paying off the loan arrived, but Solomon's father could not pay it. The merchant sprang his trap. What about an engagement between your son and my daughter? The debt will be included in the terms of the engagement, and you will receive even more.

Solomon tells us that his father was a willing dupe because it was a way of getting back at the widow Madame Rissia, who had herself reneged on her promised gifts to the groom. An agreement was made at once. The initial debt of fifty thalers was returned and torn up, and Solomon's father received an additional fifty.

Now the plot thickens. For where should the liquor merchant now go but to Madame Rissia's inn, where he always stayed when in Nesvij. Naturally she could not refrain from bragging about the great catch she had recently arranged for her daughter: "'The father of the bridegroom,' said she, 'is himself a great scholar, and the bridegroom is a young man of eleven years, who has scarcely his equal.'"[154] At which the merchant bragged himself about his great catch for his daughter and mentioned the name of Solomon Maimon. At the sound of that name, the widow cried out, "'That is a confounded lie. Solomon is my daughter's bridegroom; and here, sir, is the marriage contract.'"[155] The merchant also produced his contract.

At this point the widow called Solomon's father to court, but he did not appear. Suddenly, his wife died, and Solomon's father brought his wife's body to Nesvij for burial. Hard to believe, the widow Madame Rissia got a lien against the body to prevent interment until Solomon's father would come to court to answer her charges. At this point, Madame Rissia finally made good on her promises and gave the groom all of her promised gifts and released the body for burial.

The merchant now came to court and tried to enforce his contract. Solomon's father argued that it was null, since there was an earlier contract that he had thought she would not honor. Hardly reconciled to his loss, the merchant proceeded that night to kidnap Solomon and take him out of town, but he did it so noisily that people chased after him and retrieved the startled young groom.

Solomon actually marries the daughter of the innkeeper, Madame Rissia, and has one more revealing secret to tell us about local customs, this time, under the huppah. "I had read in a little book," he relates, "of an approved plan for a husband to secure lordship over his better half for life, he was to tread on her foot at the marriage ceremony; and if both hit on the stratagem, the first to succeed would retain the upper hand. Accordingly, when my bride and I were placed side by side at the ceremony, this trick occurred to me, and I said to myself, 'Now you must not let the opportunity pass of securing for your whole lifetime lordship over your wife.' I was just going to tread on her foot, but a certain je ne sais quoi, whether fear, shame, or love, held me back. While I was in this irresolute state, all at once I felt the slipper of my wife on my foot with such an impression that I should almost have screamed aloud if I had not been checked by shame. I took this for a bad omen."

Shortly thereafter, he continues, "I stood, however, not only under the slipper of my wife, but—what was very much worse—under the lash of my mother-in-law."[156] Unfortunately for Solomon, his wife's dowry consisted of his bride's mother's house that came equipped with his mother-in-law. She promised them six year's board, but they got only half a year's worth, "and this amidst constant brawls and squabbles. . . . Scarcely a meal passed during which we did not fling at each other's heads bowls, plates, spoons, and similar articles."[157]

Who's on Top?

From the second half of the nineteenth century in eastern Europe, too, we hear of the slipper under the huppah contest, though it has since disappeared. It resembles similar competitive behavior in ancient Roman and medieval Christian weddings, involving who gets back to the house first, bride or groom.[158]

The memoirs of Ezekiel Kotick, a writer from a Hasidic family (1847–1921), include a passage about his wedding in 1865, when he was seventeen years old, apparently not that unusual an age.[159] The great Hebrew essayist Asher Ginzberg (Ahad Ha-'Am) also reports that he "was married off before my seventeenth birthday,"[160] and the Hebrew poet laureate Hayyim Nahman Bialik says, "at the age of eighteen I came under the bridal canopy."[161]

Ezekiel tells us he was to wear "white socks, slippers and a satin caftan" for his wedding clothes[162] but instead insisted in wearing boots. But he did wear the white gown over his satin caftan.[163] The bridal party arrives the day before the wedding and stops at the groom's uncles' house, where the wedding will take place. A custom of separate pre-wedding parties with the bride or groom is described, a practice that today sometimes is carried out at what is called the Hasan's Tisch (Groom's Table) or, in some cases, the Kallah's Tisch (Bride's Table).

Here is Ezekiel describing many of the elements of the wedding celebration that are now practiced by traditional Jewish couples. "It was the custom that on the wedding day women and girls would gather at the bride's quarters at noon and stage a preliminary dance that lasted for several hours. At twilight the men folk would give a similar send-off to the bridegroom, who climaxed the event with a speech, then treated his guests to honey cake with jam and liquor. Afterwards he was led with music through the streets to the ceremonial veiling of the bride, and thence to the synagogue for the marriage ritual. After the wedding, the principals and guests repaired to the bridal quarters for supper and all-night festivities.

"If the wedding took place on a Friday, the couple was paraded home from the synagogue, and the guests left for the services. Only a small party returned to celebrate. Sabbath morning relatives and intimate friends came for the bridegroom and led him to the synagogue, where he was called upon to read from the Holy Scroll. In the evening there was the usual supper and hoopla."[164]

Ezekiel notes that his father was a strict Hasid and did not let him see the bride before the wedding. He then mentions the same custom we saw in Solomon Maimon's autobiography. "Under the wedding canopy my bride stepped on my foot. I thought it was accidental. Immediately after the ceremony, her relatives whisked her away towards the house so that she might be the first to enter it. This was done in accordance with the then current belief that the one of a newly-wedded couple who first stepped into their home would dominate the other for the rest of their conjugal life." Ezekiel reports that his friends led him home by a shortcut but the bride was already there.

They worked out a compromise, trying to enter together, and finally Ezekiel let his bride enter first.[165]

A MODERN ORTHODOX/TRADITIONAL WEDDING IN THE UNITED STATES

Before the guests arrive, the bride or the groom and each of his or her families are taking turns with the photographer in the room where the wedding will take place. Some couples are fasting on the day of their wedding and do not want to see each other prior to the ceremony at the huppah. This preference means that the photographer has to settle for separate bride-party and groom-party shots until after the wedding ceremony. Friends of the bride and groom serve as lookouts in the hallways and signal one then the other that the coast is clear so the bride or groom can emerge and be photographed with his or her family. This also means delaying the arrival of the bride and groom at the wedding celebration because the bride and groom are photographed together only after the ceremony.

Depending on whether the wedding is called for the afternoon or evening, guests arrive and are escorted either to a light breakfast of juice and pastries or a full-blown smorgasbord. In tandem with the overall reception that often precedes the ceremony, a small room is reserved for the Hasan's Tisch (Groom's Table). A long table is set up where the groom, his father and brothers, his future father-in-law and brothers-in-law, and other male relatives and friends gather. Some of the hot food is there as well as cakes and an array of drinks, especially liquor. Guests or relatives deliver words of Torah in honor of the couple, sing, and share drinks.

At some weddings, a nod to egalitarian trends, a Kallah's Tisch is provided at which the bride, her female family members, and friends also sing and hear words of Torah from various relatives and friends and personal comments about the bride and the couple.

At some point, the bride is escorted to a decorated large throne-like white wicker chair in an area at one end of the large reception room. There her friends greet her publicly, while they await the arrival of the groom and his party for the bedeken, or veiling ceremony.

Before the groom can arrive, some technical work needs to be done back at the Groom's Table. The first is the signing of the tena'im, which also involves the mothers doing something special; the other is the signing of the ketubbah, or wedding contract.

The document called the tena'im, or terms, is read and signed by both sides. Technically this document means that if the marriage were to be called off, stipulated penalties would have to be paid by the groom and his family. The mothers of the bride and groom now join the groom's party. To indicate symbolically that nothing should break the agreement just signed, the mothers break a dish. It is usually wrapped in plastic wrap and enclosed in a large cloth napkin. Both mothers take it and, while holding on to it, smash it against a chair or other hard surface. This is a symbolic act that in effect says, May this happen to us if anything goes wrong now. Alternatively, it is meant to scare away the demons hovering in the vicinity. It usually works.

The mothers leave and return to the place where the bride is seated. The men continue with a second rite, the signing of the ketubbah by two witnesses. Once it is signed, and the groom takes possession of it, the signal is given for the band to assemble the groom and his escort to leave the room of the Hasan's Tisch and proceed, while singing and dancing to blaring trumpets, into the reception hall to the seated bride. When the groom's party arrives, fathers bless the bride and the groom lowers the bride's veil, reminiscent of Rebekah and Isaac. Either the father of the bride or the rabbi pronounces the biblical verse of blessing that Laban and Rebekah's father said to her before she went off to marry Isaac.

Now and only now do the guests proceed into the room where the wedding ceremony will take place, and the wedding party assembles, groom's party first. As the guests go into the wedding hall, ushers often pass out a small folded program that has become a popular new feature of traditional weddings. It usually includes the names of the entire wedding procession. And it also contains an annotated outline of the various parts of the wedding, including those that have already taken place, and each of the parts of the ceremony and feast up to the conclusion of the seven blessings said after the meal and perhaps a reference to the ensuing week of festive wedding meals as well. Let's call the program *seder ha-hatunah* (Order of the Wedding).

The programs are important historical data and should be collected and archived somewhere for future study as should samples of the less personalized booklets containing Sabbath and wedding songs and blessings that guests will find on their tables during the wedding feast.

Sidrei ha-hatunah (plural form) are often written by the bride and groom together, and even the most traditional require some thought and decision making, if only with regard to who is listed in the processional. In more egalitarian services, especially those of traditional couples who are also egalitarian, a good deal of research and creativity come into play. The programs may involve not only explaining the standard parts of the day's events but also adding features that augment them without neutralizing the minimal Jewish legal requirements of a traditional wedding.

Ushers do not ask guests, as at many formal American Christian weddings, "Bride or groom?" which means, On which side of the aisle do you belong? Instead, most traditional weddings seat men and women on separate sides, regardless of the guest's relationship to either bride or groom.

Music announces that the procession is about to begin, usually violin, harp, trumpet. The procession of relatives starts with members of the groom's family, grandparents, siblings, and leads up to the groom, accompanied either by both of his parents or, in some super-traditional weddings, by his father and future father-in-law, who both sometimes hold long lighted candles. When the groom arrives, a special guest sings welcome, "barukh ha-ba," the same words that greeted the baby boy at his circumcision. Those who know are immediately aware of the passage of time. The same person then sings the beginning of a Hebrew poem and asks God, "the One who is all-powerful" (mi adir al ha-kol) to bless the bride and groom.[166]

The bride's family comes in next, culminating in the entrance of the veiled bride, who is accompanied either by her parents or by both mothers, who again may hold lighted tapers. While the groom awaits the bride he is helped into his kittel, a white garment that some traditional men wear on the holiest days of the year and in which some Jewish men are buried as a shroud. It is one of the mourning and atonement rituals that have become part of traditional Jewish weddings.

It is not clear how long Jewish brides have been wearing a white wedding gown, which is a Western nineteenth-century fashion statement made de rigueur by the wedding in 1840 of Queen Victoria and Prince Albert. It caught on first in England and the United States and spread around the world thanks to American fashion magazines.[167] Many posed wedding pictures that have survived from eastern Europe and America from the late nineteenth and early twentieth centuries are studio portraits of bride and groom and do not show the bride wearing a white wedding gown. Nor do most photographs record the marriage ceremony itself. Today, in contrast, photography is ever present before, during, and after the ceremony, but was much less common before World War II.

The bride is greeted with words of welcome, "berukhah ha-ba'ah," and, recently, another special poem is chanted for her, as she circles the groom seven times.[168] It has been customary that when the parents and bride or groom enter, the assembled rise to greet them and then sit down.

In Christian weddings today, it is customary for the wedding party to be seated in the front of the Church or other room where the wedding takes place. In traditional Jewish weddings, apart from grandparents and very small children, who sit in front, all of the wedding party assemble under or around the huppah.

When the bride arrives, she may circle the groom seven times, as her mother and mother-in-law hold on to her train and try to keep from tripping over it. This is frequently done today in Orthodox wedding ceremonies; sometimes she circles three times. In more egalitarian ceremonies, the bride and groom take turns going around each other. The meaning of the circling, rooted in the protective magic circle, has echoes in other life cycle events.

When the circling is over, in most Jewish American wedding ceremonies, the couple turn their back on the congregation and face the altar, if in a synagogue, and the officiant, back to the altar, faces the couple and looks out toward the congregation. This follows the common American Christian practice, in which the couple face the altar, and is often done even when the wedding does not take place in a synagogue.

In many Israeli wedding ceremonies, the couple face the congregation and the rabbi stands either facing the couple with his back to the congregation or, more thoughtfully, sideways, to the right of the couple, so that all can see them during the ceremony. In American traditional Jewish weddings, the couple block the view, and if there is no microphone, one hardly knows what is going on except from experience of what is supposed to be happening. In any case, the bride is supposed to stand at the right hand of the groom. In *Sefer ha-Roqeah,* from thirteenth-century Germany, the reason given is the verse "the queen stands at your right hand" (nizvaH sheigaL liyeminK) (Ps. 45:10), the last letters of which, read backwards, are K L H, or bride."[169]

The two parts of the ceremony each involves reciting blessings over a separate cup of wine. The person officiating pronounces the blessing over wine and then the blessing over eirusin/qiddushin and gives the cup first to the groom, who takes a sip, and then to the veiled bride, who gets some help with her veil and then takes a sip. Most times, white wine is used, since it is less likely to stain the gown if any spills.

In many ceremonies a friend of the couple serves as an emcee and announces each person who is being called up and honored to do a particular part of the rite. As the officiant asks for the two witnesses of the qiddushin, or betrothal, part of the ceremony, the emcee announces who they will be. They are needed to inspect the ring to make sure it is plain and not improper and to witness the ceremony. The officiant then asks the groom if the ring is his property and if it is worth "a penny." If he says, "Yes," the groom places the ring on the index finger of the bride's right hand, not the "ring finger" of her left hand, and he recites the formula: "Harei at . . ." Those in the know smile and whisper "mazel tov," since, technically speaking, they are married in the sense that if they stop now, the wife will need a religious divorce (get).

Before proceeding to the concluding part or nesu'in, someone is usually called upon to read the entire ketubbah or a portion of it. A tongue twister, the Aramaic document is usually read by a rabbi or religious teacher whom the couple wants to honor. Today, elaborately calligraphied hand-made or printed ketubbot are used and are often displayed after the ceremony for the guests to admire. During the ceremony, after it is read out loud, the groom takes it and gives it to the bride. It is hers. She then hands it to one of the wedding party under the huppah for safekeeping.

Again, the emcee announces each person who is honored with one of the seven wedding blessings, relatives and teachers, for example. Each comes up, recites one of the blessings over a second cup of wine filled especially for this part of the rite, and returns to his seat. After all seven have been called up, the groom and bride each take a sip.

At this point, it has become customary to modulate the tone into a moment of solemnity. Verses are sung from Psalm 137, beginning, "If I forget you, O Jerusalem, May my right hand forget its cunning" (v. 5). This remembrance of the destruction of Jerusalem is sung in anticipation of the groom's smashing the glass under foot that officially concludes the ceremony.

Note that no mention has been made thus far of any personal comments about the bride and groom and their families. Increasingly, this has disappeared from traditional wedding ceremonies and receptions and seems to be relegated to the preliminary events, such as the aufruf on the Sabbath before the wedding, and to other occasions following the wedding, such as the weeklong celebratory wedding feasts and blessings (sheva berakhot). At other weddings, of course, it is customary for the rabbi to make such comments usually right before the first part of the rite itself and for friends or family members to make "toasts" during the reception.

After the groom smashes the glass—in some egalitarian ceremonies, both bride and groom break a glass—the band and dancers appear and break out in lively dancing, which accompanies the bride and groom out of the room. They are escorted to a private room of seclusion (yihud) where, theoretically, they are alone for the first time. In some ultra-traditional communities, including some from the Muslim world, the marriage may actually be consummated at this time, and the couple arrives at the wedding party afterwards. Today, most traditional couples who practice yihud ask special friends to stand guard outside the door while the couple eats something, the first food they have had all day, and have a few moments alone to savor the significance of the moment before the bedlam of the dancing and celebrating begins. The photographer will also delay the couple a while longer and take pictures of the couple for the first time.

Meanwhile, the guests have been ushered into the banquet room, where there is some preliminary talking and eating, sometimes for quite some time, until the couple finally arrives. Then large circle dances begin, men and women separately, based on a canon of conventional melodies. Many of these songs have been composed and elaborately choreographed, during the past thirty years or so. Videos provide lessons to women on how to do the steps, for it is usually the women who do the real dancing at Jewish weddings. The men tend to shuffle behind one another in tightly packed circles, regardless of the music being played. The first dance "set" can last up to forty-five minutes. In some of the dancing sets, party costumes may appear, sparkles and streamers are thrown on the couple; someone imitates a bull and another plays matador. There is a whole repertoire of games and special dances that guests take part in, all to amuse the bride and groom, which is part of the protocol of a traditional Jewish wedding.

Dancing alternates with courses of the dinner. Before it concludes, one interruption has become customary among modern Orthodox weddings and is a sign of Jewish feminism, Orthodox style. The groom leads his friends in singing Proverbs 31, sometimes on one knee before his bride.

Once the meal is over, the Grace after Meals for a wedding and the special seven blessings begin. Guests who are still in the hall— many have given the bride or groom a gift and have left early—bring chairs over to where the bride and groom are seated. Several guests are told in advance they will be honored with one of the seven blessings recited after the wedding feast and may be given a special card with their blessing written out on it.

Although all of the blessings are the same seven that are recited under the huppah, the order is different. Under the huppah the first blessing is recited over the cup of wine used during the nesu'in, or marriage ceremony. At the Grace after Meals, the blessing over wine is first skipped and recited last as the seventh blessing. Another difference is that under the huppah a single cup of wine is used when the seven blessings are recited.

After the meal, the person who recites the Grace does so over one full cup of wine. Then he fills up a second cup of wine. It is this one that is circulated among those who recite six of the seven blessings. At the end, that second cup is returned to the person who recited the Grace, and he recites the seventh blessing over the first cup, the one that had been poured when he began to lead the Grace. Then he transfers some of the wine from each of the two full glasses to a third glass, mixing them together, and then pours some back into each of the two original glasses. The bride drinks from one and the groom from the other.

This completes the formalities of a traditional Jewish wedding. Guests continue dancing and singing, more gifts are given to the couple, and gradually everyone goes home and returns to the routine of their everyday lives.

The bride and groom may go to a hotel for the night, but they do not go on a honeymoon, at least, not for a week. That is because the Jewish wedding feast continues for an entire seven days of subsequent festive dinners. Friends of the family take a turn inviting the couple, their parents and siblings, and different groups of additional friends to a series of daily dinners to continue the celebrations. At each of them, the seven wedding blessings are recited after the Grace, and this has given the name to the set of dinners as the sheva berakhot. They can be held at homes or restaurants. Often people who were not invited to the wedding are invited to one of the sheva berakhot feasts, so as to include more people in the overall celebrations. The basic rule is that at least one new guest must be invited to each of the seven meals.

Other modern Orthodox weddings in Israel will have processions, with candles, the participation of relatives and friends under the huppah, and many of the trappings that one finds in the American traditional wedding. There, too, no personal remarks are said about the bride and groom, either during the ceremony or even at the reception. If the parents are "religious" and the couple "secular," the combination results in a brief ceremony and lots of rock music and partying at the reception.

At more egalitarian traditional weddings in America, the couple tries to create a delicate balance between older elements, which are loaded toward the acts of the groom, while enabling the bride to play a positive and active role. Apart from learned comments made at the bride's table before the ceremony, it is possible to introduce a double ring ceremony, so long as what the bride says does not affect the validity of what the groom says by implying that they are of equal weight. Clearly, the intention is to give both equal weight, but if one is not careful, the ceremony can be compromised. These are some of the opportunities that modern wedding ceremonies present to couples today. In principle, the innovative spirit that informs them is no different from that which enabled the wedding ceremony to grow and develop over millennia, often in creative response to the host culture in which Jews lived.[170]

A MORE INFORMAL ISRAELI
"SECULAR" WEDDING

Not every wedding involves such an ornate set of rites and customs. For example, in some communities in Israel today, there may not be a procession at all. In fact, the groom dressed in a suit and the bride, in her white wedding gown, go out in a specially decorated wedding car, festooned with crepe-paper bunting, to one of several locations where they are photographed before the wedding. They then proceed to have dinner in a favorite restaurant with friends before arriving at the hall, which may be located in a remote and relatively dark and isolated part of an industrial park. The guests arrived long before and have been eating, smoking, and drinking for over an hour. A portable wedding canopy has been erected in the same room, but it goes unnoticed as the disc jockey encourages the guests to dance to his electronic fare.

When the bride and groom arrive, the disc jockey takes the microphone and introduces the Orthodox rabbi who, he announces, will now preside over "tekes ha-huppah" (the wedding ceremony). The bride and groom enter to some applause, and if there is not enough to suit the disc jockey, he may introduce them again and again until the applause overtakes the talking at the many tables at which the guests sit, talk, eat, drink, and smoke throughout the ceremony.

The only ones who are standing under or around the canopy are the couple themselves, their parents, and a few close friends. The rabbi conducts the required rites of the betrothal ceremony over a cup of wine, asks for the ring, and verifies that it is the groom's property and that the groom recites the correct line in Hebrew, "harei at mequdeshet li be-tabba'at zo ke-dat moshe ve-yisrael." He has brought with him his own proper witnesses to certify that the betrothal has been conducted correctly.

Five minutes into the ceremony, the rabbi reads part of the ketubbah and immediately moves on to the seven blessings, all of which he recites himself. The conclusion is a brief reference to the destruction of the Temple, and keeping in mind that even at one's time of greatest joy one remembers the tragedy of Jerusalem in the past, and the groom smashes a wine glass wrapped in a cloth napkin underfoot. Mazel tov! Mazel tov! The disc jockey is back—perhaps ten minutes have elapsed.

Immediately, the plastic Tinkertoy-like wedding canopy is dismantled, if the photographers have not managed to knock it down in order to get a better shot of the ceremony while it is taking place. The music and dancing resume. This more or less ritually correct wedding is typical of many secular Israeli rites. The occasion is regarded mainly as a social one that must, by Israeli law, have a minimal religious ceremonial component presided over by an Orthodox rabbi.[171]

WEDDING "BENTCHERS"

At traditional Jewish weddings today, a pile of small printed booklets are placed on each guest table towards the end of the meal. They include not only the Grace after Meals (birkat ha-mazon) and the seven blessings recited after the wedding meal (sheva berakhot), but also Sabbath Eve and Sabbath Day songs that Jews sing around the table each week. The booklets also have the couple's names printed on the cover with the date of the wedding. These booklets are meant to be collectables, and they are religiously collected, taken home by the attendees, where they accumulate and are used at various occasions during the year at the Sabbath and festival table and are also continuous reminders of different weddings one has attended.

The popularity of these booklets has led to some standard ones but also to remarkable textual and artistic improvisation. Among the favored kinds is a miniaturized copy of the bride's ketubbah or some original artwork on the cover of the booklet.

A good example of how Jews take from the Christian environment and appropriate it into Judaism is the standard term used to describe this booklet that contains blessings for bride and groom as well as the standard Grace after Meals. It is called a "bentcher." The Yiddish verb for making this blessing is "to bentch." In Hebrew it is known as "birkat ha-mazon," literally the blessing over leavened bread. What is remarkable is that the term to bentch and the noun bentcher are derived from the Latin *benedictio,* which in Germany is pronounced beneditzio and became the Yiddish verb "bentchen," from which the nominative "bentcher" emerged as the name of the booklet with which one "bentches." This is yet another example of Jewish inward acculturation, as Jews take common words and gestures they see all around them and inventively Judaize them.

SIDREI HA-HATUNAH (WEDDING PROGRAMS)

The use of programs at the wedding is a recent development, perhaps a twentieth-century American Jewish invention designed to outline the contours of a traditional wedding for guests who are not familiar with one. On some scripts the order of family march is also listed in addition to explanations of the day's events; in other weddings, only the list of the family procession is printed, it being assumed that the guests know what is going to happen.

More recently, couples who have designed ritual forms that are grounded in some kind of gender equality, including among Orthodox and other traditional Jewish men and women, explain these variations in their handouts. For example, a double ring ceremony can be structured symmetrically, giving the same words and gestures to the man and woman, but this would not be suitable for a traditional wedding, in which it is the groom who "takes the bride." In weddings that want to respect that difference while at the same time giving the woman an active role, she might recite a variation of the man's betrothal formula that is stated in the passive voice and clearly not made as a condition for the effectiveness of the groom's act. Or, the bride might recite a verse from Song of Songs, "I am my beloved's and he is mine" (6:3), that has meaning to both but does not interfere with the groom's function in betrothing the woman to himself, as required.

Sidrei ha-hatunah can be based on standard explanations about what the elements in a Jewish wedding are, such as the terms for the stages of betrothal (eirusin/qiddushin) and marriage (nesu'in); the preliminary ceremonies at either the Groom's Table, where various documents are signed, or the Bride's Table, where singing and Torah lessons may take place; the appearance of the bride on her special throne (besetzen); the entrance of the groom and his escorts (*shushbinin*), who approach her and veil her (bedecken); the ceremony itself, including the groom's special white attire (kittel); the bride's circling the groom up to seven times; the ring ceremony and words of betrothal, including a double ring ceremony; if a specially designed formulation be either within or not within the asymmetry of Jewish law's view of betrothal; the ketubbah's meaning; the seven blessings of the marriage ceremony; and the mournful singing of Psalm 137:5, "If I forget you, O Jerusalem," and the groom's breaking the glass underfoot, at the end, followed by a comment about a time of privacy (yihud).

The refrain at the end of the circumcision ceremony adds to the hope that the baby will "enter the Torah" and "enter the wedding chamber," the wish that he "enter a life of good deeds." Throughout life, despite many milestones that lie ahead, there is no prescribed major life cycle rite for a couple that lives a long married life together. Judaism seems to presuppose that a married life of good deeds, with children and grandchildren, is itself the goal of growing up and maturing. The only additional major life cycle transition involves the end of life and the customs of preparation of the dead and mourning for the survivors.

4

Aging,
Dying,
Remembering

The recognition of death is universal, but each culture interprets and medi-
ates it in unique ways accompanied by many types of rituals. It is a
personal event, and it is also a profoundly social and cultural moment
that expresses the fundamental values and beliefs of a community. The
rituals of death involve what is done to prepare the body and what
the living mourners do from the moment of death. In this chapter,
I trace both more or less sequentially.

If we think of the major life cycle rites alone, the lifetime of a
Jewish person seems to go from marriage to death without any inter-
mediate lifestyle events. As we have seen, Jewish custom books tend
to shift the perspective immediately from the young adults who marry
to their new baby and his or her transitions to young adulthood and
marriage. Missing are any further transitions of the young adults themselves into work or parenthood. Having children is assumed to be
part of life as a married couple.

Rites of passage, of course, focus on times of transition. Judaism
seems to take for granted, as in the refrain at the brit ceremony, that
after marriage one "enters [a life of] good deeds," of which the first
is the biblical commandment of being fertile and then going on to

follow the other commandments of the Torah as a mature adult. Only death intervenes and prevents that from continuing. Despite the ages-of-man text mentioned in (pseudo) Mishnah Avot, no celebrations are marked out for decade birthdays, with the exception already noted of reaching age sixty, as in the Talmudic precedent.

Short of a rite, one sometimes does see behavior that marks stages of maturity. For example, some Jewish men may grow a beard at a certain age, such as forty, or grow one as mourners on the death of one of their parents, during the thirty days of semi-intense mourning (*sheloshim*), and decide to keep it afterwards as a show of maturity and family seniority.

Until very recently there was no special rite for biological changes for women in the life cycle, either at puberty or menarch, for girls, or menopause, for women, though new rites are being experimented with today. These include mourning for a lost pregnancy by miscarriage or stillbirth and prayers upon menstruation.[1] Similarly, the emergence of a gay population that wants to be explicitly involved in Jewish culture and life has generated rites of coming out as well.

PREMATURE DEATH

To be sure, death need not be associated with old age. Although most of the rites of mourning are associated with the aged who die of illness, there are ample examples throughout Jewish history of different kinds of premature death. Who can forget the vivid and poignant words of King David, who cries out: "'My son Absalom! O my son, my son Absalom! If only I had died instead of you! O Absalom, my son, my son!'" (2 Sam. 19:1).

Death struck at any age, especially at childbirth, when both mother and child were vulnerable. In the Bible, Rachel died while giving birth to Benjamin and "was buried on the road to Ephrath—now Bethlehem" (Gen. 35:19). Rabbis in ancient Palestine and Babylonia differed about the minimum age a baby should be for formal mourning rites to take place. Ashkenazic Jews followed the ancient Palestinian custom of not having a full mourning rite if the child died at less than thirty days old.[2]

From the memoirs of a Jew named Joseph who was a dealer in secondhand clothes and lived in early seventeenth-century Sienna, we learn that in one year the following died: "Messer Amadeo Betarbo, a young man of thirty-five years of age; Messer Aaron Emilio, a youth of eighteen, . . . the mother of Salvador died eight days after giving birth to a male child; a male child of my own died, aged eight months; the wife of Reuben Frosolone miscarried of a male child; and the wife of Clement Pesaro likewise miscarried of a male child."[3]

Another kind of early death that is recorded, of course, is a violent one, either from some incident that occurs in the street or home, as today, or from an anti-Jewish riot or persecution. Among the latter, is Rabbi Eleazar ben Judah of Worms's elegy written for his wife, Dulce, in the form of a paraphrase of Proverbs 31, the Woman of Valor.[4] He also wrote a tribute to his two daughters, ages thirteen and six, who were murdered with their mother in front of Rabbi Eleazar's eyes.[5] About the older girl, Belette, Rabbi Eleazar wrote that "she prepared my bed and pulled off my shoes each evening . . . and spoke only the truth." The younger daughter, Hannah, Rabbi Eleazar tells us, "recited the first part of the Shema prayer every day . . . spun and sewed and embroidered."[6]

In medieval Spain, a Jewish father lamented the early death of his son, Asher ben Turiel of Toledo, who died in the Black Death that brought death to hundreds of thousands of people in the middle of the fourteenth century.[7]

This stone is a memorial / That a later generation may know / That 'neath it lies hidden a pleasant bud / a cherished child. . . . Though only fifteen years in age. . . . But a few days before his death / He established his home; / But yesternight the joyous voice of the bride and groom / Was turned to the voice of wailing.

Another kind of violence prompted gambling-addicted Venetian Rabbi Leon Modena to write in his autobiography about the premature violent death of his twenty-year-old son.[8]

AGING

The Hebrew Bible hints that age is a blessing: "Abraham was now old, advanced in years, and the Lord had blessed Abraham in all things" (Gen. 24:1). And yet, age also brings infirmity: "When Isaac was old and his eyes were too dim to see" (Gen. 27:1); and "King David was now old, advanced in years; and although they covered him with bedclothes, he never felt warm" (1 Kings 1:1). The poignant line in the penitential sections of the Day of Atonement liturgy appeals to God "not to abandon us during our old age" (al tashlihenu be-'et ziqnah).[9]

But how old is old? The French commentator Rabbi David Kimhi of Narbonne (Radaq—1160?–1135?) was surprised that David was so weak when he was only seventy, as he himself was to embark on a major journey by horse and cart across southern France and Spain at the age of seventy-two.[10]

Occasionally, we hear of Jews who lived to an advanced age. For example, Rabbi Sherira Gaon, head of one of the rabbinical academies in late tenth-century Baghdad, is reported to have "lived a very long life, in fact for about one hundred years. . . . [and] stepped down in favor of his son. The latter was Rabbi Hai Gaon bar Rabbi Sherira Gaon. . . . After living for ninety-nine years, he passed away."[11] Rabbi Elijah Capsali mentions the elaborate ceremony that accompanied the death of his teacher, Rabbi Judah Mintz, who died in 1509, as the head of the Yeshiva in Padua, near Venice, about whom he says, in passing, "he was ninety-eight years old." And other examples can be cited.[12]

Some comments in Jewish sources refer to obvious physical decline with great years; others, to an increase of wisdom. Of the former, "Emperor [Hadrian] asked Rabbi Joshua ben Hanania why he had not attended a certain event. He replied: 'The mountain is snowy, it is surrounded by ice, the dog does not bark and the grinders do not grind'" [i. e., his hair and beard are white, his voice is feeble, and his teeth do not work].

An example that also seems to illustrate the same point is converted into an example of the advantages of old age. The Talmud continues with an account of King David, who invited his old ally and friend Barzillay the Gileadite to Jerusalem. He refused to come: "'I am now eighty years old. Can I tell the difference between good and bad? Can your servant taste what he eats and drinks? Can I still listen to the singing of men and women? Why then should your servant continue to be a burden to my lord the king?'" (2 Sam. 19:36). Although the text speaks of the infirmity of old age, the Talmud understood it differently. "Rav said: Barzillay the Gileadite was a liar. For there was a servant in Rab's house, ninety-two years old, and he could taste the dishes." Moreover, continues Rava, "Barzillay the Gileadite was promiscuous, and whoever is promiscuous gets old prematurely." The discussion concludes with the pious observation that as scholars age, they become wiser; only the ignorant get more foolish.[13]

VISITING THE SICK

Regardless of age, the onset of serious illness is a sign that death may be near, and Jewish sources place a premium on visiting the ill. For example, when Jacob becomes ill, Joseph and his sons go to visit him and Jacob blesses them (Gen. 48:1). During the divided Israelite monarchy, King Joram, son of King Ahab of the northern Kingdom of Israel, "lay ill" and King Ahazia of the southern Kingdom of Judah went to visit him (2 Kings 9:16), and when the prophet Elisha became ill, King Joash of Israel "went down to see him" (2 Kings 13:14).

It was the ancient rabbis, however, who made visiting the sick (*biqqur holim*) into a major religious obligation. The rabbis saw God as setting an example when he came to Abraham recovering from his circumcision (Gen. 18:1). Rabbi Akiva, the second-century Palestinian sage, is credited with the statement: "Whoever does not visit the sick it is as though he shed his blood," because it may hasten death. And to the third-century Palestinian sage Rabbi Yohanan is attributed the teaching that visiting the sick was one of the greatest acts of love that the Mishnah taught (M. Pe'ah 1:1); doing it resulted in unlimited reward in the next world. Among the brief Talmudic prayers to be recited when visiting the sick on the Sabbath is: "May the Almighty have compassion upon you in the midst of the sick of Israel."[14]

Relatives were to visit right away, during the first three days; others, afterwards, a distinction that would also apply to the three and seven days after a funeral for visitors of mourners.[15] Special voluntary groups or associations came into being that were dedicated to visiting the sick in the community, tending to their needs (*hevrat biqqur holim*). The first references to one are from fourteenth-century Spain, when similar Christian associations came into prominence. From there the practice spread to Renaissance Italy and northward into Prague and eastern Europe. Some Jewish congregations or communities still form voluntary biqqur holim societies.[16]

In addition, prayers are offered for the recovery of the sick in traditional synagogues. The individual's name and that of his or her mother, not father, are mentioned in a special version of a prayer beginning with the words, "He who blessed our ancestors" (mi she-beirakh). The emphasis on the name of the ill person's mother is an ancient custom, found in the Talmud, common to the old Roman notion of the certainty of maternity. Today clergy regularly visit the sick of various faiths in hospitals.[17]

CONFESSIONS

Confession of sins is an important practice in the Hebrew Bible for individuals and leaders of the people, and yet deathbed confession is not found there. Nor is any text of a confession stipulated for any occasion until the time of the Mishnah. In the Bible, dying figures call their families together to make a final blessing (Jacob), or leaders make a final oration (Moses), but they do not make a personal confession of their sins.[18]

The rabbis in the Talmud propose that individuals make a confession of sins when seriously ill, a custom that is related to last rites in the Church: "Our rabbis taught: If one falls sick and his life is in danger, he is told, 'Make confession.' For all who are sentenced to death make confession."[19] This text was expanded to include: "Many confessed their sins and did not die, and many who did not confess died; and as a reward should you confess, you will live, and he who confesses his sins has a portion in the world to come," as the Mishnah says about those who are about to be executed and make confession: "All who confess have a place in the world to come."[20]

In descriptions of early modern Italian-Jewish death rites, the institution of deathbed confession betrays Christian surroundings. For example, Leon Modena's description, written in Italian mainly for Christian readers, notes that the dying man makes confession in the presence of a rabbi, even though the rabbi is not needed. In Christian last rites, however, a priest is needed to minister extreme unction, a sacrament of the church.[21]

The confession, or *vidui,* is designed to cleanse the dying person of his sins. Those who are listening do not have any special religious power to "absolve" or in any other way assist the person's afterlife. In many ways, the death scene of Jacob in Genesis, like the wedding arrangements of Rebekah, are the model text for Jewish customs about dying and burial. The Italian Kabbalist Rabbi Aaron Berechia ben Moses of Modena wrote a special book about confession called *Ma'avar Yabboq,* named after the biblical phrase connected with Jacob's taking his family "across the ford of the Yabbok" (Gen. 32:23).[22]

JUST BEFORE DEATH

After the confession and possible blessing of children and other family members, it became traditional for the dying person to recite the verse, "Hear O Israel, The Lord our God, the Lord is one" (Deut. 6:4), the first verse of the Shema. Exactly when this became an accepted practice is not clear. In the Talmud, a narrative describes how Jacob's children recite the Shema at his deathbed scene, to reassure their father of their loyalty to the God of Israel and Jacob, and Jacob replies, "Blessed is the name of the glory of his kingdom, for ever and ever," the line recited right after Deut. 6:4 in the liturgy.[23] This is not the same thing as the dying person reciting it him- or herself with a dying breath.

A different model may lie behind the practice, whenever it appeared. A midrash pictures Rabbi Akiva, the great second-century Palestinian sage, being tortured by the Romans. When the proper time arrives to recite the evening Shema as a liturgical text, he recites it, despite the agony of being tortured. From this model of piety, the rabbis interpreted the next verse, "and you shall love the lord your God with all your heart and with all your soul [literally, life] and with all your might" (Deut. 6:5), to mean, "'with all your soul'— even if you have to give up your life," that is, be martyred, like Rabbi Akiva.[24]

There is no indication from the midrashic texts about Rabbi Akiva that a general practice yet existed for a Jewish martyr, let alone an ordinary Jew on his or her deathbed, to recite the Shema when martyrdom or death took place when the Shema was not being intentionally recited as liturgy, as in Rabbi Akiva's case. That innovation seems to have been acted out by the martyrs of the Rhineland who made the ritual leap to apply Rabbi Akiva's behavior even to the more frequent times of martyrdom when the daily Shema was not being recited liturgically. When in the spring of 1096, the Jews of the Rhineland underwent a series of massacres in the wake of the call to the first crusade, Jews are pictured as reciting the verse at the point of death or when they witness others who are martyring themselves.[25]

From that new practice in the late eleventh century, the custom apparently spread to apply the rite that the martyrs of 1096 innovated to every Jew, martyr or not, at the moment of dying even a natural death, regardless of the time of day. The pattern of transferring behaviors that originate with martyrs to the everyday world of ordinary Jewish practice, especially in northern Europe, is noticeable, for obvious reasons, in relation to rites associated with the dead.

The Jews of Germany and later on in eastern Europe and in communities derived from their descendants identified with the martyrs of 1096 and built an entire ideology about themselves as a pious community, proud of the acts of those martyrs, and ready to emulate them should circumstances arise. Religious behavior was measured against the yardstick of the more difficult act of martyrdom, for example, in *Sefer Hasidim* (Book of the Pietists), a collection of practices and opinions that expressed the views of German-Jewish Pietists in the twelfth and thirteenth centuries.[26]

The Jews of Ashkenaz remembered the acts of those martyrs on the anniversary of the deaths of each community's martyrs. In another way, however, the Ninth of Av, the anniversary of the destruction of the two Temples in Jerusalem, became a kind of Jewish All Saints' Day that the Church celebrated on November 1. Dirges (*qinot*) written to memorialize, for example, the martyrdoms of 1096 and the burning of the Talmud in Paris in 1242 were added to the canon of those that referred explicitly to the events of the Temple. Reciting the Shema upon dying is but one of many ways that the dead of 1096 affected the broader culture of medieval European Jewish memory expressed in liturgical rites and gestures.

AT THE MOMENT OF DEATH

In the *Shulhan 'Arukh,* Rabbi Joseph Karo stipulates what one may not do when a person is gravely ill but not yet dead. From this list, we can infer what was to be done when the person actually died. Some of these practices were rarely followed, such as placing on the body a bowl or a comb or a jar of water or a pinch of salt. Among those that were put into varying degrees of practice were closing the dead person's eyes, hiring professional wailers and mourners, putting the body on the cool ground on sand or pottery fragments or earth, and empty-ing vessels containing water.[27] Another sign that a death had occurred was the sound of emptying vessels containing water out the windows of the house where it had occurred. Then the windows are closed. When the body is put on the ground, a lighted candle is placed at the head. It was customary, as well, for Christians to place the body of a former monk or priest on a cross of ashes or sand on the floor with a candle lighted, but at the feet.[28]

In hospitals, this is not always possible; but if the person dies at home, these customs can be carried out by family members with the assistance of members of the hevra qadisha (burial society) or the rabbi. Many of them are mentioned in rabbinic sources, but some or all are rarely practiced except by Orthodox or other traditional Jews today. Some are practices that were ancient Christian customs and may have been adopted by Jews or vice versa.

In addition, while black is a color of mourning mentioned in the Talmud,[29] it apparently went in and out of favor among Jews. By the sixteenth century, at least in Italy, the use of black covering over the coffin seems strange, though a hundred years later, it was taken for granted. This, Leon Modena, in Venice, writes, "All mourners apparel themselves in black; but they do this, following the use of the Countries where they inhabit, and not from any Precept."[30]

Rites of mourning upon hearing of a death are dramatically recorded several times in the Hebrew Bible, and some have left their mark on practice down to the present. The abundance of acts that are described is striking, sometimes suggesting stylized forms of spon-taneity that border on frenzy.

Hearing about the death of a family member is frequently described. For example, when Sarah dies, Abraham "proceeded to mourn for Sarah and to bewail her" (Gen. 23:2), after which he buys a cave in which to bury her. In contrast to this matter-of-fact account, when Jacob mistakenly thinks that Joseph, his favorite son, has been killed, he tears his garment, puts on sackcloth, and mourns many days (Gen. 37:34). His sons and daughters tried to comfort him, but he was inconsolable.

The Bible does go out of its way to discourage customs it claims were practiced by the Canaanite nations. Among these were the prohibition on the part of Israelite priests not to "shave smooth any part of their heads, or cut the sidegrowth of their beards, or make gashes in their flesh" (Lev. 21:5). In the Book of Deuteronomy, this is extended to the whole people of Israel, who are called holy: "You shall not gash yourselves or shave the front of your heads because of the dead. For you are the people consecrated to the Lord your God" (Deut. 14:1–2).

And yet, the prophet Jeremiah reports that in the last days of the Kingdom of Judah, mourning practices included: "beards shaved, their garments torn, and their bodies gashed" (Jer. 41:5).[31] Providing food for the dead, a widespread custom in pagan cultures, is referred to in Deut. 26:12–14: "'I have not deposited any of it [tithed food] with the dead,'" as well as in the Book of Tobit, from around 200 B.C.E.: "Place your bread on the grave of the righteous but give none to sinners" (Tob. 4:17).

The tearing of clothes is the basis of what the rabbis called *qeriyah,* tearing one's garment, and it is already anticipated here: "Jacob rent his clothes, put sackcloth on his loins, and observed mourning for his son many days" (Gen. 37:34). Other reactions are illustrated when Jacob died: Joseph "flung himself upon his father's face and wept over him and kissed him" (Gen. 50:1), a custom that did not continue. The period of intense mourning of seven days appears now as well: "[Joseph] observed a mourning period of seven days for his father" (Gen. 50:10).[32]

Tearing clothes is also found elsewhere in combination with other gestures. David hears about the death of King Saul and his beloved friend Jonathan when a messenger arrives from the battle "with his clothes rent and earth on his head" (2 Sam. 1:11), and after David confirms the deaths, "he took hold of his clothes and rent them . . . they lamented and wept, and they fasted until evening" (1 Sam.

1:11–12). When he learns that his general Joab has avenged his brother's death by killing Saul's old supporter Abner ben Ner, now a supporter of the new king, David "ordered Joab and all the troops with him to rend their clothes, gird on sackcloth, and make lament before Abner; and King David himself walked behind the bier. And so they buried Abner at Hebron; the king wept aloud by Abner's grave, and all the troops wept. And the king intoned this dirge over Abner" (2 Sam. 3:31–33).

And when Job learns that his family have all suddenly been killed, he "arose, tore his robe, cut off his hair, and threw himself on the ground and worshiped" (Job 1:20). Mourners removed their shoes (2 Sam. 15:30; Ezek. 24:17, 23) or covered their faces (2 Sam. 19:5) and removed their headgear (Ezek. 24:17, 23).

The custom of covering the upper lip (Ezek. 24:22) persisted among Jews living in Muslim lands but not in Christian Europe. In contrast, not wearing leather shoes (2 Sam. 15:30) and not using cosmetic oils (2 Sam. 14:2) were both reinforced in rabbinic law.[33] Baring one's arm and shoulder was prescribed but became obsolete in the Middle Ages, along with some other public practices that rabbis thought would ridicule Judaism.[34] That motive demonstrates how the environment was both a source of practices that Judaism adopted and a reason for discontinuing others even though they had an ancient pedigree.

In the Hebrew Bible, mourning rites are invoked not only when a relative or close friend dies, but also at times of religious and social crises. For example, David acts as a mourner when the rebellion of Absalom became known: "David meanwhile went up the slope of the [Mount of] Olives, weeping as he went; his head was covered and he walked barefoot. And all the people who were with him covered their heads and wept as they went up" (2 Sam. 15:30). There he met the loyal Hushi the Archite "with his robe torn and with earth on his head" (2 Sam. 15:32). Later, when David hears of the death of his beloved son Absalom, the narrative says only that he wept, perhaps because he had already mourned when the rebellion broke out that led to the inevitable death of his traitorous son (2 Sam. 19:2). Note, too, that although wearing ashes fell into disuse in actual funerals, medieval European Jewish men put ashes on their heads on the day of their wedding, in order to fool the spirits and remind themselves of the seriousness of the occasion.[35]

In the Bible, an elaborate part of the rite of the funeral involved lamenting the dead. These sounds are described in several contexts and involve different degrees of spontaneity or standardized behavior. The northern Israelite prophet Amos refers to the rite of lament: "In every square there shall be lamenting, in every street cries of 'Ah, woe!' (Hebrew: ho ho). And the farm hand shall be called to mourn, and those skilled in wailing to lament" (Amos 5:16). A body that is found on the road is brought home "for lamentation (lispod) and burial" (1 Kings 13:29), which included: "Alas, my brother" (hoy, ahi) (1 Kings 13:30). The king would be lamented, not "alas, my brother" or "alas, my sister" (hoy ahot), but with the special refrain: "Alas, Lord" (hoy adon) or "Alas, majesty" (hoy hohoh) (Jer. 22:18; see 34:5). When Judah Maccabee was mourned, the dirge echoed the motifs of David for Saul and Jonathan: "How is the mighty fallen, the savior of Israel!" (1 Mac. 9:21; cf. 2 Sam. 1:25).

As noted, a father, like David, calls out the son's name, as when Absalom died (2 Sam. 19:1, 5).[36] Families and clans lamented in male and female groupings (Zech. 12:11–14). More elaborate than these cries of anguish was the composition of a dirge (*qinah*), a form that is best exemplified in the Hebrew Bible with the Book of Lamentations. To David is attributed such a dirge for the deaths of Saul and Jonathan (2 Sam. 1:19–27) and for Abner (2 Sam. 3:33–34), but professionals, especially women, composed and sang these hymns. The prophet Jeremiah mentions "summon the dirge-singers (ha-meqonenot). . . . Send for the skilled women (ha-hakhamot), let them come. Let them quickly start a wailing for us, that our eyes may run with tears" (Jer. 9:16–17).[37] These women were professionals and taught their daughters how to do it.[38] The practice was customary for Jews in Muslim countries into modern times.[39]

ONEIN (MOURNER UNTIL THE BURIAL OF RELATIVE)

Although biblical and some rabbinic sources provide many examples of how an individual reacts when he or she hears of the death of a close relative, the rabbis reduced the rites to just a few practical responsibilities. Upon the death of a close relative—parents, spouse, siblings, and children—but before burial, the individual becomes an onein and recites, "Barukh dayan ha-emet" (Blessed is the judge of truth).[40] At that point the mourner tears a garment as a sign of mourning or waits until just before the funeral, when a ritual tearing (qeriyah) is now customarily done. Some prefer to tear a garment; others, to tear a black ribbon that is attached to one's clothing. In either case, it is customary to wear the torn item the entire seven days of shiva. Some wear it for thirty days, but this is unusual.

A mourner who is an onein is responsible for arranging the preparation of the body—washing and cleaning it, having shrouds made, digging the grave.[41] Although traditional mourners delegate various parts of the preparations to the hevra qadisha and funeral home, with the assistance of one's rabbi, it is the mourner who is primarily responsible to see that arrangements are made. In view of this obligation, he (or she) is exempt from positive commandments until the burial.[42]

The Bible marks the paths of the dead and the living that mourn the dead as not being as absolutely different as we might suppose. In biblical religion there was no idea of a soul and a body. Life was called *nefesh* in Hebrew. The distinction is between a living nefesh and a dead nefesh. So long as the body or the bones exist, the being can sense things and is understood as a shade living in a never-never land of Sheol.[43] That is why the worst punishment that could be inflicted on a person was to leave the body unburied and a prey to animals, as in the party of the rebellious Jereboam who are to be "devoured by dogs" and "eaten by the birds of the air" (1 Kings 14:11).[44]

In Egypt, where embalming was practiced in ancient times, Joseph embalmed his father, Jacob (Gen. 50:2), and Joseph himself was also and was placed in a coffin, another Egyptian convention (Gen. 50:26). The forty days of embalming were followed by seventy days of wailing (Gen. 50:3). Embalming did not become part of traditional Judaism, and burial in a coffin was dropped for many years. Instead, Israelites and ancient Jews placed their dead on a bier (2 Sam 3:31 and Luke 7:14), a practice we see even today in the Arab world, in news reports of people carrying the partially wrapped body of the dead in public. Already in late antiquity, the preparation of the body was delegated to a hevra qadisha, but the community still is obligated to honor the dead, and a funeral takes precedence over Torah study.[45] Preparing the body has become a highly developed rite consisting of cleaning and dressing the body in a reverential manner.[46]

Modern synagogues or private associations constitute a local hevra qadisha and train members in the detailed work of preparing the purification of the body (taharah) for burial. In Israel, one of their responsibilities is to publicize the death of a local resident by pasting signs of the death on walls near the residence of the deceased. They alert the neighborhood that the person has died and indicate where and when the funeral will take place, sometimes the same day the death occurred. In the United States, for example, the family usually places a notice in the local newspaper with the time of the funeral. Some synagogues have computerized phone announcements to call the entire congregation. Others have phone squads to do this personally.

Coffins come back into Jewish practice in medieval northern Europe but were not common in medieval Spain, possibly due to earlier Muslim custom. While their use today is common in the United States, for example, they are generally not used in Israel, where bodies are buried only in shrouds unless trauma or some other reason makes this inappropriate.

FUNERAL AND BURIAL

The Hebrew Bible suggests that the dead were buried in their clothing.[47] By the first century, in the New Testament account of Jesus' burial, we find references to a Joseph of Arimethea who "took the body and wrapped it in a clean linen cloth and laid it in his own new tomb which he had hewn in the rock. He then rolled a great stone to the door of the tomb and went away" (Matt. 27:59–60). The parallel in John adds, "they took the body of Jesus and wrapped it with spices in linen cloths, according to the burial custom of the Jews" (John 19:40).[48]

In biblical times, Israel's neighbors did different things with the body, only some of which were taken up by Israelites. We do not know how quickly a body was buried in ancient Israel.[49] It must have been soon after death, a custom that has remained a central practice in traditional Judaism. Burial could be in a family burial cave in one wall of which ledges were dug out of soft rock. Presumably this is what Abraham did when he bought the cave of Machpelah from Ephron the Hittite of Hebron (Gen. 23).

What about those who were less well off? The poor or outcast were buried in the ground or even in common graves, in potter's fields located in Jerusalem in the Kidron Valley called "the burial ground of the common people" (2 Kings 23:6; Jer. 26:23). The practice of digging ledges in the walls of burial chambers apparently came into Judaism in Hellenistic times and was borrowed from the Idumeans of southern Palestine who were absorbed into the Hasmonean Jewish kingdom in the late second century B.C.E.[50]

Thus in late antiquity, burial took place either in burial niches in catacombs or caves or in the ground. If the latter, after about a year, when the body had decomposed, the bones were gathered up and placed in stone containers, called ossuaries, for secondary burial.[51] Many of these have been unearthed, and some are decorated with elaborate, even mythically inspired, bas-reliefs, for example, at Beit She'arim, the burial place of Rabbi Judah the Patriarch (third-century Palestine).[52]

Stone markers, or stelae, without any inscriptions, are mentioned already in the Hebrew Bible as a way to remember who is buried in a grave, as in the case of Rachel: "Over her grave Jacob set up a pillar; it is the pillar at Rachel's grave to this day" (Gen. 35:20). The erection of a monument seems at one point to be carried out only when there are no children, as a substitute form of remembering the dead. For example, David's son "Absalom, in his lifetime, had taken a pillar which is in the Valley of the King and set it up for himself; for he said, 'I have no son to keep my name alive.' He had named the pillar after himself, and it has been called Absalom's Monument" (2 Sam. 18:18).[53]

In contrast to pillars or stelae, mausoleums were erected over Jewish graves from the Hellenistic age, as in connection with the Maccabees at Modin: "And Simon built a monument over the tomb of his father and his brothers. . . . He also erected seven pyramids . . . erecting about them great columns, . . . and on the columns he put suits of armor . . . and besides the suits of armor he carved ships. . . . It remains to this day" (1 Macc. 13:27–30). This is but one of many examples of how the Maccabees were embedded in many features of the pagan Hellenistic culture. All the monuments in the Kidron Valley date from the late Greek or early Roman period as well.[54] Although Israelite kings were buried inside towns, the common practice was for a family burial cave or area to be outside the town, as with Abraham.

In Muslim lands, elaborate sepulchres might be erected, though more modest, flat, inscribed tombstones were more common. In medieval Christian Europe, burial in the ground with inscribed upright tombstones developed. Two of the best preserved medieval Jewish cemeteries are in Worms and Prague. Very unusually decorated gravestones are found from the seventeenth century on, as in Amsterdam and Poland.[55]

At the Cemetery

The funeral consisted of a procession to the gravesite and words of praise for the deceased, known as a *hesped*. Funerals, like weddings, were known to all by the way people behaved in public. Jews knew that someone had died by the public sights and sounds of the rites "with mourners all around in the street" (Eccles. 12:5). The procession was marked by sounds of trumpets (rams' horns) and of professional mourners, who often were women and who preceded the family and community members. David cries out to the professional women mourners, "Daughters of Israel, weep over Saul" (2 Sam. 1:24).[56] (Fig. 9)

People wrote a dirge (qinah) that they recited over the dead, as David did for Saul and his son Jonathan (2 Sam. 1:19–27). Or the survivors lamented (*sifdu*) and expressed mourning by tearing garments and putting on sackcloth (2 Sam. 3:31–35). The lament might take place after the burial: "He laid the corpse in his own burial place; and they lamented (*vayispedu*) over it, 'Alas, my brother!'" (1 Kings 13:30). Or the prophet Jeremiah warns that Jehoiakin, son of Josiah, will not be respected: "They shall not mourn (*yispedu*) for him, 'Ah, brother! Ah, sister!' They shall not mourn for him, 'Ah, lord! Ah, his majesty!'" (Jer. 22:18). (Fig. 10)

David also set the pattern for piety toward the dead when he walked behind the bier (*mittah*) of Abner, son of Ner. It is still customary, when funerals take place at a funeral chapel or synagogue, for Jews to walk behind the body as it moves toward the hearse and again, after the hearse arrives at the cemetery, to walk behind the body to the grave.

What the Bible refers to as lamentation (hesped) started as a poetical dirge (qinah) or memorial that was chanted. It continued into antiquity and in Muslim lands into modern times, but from antiquity it was complemented by a funeral oration, which came to called hesped. Professionals delivered some, and a few fragments are preserved in the Talmud.[57]

The tradition of mourners and others attending a funeral to shovel dirt on the coffin in the open grave is becoming more common today than it used to be. Each mourner who wishes to do so, takes the shovel and puts some earth on the lowered coffin. It is customary not to pass the shovel from person to person but for each to dig it into the ground after using it, and for the next person to take it out of the

9. *Funeral procession of Malka Asch, mother of Yiddish writer Sholem Asch. Kutno, Warsaw Region, 1930s. From the Archives of the YIVO Institute for Jewish Research. Reprinted with permission.*

10. *"The Oration over the Dead Man." Painting from the Prague Burial Society (Hevra Qadisha), about 1780, inv. No. 12.843/9. Collection of the Jewish Museum in Prague. Reprinted with permission.*

earth. In Israel, where coffins are not used, the earth is put directly over the covered body. Among the other customs that developed in post-Talmudic times are washing hands when leaving the cemetery or entering the house of mourning and lighting a memorial candle.[58]

After the burial, the Talmud reports that mourners used to stand while the other people passed by to comfort them, as at a receiving line. But two families in Jerusalem used to argue about who should get precedence to comfort the mourners after the burial, and the rabbis established the rule that the people should remain standing in a row and the mourners should pass by them. Subsequently, the practice developed of those attending the funeral should form two parallel lines facing each other, and the mourners pass between them and are greeted with words of comfort.[59]

These formulaic words of comfort, also said today when a visitor leaves the house sitting shiva, are relatively recent, but they are based on earlier shorter formulas of consolation or blessing. In the Talmud, one tells mourners merely, "be comforted" (*titnahamu*).[60] Or they are greeted when people leave the cemetery with the blessing, "May the master of consolation comfort you, blessed is He who comforts mourners."[61] In the late Palestinian midrash, *Pirqei de-Rabbi Eliezer,* the phrase appears, "May He who dwells in this house comfort you" (ha-shokhen be-bayit zeh yenahemkha), and this is the language cited by Rabbi Jacob ben Asher, in his code, *Arba'ah Turim,* in fourteenth-century Spain.[62]

Closer yet to the formula used today among Ashkenazic Jews is the comment in the gloss of Rabbi Joshua Falk (1555–1614), author of commentaries on the *Arba'ah Turim* and *Shulhan 'Arukh,* of which part of the former commentary is known as "Derishah u-Ferishah" (Inquiry and Explication). He comments: "Based on this there is a bit of support for our way of consoling mourners, when generally speaking the mourner does not begin to speak at all but rather people enter the house and sit awhile and then say: 'May the Lord comfort you along with the other mourners of Zion.' ('H yenahemkha 'im she'ar aveilei zion')."[63] The phrase as it is usually said today is evidently later still and perhaps based on the merger of another traditional formula.

In Shem Tov Gagin's compendium of the customs of the Sefardic synagogues in London and Amsterdam, to which he adds many variations from other Sefardic or Mediterranean communities, he notes that the phrase "May the Place [God] comfort you" (ha-maqom yenahem etkhem) is offered as an expression of consolation by Jews in the Land of Israel. In Egypt, Jews say "be comforted from Heaven" (tenuhamu min ha-shamayim). The Ashkenazic expression seems to have combined the former, "May the Place comfort you," with the continuation of the earlier Ashkenazic phrase, changing "im" (with) to "betokh" (among) and adding to the phrase "mourners of Zion" the redundant "and Jerusalem."[64] This yields the current formula: "ha-maqom yenahem etkhem betokh sh'ar aveilei zion virushalayim" (May the Place comfort you among the rest of the mourners of Zion and Jerusalem).

Sefardim today often say an adaptation of two Talmudic phrases. The first, mentioned above, is "Be comforted" (titnahamu) and a second, "From Heaven may they have mercy" (min ha-shamayim yerahamu). The result: "May you be comforted from Heaven" (min ha-shamayim terahamu or terahamu min ha-shamayim).[65]

Other cemetery customs involve people either uprooting and throwing grass and pebbles behind them or putting grass or pebbles on a tombstone. The first, still done in some traditional burials, is to pluck a bunch of grass and throw it into the air. It is mentioned already in the twelfth-century *Mahzor Vitry,* a rabbinic collection of liturgical customs derived from Babylonian rites and augmented in northern France in the twelfth and thirteenth centuries in various versions of the final book. After presenting the form of the burial Kaddish that was used then, the author continues: "There are those who pluck up grass from the ground and say [the verse], 'Let men sprout up in towns like grass of the field'" (Ps. 72:16).[66]

Immediately after this, an historical anecdote is reported by Rabbi Isaac ben Dorbello (mid-twelfth-century northern France), a student of Rabbi Jacob ben Meir (Rabbeinu Tam). Apostates complained to the French king (Louis VII) that Jews threw the grass behind them in order to cast a spell on Christians to cause their death. In a report of a meeting between Rabbi Moses of Paris and the king of France, the rabbi explains that the reason for the custom is to affirm the Jews' belief in the resurrection of the dead. Just as the grass will come back to life in the spring, so the dead will in the end of days. The king supposedly was impressed. Some Jews, Rabbi Isaac continues, hesitated to do the rite for fear of Christian repercussions.[67]

The more popular related but different custom today of Jews picking up pebbles and placing them on tombstones is not mentioned in the *Mahzor Vitry* and apparently dates from the late Middle Ages in Germany. In his short commentary on the *Shulhan 'Arukh,* known as *Be'er Heiteiv,* Rabbi Judah ben Simeon Ashkenazi (eighteenth century) cites *Derashot Maharash,* a work by Rabbi Shalom mi-Neustadt, a late fourteenth-century authority, and teacher of Maharil, but the custom is not found in the published collections of Rabbi Shalom's rulings. On Orah Hayyim 224:12, Rabbi Judah says: "It is written in *Derashot Maharash* . . . that the reason people pull up grass or a pebble and *put it on the gravestone* is purely out of respect for the dead, to show that he was at the grave" (italics added).[68]

Although Christians today place flowers on the grave, the custom of placing a small stone on the tombstone was widely followed by Jews in medieval Christian lands and may have ancient pagan roots. One explanation is that the stone protects one from harm that comes from demons if one reads a tombstone inscription, a neutralization of bad luck. There are other explanations and modern homiletical accommodations, but the origins seem veiled in ancient pagan practices. Today it is viewed as a sign of respect for the dead. Although traditional Jews today do not usually put flowers on graves, some Jews do place all kinds of objects on the grave of a small child including baskets of stuffed animals, something we have seen at the memorial sites of terrorist bombings in which children were killed, as in Oklahoma City.[69]

SHIVA

Unless a death occurs during some Jewish festivals or just before one, when special rules apply, the mourners return from the cemetery and "sit shiva" for nearly a whole week. Among the differences between Babylonia and Palestine in Geonic times, in Babylonia a man need not sit shiva anymore if he did so even one hour before a festival begins; in Palestine, three days were needed before the festival to cancel shiva. The Babylonian custom prevailed.[70]

The remainder of the day of the funeral counts as the first day. It is followed by the next five whole days, and it concludes with the first part of the morning of the seventh day, when the mourners "get up from shiva." If the seventh day is a Sabbath, the shiva usually concludes just before the Sabbath begins. In some communities, it is traditional for the mourner to complete the rite by going outside and walking "around the block," thereby making a symbolic gesture of wholeness to mark a return to the outside world.

The biblical Book of Ecclesiastes preaches: "Better to go to the house of mourning than to a house of feasting" (Eccles. 7:2). Biblical texts emphasize mourning for seven days. For example, fasting is noted as a sign of mourning, for one day, by David (2 Sam. 1:12; 2 Sam. 3:35), but for seven days for Saul (1 Sam. 31:13). Seven days of mourning, without the fasting, remained customary through the centuries. We see it in the Pentateuch with Joseph for Jacob: "and he observed a mourning period of seven days for his father" (Gen. 50:10); in the post-biblical Book of Judith about whom it is said, "the house of Israel mourned her for seven days" (Jth. 16:24); and in the Book of Ecclesiasticus, or Ben Sira, ca. 200 B.C.E., "mourning for the dead lasts seven days" (Ecclus. 22:12). The seven-day period is yet another rite built on that number, complementing the shevua ha-ben after the birth of a son, and the seven days of feasting after a wedding.

Fasting was not practiced already in the time of Jeremiah and Ezekiel (late sixth century B.C.E.). In fact, mourning involves breaking bread for the mourner as a form of comfort. Jeremiah mentions that "a cup of consolation" is offered to the mourner "for the loss of his father or mother" (Jer. 16:7), and Ezekiel refers to "the bread of comforters" (Ezek. 24:17, 22).[71] This meal is called *se'udat havra'ah* (healing meal) and is a shift from feeding the dead to feeding the living.

Today, some synagogue communities provide not only the first meal but all subsequent meals as well and if possible also a prayer quorum for evening and morning daily services in the mourners' home. The practice of covering mirrors in the house is modern, practiced by Ashkenazic and Sefardic/Mediterranean Jews.[72]

The Talmud distinguished between the first "three days of weeping" and the other four days.[73] This distinction survives at least in Israel today, where it is customary only for family to visit the first three days, and for friends to come later in the week. Rabbinic law prohibits behavior during the shiva period that is also forbidden on the Day of Atonement: working, bathing, cosmetics, engaging in sexual relations, and wearing leather shoes. In addition, study of Torah, considered a great pleasure, is prohibited.[74]

Other Signs of Mourning

Many customs about shiva developed or were eliminated in medieval and early modern times. The week is one of confinement from routine duties and allowing oneself to be taken care of by other family members and especially close friends and members of the community.

In both Talmuds it is taught that during the shiva the mourner is supposed to overturn his or her bed and sit on it or sleep on the ground: "Bar Kappara taught [God says]: I have set the likeness of my image on them and through their sins have I upset it; let your couches be overturned on their account."[75] Behind this gesture is the idea that although humans were created in the image of God, death is related to sin and this upsets the human condition. To act this out, mourners are to sleep with beds turned upside down.[76]

Despite the urging of Maimonides and Joseph Karo that mourners should do this for at least part of the seven-day period, Ashkenazic and Sefardic rabbis ruled that it was no longer to be done. For example, even in Germany, where many Christian practices were adopted into Judaism, Rabbi Meir of Rothenburg (d. 1293) wrote, "today one does not overturn the beds, since we live among (Christians) and they would suspect us of witchcraft."[77] Even Joseph Karo conceded that "upsetting the bed is no longer done because the Gentiles will say it is witchcraft and our beds are not made the way the beds were made in ancient times."[78]

The practice today is for mourners not to sit on regular chairs or couches. This is based on the behavior of Job's friends who "'sat with him towards the ground (la-aretz) seven days and seven nights' (Job 2:13). The text does not say *on* ('al) the ground' and that means on something *close* to the ground."[79] Synagogues or funeral parlors today provide mourners who are sitting shiva with low folding chairs.

Yet another mourning custom is inferred in the Talmud from a biblical verse: "A mourner is obligated to wrap his head. Since the Merciful told Ezekiel [the opposite], namely, 'And cover not your upper lip' (Ezek. 24:17), we infer that other mourners are obligated [to do so]."[80] The passage in Ezekiel also mentions several other commonly practiced modes of mourning, all of which God tells Ezekiel not to perform when his wife dies: "'But you shall not lament or weep or let your tears flow. Moan softly; observe no mourning for the dead; Put on your turban and put your sandals on your feet; do not cover over your upper lip (ve-lo ta'teh 'al safam), and do not eat the bread of comforters'" (Ezek. 24:16–17).

The Jerusalem Talmud explains that the requirement to cover the upper lip means covering the mouth.[81] In Babylonia, Shmuel (third century) describes the difference between wrapping the head on weekdays and on the Sabbath, which is not to be a time of public mourning. On the Sabbath, a mourner wraps the head but shows hair; during the rest of the week, he wraps his head completely, in the manner of the Arabs.[82] The custom of covering the lip by specially wrapping a tallit or cloth around the head is to begin after the burial, according to Rabbi Natronai bar Hilai Gaon (of Sura, 853–58).[83]

The northern French Talmud commentators, the Tosafists, observed that this ancient custom, like overturning the beds, is no longer done. The basis for not covering the head or overturning the bed anymore is the passage in the Jerusalem Talmud: "a traveler (akhsana'i) is not obligated to overturn his bed, so that people do not say he is a sorcerer (harash)." "Moreover, we live among [Christians] and we have men and women [Christian] servants. . . . Another reason for not covering the head is that it would bring ridicule on us, since it looks like the Muslim way of wrapping the head."[84] Not surprisingly, Maimonides, in Muslim Egypt, ruled that it should continue, as did Joseph Karo in Ottoman Palestine, and it did continue in Muslim lands and among some Jews who grew up there. In Christian Poland, Rabbi Moses Isserles commented that it is not done.[85]

In some parts of the Muslim East, mourners went to the synagogue for daily prayers during shiva instead of having services in the mourners' house, especially when there were not enough people to make a minyan both in the synagogue and in the house. Again, there was a difference between the customs of Babylonia and Palestine. In Babylonia, the mourner was able to go to the synagogue throughout the shiva; in Palestine, only on the Sabbath.[86] The practice depended on how different rabbis interpreted the words "shabbat rishonah" (either first Sabbath or first week) in the following Talmudic teaching: "Our Rabbis taught: On/During the first shabbat a mourner does not go out of the door of his house; the second week he goes out but does not sit in his [usual] place (in the synagogue); the third week he sits in his [usual] place but does not speak; the fourth week he is like any other person."[87]

In Iraq, Rabbi Paltoi ben Abbaye Gaon (fl. 842–57) wrote that unless a person is an important public figure who has many students and relatives who come to comfort him at home, he should go to synagogue to be comforted there, as is done in "all the villages in Babylonia and in the other lands." Apparently he meant the entire week, not just the Sabbath. This ruling was made for the practical reason that in small Jewish communities, providing two simultaneous prayer quorums then was as difficult as it is today.

Rabbi Hai ben Shrira Gaon (939–1038) ruled there that people should follow the local custom during the first week and that "in Babylon everyone goes to the synagogue, but in large cities and districts most pray at home." In Muslim Spain, Rabbi Isaac Ibn Ghayyat (1038–89) reported the words of the two distinguished Babylonian rabbinic authorities, but he added that "it was the custom of our predecessors to go to the synagogue to pray" (during shiva).[88]

Writing later in Christian Gerona, in Catalonia, Rabbi Moses ben Nahman (Nahmanides) (1194–1270) says that mourners should pray at home the first week except on the Sabbath,[89] but Rabbi Isaac bar Sheshet (1326–1408) points out: "there are different practices in these lands. In all of Catalonia, this is observed only on weekdays, when one prays at the house of a mourner; but on the Sabbath morning, the mourner may go to the synagogue, since mourning does not take place on the Sabbath, and he does not sit in his usual place." In Valencia, he continued, "it is customary not to go to synagogue the first week even on the Sabbath," while "in Saragossa mourners usually go to the synagogue all seven days of the week in the morning and evening. After services they return to their house accompanied by most of the community who stop at the entrance to the courtyard, the keener (*ha-meqonenet*) wails and beats a tambourine in her hand and the women mourn and clap their hands together. They do this to honor the deceased, and their custom is not to be stopped."[90]

In the *Shulhan 'Arukh,* Rabbi Joseph Karo rules "but the first week (*shavua ha-rishon*) he does not leave his house even to hear the blessing of a huppah (wedding) or a circumcision."[91] On this, Rabbi Moses Isserles comments: "These days, it is the custom not to sit in one's own seat [in the synagogue] the entire thirty days [of mourning for a relative other than a parent], and for one's father or mother, the entire twelve months. This custom has no basis [in any rabbinic authority], but we should not change it, since [we follow the general principle] 'every place should follow its own custom.'"[92]

Today, those mourners who wish to participate evening and morning in daily services, theoretically may do so without going to the synagogue, if a quorum of men (or women, in egalitarian communities) takes turns coming to the mourners' house all week. On the Sabbath, it is customary now for the mourner to attend synagogue, but to wait outside the main hall during the preliminary Qabbalat Shabbat Friday evening service and be greeted with traditional words of comfort just before the formal part of the evening service (*ma'ariv*) begins.

Despite the ruling in the Talmud about where a mourner should pray during all or part of the seven days of shiva, practice clearly varied, even among sages in Baghdad and in medieval Spain. In addition, ordinary Jews followed various local customs derived from either Muslim or Christian practices, and rabbis were powerless to stop them. In some cases, they threw up their hands and did not even try.

Rabbi Isaac bar Sheshet also commented that Jews in one community in Christian Spain follow a Muslim custom of which he disapproves: "You also asked me to instruct you about the wicked custom which people do in that land to go out to the cemetery the morning of the seven days of mourning each and every morning. They have taken this custom from the Muslims and you should tell them that it is forbidden."[93]

Today, the most typical feature of shiva occurs between meal times and religious services, when visitors drop by during the day or early evening to pay respects. They are not required to say anything to a mourner; the mourner takes the initiative. Just sitting near the mourner is enough. Visits usually last about a half hour, depending on how crowded the room is with new arrivals.[94]

SHELOSHIM (THE "THIRTY DAYS" AFTER THE BURIAL)

The period of mourning continues, with fewer restrictions, up to thirty days as the mourner gradually goes back into the world of work and society. The number thirty is found in the Bible in connection with mourning for Aaron, "All the house of Israel bewailed Aaron 30 days" (Num. 20:29), and for Moses, "And the Israelites bewailed Moses in the steppes of Moab for 30 days" (Deut. 34:8).

A person may not shave or cut the hair for the entire month, unless it becomes something socially intolerable. The rabbis derived the law of the mourner not cutting the hair for thirty days by using the exegetical technique of comparing two different biblical verses in which the same word appears (*gezeirah shavah*). This permits them to apply to both cases a condition stipulated in only one of them. Thus the root PR' (let [hair] grow wild) appears in a verse that refers to mourning (Lev. 10:6) and to one that speaks about the Nazirite (Num. 6:5), where it implicitly says that a person who takes on an ascetic way of life is supposed to let his hair grow long for thirty days. Based on the exegetical rule of comparison, the rabbis infer that a mourner is also to let his hair grow for thirty days.[95]

During the thirty days, one is restricted mainly from attending celebrations, especially any with live music. If the dead is a sibling, a spouse, or a child, mourning ends after thirty days; for a parent, only after a year.[96] The end of sheloshim, at least in Israel, is a time of holding family or public memorials (*askarot*) dedicated to study and remembering the dead (see "Unveiling," below).

RITES OF MEMORIALIZATION: GERMAN-JEWISH INNOVATIVENESS

Although mourning ends after a stipulated period, remembering continues in different ways through the lifetime of a surviving relative. One of the most observed rites of Judaism today, even among Jews who otherwise are not involved in traditional Jewish religious practice, is the observance of Yahrzeit (literally, time of the year), the anniversary of a parent's death, on which Jews customarily used to fast, though this is not often mentioned today, light a memorial candle that burns all day, attend synagogue services that day, and recite the Kaddish (the best-known custom), even if it is done by painstakingly reading a transliteration in roman letters of the Aramaic and Hebrew text. The popularity of this observance, among otherwise non-traditional American Jews today, can be compared only to attending a Passover Seder or to going to the synagogue on the Jewish New Year and Day of Atonement.

Also popular is the memorial prayer known as Yizkor ("May He remember"). On the Day of Atonement and on the three major festivals of Pesah (Passover), Shavuot, and Sukkot, Jews traditionally recite a sequence of memorial prayers for the martyrs of Jewish history and for individual members of one's own family who have died. Many Jews go to the synagogue on those holidays just to recite "the Yizkor prayers," and synagogue bulletins stipulate clearly in the holiday calendar just when the Yizkor service will take place.[97] A candle that lasts all day is lit in the home.

Traditional or not, modern Jews have personal reasons for observing some or all of the rites of remembering the dead in one's family, especially parents. It is true that a tradition interprets the basic biblical injunction to honor your father and mother (Exod. 20:12; Deut. 5:16) to mean, especially, to honor their memory after they have died, but the background of these and other rites of memory lies elsewhere.[98]

Interwoven with remembering one's own family are traditions that involve recalling the memory of Jews who died as martyrs. As in the Christian Church, memorials to the souls of the departed and to the saints are often connected, and the rites that Jews invented in order to remember each category of the dead are related, in ways still to be unraveled, to the ways the Church did so.[99]

A second powerful motivation to create and to follow rites of memorialization of the dead is the ancient belief, still held by some Jews today, that an active relationship exists between the living and the dead, such that the two could affect one another in significant ways. In the biblical view, when a person died, the sentient part went into a storage area known as Sheol, an ill-defined place. It is not clear what happened there. The Psalmist notes, "The dead cannot praise the Lord, nor any who go down into silence" (Ps. 115:17), and there is no sign in the Hebrew Bible of an afterlife that resembles Heaven or Hell.

The Hebrew Bible includes descriptions of the prohibition that the living should use intermediaries to contact the dead (Lev. 19:31; Deut. 18:11; Isa. 8:19) and records episodes of worthy people who do so anyway. A good example is King Saul, who asks "a woman who consults ghosts . . . in En-dor" (1 Sam. 28:7) to contact Samuel, who had recently died, about how to fight the Philistines (1 Sam. 28:3–25). Saul is portrayed as doing this even though he himself "had forbidden [recourse to] ghosts and familiar spirits in the land" (1 Sam. 28:3; cf. 1 Chron. 10:13). The king's desperate behavior suggests how ineffective such laws were and that the practice of using such mediums was a persisting one in ancient Israel.[100]

There is a hint in late biblical writings of the resurrection of the dead (Dan. 12:2), but only after the Hebrew biblical canon was sealed did some Jews think that the living could atone for the sins of the dead and lessen their punishment. The book known as 2 Maccabees (first century B.C.E.) refers to Judah making atonement for his dead soldiers who had sinned: "Therefore he made atonement for the dead, so that they might be delivered from their sin" (2 Macc. 12:45). They pray and send money to Jerusalem for a sin offering (12:42–43).

As will soon become clear, it is not surprising that some of the ancient kernels of Jewish rites about the dead were shaped into a set of rites of memorialization of the dead in northern Europe, especially from the twelfth century on. This was due to the combined effects of a specific set of experiences that triggered an ideology of Jewish martyrs, and the rites that developed internalized familiar Christian practices, including lighting candles at the point of death, during shiva, on the anniversary, and on the days of Yizkor, just as monks did when they remembered the dead in their monastic family.

Apart from the specific conditions in medieval Germany that generated memorial rites, there was an ancient Jewish set of assumptions about a relationship between the living and the dead that the Jewish communities in Ashkenaz accepted and nurtured more than the Jews of Muslim lands. Although scholars know that relations between the living and the dead are described in biblical and other ancient Near Eastern texts, most people today are unfamiliar with these references and are surprised that this pattern is part of ancient and later traditional expressions of Judaism. Without acknowledging these beliefs, however, it is hard to understand the staying power of memorials for the dead even today among admittedly modern men and women.

In contrast, the Jews of medieval Iraq and Spain under Islam, and their descendants, even under Christian rule in Spain, were relatively untouched by these features of the Jewish cult of the dead in all of the forms that developed in northern Christian Europe, where they originated. Some of them did penetrate into medieval Spain, but others did not, such as reciting the prayer that begins, "av ha-rahamim" (Merciful Father), on the Sabbath.

This Life and the Afterlife

Rabbinic sources do not agree if a person's sins can be atoned after death. One view holds that death itself atones, and there is no further possibility (or need?) of atonement after death.[101] This view had adherents in the Muslim East and West, and may have inhibited the development there of a full set of rites in memory of the dead.

But the contrary notion that the living can atone for the sins of the dead was also a rabbinic teaching. In the midrashic comment on a verse in Deuteronomy, the *Sifrei Devarim* says: "'Absolve, O Lord, Your people Israel whom You redeemed' (Deut. 21:8); 'Absolve . . . Your people' [refers to] those who are now alive; 'whom You redeemed' [refers to] those who are dead. This indicates that the dead, too, require atonement."[102] The idea is found in the Talmud[103] and in *Midrash Pesiqta Rabbati,* in a long discussion about how a person may be compared to the twelve signs of the zodiac: "Perhaps you will say that once a man is plunged into Gehenna, there will be no coming up for him. When mercy is besought on his behalf, however, he is shot up from Gehenna as an arrow from the bow [=Sagittarius]."[104]

In Palestine and medieval Ashkenaz, these ideas generated different Jewish memorial rites that enabled a Jew to remember a dead
parent or other relative as well as the martyred dead. Customs for
remembering both begin in early medieval Palestine and then developed liturgically in the wake of the 1096 anti-Jewish riots and acts
of Jewish martyrdom in the Rhineland that accompanied the call to
the First Crusade (av ha-rahamim [Merciful Father]), once again, after
the geographically more extensive mass murders perpetrated on the
Jews of the German Empire at the time of the Black Death (1348–50)
(Yahrzeit, saying Yizkor four times a year instead of just on Yom Kippur), and, once again, after the pogroms carried out by the Cossacks
under the leadership of the Ukrainian leader Bogdan Chmielnitzki
in 1648–49 (el malei rahamim). I now turn to each of the elements
that came to constitute an elaborate cult in memory of the dead, especially in Christian Europe.

Early Medieval Practices

The Palestinian *Midrash Tanhuma* combines the midrash in *Sifrei
Devarim* and the one also found in *Pesiqta Rabbati* to justify different
specific ritual practices that we hear about for the first time. These
are said to enable the living to reduce the punishment owed to the
dead:

> *We are accustomed to recall the {names of the} dead on the Sabbath so that
> they do not return to Hell.* It is written in Torat Kohanim [*sic;* read: *Sifrei*]
> [on the verse] "Absolve, O Lord, Your people Israel [whom You
> redeemed]" (Deut. 21:8)—"'Your people Israel,' are the living; 'whom
> You redeemed;' are the dead. From this we learn that the living can
> redeem the dead."
>
> *This is why we are accustomed to recall the [names of the] dead on Yom
> Kippur and to give charity on their behalf.* For we have learned in *Torat
> Kohanim* [*sic;* read: *Pesiqta Rabbati*] "Perhaps charity does not help them
> after they died? Learn [that it does, from the verse] 'whom You

redeemed' (ibid.). From this [we learn] that when we give charity for them, they immediately rise up [from Hell] like an arrow from a bow [of the Archer=Sagittarius], immediately [they] are made pure and innocent like the Kid [=Capricorn], and become pure as on the day [they] were born, pure water is poured on [them] from the pail [of the Waterbearer]."[105]

The first part of the passage in *Midrash Tanhuma,* basing itself on a midrash in *Sifrei Devarim* on Deut. 21:8, says that Jews have the custom of remembering or mentioning in public the (souls of the) dead on the Sabbath "so that they [the dead] do not return to Hell." Underlying this teaching is the rabbis' assumption that a relationship exists between the Sabbath and the souls of the living and of the dead. Thus, the third-century Palestinian Amora Simeon ben/Resh Laqish taught that on Friday a living Jew is given an "additional soul" for the Sabbath and when the Sabbath ends that soul is taken away.[106]

The special relationship between the Sabbath and the souls of the wicked who have died is made explicit in the *Tanhuma* passage where it says that the souls of those being punished in Hell are temporarily reprieved on the Sabbath, but at the conclusion of the Sabbath, they return there. This notion, in turn, is predicated on the rabbinic idea concerning the punishment of the "wicked" for twelve months: "for full [twelve months] the body is in existence and the soul ascends and descends; after twelve months the body ceases to exist and the soul ascends but never descends again," that is, into Hell.[107] When the living mention the names of the dead on the Sabbath, their return to Hell is delayed.[108] The practice of "mentioning the dead" on the Sabbath in the *Tanhuma* text, otherwise unattested until much later, underlies what would eventually lead to the introduction of different rites of mentioning the dead in the synagogue right after the Torah reading on the Sabbath.[109]

The second rite mentioned in *Midrash Tanhuma,* this time based on a passage in *Midrash Pesiqta Rabbati,* another early medieval Palestinian text, refers to the specific acts of giving charity and remembering the dead on the Day of Atonement. This practice became the basis of the Yizkor memorial service that for centuries took place after the reading of the Torah only on Yom Kippur. In early modern central and especially eastern Europe, it was expanded so that the prayers were also recited on the last day of each of the three major festivals: Sukkot (Tabernacles—on Shemini Azeret), Pesah (Passover), and Shavuot (Pentecost).

Hazkarat Neshamot *(Remembering the Souls of the Martyrs)* (qedoshim)

In addition to continuing the practice of mentioning the names of the family dead on the Sabbath, mentioned in *Midrash Tanhuma,* two different prayers in memory of the dead emerged in medieval Germany. One, "av ha-rahamim" (Merciful Father), was written for the martyrs or saints (qedoshim) who died in 1096 in the Rhineland towns. Another, beginning with the words "yizkor ehohim" (May God remember), was dedicated to remembering the souls of family dead on the Day of Atonement.

None of these now traditional practices of memorialization connected with the dead of one's own family is clearly found in the Bible or Talmud. Jews developed earlier hints they "found" in traditional sources when they internalized and transformed local Christian customs and practices in order to affirm their own Jewish continuities and meanings. As in customs of childhood and forming a new couple and family, death too connects the individual to the larger whole of a Jewish community situated in a non-Jewish culture. It also ties the individual to sources of transcendent meanings that people express in dramatic rituals and ceremonies.

The primary prayers and customs associated with martyrs or mourning—av ha-rahamim, Yizkor, Yahrzeit, and the Orphan's Kaddish (kaddish yatom)—all developed in medieval Germany and spread to varying degrees to the rest of the Jewish world. They developed there because that is where a cult of the local Jewish martyrs of

1096 emerged as a coherent set of practices that became part of a regional Jewish collective memory. The rites designed to remember the special martyrs of Germany developed in central and eastern Europe into broader memorializations of the dead of every Jewish family. The relative absence of this cult in memory of the dead among Jews from Muslim lands points to the regional origins of these rites and prayers.

1096 and Av Ha-Rahamim (Merciful Father)

The formation of a Jewish cult in memory of the dead was accelerated after a traumatic episode in German Jewish history. Before well-organized armies of knights left for the East in the late summer of 1096, other knights and mobs marched from France and areas of Germany into the Rhineland. In the late spring and early summer, they attacked the growing Jewish communities living in Speyer, Worms, and Mainz, on the Rhine, Trier, on the Moselle River, the villages on the lower Rhine to which the Jews of Cologne had fled, and Regensburg on the Danube. With the exception of the Jews of Speyer, most of whom were saved, or of Regensburg, further southeast, in Bavaria, who were forced into the Danube and baptized en masse, most Jews either temporarily converted or died. The attackers killed some Jews, as other Jews engaged in acts of ritual killing of their families and committed suicide, rather than be forcibly converted to Christianity.[110]

The riots and acts of martyrdom and conversion are known to us from short passages in Latin chronicles of the Crusaders' trek to Jerusalem and from three types of Hebrew sources: liturgical poems, memorial lists of martyrs, and unusually detailed narratives or chronicles. Together, the Hebrew texts created a liturgically structured, lasting collective memory of the very character of the culture of Ashkenaz.

The oldest and most influential genre is the liturgical poetry (*piyyutim*) written in the form of dirges (*qinot*). Perhaps as many as twenty-five such laments about the 1096 martyrs were composed in the early twelfth century. Some have remained in the German and Polish/ Lithuanian liturgies for the Ninth of Av, the fast day that marks the destruction of both ancient Temples in Jerusalem, now linked to Germany in 1096 as well.[111] The martyrs of 1096 left a scar in Jewish collective memory in the German Empire and in Christian reports about the various episodes accompanying the First Crusade. Some traces are in narratives that made their way into Jewish anthologies about accounts of past significant events worthy of being recorded and remembered.[112]

The expansion of certain memorial rites from remembering the martyrs of 1096 to remembering the dead relatives, especially parents, of every Jewish family was a gradual process that contributed to the intensive cult in memory of the dead that persists especially in Ashkenazic Jewish practice.

Liturgical poems were crucial in achieving this collective group consciousness, which persisted in special ways among the Jews of Frankfurt am Main, for example, into the twentieth century. One of the poems written about 1096 entered the Sabbath liturgy and replaced the earlier custom of remembering the names of family dead on the Sabbath, as in *Midrash Tanhuma.*

Called av ha-rahamim, it is still recited on most Sabbaths in the Polish/Lithuanian rite, but in the synagogues of Germany it was said only twice a year: on the Sabbath prior to Tisha Be-Av and on the Sabbath before Shavuot, when the Jews of Mainz were attacked in 1096. It is omitted if there is a special reason for not remembering tragedy, as on Sabbaths when one blesses the new moon, for example. This has remained the practice regarding av ha-rahamim in most Ashkenazic synagogues to this day. It is not recited in most Sefardic and Mediterranean synagogues, where the earlier custom continued.

It reads in part:

May the Merciful Father, Who dwells on high, in His mighty
  compassion,
Remember those loving, upright, and blameless ones,

The holy congregations, who laid down their lives for the
    sanctification of the divine Name,
Who were lovely and pleasant in their lives, and in their death were
    not divided;
Swifter than eagles, stronger than lions to do the will of their Master
    and the desire of their Rock.
May our God remember them for good with the other righteous
    of the world,
And render retribution for the blood of his servants which has been
    shed.[113]

It also became the custom in Germany to recite annually the names
of the local martyrs on the anniversary that they died in each community. This practice is mainly derived from the Christian monastic practice of compiling and reading necrologies, lists of the dead
arranged according to the date of their death. Jewish martyrs' names
were preserved in communal *Memorbücher* (memorial books), a practice adapted from monasteries that preserved the dates of the deaths
of members in *libri memorialis,* recited on the *dies natalis,* literally,
"birthday," meaning the day the saint died and was born to eternal
life.

The custom was accompanied in the Church by lighting candles,
a practice northern Jews adopted as well on the anniversary of the
dead.[114] These practices reflect the Jews' close awareness of their Christian neighbors' rites that they sometimes turned into a cultural
polemic. Reading out the memorial lists on the anniversaries of the
Jewish martyrs' deaths was a way of affirming the truth of Judaism
and denying any Christian claims.

Although av ha-rahamim, generated by martyrs, came to displace
the early medieval custom of remembering one's family dead on the
Sabbath, forms of the ancient family memorialization on the Sabbath
persisted, but only for Ashkenazic mourners and for Sefardic Jews.
Whereas all members of a congregation recite during the Sabbath
morning service most weeks the prayer av ha-rahamim, which

emphasizes the deaths of Jewish martyrs, mourners continue to remember their dead for at least thirty days (sheloshim), by having a special memorial prayer said in their memory when the Torah is read in the synagogue on Monday and Thursday mornings and on Sabbath afternoons. Sefardic Jews continue the practice mentioned in *Midrash Tanhuma* and recite a prayer for their dead on the Sabbath after the Torah is read and generally do not recite av ha-rahamim. Their practice, uninfluenced by the regional events of 1096, is in contrast to that of Ashkenazic Jews, whose memorial liturgy was greatly expanded in their wake.

Yizkor

A second prayer, written in memory of family dead, begins with the words, "yizkor ehohim" (May God remember). It is found in many medieval prayer books and at first was to be recited only on the Day of Atonement, immediately after the reading of the Torah:

> May God remember the soul of my father/mother who has gone to his/her eternal [rest] for that, I now solemnly offer charity for his sake; in reward of this, may his soul enjoy eternal life, with the souls of Abraham, Isaac, and Jacob; Sarah, Rebekah, Rachel, Leah, and the rest of the righteous males and females that are in Paradise; and let us say, Amen.[115]

By the early fifteenth century, remembering the dead this way was extended to the three major festivals. Rabbi Jacob ben Moses (Maharil) notes: "In Austria, we do it also on three festivals and say av ha-rahamim."[116] The expanded practice did not catch on in Germany, where Yizkor often continued to be recited only on Yom Kippur. In eastern Europe, on the other hand, four times a year became the norm by the late seventeenth century.

Around that time, special prayers, beginning "el malei rahamim" (O God, full of Mercy), were written in memory of martyrs of specific communities who were murdered, especially in the Cossack riots perpetrated in the Ukraine by Bogdan Chmielnitzki in the mid-seventeenth century.[117] One version of this prayer also became standard for Jewish family memorial services, with slightly differing wording, depending on whether the prayer is recited by an officiant at a funeral service or by a surviving spouse, for example, at an appropriate subsequent time of the year. The text recited by a person such as a cantor reads:

> O God, full of mercy (el malei rahamim), who dwells on high, Grant perfect rest beneath the wings of Your Divine Presence, in the highest [places of the] holy and pure ones, who radiate as brightly as the heavens, to the soul of ——— who has gone to his/her eternal home. *Because they have pledged (to give) charity for mentioning the name of his/her soul,* may his/her rest be in Paradise. Therefore, O Lord of compassion, shelter him/her forever under the protection of Your wings, and let his/her soul be bound up in the bond of life, and may he/she rest in peace upon his couch; and let us say Amen.[118]

In the ones recited by a surviving spouse, for example, the individual says: "Because I pledge charity for his/her sake, as a reward may his/her soul be bound up in the bond of life."

In some ways, Yizkor, also known in Hebrew as hazkarat neshamot, remembering the souls, is a Jewish equivalent to the Christian All Souls' Day, celebrated in the Roman calendar on November 2, when Christians pray in public for the souls of all who have died. It is a feast that follows All Saints' Day on November 1, preceded by All Hallows' Eve, or the modern Halloween. The memorial prayers for the martyrs of 1096 resembles the Christian institution of All Saints' Day (November 1). In the Jewish adaptation, the occasion was marked in Germany on the anniversary of the dates the attacks happened in individual communities. Yizkor is a combination of both Christian rites, since different Yizkor prayers are said for martyrs and for one's own family.[119]

On All Saints' Day and All Souls' Day, candles are lighted and special masses are recited for the dead. Lighting memorial candles that burn all day on Yom Kippur, when Yizkor was first said exclusively, is first mentioned by Rabbi Joseph ben Moses (fifteenth-century Germany), who says, "And I recall that there is a custom in Marburg to light oil lamps [to burn on] Yom Kippur for relatives who have died."[120] The Yizkor memorial lamp became standard Ashkenazic practice from that point on and was extended to all four days Yizkor prayers came to be recited, as well as on the day of the anniversary, the Yahrzeit.

In Muslim Lands: Hashkavah

Remembering the dead had a different history in the Muslim East and Spain from that in Christian northern Europe. The geonim and Jews of Spain refer to a form of prayer for the recent dead, called "hashkavah" (putting to rest), that mourners recite during the first year. In it they also mention family members who died earlier.[121] Rabbi Natronai Gaon stands by the principle that "the dead are forgotten after twelve months"[122] and stipulates at which semiannual assembly one should eulogize (maspidin) and pray for the rest (mashkivin) of the rabbi who has died, apparently a reference to two different rites. The latter took place at the end of the first year. Though the language of the prayer is not provided, its name is referred to in Aramaic as "ashkavta" (Hebrew=hashkavah). Rabbi Natronai also adds that if an important Jew dies in Babylonia, the Jews who live in Spain or France do not have to take note of it in any way, since it takes at least twelve months for word to reach them there.[123]

We find references in documents from the Cairo Geniza to prayers of praise for Jews who made contributions to the poor, and the language of praise includes mention of the names of the donors' relatives who have died.[124] In one Geniza document from twelfth-century Egypt there is a list of names that begins, "a good memorial" (dukhran tav).[125] In Muslim Spain and in the subsequent Sefardic culture, mourners recited ashkavah prayers during the seven days of shiva, twice a day, and whenever a mourner was called to the Torah during the first year after the death.[126] The individual was blessed, and in the course of the blessing his departed relatives were mentioned. No special ceremony, like Yizkor in northern Europe, existed for remembering the souls of the dead in a collective way.[127]

In Muslim lands, it was also not always clear what effect Jews thought prayer or some other way of remembering the dead had on the dead. Thus Rabbi Hai Gaon was asked if living relatives can pay off a dead relative's monetary debts and other sins against people, so as to reduce their punishment in the afterlife. He writes that they can and that a righteous person can even alleviate somewhat the punishment owed for sins committed against God, but no living person can add to the reward a dead person will receive. That is determined solely by their meritorious behavior while alive.[128] In Christian Spain (Barcelona), however, Rabbi Abraham bar Hiyya (d. ca. 1136) wrote that the living who give charity can affect the punishment the dead deserved by returning what the dead had stolen or by counting the amount of Torah they taught.[129]

Even in early thirteenth-century Germany, Rabbi Eleazar ben Judah of Worms seems to struggle with why giving charity for the dead is effective and why it is done only on the Day of Atonement and not on the festivals, perhaps a sign that some Jews wanted to curtail the practice, while others wanted to expand it to four times a year: "The reason we donate charity for the [benefit of the] dead on Yom Kippur and not on the festivals has scriptural support. . . . But what good is it to the dead when the living give charity? God examines the motives of the living and the dead. If that dead person, while he was alive, used to give charity or if he was poor but had a good heart and would have given had he had the means to do so, then he derives a little benefit because the living can ask [God] to lighten his sentence."[130] Rabbi Eleazar seems to resist the earlier assumption that the living can ameliorate the fate of the dead simply by giving charity. For him, there must also be a relationship to the character

234

of the dead as well. In any case, the practice of doing this on festivals, mentioned by Rabbi Eleazar, sometimes takes the form of charitable "Yizkor appeals."[131]

Yahrzeit

The midrash in *Tanhuma* contains the ideas that the living can atone for the dead by remembering them either on the Sabbath or on Yom Kippur and by giving charity for their benefit. Although there are teachings in the Talmud that sons are to remember the parents and affect their fate in the afterlife, the institution of memorialization of the dead in the form of Yahrzeit built on an ancient notion and an early medieval one. The ancient text was the teaching that a student or child was supposed to fast on the anniversary of the death of a teacher or parent. In the Talmud, one took an oath not to eat meat or drink wine on the anniversary of "the day that my father died, or on the day So and So died, or on the day that Gedaliah, son of Ahikam, was killed, or on the day that I saw Jerusalem in its destruction, he is prohibited [from eating]."[132] But, as far as we can tell, that text did not generate any continuous annual rite that lasted.

Perhaps no aspect of Jewish identity brings Jews into the synagogue of their youth more than the annual date memorializing the death of one's parent, the Yahrzeit. The recitation of the mourner's Kaddish in memory of the dead relative moves some Jews during their eleven-month mourning cycle for a parent to arrange their busy schedules as lawyers or businesspeople or physicians around synagogues mornings and late afternoons. People are nearly obsessed with the daily thought: can I find a minyan for Kaddish, the quorum of ten Jews required to say the prayer at a Jewish service.

It is still a custom for a person marking what came to be called a Yahrzeit for a parent's day of death to fast. In addition, an all-day candle is lighted at home, and the person who has a religious obligation that day (*hiyyuv*) may either lead services or, if the Torah is read, receive an 'aliyah. The historical context that generated or reinforced these customs emerged in medieval Germany, not in Talmudic times. This practice was already going on there in the thirteenth century, as attested by *Sefer Hasidim,* which refers to cases when a person should not take on a private fast when a town is besieged, when the midwife is called for, or when a person takes care of an aged mother or father or a sick person relies on him, but he can fast with the community or "fast as a person is accustomed to fast on the day one's father died."[133]

Reinforced in fourteenth-century German riots and massacres accompanying the fifty years of turbulence culminating in the Black Death in 1348–50, a new diffusion of the memorialization of the martyrs of Germany was transferred to remembering annually one's own family who died. Among such precedents also was the rabbinic notion of the death of Moses on the 7th of Adar. This anniversary became the date for hevra qadisha societies to fast and then hold a banquet in the evening.

Following the German-Christian terminology of remembering the souls of the dead annually on the date of their death, Jews began to refer to that anniversary by the same name, Yahrzeit. Rabbi Moses ben Isaac Mintz (ca. 1420–?), a German Talmudist, refers to "yahr zeit," in two words, in the context of what to do when people with different kinds of mourning statuses each want to recite the mourner's Kaddish or lead the services at the same time. One person is sitting shiva, another is in the first month of mourning, and a third is observing the "twelve months" anniversary. Mintz says that the man sitting shiva should have priority to say mourner's Kaddish the whole week, even if during that week "falls the anniversary of the death of another man's mother or father, which in the German language is called 'yahr zeit'" (two words).[134]

This practice is recorded as common when Rabbi Jacob ben Moses Ha-Levi (Maharil) ruled further in Mainz that "one fasts for the anniversary of one's father's or mother's death, not the day of the burial."[135] This suggests that the custom was not consistently being followed in his time. The anniversary became a day of saying mourner's Kaddish and leading the prayers in the synagogue. At home, one lights a long-burning candle, preferably of wax.[136]

Kaddish as Orphan's Prayer of Mourning

In the Middle Ages, the multiplication of masses for the dead became a major concern of Church leaders, as the powerful and wealthy ordered multiples of masses to assist the dead in purgatory, a concept that developed especially in the twelfth century. The Jewish liturgy today also offers many opportunities for a mourner to say Kaddish: at the beginning and end of every daily and holiday morning service and at the end of the afternoon and evening services, a reflection of the similar motive to say it in order to help or honor the dead.

How did this all get started? The earliest references that such a practice was to be followed is traditionally grounded in a story told, usually about the great second-century Palestinian sage Rabbi Akiva.[137] The account is found, for example, in *Mahzor Vitry,* though it is preserved in early medieval texts in many versions.[138] The core of the story is that Rabbi Akiva met a person walking in a cemetery, carrying a heavy load of wood, and offered to help him. The person reveals that he is dead and is being punished for the sin of having been a merciless tax collector when alive. The only way he can be saved, he tells Rabbi Akiva, would be if he had a son who could stand up in the congregation [as prayer leader] and say, "Blessed be the Lord, who is blessed" (barekhu et YHWH ha-mevorakh), after which the congregation would respond after him, "May His great name be blessed" (yehei shemei rabbah mevorakh). Then he would be released at once from his punishment.

Rabbi Akiva inquires into the dead man's family and discovers that his wife, who had been pregnant when he died, did deliver a son. And though the son had not been circumcised and did not practice Judaism, Rabbi Akiva saw to it that the son returned to Judaism, studied Torah, and "stood before the congregation and said 'Blessed'

(barekhu) and was answered, 'Blessed be the Lord, who is blessed.'"
At that very moment, the father was released from his punishment.

The dead person appeared to Rabbi Akiva in a dream to thank him for "saving me from my punishment in Gehenna." And, concludes the narrator in the twelfth-century northern French liturgical compilation *Mahzor Vitry:* "That is why people were accustomed to set before the Ark [as leader of prayers] on the night after the Sabbath a man who has no father or mother to say 'blessed' (barekhu) or Kaddish."[139]

In addition to basing itself on the principle that a son can alleviate the punishment a father is suffering in the afterlife, the story indicates that the remedy is for an orphan to lead the evening services after the conclusion of the Sabbath. In particular, the opening prayer that begins with the word "barekhu" (bless) or the "Kaddish" is said to have this effect. This practice included the recruitment even of a young boy (not yet thirteen) to lead this service. In part, this was because according to Jewish tradition the evening service (ma'ariv) was optional (reshut) as a public service. But it also became customary in northern Europe, at least, because of the story about Akiva and the power ascribed to the orphan reciting either barekhu or Kaddish prayer as a way to help offset the parent's punishment in Hell.

Although this special Sabbath night barekhu prayer was associated with orphans since early medieval times as a way to ameliorate their dead parents' sins, the Kaddish prayer became an introduction to the barekhu. At some point, the two prayers separated into two distinct, independent liturgical units. The Kaddish was no longer understood as an introduction to the barekhu prayer and instead acquired the new function of serving, not as an introduction to something, but as the conclusion of the prayers that preceded it, as today.

The barekhu prayer remained the opening of the evening service, and orphans continued to be associated with leading the prayers on Sabbath night well into early modern times. Simultaneously, the special function that an orphan's reciting the Kaddish-barekhu together had enjoyed came to be attached either to an orphan leading the post-

Sabbath evening service or to his reciting the "orphan's Kaddish" at the end of the service. Although barekhu was the earlier prayer recited by orphans to ameliorate their dead parents' suffering, the Kaddish developed into the most well known prayer associated in Judaism with ceremonies connected with memory of the dead, not just by minor orphans, but by any mourner. Hence, the mourner's Kaddish.

The word "Kaddish" means "sanctified" and is written mainly in Aramaic, with some Hebrew, and contains no reference to the dead, though its earlier part, as we have seen, was associated with ameliorating the punishment of the dead in the afterlife. It is a prayer about the sanctity of God and hopes for Israel's redemption.[140] It exists in ancient, Ashkenazic, and Sefardic versions and functions in three primary ways: (1) it is recited after one studies classical Jewish texts (kaddish de-rabbanan, or scholars' Kaddish); (2) it marks transitions during sections of the prayer services, such as before and after the Shemoneh Esreh, which is the required prayer of each service; and (3) it came to be recited as the prayer of mourners, the Kaddish yatom.

The original line of the Kaddish is the short ancient prayer that probably goes back to the days of the Temple, before 70 C.E.: "May His great name be blessed for ever and ever" (yehei shemei rabba mevorakh le-'olam u-l-'olemei 'almaya). According to midrash *Sifrei Devarim* on Deuteronomy, that line was to be broken into two parts and recited entirely in Hebrew as an antiphonal or responsive reading between the reader and others: "We say, 'May His great Name be blessed' (yehi shemo ha-gadol mevorakh), and this is to be followed by the refrain, 'for ever and ever' (le-'olam u-le-'olemei 'olamim)."[141]

This original line of what developed into the Kaddish echoes biblical verses, especially the Aramaic verse in Daniel: "'Let the Name of God be blessed for ever and ever'" (lehevei shemei di-elaha mevarakh min-'alma ve-'ad 'alma) (Dan. 2:20) and the Hebrew verses "Let the name of the Lord be blessed now and forever" (yehi shem YHWH mevorakh mei-'atah ve-'ad 'olam) (Ps. 113:2), and "'blessed be the name of the Lord'" (yehi sheim YHWH mevorakh) (Job 1:21).

These motifs are also reflected in the beginning of the "Lord's

Prayer," which begins, "Our Father who is in heaven, hallowed [i.e., blessed] be Your name" (Matt. 6:9; cf. Luke 11:2). In the Gospel of Luke, the canticle known as the Magnificat begins: "'My soul *magnifies the Lord,* and my spirit rejoices in God my Savior. . . . for the Mighty One has done great things for me, and *holy is His name'*" (1:46–49).

That was the base text of the prayer to be said for the benefit of the dead in the Talmud. Rabbi Joshua ben Levi (third-century Palestine) claimed that this short prayer had cosmic powers: "Rabbi Joshua ben Levi said: He who responds 'Amen. May His great Name be blessed' with all his might, the sentence decreed for his [sins] is annulled, as it is said, 'When retribution was annulled in Israel, when people dedicate themselves—bless the Lord' (Judg. 5:2). [The verse means that] retribution [was] annulled *because* they blessed the Lord, that is, by saying the formula, 'Amen. May his great name be blessed.'"[142]

Originally, the Kaddish was a short Aramaic prayer that scholars recited after a public Aramaic homily in the house of study; it was not a synagogue prayer at all. The power of this line is such that when recited after a study session, the world continues to exist: "How can the world endure? . . . [in the response] 'May his great name [be blessed]' [which is said] after studying aggadah."[143] This function persists as the "kaddish de-rabbanan" (literally, Kaddish for our rabbis), and it still is recited after Jews recite or study a section of rabbinic teaching, most prominently, as part of every daily service in the morning.

The Hebrew introduction to the prayer was added to lead up to the ancient formula. It begins: "May his great name be magnified and sanctified" (yitgadal ve-yitkadash shemei rabba), based on, "Thus will I manifest My greatness and holiness" (ve-nitgadalti ve-nitqadashti) (Ezek. 38:23) and "his name is holy and awesome" (qadosh ve-nora shemo) (Ps. 111:9).

Only in the post-Talmudic *Masekhet Soferim,* on the liturgy, do we hear for the first time that a prayer called "Kaddish" is part of the synagogue service, as opposed to the study hall. It is mentioned in the context of synagogue prayer, but it is not a prayer for mourners.

By geonic times, ten adult males (minyan) are necessary for someone to recite it publicly in the synagogue.[144]

Even though there are ancient and medieval elements of saying some Kaddish text in the liturgy, the events of 1096 greatly intensified this, at least in the German Empire. That cult of the martyrs of 1096 eventually generated or elaborated the widespread cult of remembering the dead of every household.

As we have seen, in the first half of the twelfth century we find for the first time in the *Mahzor Vitry* the custom of an orphan leading the evening prayers after the Sabbath and reciting Kaddish or barekhu. It still was not accepted custom in the fourteenth century,[145] and the Maharil wrote that it was permissible for someone who was not an orphan to lead the Sabbath night services and say Kaddish, again, indicating that the earlier practice was still a live option that he had to oppose.[146] Extending the end of the Sabbath, after which Jews in Ashkenaz believed that the souls of the dead returned to Hell, involved prolonged pronunciation of the word barekhu, as Rabbi Eleazar of Worms noted.[147]

YAHRZEIT AND KADDISH OBLIGATIONS

Jews made a point of remembering to say Kaddish. An extreme case is illustrated with Glueckl of Hameln's *Memoirs.* She tells us how her pious businessman husband acted when her father-in-law died: "Straight after the seven days of mourning he engaged ten Talmud scholars, and fitted up a room in our house where services were held; and he devoted his days and nights to the Torah. He gave up his business travels throughout the whole year of mourning, in order not to miss a single *kaddish.*"[148]

For parents, mourned for an entire twelve months, Kaddish is recited only for eleven.[149] Rabbi Jacob ben Moses (Maharil) attributes it to the influence of the Mishnaic rule that the wicked will spend twelve months in Hell. He also points out that in the Rhineland, mourners wore a special poncho-like hooded mourning garment known as a mitaron for the full twelve months for parents and thirty days for other close relatives for whom one mourns.[150]

One sign of how recent were different rites of memorialization even in late medieval Germany is a question about who gets precedence in the synagogue when more than one kind of mourner is there at the same time. The tensions over rival claims are alluded to in Rabbi Moses ben Isaac Mintz's responsum about the competition among mourners of different status: natives or visitors; those sitting shiva, or sheloshim, or marking the Yahrzeit. He also refers to a mourner's Kaddish that is said inside the synagogue and the mourner's Kaddish that is recited outside the entrance to the synagogue, a distinction that no longer exists.

At first he seems to follow the Talmudic rule that would permit whoever gets there first to be able to recite the Kaddish outside, but eventually he decides that a set of rules of precedence will determine which of the mourners is to be able to recite it. Priority goes to those sitting shiva. If two men have the same status, they draw lots. The complexity of the discussion suggests that there was a great deal of tension over who should get precedence.[151]

Eventually, the rabbis ruled that everyone with an obligation should be accommodated: those saying Kaddish should do so together, the present practice. Those who lead the services are accommodated during the week in their homes, if possible, and on the Sabbath, it was not a problem since mourning is not appropriate for the Sabbath, and so, someone sitting shiva did not need a special honor that day. Those who were marking the anniversary, or Yahrzeit, however, were entitled to be called to the Torah or to lead services, and if more than one had such a religious obligation (hiyyuv), the spoils were divided (evening, morning, additional, afternoon) on the Sabbath, and so on.[152]

The rite of remembering can, but need not, continue to the third generation. The mourning by grandchildren is discussed, and some prayer books have formulas to include grandparents in Yizkor prayers. To perpetuate the memory of earlier generations synagogues developed the custom of erecting memorial plaques inside the synagogue with small lights that are lit on the Yahrzeit. Tombstones weather, synagogues are sold or dismantled, and with them memorial plaques of a community that no longer exists may be set aside. Families pay cemeteries for the "perpetual care" of a parent's grave, but children themselves die, and grandchildren may not even know where grandparents are buried. Despite the elaborate customs and rites that accompany death, there are limits to memory of individuals who were not martyrs.

Synagogues keep records of the Yahrzeit file that are updated regularly. One such notice reads: "We are updating our Yuhrzeit [*sic*] file. In order that we may accommodate you with a notice on the anniversary of the death of your loved one, can you please fill out the information below and send to the Shul office."[153] Synagogues send members regular reminders a few days prior to the date, and Jews are called up to the Torah on the Sabbath prior to the day during the following week.

A Reform temple sends out to members reminder cards that have a brief description:

> The Kaddish, known as "The Orphan's Prayer," is one of the oldest and most highly cherished prayers of Israel. While originally used in Synagogue and School as a praise of God, it has come to be associated through the centuries with the memory of our beloved dead . . . The Memorial Kaddish will be read in remembrance of (name) during the Sabbath Services on Friday evening, (date) at 8:30 P.M. and Saturday morning at 11:00 A.M.[154]

A Conservative synagogue sends out a notice as follows about a month in advance of the date:

> Dear ———, We wish to inform you that yahrzeit for your beloved father (named) will begin on Thursday evening, (date). Evening services begin at 5:30 PM and morning services commence at 7:00 AM. We hope that you can be present.

In addition, the giving of Tzedakah (charity) to a worthy Jewish cause, and lighting a yahrzeit candle at home, are traditional ways of memorializing our loved ones. Sincerely, (name) Assistant Cantor.[155]

A MODERN ORTHODOX/TRADITIONAL FUNERAL AND BURIAL

The family gathers around the dying loved one either in the hospital or hospice or, as in this case, at home. The first thing is to call the rabbi, who will come over and help with the arrangements. The rabbi may ask if the family wants to have a traditional funeral. If so, he will call the hevra qadisha to arrange for the purification and guarding of the body before the funeral, and he will also call the funeral director and introduce a family member, as necessary. If one is aware of Jewish customs, a family member closes the eyes, places the body on the ground, places a lighted candle near the head, and opens the windows even before the burial society member comes over.

The rabbi may also call the police department and indicate that he knows the family and that they are at such and such an address. When the police come and take a look, a release is signed that permits the body to be removed from the premises without need for a medical examiner's autopsy.

The hevra qadisha or someone from the funeral hall comes over and removes the body to begin the process of purification (taharah) and guarding (shemirah) that will take place before the funeral service. The family members check to see that they have the deed to the burial plot or make arrangements for burial in Israel, a complication requiring plane tickets and international calls.

The details of washing and dressing the body are done with precision and respect by a group of volunteers who are trained to do this work. After the body is dressed, it is guarded by members of the hevra qadisha who are ever present and recite Psalms round the clock until the funeral. A special candle is lighted as well near the body.

The family members speak to the funeral hall and arrange the time for the service and select a coffin. Traditionally, this is a simple pine box. A family member calls the local newspaper of record and places an obituary that indicates when the funeral will take place. The cemetery is called, the ownership of the plot verified, and the arrangements made for the grave to be dug on the day of the funeral.

The funeral is planned as quickly as possible. The family will talk to the rabbi and indicate some special memories they would like him to include in his remarks or indicate that one or more family members will also be speaking.

In the United States, there may be a delay for relatives to fly in from far away, but time is important. The funeral takes place usually in a funeral chapel, though sometimes in a synagogue. The coffin has been brought into the chapel and is draped in a black cloth. The name of the hevra qadisha may be marked on it in a decorative embroidery such as "hevra qadisha de-hevrat biqqur holim de-boro[ugh] park," one of many such organizations just in Brooklyn, New York, today. A candle is lighted and a member of the hevra qadisha is nearby reciting Psalms.

The family members arrive from their houses by limousine and are seated in a waiting room to be greeted by guests who arrive in time to see them before the funeral service. Guests sign a book indicating they were there to pay their respects. Mourners are seated and are greeted by those who come by.

At some point, the funeral director indicates that all but the mourners and their families should take their seats in the chapel, and the mourners remain behind with the rabbi. In most funerals today, the rabbi presides over the rite of tearing a garment of the mourners (qeriyah). Approaching each mourner in turn, the rabbi begins a tear with a razor either on an indicated garment such as a tie or lapel or on a specially attached black ribbon, and the mourner continues the tear by him- or herself. Together, then, they say the blessing over God's justice recited after hearing about a death, "Blessed are You . . . Judge of truth."

The mourners are led into the chapel and take seats in the first row, closest to the body. Except for the funerals of his own parents, a Jew who is a Kohen may not be present where the body is in the same enclosed space, either at the funeral or at the cemetery. When the mourners enter, the guests all stand up.

Then everybody is seated, and the person presiding over the funeral service, usually the family rabbi, begins by reciting one or two traditional Psalms that mention the fragility of life. Many consider the twenty-third Psalm, "The Lord is my shepherd," to be the most appropriate. Others also read any number of other Psalms to evoke the mood of solemnity and the impermanence of life.

In the past, it was the practice of just the rabbi to make a eulogy about the deceased based on firsthand knowledge and notes gone over with surviving family members. More recently, it has become accepted for family members, sometimes one from each surviving generation, to make such remarks of a more personal kind as well. In some of these comments, individuals may recall personal experiences or describe the biographical details of an aged mother or grandmother and what their life meant to them.

Toward the end of the service, a cantor or the rabbi or a relative chants the memorial prayer, written sometime in the seventeenth century, el malei rahamim (God, Full of Mercy) and invokes God's blessing on the soul of the departed family member, whose name is mentioned in the prayer. The Kaddish prayer usually is not recited at the funeral service.

The person presiding over the funeral then announces when and where the burial will take place and that those who are going to the cemetery should form a cortege behind the hearse with their headlights on. This is a modern version of the ancient torch-lighted funeral procession to the cemetery. He also announces where family members will be sitting shiva. Sometimes this is in more than one location or for different numbers of days, depending on where survivors live.

The body is then moved out of the funeral chapel and placed into the hearse. Sometimes grandchildren are honored as pallbearers and help guide the body, placed on a movable bier on wheels, out the door of the chapel towards the hearse. Mourners who wish to practice the tradition of accompanying the body may go outside and follow the hearse on foot for a while as it moves into position to lead the cars going to the funeral.

Those who wish to follow the tradition, arrive at the cemetery and walk again behind the body, stopping seven times, to recite different Psalms, before reaching the grave site that has been prepared by the grave diggers employed by the cemetery.

As people crowd around the newly dug burial plot, the coffin is already lowered into the grave and the burial service begins. The rabbi or whoever is presiding reads another Psalm and the mourners recite together either the special burial Kaddish or the usual Kaddish prayer, depending on the time of the year. Even when the burial Kaddish is appropriate, many traditional families prefer to recite the standard mourner's Kaddish, but others insist on saying the burial Kaddish when it is permitted. The memorial prayer is recited once again, naming the deceased.

At this point, mourners and other family members and friends take turns shoveling dirt over the coffin until it is completely covered. This practice has become more popular in the past few years than before, just as family participation in the funeral service has. It is considered bad luck for one person to hand the shovel to the next, and so as each finishes shoveling some dirt on the grave, he or she puts the shovel into the ground and the next person takes it up anew until enough has been shoveled.

The service ends and people step back from the grave to form two parallel lines facing each other. In between these two lines, the mourners walk, and those present console them with the formula of consolation: "May you be comforted among the rest of the mourners of Zion and Jerusalem," the same message of consolation they will use when they leave the house of mourning during the seven days of the shiva that are about to begin.[156]

UNVEILING: A MODERN CUSTOM

The name comes from the modern custom of covering a tombstone just prior to a brief ceremony at which someone removes the temporary covering or veil and reads the inscription for the first time to family and friends of the deceased who gather for this purpose around the graveside. The custom has no Jewish sources. Apparently, it is derived from the widely practiced custom all over the world to dedicate a new work of sculpture or a commemorative plaque by first covering it and then unveiling it at a special ceremony. This custom has been taken into Judaism in modern times.

In the United States, the erection of a funeral monument, with the name and dates of the deceased, is done about a year after the burial. In Israel, it is common to put up the stone monument as soon as possible, often at the end of thirty days, the end of mourning for all but parents, sometimes even earlier.

No prescribed ceremony exists except recently invented combinations of Psalms and words of memorial. Some say the Kaddish, "for the last time"; others do not, since it may not be the end of the mourning period (e.g., for a parent in Israel, after thirty days). In some ways, the unveiling brings a measure of "closure" to the period of mourning, at least in the United States, though the strict mourning period may have been over for months if the deceased is a relative other than a parent. That is why the general practice in Israel, to have the monument erected by the end of sheloshim, makes liturgical sense even for a parent, but this has not caught on in most Jewish communities outside of Israel.

Conclusions

As we have seen, the Jews have developed a rich variety of life cycle ceremonies.
The Jewish life cycle contains powerful rites that have shaped Jewish lived experience for centuries and been modified by it. Some, like
infant male circumcision, began in biblical times and were renewed
and augmented over millennia of Jewish living. Others, like the rite
of bar mitzvah for a thirteen-year-old boy's onset of ritual participation drew on earlier precedents but came into its own only in early
modern times in central Europe and enjoyed close to universal practice only within the last two hundred years, surprising as that may
be. Weddings and funerals build on biblical, rabbinic, medieval, and
modern reinterpretations of gestures and terms and vary from Jewish community to community, though the outlines of both are recognizably Jewish everywhere.

Although each life cycle rite has its own characteristic vocabulary,
some idioms are common to more than one rite. For example, the
belief that a circle protects the vulnerable from danger helped generate the custom of making circles around the participants in more
than one important life cycle rite of passage. A circle is drawn around
the newborn boy between the birth and the brit; the bride circles
three or seven times around the groom; and the burial society or

mourners circle the grave seven times at the burial, a custom rarely seen today. Seven also features in days of celebration, as in seven days after the birth of a son or daughter in ancient times, the seven days of the wedding feast, and the seven days of shiva after a death, the last two of which are still done.

Several of the rites of passage appropriately act out a ritualized "journey" from one place and status to another. The baby is brought from his mother to the male gathering for the circumcision, either in a different part of the house or at the synagogue. The boy who is to begin his schooling is wrapped like a Torah scroll and carried from his mother's domain at home to the male world of the schoolteacher and future male classmates. The bride is marched in torchlight procession from her father's house to the wedding and to the new home with the groom and her new family. And in the end, the body is accompanied through town, also with lighted torches, from the place of purification to the grave site.

The transformation from a natural to a cultured stage of being is often indicated by gestures of removal or cutting. The newborn boy is circumcised and made into a perfect Jewish male; the long curly hair of a girl-like boy of three is cut for the first time, creating the sidelocks (pe'ot) of an Ultra-Orthodox Jewish boy. The wedding ceremony is completed with the breaking of a glass and the sexual consummation of the rite. And mourners tear their garment and rip up grass and throw it behind them at a funeral.

At other times, an act of addition makes the difference. The boy goes to school for the first time and is fed cakes and other special Torah foods; the bar mitzvah boy starts to wrap himself in the leather straps of tefillin; the groom gives the bride a ring or equivalent to bond them together; family and friends feed mourners during the shiva and male mourners grow beards; a monument is erected over the grave that was part of a field before.

Sometimes gestures that are originally more appropriate for one rite are transferred to another, suggesting that the latter is metaphorically or symbolically like the former. Wedding customs, like throwing grain at the bride and groom, a wish for fertility, becomes throwing candy at the bar mitzvah boy when he is honored in the synagogue. The transferred setting creates a new mixed symbol of early adolescence: childish candy combined with the hint of future sexual activity and fertility. Similarly, raising the bar mizvah boy on a chair at the party is an echo of the more traditional elevation of the bride and groom at the wedding celebration. Holding the bar mitzvah ceremony under a four-poled canopy, as at outdoor weddings, at Israeli historical outdoor locations, such as on the mountain fortress of Masada, also points to the wedding.

A remarkable number of wedding customs incorporate mourning practices. The ancient belief that demons lurk about when people celebrate joyous events underlies many of these adaptations, but other rationales developed as well, emphasizing the seriousness of the occasion. Before the modern fashion requiring a bride to wear a white wedding gown, Jewish grooms and brides wore white as a reminder of death and humility; the groom wore ashes on his forehead; the bride and groom may fast on the day of the wedding, as on the day of a funeral; the tallit may be used to cover the bride and groom and is used as part of a man's burial shroud.

Although Jews performed many of these rites by internalizing aspects of non-Jewish rites that they saw all around them, most also represent a Jewish adaptation or reinterpretation of earlier Jewish practices or literary motifs. The midrashic or elaborative quality of Jewish rites of passage evidences how Jewish life has evolved over the centuries in many new directions, while at the same time remaining recognizably Jewish, even biblical. As part of the dynamic of Jewish cultural persistence, we find metaphoric and symbolic expansions of ancient themes, not literal continuity. For example, the biblical notion of covering the bride and groom in a huppah evolved from a tent, into a bridal chamber, then into a garment draped over their heads, before it became the familiar four-poled canopy, sometimes combined with one or more of the other acted-out interpretations.

The history of Jewish life cycle rites illustrates the fact that Jews have not been dry literalists. Rather, they have followed the muses of biblical examples, rabbinical prodding to sanctify important events with words and gestures of gratitude, the colorations of Christian and Muslim cultures, and the individualism of modern lifestyles.

As a result, each age has contributed important rites of passage or stages in their development. Our own time is no exception. In the nineteenth and twentieth centuries, we see emerge not only different kinds of bat mitzvah rites as gestures for young girls to mark their coming of age religiously as Jews, but the diffusion of the bar mitzvah ceremony as well as a Jewish adaptation of the goal of continued adolescent religious education in various forms of a Jewish confirmation ceremony during high school years. This emphasis especially among non-Orthodox Jews on bar and bat mitzvah suggests the importance in modern times of choices being made by a culture in which people are approaching the age of decision making. It is a culture of youth movements, summer camps, afternoon or day schools, trips to Israel or eastern Europe.

The cutting edge of innovation among the Ultra-Orthodox lies elsewhere. Often thought to be conservative practitioners of ancient customs and rites, an entirely new custom has developed at the very end of the twentieth century, and it emphasizes the beginnings of a small boy's religious schooling at age three. The new ceremony combines the independently developed customs associated with the first haircut of a boy of three and the first time a boy learns the letters of the Hebrew alphabet. Before the 1980s Jews did not combine the two early childhood initiations into a single ceremony. Ultra-Orthodox Jews in Brooklyn and Israel innovated by doing this. If a small child can be attracted to Judaism by associating learning with honey and other symbolic sweets, the child will be encouraged to stay in school and grow up in the Torah.

So far boys. What about girls and women in Judaism? No movement within modern times has had the effect that the women's movement has had on all parts of the Jewish religious spectrum. As a litmus test of Jewish cultural vitality, life cycle innovations mark the impact the changing role of women has had in modern Jewish practice. This is true of Orthodox and non-Orthodox Jewish women alike.

Orthodox Jewish women are experimenting with new kinds of prayer services that include women being called to the Torah and reading the Torah. Some are all-female services; others are in services where men are seated separately. These changes are transforming the Orthodox bat mitzvah celebration, which now usually consists of a learned Torah talk delivered at a festive meal, into a liturgical rite that will resemble the bar mitzvah setting.

If ritual innovation is a measure of a culture's vitality, then the study of Jewish rites of passage should make one hesitate before throwing up one's hands in despair over the future of the present Jewish community.

Glossary

All terms are Hebrew unless specified otherwise.

Aron. Coffin, traditionally made of plain pine.

Aufruf. Call up [to read the Torah]. German/ Yiddish. Honor a groom receives the Shabbat before the wedding. *See* Shabbat Hatan; Spinholtz.

Aveil/Aveilah. Mourner. The child, spouse, sibling, or parent of one who dies.

Ba'al Brit/Ba'alat Brit. *See* Sandeq.

Bar Mitzvah. Obligated male. Came to mean a boy of thirteen years and a day who becomes religiously obligated for the first time to perform the commandments of Judaism.

Bat Mitzvah. Obligated female. Girl obligated to perform the commandments of Judaism from either age twelve years and a day or thirteen years and a day. A modern term based on Bar Mitzvah.

Bedeken. Yiddish: Covering that veils the bride prior to the marriage ceremony.

Bentcher. To bentch; Yiddish, from Latin. Booklet of blessings, including Grace after Meals, with special phrases used at a meal after a wedding or circumcision; to recite Grace after Meals.

Brit Banot. Covenant for daughters. Recent experimental rites to provide a baby girl with a religious initiation into Judaism.

Brit Milah. Covenant of circumcision. Rite of circumcision.

Confirmation. Jewish rites inspired either by Catholic sacrament, as in Italy, or by Protestant theological training, as in Protestant Europe and the United States, to provide an initiation of teenagers into Judaism; often held on the feast of Shavuot (Pentecost).

Erusin (also known as Qiddushin). Betrothal. The groom symbolically acquires a bride by giving her a token, observed by two proper witnesses. Breaking it off requires a religious divorce; before cohabitation, the additional ceremony of nesu'in (marriage) is required.

Get. Bill of divorcement. Document a Jewish husband has written out for his wife in a rite if their marriage is terminated.

Halaqa. Arabic: Haircut. *See* Upsherenish.

Hasan's Tisch. Yiddish: Groom's Table. Celebration of male relatives and friends of the groom, who study, sing, drink, and eat together in a private room prior to the wedding ceremony. If there are formal tena'im, this is when they are signed and the mothers-in-law break a plate; the witnesses sign the ketubbah. *See* Kallah's Tisch; Tena'im; Ketubbah.

Hesped. Eulogy at a funeral.

Hevra Qadisha. Aramaic: Holy society. Especially a group of pious men and women volunteers who are trained to wash and dress the bodies of Jewish men and women, respectively, prior to burial.

Hollekreisch. German: Crying "Holle." German custom of giving a boy or girl a secular name by having young boys or girls raise the month-old infant in the cradle three times while screaming out "Hollekreisch" each time.

Huppah. Overhead covering. By sixteenth-century Germany, an open four-poled canopy under which wedding ceremony takes place.

Kaddish. Sanctified. Here refers to specific text used by mourners and other Jews on the anniversary of a parent's death. A special version is often recited at the graveside.

Kallah's Tisch. Yiddish: Bride's table. Private celebration of female relatives and friends of the bride, who may sing, study, drink, and eat together, prior to the wedding ceremony.

Kefatter. Yiddish: Godfather. Secondary honor at brit, given to a male relative or friend. *See* Sandeq.

Kefatterin. Yiddish: Godmother. Honor at brit, given to female relative or friend.

Ketubbah. Written document. Pre-nuptial agreement a groom gives his bride during the wedding ceremony, in which he agrees to give her a certain amount of property if the marriage ends by either his death or their divorce due to no fault of hers.

Kittel. German/Yiddish: White outer garment. Worn by some grooms and by some male Jews on holiest days of the year.

Klezmer. Yiddish (from Hebrew: *kelei zemer:* musical instruments). Wedding musicians. Eastern Europe, revived in late twentieth century as de rigueur at traditional weddings.

Knasmahl. Penalty meal. Ceremony at arrangement/engagement (shiddukhin), where document (tena'im) is signed, with penalties if marriage is canceled, and marked by future mothers-in-law breaking a plate together.

Lilith. Demon jealous of newborns; amulet written to protect newborn son and mother from Lilith, especially before the brit.

Mohel. One who performs a brit.

Nesu'in. Marriage. Second stage of betrothal-marriage ceremonies. Husband and wife now live together as a married couple. *See* Erusin.

Onein. A person who has not yet buried a close relative who has just died.

Pidyon ha-Ben: Redeeming the son. Ceremony for a specially defined firstborn son on the thirty-first day after his birth. A Kohen releases the child back to his parents in return for a symbolic payment of redemption, traditionally five units of money.

Qeriyah. Tearing [a garment]. A mourner's symbolic rending of a garment just before the funeral.

Qiddushin. *See* Erusin; Nesu'in.

Sandeq (Greek); **Ba'al Brit** (Hebrew). Godfather. Primary male honoree at brit. Usually holds the infant securely on his lap during the surgical part of the rite. Prior to the late thirteenth century, women also could receive this honor (ba'alat brit).

Seder ha-Hatunah (plural: sidrei hatunah). Wedding program. Proposed Hebrew name for the pamphlet that brides and grooms prepare, containing the order of the wedding procession and the sequence of the parts of the wedding day.

Shabbat Hatan. Groom's Sabbath. Special Shabbat before or after the wedding. The groom is called to the Torah and candy is thrown on him. *See* Aufruf; Spinholtz.

Shadkhan. Marriage broker who arranges matches for a fee.

Shalom Zakhar. Party for a boy. Ashkenazic name for celebration in the home, usually the Friday evening after the birth of a son, at which there is study and refreshments are served. *See* Zeved ha-Bat.

Sheloshim. Thirty. The thirty days of mourning for close relatives. Parents are mourned for an additional eleven months; siblings, spouses, and children for only thirty days.

Shemirah. Watching. The vigil over the body prior to the funeral. A candle burns and Psalms are recited.

Sheva Berakhot. Seven blessings. Seven blessings recited during the marriage ceremony (nesu'in); the seven festive meals during the week after the marriage, at which the seven blessings are recited during the Grace after Meals.

Shevu'a ha-Ben. Week for the Son. Talmudic week of celebrating after a boy is born; was misunderstood in medieval times as celebration for the brit, which takes place a week after the birth.

Shevu'a ha-Bat. Week for the Daughter. Week of celebrating after a girl is born. Not clear when observed.

Shiddukh. Yiddish: A brokered marriage. A good match, regardless of how it came about.

Shiddukhin. Arrangements. From Talmudic times on, the practice of parents coming to a written agreement that their children would marry. *See* Tena'im.

Shiva. Seven. The first seven days of mourning at home, where people come to comfort the mourner.

Simhat ha-Bat. Joy over a daughter. Sefardic custom to name a girl in the home at a party celebrating her birth.

Spinholtz. Unknown. German. Early name for aufruf.

Taharah. Purification and washing. Preparing the body for the funeral and burial.

Takhrikhin. Shrouds. White garments in which the body is dressed.

Tena'im. Conditions. Pre-nuptial agreement written between families of the bride and groom, stipulating payments if the engagement is terminated. *See* Ketubbah.

Upsherenish. (often pronounced "upsheren"). Yiddish: Haircut. First haircut of a Jewish boy, usually after he reaches his third birthday.

Vidui. Confession on deathbed.

Wachnacht. German: Night watch. A meal and nightlong visit to the home of a mother the night before the brit of her son; developed to protect the mother and child from harm.

Wimpel. Yiddish: Binder. Cloth binding in which baby is wrapped during circumcision; used again to wrap Torah at his bar mitzvah. Early modern Germany. Boy's name and designs alluding to life cycle are embroidered on it. After the brit, it is stored in the synagogue.

Yahrzeit. German/Yiddish: Time of the year. Anniversary of the death of a parent. Customary to fast, recite mourning prayers, and light a Yahrzeit lamp that burns all day.

Yizkor. Prayer beginning "May He remember," recited in synagogue four times a year to remember family dead and Jewish martyrs.

Zeved ha-Bat. Gift of a daughter. Sefardic name for celebration in the home the Friday evening following the birth of a daughter. There is study and refreshments are served.

Notes

INTRODUCTION

1. Patterson, *Negotiating the Past.* I am also grateful to David Roskies for helping me come to this formulation.

2. Marcus, *Rituals of Childhood,* chap. 1.

3. B. Megillah 9b.

4. See Cohen and Horowitz, "In Search of the Sacred"; Marcus, "Jewish-Christian Symbiosis"; and Valensi, "Religious Orthodoxy," for the argument that Jews and Christians in medieval Christian Europe (Cohen and Horowitz, Marcus) as well as in the Muslim world (Valensi) lived side by side on close terms with one another, not in segregated areas. For the important notion of a common "vernacular tradition," see Valensi, "Religious Orthodoxy," 67.

5. A case study is Marcus, *Rituals of Childhood.*

6. Schwartz, *Imperialism.* On cultural hybridity, see Bhabha, *Location of Culture;* Boyarin, *Dying for God;* and Young, *Colonial Desire.*

7. See the examples in Marcus, "Jewish-Christian Symbiosis."

8. Unless I specify the Babylonian or Jerusalem Talmud, the word by itself refers to both.

9. Cohen, "Blessing of Assimilation." The argument is better under-

stood if we substitute the term "(inward) acculturation" for Cohen's more provocative "assimilation," which is the burden of this introduction and book.

10. See Silber, "Emergence of Ultra-Orthodoxy"; Soloveitchik, "Rupture"; Friedman, *Ha-Hevrah ha-Hareidit;* and Dan, "Ultra-Orthodoxy."

11. On body gestures in Judaism, see Zimmer, "Body Gestures"; Ehrlich, *"Kol 'Azmotai."*

12. On various schemas of age division, see Löw, *Lebensalter,* 26–36; and cf. Sears, *Ages of Man.*

13. See Kugel, *Great Poems,* 311, who prefers the literal meaning of the Hebrew, but it is not parallel to the second part of the line, which refers to dying, not killing or ending life.

14. Num. 1:3; 26:2–4; see, too, Num. 14:29; 32:11; Ezra 3:8; 1 Chron. 23:24, 27;2 Chron. 25:5; 31:17.

15. See, too, Exod. 38:26.

16. T. Megillah 3 (4): 15, 357.

17. B. Shabbat 129b.

18. B. Gittin 65a; and see B. Sukah 42b.

19. *Eivel Rabbati* (= *Masekhet Semahot*) 3:1–8; *Tractate Mourning,* trans. Zlotnick, 5–6 (Hebrew) and 37–39 (English).

20. *Qohelet Rabbah* 1:2, translated up to the stage of old age in Kraemer, "Images of Childhood," 76–77, which I have slightly modified.

21. *Living Talmud,* ed. and trans. Goldin, 222.

22. Abraham Ibn Ezra, "Ben adamah yizkor be-moladeto," in *Shirei ha-Qodesh,* ed. Levin, 2:544, lines 23–38; and Schirmann, *Ha-Shirah ha-'Ivrit,* 1:2, 589–90, lines 23–43, translated in Talmage, "So Teach Us to Number Our Days," 59–60. See, too, Shemuel Ha-Nagid, in Schirmann, *Ha-Shirah ha-'Ivrit,* 1:132, reprinted and translated in Scheindlin, *Wine,* 165, and R. Isaac b. Yedaiah's scheme that correlates seven human decades with seven millennia of world history in Saperstein, *Decoding the Rabbis,* 114–16.

23. Shakespeare, *As You Like It,* 2.7.139–66, 857.

24. See, e.g., Shemuel Ha-Nagid's poem, "she'ei minni" refuting a critic who chastises him for serving a human king, instead of God, in Schirmann, *Ha-Shirah ha-'Ivrit,* 1:109–11, and translated in Cole, *Selected Poems,* 49–51.

25. B. Qiddushin 29a; *Mekhilta de-Rabbi Yishmael,* Bo, Pisha 18; *Sefer ha-Aggadah,* 635:238.

26. See Chap. 1.

27. van Gennep, *Rites of Passage.*

28. Pardes, *Biography.*

29. *Sefer Minhagim.* See Wolfthal, "Imaging the Self"; [Zotenberg], *Catalogues.*

30. Pollack, "Historical Explanation."

31. Carlebach, *Divided Souls.*

32. Yaakov Deutsch, of the Hebrew University, is researching this subject.

33. Cf., e.g., the order in *Mahzor Vitry* (mourning comes after fasts, and, later on, betrothal and marriage are followed by circumcision, and schooling); *Tanya Rabbati,* pars. 89–91 (marriage) and pars. 92–100 (children); Juda Löw Kirchheim, *Minhagot Vermaiza,* 78–82 (marriage), and 82–86 (children); Shalom mi-Neustadt, *Halakhot u-Minhagim,* 206–18, for the same order; Yuspa Shamash, *Minhagim,* etc.; Leon Modena, *History of the Rites,* pt. 4 (marriage, then birth); pt. 5 (death), on the one hand, and the order in Bodenschatz, *Kirchliche Verfassung,* pt. 4, chaps. 3 (birth), 4 (marriage), and 5 (death), and Kirchner, *Jüdisches Ceremoniel,* same, etc., on the other. Exceptions are the sequence, circumcision, and marriage, in *Seder Rav 'Amram Gaon,* 179–82, and birth, marriage, and death in Rabbi Aaron ben Jacob Ha-Kohen of Lunel, *Sefer Orhot Hayyim,* pt. 2.

34. Hsia, "Christian Ethnography of Jews"; Carlebach, *Divided Souls,* 178–79.

35. Burnett, *From Christian Hebraism,* 55–102; Cohen, "Leone da Modena's *Riti,*" 292–93.

36. Cohen, "Leone da Modena's *Riti*"; and Cohen, *Jewish Icons,* 28.

37. Cohen, *Jewish Icons,* 34–43, on Romeyn de Hooghe's drawing, "Circumcision in a Sephardic Family" (1668); Johannes Leusden's engraving of a circumcision in *Philologus Hebraeo-Mixtus* (1682); and Jan Luyken's etching, "The Circumcision," published in the Dutch edition of Leon Modena, *Historia de' riti hebraici* (1683).

38. On Picart, see Cohen, *Jewish Icons,* 43–52.

38. Cohen, "Leone da Modena's *Riti,*" 288; and Carlebach, *Divided Souls,* 205–9.

40. Cohen, *Jewish Icons,* 52–66.

41. Güdemann, *Geschichte des Erziehungswesens,* which deserves to be translated into English; Lauterbach, *Studies in Jewish Law;* Gutmann, "Christian Influences"; and Ta-Shema, *Minhag Ashkenaz.*

42. *Jewish Catalogue.*

43. See, too, Rubin, *Tiqsei Leidah,* and his *Qeiz ha-Hayyim.*

44. See, e.g., Grossman, *Hasidot u-Moredot;* Baumgarten, "Imahot," *Mothers;* Kraemer, *Meanings of Death.*

45. On the invention of Ultra-Orthodoxy, see esp. the brilliant essay by Michael Silber, cited earlier (see n. 10 above).

1 / BIRTH, "BRIS," SCHOOLING

1. See de Vaux, *Ancient Israel,* 1:24; *Ancient Near Eastern Texts,* 172, par. 138.

2. See Grimes, *Deeply,* 16. For later examples of Jewish birthing amulets, see Sabar, "Childbirth and Magic."

3. Baumgarten, *Mothers,* 48–49; and Matras, "Contemporary Amulets." On birth magic, e.g., B. Sotah 22a. For Christian practices, Orme, *Medieval Children,* 16 and 65n75. On Lilith, see below.

4. Cassuto, "Avnayim. 1:58–59.

5. Ibid., 1:58.

6. See the illustrations from sixteenth- and seventeenth-century England in Cressy, *Birth, Marriage and Death,* 52–53.

7. de Vaux, *Ancient Israel,* 1:42, doubts that this is what the text means, but that is what it says.

8. B. Niddah 31b.

9. See M. Shabbat 18:3 and B. Shabbat 128b; M. Rosh ha-Shanah (*hakhamah*); M. Niddah 10:5; Bava Qama 59a, B. Sotah 11b (*hayyah*). On medieval Jewish and Christian midwives, see Baumgarten, *Mothers,* 43–54.

10. M. Shabbat 18:3. For midwives in later Jewish history and the expertise women acquired in deliveries, see Baumgarten, "'So Say the Expert Midwives.'"

11. The passage from Ezekiel is discussed in B. Shabbat 129b and translated in Cooper, *Child,* 12. On abandonment, see Boswell, *Kindness.*

12. Boswell, *Kindness,* 146n27; Cooper, *Child,* 13; Morgenstern, *Rites of Birth,* 8–9, 13–14 and 196–98n27.

13. On salt in magic, see Trachtenberg, *Jewish Magic,* 160–61.

14. B. Niddah 31a.

15. Shahar, *Childhood,* 41; Baumgarten, *Mothers,* 52; Orme, *Medieval Children,* 28.

16. For the Christian practice, see Shahar, *Childhood,* 85–88, and Alexandre-Bidon and Closson, *L'enfant à l'ombre des cathédrales,* 94–99.

17. For 'arisah, see T. Makkot 2:4 ("tinnoq ba-'arisah ve-yashav 'alav ve-harago"); B. Shabbat 58b.

18. *Mahzor Vitry,* 628.

19. See, e.g., T. Shabbat 6:2, 22–25; Blau, *Altjüdische Zauberwesen;* and Trachtenberg, *Jewish Magic.*

20. Blau, *Altjüdische Zauberwesen.*

21. See Rosman, *Founder of Hasidism.*

22. See Schauss, *Lifetime,* 21; *Sefer Raziel.*

23. Josephus, *Against Apion,* 2:25.

24. B. Gittin 57a.

25. Y. Ketubbot 1:5, 25c, 958; B. Sanhedrin 32b; Rashi on B. Bava Batra 60b s.v. "le-shevu'a ha-ben": "milah (circumcision), which takes place after seven [days]," and Rashi on B. Bava Qama 80a s.v. "shevu'a ha-ben."

26. We do not know when he got that name or why. In twelfth-century sources he is called "Our Rabbi Jacob" (rabbeinu ya'aqov). Why he came to be called "Rabbeinu Tam" and not, for example, RIBAM, the acronym for Rabbi Jacob ben Meir, in keeping with the way other medieval rabbis were known, is not clear. It was equivalent to calling him "Saint Jacob." Rashi's acronym, too, is an exception, since it should have been RaSHBI, Rabbi Shlomo ben Yizhaq. One possible reason Rabbeinu Tam's name was linked to the partriarch Jacob's (and Job's) epithet of being innocent (*tam*)

is the story claiming he was attacked by crusaders in his house in Ramerupt and was nearly martyred there. See Marcus, "Jewish-Christian Symbiosis," 493–95.

27. Tosafot to B. Bava Qama 80a, s.v. "le-vei yeshu'a ha-ben."

28. See, e.g., *Masekhet Semahot,* supplement, 231; and the references in Hoffman, *Covenant,* 177–79.

29. Löw, *Lebensalter,* 89; Bergmann, "Schebua ha-ben"; and Mann, "Rabbinic Studies," 325n3.

30. *Midrash Ruth Rabbah* 6:6; *Midrash Qohelet Rabbah* 3:4, etc.; Schauss, *Lifetime,* 25–27.

31. *Pirqei de-Rabbi Eliezer,* chap. 29, 65a–65b, trans. Friedlander, 207–8, and the reading by Rabbeinu Tam in Tosafot to B. Berakhot 130a s.v. "sas anokhi"; *Midrash Tehillim,* 468, cited in Baumgarten, *Mothers,* 2172n34, and *Midrash on Psalms,* trans. Braude, 211; *Tanya Rabbati sec.* 96, 101b. All of these texts are from Byzantine early medieval Palestine or southern Italy. The proof text is also quoted in *Mahzor Vitry,* par. 506, 627, right after mentioning the new custom that the ba'al brit provides a meal in the home the night before the brit.

32. Israel Isserlein, *Terumat ha-Deshen,* 1:269, 49c, quoted by Isserles, on *Shulhan 'Arukh,* Yoreh De'ah 265:12. See B. Niddah 31b for the teaching about boys and peace; Schauss, *Lifetime,* 56. It is not clear how old either term is for the Friday night celebration after a boy is born.

33. See Dobrinsky, *Treasury,* 11 and 20 (home), and cf. 3–4 and 25 (synagogue). My thanks to Sol Steinmetz. Texts and some customs can be found in Cohen, *Zeved ha-Bat.*

34. For the custom in eastern Europe to weigh a child each year on his or her birthday and to give the equivalent amount of bread to the poor, see Schauss, *Lifetime,* 80–81.

35. See Chap. 4.

36. B. Mo'ed Qatan 28a.

37. Rabbi Joseph ben Moses, *Sefer Leqet Yosher,* 2:40. Zimmels, *Ashkenazim,* 166. For seventy, see Bacharach, *Havvat Ya'ir,* 1:214, par. 70, cited in Ta-Shema, "Jewish Birthday," 21n10, but it is not clear from the text itself that this custom was "widespread in his time" (ibid.).

38. See Ariès, *Centuries,* 16–17, cited by Baumgarten, "Imahot," 323; and Orme, *Medieval Children,* 48.

39. See Rabbi Menahem ben Shlomo, *Midrash Sekhel Tov;* Vayeshev, chap. 40, 2:247; Baumgarten, "Imahot," 323, citing oral communication from Israel Ta-Shema; and Ta-Shema, "Jewish Birthday," 21.

40. E.g., see Rabbi Joseph Hayyim ben Elijah (al-Hakam), *Sefer Ben Ish Hai,* Re'eh, 291, who says, "some are accustomed to make a holiday on their birthday. It is a good thing and we do it in our family." He also says there that some hold a feast on the anniversary of their circumcision. He approves but says members of his family do not do it.

41. See Shamgar-Handelman and Handelman, "Celebrations of Bureaucracy."

42. Interview on August 14, 2000, with informant who was born in Warsaw.

43. See Ta-Shema, "Jewish Birthday," who does not consider why some pagan practices were avoided and others were adopted into Jewish practice. It is not enough to refer to rabbinic legal norms and definitions to explain Jewish behavior, since Jews did not necessarily follow norms, either as biblical Israelites or since. For one attempt to deal with this complex issue, see Katz, *Exclusiveness and Tolerance,* and next note.

44. Goitein, *Mediterranean Society,* 5:27–28 and 512n82. Cf. Ta-Shema, "Jewish Birthday."

45. Baumgarten, *Mothers,* 53.

46. See Klein, *Guide,* 421–24. The stages of the operation are referred to in the context of doing them on the Sabbath in M. Shabbat 19:2 and B. Shabbat 133a, 137a–b, where the blessings are also found. See, too, the medieval manual, Rabbi Jacob Ha-Gozer, *Zikhron Brit Rishonim.*

47. Grimes, *Deeply,* 19.

48. See Belmont, "Levana," 1–2.

49. Lynch, *Godparents,* 126.

50. See Macrides, "Byzantine Godfather"; Lynch, *Godparents,* 117–40; and Baumgarten, *Mothers,* 55–91.

51. See Ben-Yehudah, *Millon,* 2839 s.v. "mohel"; Rabbi Jacob ben Asher, *Arba'ah Turim,* Yoreh De'ah 264, par. 2.

52. B. Shabbat 135a (singular); 156a (plural); B. Shabbat 130b ("ha-gozer"); and see B. Bava Batra 21a: "rofei," which Rashi glosses, "mohel."

53. Karo, *Shulhan 'Arukh,* Yoreh De'ah 264:1 (Beit Yosef), who cites Rabbi Isaac Alfasi (eleventh-century Spain and North Africa) and Rabbi Asher ben Yehiel (Germany and Spain, early fourteenth century) as the authority for his ruling. See B. 'Avodah Zarah 27a.

54. E.g., Rabbi Eliezer ben Joel Halevi (Raviah), *Sefer Raviah* 1:360, in thirteenth-century Germany, circumcised his own son.

55. Wensinck, "Khitan," 20–22.

56. de Vaux, *Ancient Israel,* 147. See Ben-Yehudah, *Millon,* 2:1827, s.v. "hatan"; and Wensinck, "Khitan."

57. de Vaux, *Ancient Israel,* 147; Propp, "Origins"; idem, "Bloody Bridegroom."

58. Samuel Cooper, comments at luncheon workshop of Department of Sociology, Hebrew University of Jerusalem, 1996, and "Laws of Mixtures," 69; *Pirqei de-Rabbi Eliezer,* chap. 29, 64b, trans. Friedlander, 206–7; Bilu, "From Circumcision to Word," 22.

59. Heilman, *Defenders of the Faith,* 134 and below.

60. *Avot de-Rabbi Natan,* chap. 2, 6b; *Fathers,* trans. Goldin, 22–23, who also cites M. Nedarim 3:11.

61. On classical authors and early Christian writers on circumcision, see Cohen, *Beginnings,* esp. 39–49, 363–77. Only one source in antiquity refers to Jewish female circumcision in Egypt, and there is no evidence that it was practiced. See Strabo, *Geography,* 16.2.37=16.4.9=17.2.5, in Stern, *Authors,* nos. 115, 118, 124=I:300, 312, 315; Cohen, *Beginnings,* 39n48; and Goitein, *Mediterranean Society,* 3:233.

62. Ta-Shema, "Blessing on Circumcision," 331n13.

63. *Mahzor Vitry,* pars. 502, 506, cited in Baumgarten, *Mothers,* 99. See Horowitz, "Eve of Circumcision."

64. Baumgarten, *Mothers,* 99–100.

65. On Frau Holle in medieval Europe, see Kummer, "Frau Holle," and other sources mentioned in Baumgarten, *Mothers,* 97–99; Trachtenberg, *Jewish Magic,* 42.

66. See Schauss, *Lifetime,* 309n49.

67. Scholem, "Lilith"; Dan, "Samael, Lilith"; Brill, *Lilith;* Hurwitz, *Lilith;* and Baumgarten, *Mothers,* 99–100.

68. See Trachtenberg, *Jewish Magic,* 101; Leon Modena, *History of the Rites,* 4.8.1, 201; Wengeroff, *Memoiren,* 1:107.

69. Information provided, early 2002, by Judith R. Marcus, M.D.

70. See T. Berakhot 6:12, 37; Y. Berakhot 9:3 14a, 73; Lieberman, *Tosefta Ki-Feshuta,* Zeraim, 114; B. Shabbat 137b and *Diqduqei Sofrim,* Shabbat, 320, on that passage; *Seder Rav 'Amram Gaon,* 179. Rabbeinu Tam reads: "as he [the father] entered him," still referring to the father, not the baby. As Hoffman, *Covenant,* 79–80, points out, the last phrase, "and good deeds," which is syntactically awkward in a series governed by the verb "to enter" (what does it mean to enter good deeds?), is not original.

71. See Baumgarten, *Mothers,* 65–70, on *Midrash Tehillim,* Psalm 35, sec. 2, 248; *Midrash on Psalms,* trans. Braude, 1:414. "I become a godfather [syndiknos] to children who are circumcised on my knees"; and Macrides, "The Byzantine Godfather." "Ba'al brit" is common in the twelfth through the fifteenth centuries, as in *Mahzor Vitry,* par. 506 (ba'al brit); Eleazar ben Judah, *Sefer ha-Roqeah,* par. 108, who explains the strange Greek term in *Midrash Tehillim* with ba'al brit, which was the more familiar term to him. That women served as *ba'alot brit,* see Baumgarten, *Mothers,* 70–77; Spiegel, "The Woman as Circumciser."

72. *Pirqei de-Rabbi Eliezer,* chap. 29; trans. Friedlander, 214. Hoffman, *Covenant,* 73.

73. Schauss, *Lifetime,* 34–37. For Christian descriptions, see Lasker, "Transubstantiation," 32–33, quoting Yom Tov Lipmann Muehlhausen (Prague, 1400), and see Addison, *Present State,* 62: "Upon the day when Circumcision is celebrated, there are two seats set close by the Ark in the Synagogue; the one for Elias whose presence they still expect at this Solemnity, and another for the Baal-Brit, or Godfather." For illustrations of double seats and small raised seats, see Sabar, *Birth, Childhood, and Bar-Mitzvah,* 44–53. On the relationship between the two, see Jacoby, "Relation."

74. *Pirqei de-Rabbi Eliezer,* 29, and see *Ha-Hilluqim,* ed. Margaliot, no. 17, 80–81 and 125–27; Rabbi Isaac ben Moses of Vienna, *Sefer Or Zaru'a,* vol. 2, sec. 107, 27b; *Shulhan 'Arukh,* Yoreh De'ah 265:10; Addison, *Present*

State, 63: "The Foreskin being cut off, the Mohel casts it into the dish of Sand"; Sperber, *Minhagei Yisrael,* [1]:90–94.

75. For a female as *ba'alat brit,* see Baumgarten, *Mothers,* 70–77. For medieval German descriptions of the ceremony; see Schauss, *Lifetime,* 40–43.

76. Lynch, *Godparents,* 6.

77. Ruderman, *World of a Renaissance Jew,* 28.

78. Bonfil, *Jewish Life in Renaissance Italy,* 251–52; and cf. Leon Modena, *History of the Rites,* 4.8.6–7, 205–6, with some variations.

79. *Mahzor Vitry,* 628. The verse in Ezra ends with the phrase, "Torah of *Moses.*"

80. Gendler, "Sarah's Seed," 73; Orenstein, *Lifecycles,* 53–82; and Cohen, *Celebrating Your New Jewish Daughter.*

81. Ner-David, *Life on the Fringes,* 26–27.

82. See esp. Lauterbach, "Naming."

83. See Noth, *Israelitischen Personennamen,* 63; and Meek, *Hebrew Origins,* 32–33.

84. Porten, *Archives,* 235–36.

85. See Schauss, *Lifetime,* 27–29, 43–44. Early examples of names repeating from grandfather to grandson are the Hasmoneans and rabbis claiming descent from Hillel the Elder, M. Avot, passim.

86. Zimmels, *Ashkenazim,* 165; Lauterbach, "Naming."

87. Cf. Grimes, *Deeply,* 44, for the Muslim *aqiqah* naming ceremony after a child is seven days old, though circumcision in Islam can take place any time from one week to thirteen years.

88. See the qualifications in Cohen, *Beginnings,* 39–49. Still, of all the commandments of Judaism that are chosen for polemical discussion in the earliest Christian writings, Paul's Letters, circumcision is discussed frequently and reinterpreted as a spiritual, rather than physical, sign.

89. Cohen, *Beginnings,* 39–40.

90. Schwartz, *Imperialism,* 109–10.

91. See B. Shabbat 134a.

92. *Pirqei de-Rabbi Eliezer,* chap. 48; trans. Friedlander, 378.

93. See *Seder Rav 'Amram Gaon,* 178; *Siddur R. Saadja Gaon,* 99, and the

notes there to the Hebrew prayer, beginning with the words, "Qayyem et ha-yeled" (Keep alive this boy), in which the boy is publicly named for the first time. This prayer replaced an Aramaic text for the health of the mother, as found in prayer books of Amram and Saadia. On the texts, see Hoffman, *Covenant.*

94. See a new weaning rite in Orenstein, *Lifecycles,* 272–75. This is a return to a biblical tradition; *Mahzor Vitry,* par. 506, 626.

95. Lev. 12:1–8; Jubilees 3:8–14. For rabbinic times, see M. Niddah 3:7; and Schauss, *Lifetime,* 18–19.

96. M. Sheqalim 6:5; M. Sotah 1:5; B. Eruvin 32a; Löw, *Lebensalter,* 111; Zimmer, "Days of Impurity."

97. See Orme, *Medieval Children,* 31–33.

98. B. Niddah 31b.

99. Löw, *Lebensalter,* 104.

100. Moses ben Isaac Mintz, *Teshuvot,* no. 19, fol. 19b–19c; and see no. 64, fol. 60d; Löw, *Lebensalter,* 389n98. See Schauss, *Lifetime,* 46–47; Hamburger, *Shorashei Minhag Ashkenaz,* 1:415–55.

101. Löw, *Lebensalter,* 105; Schauss, *Lifetime,* 45; Pollack, *Jewish Folkways,* 27–28 and notes.

102. Marcus, *Rituals of Childhood,* 77, 124; Kirshenblatt-Gimblett, "Cut That Binds," 138–39; Goldberg, "Torah and Children," 112; Sperber, *Minhagei Yisrael* 2:197; Orme, *Medieval Children,* 33; Hamburger, *Shorashei Minhag Ashkenaz* 2:322–604; Feuchtwanger-Sarig, "Torah Binders from Denmark," and "'May He Grow to Torah.'"

103. In the Bible, the recording of firstborn males is to take place at the thirtieth day, as in Num. 3:40. See, too, Num. 8:14–17.

104. B. Bekhorot 51b; Rubin, "Price of Redemption." The rite takes place on the thirty-first day so that a full thirty days after the first have elapsed.

105. B. Pesahim 121b.

106. Jacob ben Moses Ha-Levi Molin, *Sefer Maharil, Minhagim,* 489–93; on pidyon ha-bat, see Isaacs, *Rites of Passage,* 56–59, for a description and liturgical texts.

107. Kafka, "Before the Law," 392–93, emphasis added.

108. For the texts, see Marcus, *Rituals of Childhood,* chap. 1, and the

illumination, fig. 3 above p. 70; Marcus, "Honey Cakes and Torah"; for additional allusions to the ceremony preserved in Hebrew manuscripts, see Marcus, "Jewish-Christian Symbiosis." My thanks to Drs. Elisheva Baumgarten and Ephraim Shoham-Steiner, who called these manuscripts to my attention.

109. For honey and wisdom in antiquity, see the references to Philo in Schneider, "'Joseph and Osnat,'" 330. My thanks to Moshe Idel and Michael Schneider. The other sources are noted in Marcus, *Rituals of Childhood,* 53–73. On metaphor and ritual, see Fernandez, "Performance of Ritual Metaphors."

110. For the expression "the Torah of our ancestors is valid" (minhag ovoteinu torah hi), see Ta-Shema, *Minhag Ashkenaz,* 28–29; Sperber, *Minhagei Yisrael,* 4:275–76; and cf. Ta-Shema, "Rite of Initiation," 597, who reduces the phrase to an autobiographical comment, without offering any evidence.

111. The entire alphabet is considered a name of God, and the child who licks the alphabet off the tablet symbolically eats the name of God. See Marcus, *Rituals of Childhood,* 157n27, esp. references there to Scholem and Idel, and cf. Ta-Shema, "Rite of Initiation," 597 (no. 5).

112. For other examples of a Jewish awareness of the Eucharist, see Marcus, *Rituals of Childhood,* 155n89.

113. Robinson, *Readings,* 1:427; for Rigord, *Oeuvres,* 1:13, 25, cited in Shatzmiller, "Desecrating the Cross," 160n3.

114. See Parma, Biblioteca Palatina, Hebrew MS De Rossi no. 1033, fol. 25, col. 2, which Elisheva Baumgarten pointed out to me.

115. Weiser, *Handbook,* 251; Gaudin, "Colybes."

116. The two manuscripts are Paris, Bibliothèque Nationale, Hebrew MS 353, fol. 81v, published in Assaf, *Meqorot,* 1:1, and *Sefer ha-Asufot* fol. 67r. See Marcus, *Rituals of Childhood,* 110. Ta-Shema, "Rite of Initiation," 597, observes that this pattern can be explained simply as the result of the fact that Jews double the ends of some liturgically recited passages. This "simple explanation" is no better than R. Leontin's in MS Paris. There a forced explanation about doubled letters in the verse proves that he was not thinking about some final liturgical phrases being doubled. Moreover, the

meaning of the specific duplication—QRSHT—is not elucidated by invoking doubling the ends of passages, a practice that is not common even in the liturgy.

117. Weiser, *Handbook,* 303.

118. Levin, *Childhood in Exile,* 49–50. My thanks to Elliott Horowitz for reminding me of this passage. See, too, Marcus, *Rituals,* 140n4, for Levin's ordeal with learning the Hebrew alphabet backwards, a feature of the medieval ceremonies; and also Levin, *Childhood in Exile,* 71. For other recollections of remnants of the ceremony in eastern Europe, see Schauss, *Lifetime,* 107–9.

119. Motzki, "Das Kind," 415–16; Juynboll and Pedersen, "'Akika." There was an early medieval pagan rite of the first time the hair or beard was cut, but it was replaced by Christian initiations. See Nelson, "Parents," 99; and Bartlett, "Symbolic Meanings." Cf. 2 Sam. 14:25, where David's son Absalom cut his long hair every year and weighed it.

120. *Midrash Tanhuma,* on Lev. 19:23, 40a.

121. E.g., see the description in Heilman, *Defenders of the Faith,* 131–35. The following reconstruction is mainly based on Benayahu, "Customs of Safed Kabbalists in Meron." Cf. Ya'ari, "History of the Festival in Meron." Note that references to a first haircut as a way of fulfilling the religious commandment of cutting all but the earlocks (pe'ot) are not the origin of the early modern practice, which is from Arab, as well as Jewish, legal and pietistic inspiration. See, e.g., Tosafot to B. Nazir 41b, s.v. hashta: "when they cut the hair of young boys in order to leave much hair on the sides." That comment has nothing to do with the early modern custom of a first haircut that began in Meron. Religious scholars have always tried to connect customs to a legal basis, even though the former was not based on the latter. The commandment is found in Lev. 19:27 and B. Makkot 20b.

122. The plague is mentioned in B. Yevamot 62b and *Midrash Bereishit Rabbah,* chap. 63, sec. 3, 660; for the interruption on Lag ba-Omer, in *Ozar ha-Geonim* 7:140–41. On the period between Passover and Shavuot, known as Sefirah (counting), see Sperber, "Customs of Mourning." The medieval tradition that says that weddings are prohibited during Sefirah stipulates

only *nesu'in,* the completion of the actual marriage, not *eirusin,* or betrothal. Once both ceremonies were combined into a single ceremony, the entire rite was prohibited. I discuss this change in Chap. 3.

123. For cutting as symbolic act, see Bilu, "From Circumcision to Word," 22; Rubin, *Reishit ha-Hayyim,* 144, who does not refer to additions as well as subtractions.

124. For the combined rite, see Bilu, loc. cit., 33, who refers to it as "modern." In an email exchange (August 2002), Bilu confirmed my impression that it appears to be very recent, perhaps as late as the 1980s, in Ultra-Orthodox communities in the United States and in Israel. Two books published in 1991 are Gottlieb, *My Upsheren Book,* and Geller, *Upsherin,* both in English, which Judith Marcus found for me, and from around the same time, Abramowitz, *Sefer Zon Qodashim,* in Hebrew, which Yoram Bilu called to my attention. Another example is a coloring book, published in Monsey, New York, mainly in Yiddish with some English, Brandwein, *Ich Bin Alt 3 Yahr,* from around the same time. My thanks to Chava Weissler for a copy of this booklet. A thorough ethnographic-historical study is needed. The Italian custom is based on a conversation, June 12, 2002, with an informant born in southern Italy.

125. Kessler, "Return," 14.

126. Silber, "Emergence of Ultra-Orthodoxy."

2 / BAR MITZVAH, BAT MITZVAH, CONFIRMATION

1. Kraemer, "Images of Jewish Childhood," 72–74; e.g., Exod. 38:26; Num. 1:3; Ezra 3:8; 1 Chron. 23:24, and elsewhere.

2. See Epstein, *Mavo,* 978.

3. Gilat, "Age Thirteen." Cf. *Midrash Bereishit Rabbah,* sec. 63:27, 692–93, on Jacob and Esau, who were indistinguishable in character until they turned thirteen.

4. T. Hagigah 1:2.

5. This concept is invoked to resolve contradictory teachings as to whether a minor is or is not supposed (1) to see the Temple sacrifices on fes-

tivals (B. Hagigah 4a on M. Hagigah 1:1); (2) to dwell in a sukkah on that festival (B. Sukkah 28b on M. Sukkah 2:8); (3) to hear the reading of the Book of Esther on Purim (B. Megillah 19b on M. Megillah 2:4); (4) to hear the ram's horn blown on Rosh Hashanah (B. Rosh Hashanah 33b on M. Rosh Hashanah 4:8). For the discussion of the minor and religious practices before the thirteenth century, see Goldin, *Ha-Yihud,* 111–12.

6. B. Sukkah 42a. See, too, B. 'Arakhin 2b; Y. Sukkah 3 (end) 54a, 649; T. Hagigah 1:2, 374. The lulav is the palm branch, myrtle, and willow, bound together, that is part of the rite of the fall festival of Sukkot (Tabernacles); the tallit, a fringed prayer shawl; tefillin, parchments of biblical passages, enclosed in black leather boxes to which leather straps have been attached for binding one to the upper arm, near the heart, and the other around the head.

7. B. Megillah 23a; Karo, *Shulhan 'Arukh,* Orah Hayyim 282:3.

8. On tefillin, see Tosafot on B. Berakhot 20a, s.v. u-qetanim. The commentator extends the concept of a minor who has been trained (qatan she-higi'a le-hinukh) to put on tefillin, even though the Talmud applies that term to different cases, as above. On a minor's being called to read the Torah, M. Megillah 4:6 permits it, and later authorities insisted that minors, whether they "had been trained" or not, could do so. See Rabbi Isaac ben Moses of Vienna, *Sefer Or Zaru'a,* pt. 1, par. 752, 108b–108c. The fact that he had to reiterate a view that is stated clearly in the Mishnah implies that there was opposition to it.

9. Schechter, "Child," 22–24; Goitein, *Mediterranean Society,* 2:556n9; Goitein, *Sidrei Hinukh,* 36. One early medieval Palestinian opinion held that a minor should not read the Torah until thirteen, but it did not have any influence. See *Masekhet Soferim,* 16:9, 295–96. The religious significance of thirteen as the time of decision making was emphasized in *Avot de-Rabbi Natan,* chap. 16, ed. Schechter, 31b; *Fathers,* trans. Goldin, 83.

10. *Mahzor Vitry,* par. 81, 51.

11. B. Berakhot 47b and Tosafot to B. Berakhot 48a, s.v. ve-lit hilkheta, where Rabbeinu Tam opposes this practice by pointing out famously, "Is a Pentateuch a man?" (atu humash gavra hu?).

12. See Schauss, *Lifetime,* 115, who proposes the principle that a rite of

passage like bar mitzvah requires a distinction between behavior that is permitted to children before and after the age of thirteen. How this divide was created is still not sufficiently clear, since the rite developed in jumps and starts and apparently did not become widespread until the nineteenth century outside of parts of central Europe.

13. Extensive research is needed to track this in Europe, America, and the Muslim Jewish communities down to the mid-twentieth century, by which time it had become commonplace throughout nearly all of the Jewish world.

14. When these and other methodological distinctions are ignored, the result is that naive assumptions, grounded in pious wishful thinking, substitute for historical analysis. I agree with the critical comments by Weinstein, Review, 395n14.

15. Goitein, *Mediterranean Society,* 5:512n83. For the ceremony that Momigliano discusses, see below.

16. Pardes, *Biography,* 171n5.

17. *Masekhet Soferim* 18:7, 318–19; paraphrased in Schechter, "Child," 24: "there was the godly custom to initiate children with the beginning of the 13th year by fasting the whole Day of Atonement. During this year they took the boy to the priests and learned men that they might bless him, and pray for him that God might think him worthy of a life devoted to the study of the Torah and pious works." Rivkind, *Le-Ot,* 16, takes Schechter's enthusiasm for this passage as a begrudging endorsement of his own view that the bar mitzvah ceremony was ancient, even though he admits the term did not mean a bar mitzvah boy's initiation ceremony in antiquity or in the Muslim Middle Ages. Schauss, *Lifetime,* 114, was also misled by this text.

18. See Lieberman, Review, 56–57; and Gilat, "Age Thirteen," 44–45.

19. Gilat, "Age Thirteen," notes the various commandments that are required at different ages and the relationship between physical signs of puberty and age as markers of religious majority for males and females. See, e.g., B. Qiddushin 16b.

20. *Midrash Bereishit Rabbah,* sec. 63, 2:693.

21. The father's practice is mentioned by Rabbi Isaac ben Abba Mari of Marseilles, from late twelfth-century Provence: "In some places, when a

son reaches age thirteen, the father says the complete blessing, with [God's] name, 'that he exempted me from the punishment of this one.'" See *Sefer ha-'Ittur,* Hilekhot Milah, 53a (not 53c, as in Ta-Shema, "Rite of Initiation," 593).

22. Aaron ben Jacob Ha-Kohen of Lunel, *Sefer Orhot Hayyim,* pt. 1, 40c, par. 58.

23. Marcus, *Tiqsei Yaldut,* 167.

24. Grossman, *Hakhmei Ashkenaz,* 287.

25. The text uses the verb "peda'ani" (redeemed me); in *Midrash Bereishit Rabbah* and subsequent liturgical practice, the verb is "petarani" (exempted me).

26. The text is quoted in "Hora'ot Mei-Rabbanei Zarfat z l," 82.

27. Jacob ben Moses Ha-Levi Molin, *Sefer Maharil, Minhagim,* 453. The editor of this text points to the thirteenth-century "Hora'ot mei-Rabbanei Zarfat" as the source, where Rabbi Judah ben Barukh is cited (ibid., 454n9).

28. See, e.g., B. Gittin 22a; and Weinstein, "'Ad Ya'avor,'" 57–61, and notes there.

29. See Gilat, "Age Thirteen," 44–45; Schäfer, "Ideal of Piety"; Marcus, "Dynamics of Jewish Renaissance," 38–39.

30. Judah ben Samuel, He-Hasid, *Sefer Hasidim,* ed. Wistinetzky, par. 216; Ta-Shema, "Children," 277–78.

31. Asher ben Yehiel (Rosh), *She'elot u-Teshuvot,* kelal 16, p. 79.

32. Boswell, *Kindness,* 314–15.

33. B. Sukkah 42a; and Isaac ben Abba Mari of Marseilles, *Sefer ha-'Ittur,* 61c. Regardless of how Rabbi Isaac interprets the Talmudic passage, Rabbi Moses Isserles correctly understood the implication of his comment: boys under the age of thirteen years were not to put on tefillin.

34. See Mordekhai ben Hillel, *Sefer ha-Mordekhai,* on Berakhot, par. 60, which includes Jacob ben Meir's view too. Cf. the tannaitic requirement for a responsible minor to do so in *Mekhilta de-Rabbi Shimon bar Yohai,* 41; *Mekhilta de-Rabbi Yishmael,* 68; and Gilat, "Age Thirteen," 45.

35. Karo, *Beit Yosef* on *Sefer Arba'ah Turim,* Orah Hayyim, 37:4; Isserles, *Darkhei Moshe* on *Sefer Arba'ah Turim,* Orah Hayyim, 37. Cf. Ta-Shema,

"Rite of Initiation," 593, who interprets the implications of the passage in *Sefer ha-'Ittur* differently from the way Isserles does. For the basic definition of religious minhag as a norm not prescribed in the Talmud, see Ta-Shema, *Minhag Ashkenaz,* 21. Isserles's comment is a good example of this meaning of minhag, since, according to the Talmud, boys who can take care of tefillin *are* supposed to put them on.

36. See, e.g., B. Bava Batra 96a; and Löw, *Lebensalter,* 211.

37. See Isserles on Karo, *Shulhan 'Arukh,* Orah Hayyim, 55:10; Karo, loc. cit. On this custom, see Ta-Shema, "Some Matters," 566–68.

38. See Isserles, *Darkhei Moshe* on *Arba'ah Turim,* Orah Hayyim, 225:1; and Isserles on Karo, *Shulhan 'Arukh,* Orah Hayyim 225:1. See, too, Isserles on Karo, *Shulhan 'Arukh,* Orah Hayyim, 55:10: "when he becomes bar mitzvah," without any elaboration.

39. Isaac ben Moses of Vienna, *Sefer Or Zaru'a,* pt. 2, par. 43, 11c; pt. 1, par. 753, 108a–108b.

40. See Baumgarten, *Mothers,* 71–72, and sources cited there, esp. Rabbi Shimshon ben Zadoq, *Sefer Tashbez,* par. 397, 38a; Hoffman, *Covenant,* 190–202.

41. On the history of this Palestinian Jewish custom, and Rabbi Meir's opposition to it in its waning days in Germany, see Ta-Shema, "By the Power of the Name"; Rabbi Meir ben Barukh, *Sefer She'eilot u-Teshuvot,* no. 268, 21a; and Ta-Shema, "Rite of Initiation," 592. Origins, of course, do not explain later historical developments. How one rabbi (Rabbeinu Tam) can decide the fate of one practice and another rabbi (Rabbi Meir ben Barukh) not decisively influence another practice is a mystery not explained in Ta-Shema, "Rite of Initiation," 597–98, and "By the Power of the Name," 394–95.

42. Luria, *Yam shel Shlomo,* to Bava Qama 7:37, 98a.

43. Yuspa Shamash, *Minhagim,* 164.

44. Luria, *Yam shel Shlomo,* to Bava Qama 7:37, 98a. See Rivkind, *Le-Ot,* 40; Rappoport, "Differences," 36; Ta-Shema, "More," 261.

45. Löw, *Lebensalter,* 210, already correctly noted the German origins of bar mitzvah: "Deutschland ist ihre Heimat."

46. See "Herman-Judah's Account," in Morrison, *Conversion and Text,*

77; and Momigliano, "Medieval Jewish Autobiography," 229; Cooper, *Child,* 185.

47. Rabbi Avigdor ha-Zarfati, *Peirushim u-Pesaqim,* 4, and two passages that Israel Ta-Shama claims are in *Zohar Hadash* (Midrash ha-Ne'elam) on Genesis, both quoted in Ta-Shema, "More," 261, repeated in Ta-Shema, *Ha-Nigleh,* 34–35, with a Hebrew translation. The first quotation is not in *Zohar Hadash* (Midrash ha-Ne'elam), Genesis, 19b. The second quotation he says is found "ibid., further on" is found on 16d! On the first edition of Ta-Shema, *Ha-Nigleh,* see Liebes, "The *Zohar* as a Book of Jewish Law."

48. Yuspa Shamash, *Minhagim,* 167; *Rabbi Juspa, Shammash of Warmaisa* (Worms), 25.

49. See Assaf, *Meqorot* 2:114, translated in Bonfil, *Jewish Life in Renaissance Italy,* 130.

50. Leon Modena, *History of the Rites,* 4.10.4, 214; Leon Modena, *Autobiography.*

51. Johann Buxtorf, *The Jewish Synagogue,* 69–70, quoted in Cooper, *Child,* 185. This is very different from anything mentioned by Polish rabbis from the sixteenth or seventeenth century. Rabbi Jacob Emden (eighteenth-century Germany) says in his autobiography, "at that time I became bar mitzvah," which means, he turned thirteen. See Emden, *Megillat Sefer,* 57.

52. See Deutsch, "'A View of Jewish Religion,'" 282.

53. See Morosini, *Via,* 165, translated into Hebrew in Weinstein, "''Ad Ya'avor,'" 69. On Morosini, see Ravid, *"Contra Judaeos."* It is not clear how common this ceremony was even in the late seventeenth century in parts of Italy. Northern Italy was a center of German-Jewish settlement. Two other Christian sources from eighteenth-century Germany mention it: Anton, *Kurzer Entwurf* 1:36–58, and Selig, *Der Jude,* 1:411–13. My thanks to Yaakov Deutsch for this information. The rite described in Buxtorf is barely another example.

54. There is a vast literature in the field that Ariès' book helped create. His classic is Ariès, *Centuries.* For criticism, see Shahar, *Childhood;* Kanarfogel, *Jewish Education,* 33–36; Kanarfogel, "Attitudes toward Children"; but see Ta-Shema, "Children," whose observations support Ariès. The whole debate is transformed in Schultz, *Knowledge of Childhood,* 1–20, who argues

persuasively for the existence of different historical conceptions of childhood and children. See, too, Cunningham, "Histories of Childhood."

55. Goitein, *Mediterranean Society,* 5:28, and 512n83. But see the description from Yemen quoted in Rivkind, *Le-Ot,* 68–69; and see Hazan, *Ha-Shirah ha-'Ivrit,* 79–82, pointed out to me by Menachem Schmelzer.

56. Levin, *Childhood in Exile,* 269–70; Schauss, *Lifetime,* 115–19.

57. For similar impressions, see Rivkind, *Le-Ot,* 60–72.

58. For Warsaw's "first confirmation . . . that is, a bar mitzvah celebration for girls," see Shatzky, *Geshikhte,* 2:146, for which I thank Gershon Hundert. For the celebration in 1902 of a bat mitzvah in Lemberg (Lvov) in the synagogue of a progressive rabbi, see Sadan, "Bat Mitzvah," 59, where there is no mention of anything other than a party (*hagigah*). My thanks to Jonathan Sarna and Benjamin Ravid. See, too, Breuer, "Chapters," 61n25. For a description of a ceremony of initiation for young girls into the synagogue on the first day of Passover in Verona in 1844, see Conigliani, "Iniziazione religiosa," where the author acknowledges the influence of a Catholic girl's celebration of First Communion. My thanks to Robert Bonfil for the nineteenth-century press accounts of various Italian ceremonies. For Hebrew texts and English translations of these ceremonies, see *Bat Mitzvah,* 16–18.

59. See the Baghdad authority, Rabbi Joseph Hayyim ben Elijah al-Hakom, *Sefer Ben Ish Hai,* on Re'eh, sec. 17, 291, quoted in Rappoport, "Difference," 31.

60. Hyman, "Introduction of Bat Mitzvah," 133; Diner and Benderly, *Her Works Praise Her,* 245, "the world's first bat mitzvah," where the date should be 1922. Note, too, that Kaplan may have thought "that his daughter, Judith, deserved the same synagogue honors as a boy of her learning and age" (ibid.), but that is not what happened at her bat mitzvah.

61. Eisenstein, "'No Thunder,'" 32.

62. Scult, *Judaism Faces,* 300.

63. Ibid., 30.

64. Kaplan, *Communings,* 159.

65. Eisenstein, "'No Thunder,'" 31; Scult, *Judaism Faces,* 301.

66. Eisenstein, "'No Thunder,'" 32.

67. Ibid., 30.

68. Ibid., 31.

69. See Kaplan, *Communings,* 159.

70. Eisenstein, "'No Thunder,'" 32.

71. Scult, *Judaism Faces,* 301.

72. Ibid., 415n31.

73. Eisenstein, "'No Thunder,'" 32; Scult, *Judaism Faces,* 302.

74. Kaplan, *Communings,* 506.

75. Scult, *Judaism Faces,* 302; Mel Scult, personal communication, December 12, 2002. He also reports that a relative of Mordecai Kaplan's wife, who turned thirteen in 1929 never considered having a bat mitzvah.

76. See Leon Modena, *Autobiography,* 83. For the information about a bat mitzvah at Havdalah, my thanks to Joel Rascoff.

77. Scannell, "Confirmation." On the age of the child at confirmation, see Fisher, *Christian Initiation,* 135; Taglia, "Cultural Construction."

78. Segre, *Memoirs,* 22–23. Cf. the absence of any ceremony in the memoir of Pauline Wengeroff, *Memoiren,* 1:53, who comments that at age twelve girls began to light candles for the Sabbath and holidays.

79. Machlin, "Pitigliano," 35. My thanks to Chava Weissler for the reference to this book, which I found in the library of the Beth El Synagogue Center (New Rochelle, N. Y.), and to librarian Ruth Kaufman for her assistance.

80. Kaplan, *Communings,* 163–64.

81. See Meyer, *Response,* 39–40; Eliav, *Ha-Hinukh,* 264; and Orsborn, "Initiation of Confirmation, 44n75 and 91–98. For the new catechism, see Orsborn, loc. cit., 31; and Petuchowski, "Manuals and Catechisms."

82. Meyer, *Response,* 39–40, 170, 175, 238.

83. Schauss, *Lifetime,* 121.

84. See Hyman, introduction to "Bat Mitzvah"; Hyman, "Bat Mitzvah"; and Stein, "Road to Bat Mitzvah." Shavuot had already appealed to German Reformers. See Orsborn, "Initiation of Confirmation," 226.

85. See, e.g., Schoenfeld, "Some Aspects," "Folk Judaism," and "Theoretical Approaches"; Davis, "Bar Mitzvah"; Kraemer, "What Does Bar/Bat Mitzvah *Really* Signify?"; Mason, "Adult Bat Mitzvah"; Weissler, "Coming of Age."

86. See Cohen, "Celebration"; Brown, "Bat Mitzvah"; Wolowelsky, *Women, Jewish Law,* 51–56. My thanks to Sid Z. Leiman for the references. See, too, Elper, *Traditions and Celebrations;* and Friedland Ben Arza, *Bat-Mitzvah.*

87. See texts and illustrations of an Orthodox girl's bat mitzvah at an all-women's service, where the girl reads the Torah, in *Bat Mitzvah,* 2–10, and the learned discussion, not offered as a rabbinical opinion, in Shapiro, "Qeri'at ha-Torah [Public reading of the Torah] by Women." The rabbinical opinion of Rabbi Aaron Blumenthal, defending giving women an 'aliyah in Conservative synagogues, was published in 1955.

88. For another relatively new rite for adolescents, see Grimes, *Deeply,* 128, on "la qinceañera" celebrated by fifteen-year-old Latina girls. An older American rite is the Sweet Sixteen party.

89. See Rivkind, *Le-Ot,* 62 and 69.

90. Weinberger, quoted in Sarna, *People Walk,* 14–15.

91. See Weinberger, *Jews and Judaism,* 76. My thanks to Jonathan Sarna for the reference; Joselit, *Wonders,* 89–133.

92. See the description of such a ceremony at a Russian-American adult's bat mitzvah ceremony in Markowitz, "Bat Mitzvah," 129–30.

93. Schoenfeld, "Integration into the Group."

94. Zhao, "New Age," and "Episcopal Church;" Bernstein, "You Don't."

95. In eastern Europe, just a few generations ago, the age of marriage was not much different from bar mitzvah, and the two were sometimes celebrated at the same time. See Schauss, *Lifetime,* 179.

96. *Heilman, Defenders of the Faith,* 47–69, esp. 55, where putting on tefillin for the first time is mentioned. The event took place on a weekday morning.

3 / ENGAGEMENT, BETROTHAL, MARRIAGE

1. Michal is the only woman in the Bible who is presented as actually being in love with a man, perhaps a violation of the Bible's Near Eastern sense of etiquette and not necessarily a compliment to her. The usual form

is for a man to express love for a woman. The verb A-H-V otherwise never appears with a single feminine subject. See Alter, *David Story*, 115n20. See, too, Orme, *Medieval Children,* 337, on love in marriage arranged by matchmakers or parents.

2. *Pesiqta de-Rab Kahana,* 2:4, 18–19; *Midrash Bereishit Rabbah,* 68:4, 771–72; *Midrash Vayyiqra Rabbah* 8:1, 164–65; *Book of Legends,* 510:56.

3. M. Ketubbot 1:1 and B. Ketubbot 2a.

4. For the biblical view of multiple wives and concubines, see de Vaux, *Ancient Israel,* 1:24–25.

5. See Cohen, *Be Fertile and Increase,* passim.

6. See de Vaux, *Ancient Israel,* 1:27, who cites Exod. 21:7–11.

7. For comparable laws in Babylonia and Assyria, see de Vaux, *Ancient Israel,* 1:27–28, and *Ancient Near Eastern Texts,* 173–74, 182. In none of these cases does the groom own the bride/wife.

8. See Michal, e.g., Saul's younger daughter (1 Sam. 18:20–29), or rabbinic sources about young women going out in search of husbands on the fifteenth of the month of Av and on the Day of Atonement—M. Ta'anit 4:8; B.Ta'anit 31a; Y. Ta'anit 4:8, 69c, 738—a Jewish equivalent of Sadie Hawkins Day; and cf. Jud. 21:19–21.

9. See Gen. 24:4 (Isaac), Gen. 28:2 (Jacob), Laban's comment preferring relatives (Gen. 29:19), and Samson's father's disappointment (Judg. 14:3), as well as Tobit, who advises his son to choose from within his clan (Tob. 4:12–13), noted in de Vaux, *Ancient Israel,* 1:30–32.

10. See esp. Ezra 9–10; Neh. 10:31, 13:23–27.

11. Songs 3:11; cf. Isa. 61:10.

12. Feuchtwanger, "Coronation of the Virgin"; Marcus, "Jewish-Christian Symbiosis," 496–500.

13. The noun is found in the context of a marriage in Gen. 34:12, Exod. 22:16, and 1 Sam. 18:25.

14. *Ancient Near Eastern Texts,* 173, par. 160.

15. See B. Ketubbot 102a. Rashi, s.v. "lo bi-shetarei pesiqa," refers to the terms as "tenai'm."

16. B. Qiddushin 50b.

17. B. Qiddushin 12b.

18. See B. Yoma 18b; B. Yevamot 37b; Grossman, "Historical Background," 12; Marcus, "Jewish-Christian Symbiosis," 473.

19. Y. Qiddushin 3:8, 64b, 1174 (bottom).

20. B. Ketubbot 23a.

21. M. Ketubbot 1:1; B. Ketubbot 2a.

22. Goitein, *Mediterranean Society,* 3:54.

23. Ibid., 3:55.

24. Kraemer, "Life," 418.

25. For the Kurdish custom, see Bar'am-Ben-Yosef, *Bo'i Kallah,* 44-44; on Knasmahl, see Lauterbach, "Ceremony," 25n36, who refers to a seventeenth-century author, Rabbi Yomtov Lippmann Heller (d. 1654), for the earliest description of this custom.

26. Leon Modena, *Autobiography,* 91 and 199–200 at note y; and idem, *History of the Rites,* 4.3.4, 174.

27. Bacharach, *Havvot Ya'ir,* vol. 1, sec. 70, 74a; Yuspa Shamash, *Minhagim,* 2; Falk, *Jewish Matrimonial Law,* esp. 38–85; Schauss, *Lifetime,* 165; Pollack, *Jewish Folkways,* 29 and references 218n82.

28. Goitein, *Mediterranean Society,* 3:72.

29. B. Gittin 89a; cf. M. Pesahim 3:7: "to eat the betrothal festive meal in the home of his in-laws."

30. Klein, *Guide,* 391, mixes up the terminology and chronology. For an example of eirusin as betrothal, see M. Ketubbot 5:1, where it is contrasted to nesu'in (marriage).

31. See Ezra 9, and cf. the reaction and the use of the verb *ma'al* (desecration of something holy) in Joshua 7. The late Gerson D. Cohen pointed out this relationship in seminars about the Second Commonwealth that he taught in 1969.

32. B. Ketubbot 57b.

33. M. Ketubbot 5:2.

34. B. Ketubbot 57b.

35. Goitein, "Trousseaux," 83–85.

36. M. Qiddushin 1:1; B. Qiddushin 2a.

37. B. Qiddushin 12b.

38. T. Qiddushin 1:1, 276, in which variations of the man's declaration are found and the stipulation that if the woman says something equivalent, it has no effect.

39. Qiddushin 6a; Freimann, *Seder,* 3.

40. Freimann, *Seder,* introduction.

41. B. Qiddushin 2b.

42. B. Ketubbot 7b. See Freimann, *Seder,* 10n3.

43. This is the formula in *Siddur R. Saadja Gaon,* 97.

44. Hildesheimer, "History of the Blessings," 110.

45. See Rabbi Aha bar Shabha, *She'iltot,* Bereishit, Hayyei Sarah, sec. 16, 110; Hildesheimer, "History of the Blessings," 111.

46. David ben Joseph Abudarham, *Sefer Abudarham,* 2:408.

47. Schauss, *Lifetime,* 161 and 317n192. See Harkavy, *Teshuvot ha-Geonim,* par. 65, 30; Tosafot to B. Qiddushin 9a, s.v. ve-hilkhata.

48. Others have argued that these elaborate precious communal treasures are not wedding rings or at least were not used as rings of betrothal. See Abrahams, *Jewish Life,* 180–84; Gutmann, *Jewish Life Cycle,* 15–16; and Sperber, "Wedding Rings." It deserves a new study.

49. See, e.g., Gutmann, "Jewish Medieval Marriage Customs," 54, fig. 4. My thanks to Elliott Horowitz for telling me about the absence of written sources about this illustrated custom. See, too, Metzger and Metzger, *Jewish Life,* nos. 187 and 335.

50. Leon Modena, *History of the Rites,* 4.3.1, 174.

51. This would include Princeton, Garrett MS 26, fol. 14, reproduced in color in Horowitz, "Giotto in Avignon," 102, fig. 2.

52. For the Talmud, see B. Ketubbot 7b; the *She'iltot* is quoted in *Ozar, ha-Geonim,* ed. Levin, Ketubbot, 13. See Rav Aha bar Shabha, *She'iltot,* sec. 16, Hayyei Sarah, ed. Berliner, 95a. On this reading and the fact that, even if a late addition to Rav Aha's work, it was known to Rabbi Shmuel ha-Nagid, see *Ozar ha-Geonim,* ed. Levin, and Freimann, *Seder,* 17.

53. See *Siddur R. Saadja Gaon,* 96–97, cited in Freimann, *Seder,* 16. This custom is not mentioned in *Seder Rav 'Amram,* 181.

54. 1 Macc. 9:39–41; Glick, *Or Nagah 'Aleihem,* 37.

55. See Glick, *Or Nagah 'Aleihem,* 36–39.

56. See Modrzejewski, *Jews of Egypt,* 141–43; and see, too, 3 Macc. 4:6–8 in *Old Testament Pseudoepigrapha,* 2:522, and 3 Macc. 1:18 at 2:578.

57. Matt. 25:1–4; John 3:29; Treggiari, *Roman Marriage,* 163; B. Ketubbot 17a; Schauss, *Lifetime,* 155–57; Glick, *Or Nagah 'Aleihem,* 97–106; Valensi, "Religious Orthodoxy."

58. B. Gittin 57a.

59. See Abrams and Ta-Shema, *Sefer Gematriot,* fol. 33b–34a, 90–91; and Sperber, "Throwing Wheat," 4:150–56, who reproduces the image from Bodenschatz, *Kirchliche Verfassung,* no. 11, 4:127c, in the miniature in the upper-left corner.

60. Treggiari, *Roman Marriage,* 166–68; Leon Modena, *History of the Rites,* 4.3.4, 176; and Ritzer, *Formen, Riten,* 205, cited by Schmelzer, "Wedding Poems."

61. M. Ketubbot 2:1. Other signs were that she went out of her father's house with long hair and that she was accompanied by song (be-hinuma). On the phrase "be-hinuma," see Bonfil, "'What Is Hinuma?'"

62. T. Shabbat 7:16; *Masekhet Semahot* 8:4, 150; B. Berakhot 50; and cf. Y. Ketubbot 2:1, 26b, 961.

63. Rabbi Eleazar ben Judah, *Sefer ha-Roqeah,* par. 352. For throwing wheat as a medieval innovation, see *Mahzor Vitry,* 598; Tosafot to B. Berakhot 50b, s.v. ve-lo: "now it is their custom to throw wheat at a wedding"; and esp. Rabbi Eliezer ben Joel Halevi, *Sefer Raviah,* sec. 137, 1:126, who distinguishes between what is now customary (nahug) in contrast to the Talmudic custom of throwing "roasted heads of wheat and nuts in their time" (bi-meihem).

64. For related customs, see Moser, "Maibaum und Maienbrauch."

65. Rabbi Jacob ben Moses Ha-Levi Molin, *Sefer Maharil, Minhagim,* 464; Schauss, *Lifetime,* 176–77.

66. Y. Demai 4:2, 24a, 129; Y. Shevi'it 4:10, 35c, 192; and see *Pirqei de-Rabbi Eliezer,* chap. 17 (end), fol. 41b; and Friedlander, *Pirke de Rabbi Eliezer,* 123.

67. See Schauss, *Lifetime,* 166, 175; Gaster, *Holy and Profane,* 88–89; Treggiari, *Roman Marriage,* 147–53. Pollack, *Jewish Folkways,* 32, says it is from Talmudic times without any evidence.

68. Hahn (Nordlingen), Joseph Yuspa ben Phinehas Seligmann, *Yosif Omez,* sec. 657, 146, who recalls this from his own experience in Frankfurt am Main in the early seventeenth century; Yuspa Shamash, *Minhagim,* par. 227, 2:3–9; Holzer, "Aus dem Leben," summarized in Schauss, *Lifetime,* 175.

69. Glick, *Or Nagah 'Aleihem,* passim.

70. Glick, *Or Nagah 'Aleihem,* 76; Addison, *Present State,* 53. On Addison as an armchair ethnographer, see the caveats of Horowitz, "'A Different Mode'"; and Marcus, *Rituals of Childhood,* 20–25.

71. See Glick, *Or Nagah 'Aleihem,* 74–79. For kapparot and the Day of Atonement, see Lauterbach, "Ritual for the Kapparot Ceremony"; Gutmann, "Strange History." I saw "making kapparot" over dropped eggs some years ago in Jerusalem in the Rehavia fruit store known as "Yom Tov."

72. Rabbi Isaac ben Judah Ibn Ghayyat, *Sha'arei Simhah* (=*Me'ah She'arim*), 2, Hilekhot Aveil, 71; Rabbi Jacob ben Asher, *Arba'ah Turim,* Yoreh De'ah 345; Sperber, *Minhagei Yisrael* 4:103n40; Glick, *Or Nagah 'Aleihem,* 127–28, 131–39; Markon, "The Kitl."

73. See Lieberman, *Yevanit,* 80, cited in Glick, *Or Nagah 'Aleihem,* 112n5. Each individual and community work out the relationship between a custom's original and acquired meanings and whether to continue or modify or drop a particular custom or its interpretations. Most Orthodox Jews, for example, do not celebrate Halloween in America. They note its original and continuing meaning in the Christian calendar as the Eve of All Saints' Day. Most other American Jews ignore the Christian calendrical meaning and consider it a secular children's holiday.

74. B. Bava Batra 60b.

75. *Midrash Tehillim,* Ps. 137, 525; *Midrash on Psalms,* trans. Braude, 336–37.

76. Glick, *Or Nagah 'Aleihem,* 113nn7–10.

77. See Rabbi Jacob ben Moses Ha-Levi Molin, *Sefer Maharil, Minhagim,* 465, but the motive is not mentioned. The lengthy description of a wedding in Mainz is translated in Abrahams, *Jewish Life,* 204–10, and paraphrased in Schauss, *Lifetime,* 170–74.

78. Rabbi David ben Joseph Abudarham, *Sefer Abudarham,* Birkat Eirusin, 412.

79. Rabbi Joseph Karo, *Shulhan 'Arukh,* Orah Hayyim 560:2, and Isserles, loc. cit.

80. Arend, "Bride's Circling the Groom," 7–8.

81. Addison, *Present State,* 52, 53.

82. See Bonfil, "'What Is Hinuma?'"

83. M. Ketubbot 2:1.

84. B. Ketubbot 7b.

85. Ibid.

86. B. Ketubbot 8a.

87. M. Ketubbot 5:2 (end).

88. B. Ketubbot 8a.

89. See Flusser, "Tuvia," 3:371.

90. See *Teshuvot ha-Geonim,* ed. Harkavy, par. 65, 30, cited in *Ha-Hilluqim,* ed. Margaliot, 144n3.

91. See *Ha-Hilluqim,* ed. Margaliot, no. 28, 143, and notes.

92. See *Seder Rav 'Amram Gaon,* 181.

93. Falk, *Jewish Matrimonial Law,* 68n1.

94. See, e.g., Mal. 2:14, Prov. 2:17, and Ezek. 16:8.

95. Grossman, "Historical Background."

96. See Porten, *Archives.*

97. See Porten, *Archives,* 235–63.

98. *Ancient Near Eastern Texts,* 222.

99. On the unit of the detachment (*degel*), see Porten, *Archives,* 28–31.

100. Porten, *Archives,* 247.

101. *Ancient Near Eastern Texts,* 491.

102. *Ancient Near Eastern Texts,* 222–23.

103. Porten, *Archives,* 252–53.

104. de Vaux, *Ancient Israel,* 133.

105. The institution of the ketubbah is traditionally attributed to the first-century B.C.E. Pharisee Simeon ben Shetah, but this tradition itself is no older than the source layer in which it is found, that is, from the first or second century C.E. On the early ketubbah, see Satlow, *Jewish Marriage,* 213–16; M. Ketubbot 5:1, the earliest reference in rabbinic literature; and for

the Greek marriage contracts associated with the Jewish woman, Babatha, from the early second century, see Schwartz, *Imperialism,* 69–71.

106. Letter of Rabbi Meshullam ben Natan to Rabbi Jacob ben Meir (Rabbeinu Tam), in Rabbi Jacob ben Meir, *Sefer ha-Yashar,* par. 44, 92, perhaps attributing this practice already to Rashi ("rabbeinu shlomo"); Freimann, *Seder,* 41; Sabar, "Beginnings," 99n25.

107. Sabar, "Beginnings," 98–100.

108. Landsberger, "Illuminated"; Sabar, "Beginnings"; and Sabar, *Ketubbah,* 3–32.

109. See Sabar, *Ketubbah,* 27.

110. T. Ketubbot 1:4, 57; Y. Ketubbot 1:4, 25c, 958; B. Ketubbot 12a.

111. Eleazar ben Judah, *Sefer ha-Roqeah,* par. 354, 240; Jacob ben Moses, *Ha-Levi Molin, Sefer Maharil, Minhagim,* 466.

112. Karo, *Shulhan 'Arukh,* Even ha-'Ezer 55:1 and Isserles, ad loc.; Freehof, "Chuppah," 187.

113. B. Gittin 57a. For a thorough discussion, see Lauterbach, "Ceremony." His assumption of the continuous observance of the ancient rite into medieval times, ibid., 15, is not demonstrated.

114. Slonik, *Mas'at Benyamin,* no. 90, p. 182; Shulman, *Authority and Community,* 18, 162.

115. B. Berakhot 30b and 31a.

116. B. Bava Batra 60b.

117. Tosafot to B. Berakhot 31a, s.v. "ayytei kasa de-zugita hivrata."

118. *Mahzor Vitry,* par. 470, 589.

119. B. Berakhot 31a.

120. Rabbi Eliezer ben Natan (Ravan), *Even ha-Ezer=Sefer Ravan,* par. 177, 96c; Lauterbach, "Ceremony," 15; Rabbi Eleazar ben Judah of Worms, *Sefer ha-Roqeah,* pars. 353 and 355, 240.

121. *Kol Bo,* par. 62, 83d; and Rabbi Aaron ben Jacob ha-Kohen of Lunel, *Sefer Orhot Hayyim,* pt. 1, Laws of Ninth of Av, 95b; cf. pt. 2, 67. On laxness in men wearing tefillin, and other ritual commandments in thirteenth-century Spain, see Rabbi Moses ben Jacob of Coucy, *Sefer Mizvot Gadol,* Positive Commandments, par. 3, 96d.

122. Rabbi Jacob ben Moses Ha-Levi Molin, *Sefer Maharil, Minhagim,* 467.

123. Rabbi Moses ben Isaac Mintz, *Teshuvot Maharam Mintz,* par. 109, 125c.

124. Isserles on *Shulhan 'Arukh,* Orah Hayyim 560:2.

125. Rabbi David ben Samuel Halevi, *Turei Zahav* [Taz], par. 4 on *Shulhan 'Arukh,* Orah Hayyim 560:2; Yuspa Shamash, *Minhagim,* 40.

126. Isserles on *Shulhan 'Arukh,* Even ha-'Ezer 65:3. Leon Modena, *History of the Rites,* 4.3.4, 176, refers to spilling out the second cup, which "the Bridegroom . . . takes and dasheth it with all his might against the Ground," as a momento mori, not of Jerusalem.

127. See Gutmann, *Jewish Life Cycle,* pls. 31a and 31b.

128. Apple, "Marriage: The Concept," for drawing of groom about to throw a glass at a metal plate on the ground (1721); also Gutmann, "Jewish Medieval Marriage Customs," fig. 3; and Gutman, *Jewish Life Cycle,* pl. 32a; pl. 32b shows a silver wedding plate from Gouda, Holland, ca. 1730.

129. Schauss, *Lifetime,* 194.

130. See example in Mann and Bilski, *Jewish Museum,* no. 122, 91: Double Marriage Cup, Augsburg, ca. 1650–60.

131. Teomim, *Mishbezot Zahav* on *Shulhan 'Arukh,* Orah Hayyim 560:4, cited by Lauterbach, "Ceremony," 365.

132. See Leon Modena, *Autobiography,* 90.

133. Ibid., 91.

134. Ibid.

135. Ibid., 92.

136. For the text, see Glueckel of Hameln, *Memoirs;* Schechter, "Memoirs of a Jewess; and Davis, "Glikl bas Judah Leib," 5–62 and notes.

137. Glueckel of Hameln, *Memoirs,* 10.

138. Ibid., 23, 25.

139. Ibid., 95; see, too, 111 for another brokered match.

140. Ibid., 96.

141. Ibid., 98.

142. Ibid., 97–98.

143. Ibid., 99.

144. Ibid., 110.

145. Ibid., 111.

146. Ibid.

147. Ibid., 111–12.

148. Ibid.

149. Maimon, "Struggle," 193.

150. Ibid., 194.

151. Ibid., 195.

152. Ibid., 195–96.

153. Ibid., 196–97.

154. Ibid., 198.

155. Ibid.

156. Ibid., 199.

157. Ibid., 200.

158. Treggiari, *Roman Marriage*, 166.

159. Kotick, "Love Found a Way," 233.

160. Ahad Ha-'Am, "Memories," 252.

161. Bialik, "Before Thirty," 267.

162. Ibid., 233.

163. Ibid., 235.

164. Ibid., 234.

165. Ibid., 235.

166. Davidson, *Ozar,* mem 982, 3:114; Kaufmann, "Chant nuptual."

167. Grimes, *Deeply,* 155–56.

168. See Lewy, *Sefer Minhag Yisrael Torah,* 4:171.

169. Rabbi Eleazar ben Judah of Worms, *Sefer ha-Roqeah,* par. 353. These exegetical techniques were characteristic of Rabbi Eleazar and the circle of German Jewish Pietists known as *hasidei ashkenaz.* See Marcus, "Exegesis for the Few."

170. For an Ultra-Orthodox wedding, see Heilman, *Defenders of the Faith,* 277–90.

171. The rite of divorce and the relatively esoteric laws of the levirate marriage are discussed in Klein, *Guide,* 450–508 and 387–89.

4 / AGING, DYING, REMEMBERING

1. Orenstein, *Life Cycles,* 45–51, 94–95.

2. See *Ha-Hilluqim,* ed. Margaliot, no. 2, 75; *Shulhan 'Arukh,* Yoreh De'ah 340:30.

3. Joseph da Modena, "Trouble," 102.

4. Marcus, "Mothers, Martyrs, and Moneymakers," 41–42, retranslated by Baskin, "Dolce of Worms," 435–36.

5. See Carmi, *Penguin Book,* 387–88; and Baskin, "Dolce of Worms," 436–37.

6. Baskin, "Dolce of Worms," 436–37.

7. Marcus, *Jew in the Medieval World,* 47–48.

8. Bonfil, *Jewish Life in Renaissance Italy,* 265; Leon Modena, *Autobiography,* 120–21, and for the deaths of other children, 97, 109–11.

9. Psalm 71:9, turned from the first-person singular into first-person plural. See the introduction to the confession in Goldschmidt, *Mahzor le-Yamim Nora'im,* Yom Kippur, 44, etc.

10. On 1 Kings 1:1 in standard rabbinic Bibles, see Talmage, "So Teach Us," 50.

11. Abraham Ibn Daud, *Sefer ha-Qabbalah,* 43 (Hebrew) and 58 (English).

12. Eliyahu ben Elqana Capsali, *Seder Eliyahu Zuta,* 2:254, translated in Bonfil, *Jewish Life in Renaissance Italy,* 268. See, too, Leon Modena, *Autobiography,* 107: "my revered uncle, the gaon Rabbi Abtalion of Modena, of blessed memory, died in Ferrara at the age of eighty-two."

13. B. Shabbat 152a. For old age in medieval Europe, see Sheehan, *Aging,* and Shahar, *Growing Old.*

14. B. Nedarim 40a; B. Shabbat 127a; B. Shabbat 12b.

15. Y. Pe'ah 3:7 17d, 93; on shiva, see below.

16. *Encyclopedia Judaica* 14:1498; Marcus, *Communal Sick-Care,* 63–66; Horowitz, "Membership."

17. B. Gittin 61a; B. Shabbat 66b.

18. M. Yoma 3:8. For individual confession, see Gen. 4:13; Gen. 38:26; Josh. 7:19–21; 1 Sam. 15:24–25. For leaders, see Exod. 32:31; the confession of the high priest on the day of atonement, Lev. 16:6–21, which

influenced the liturgy on that day, and Ezra 9:6–15 and Neh. 1:6–7; 9:2, 33–35, and other cases mentioned in *Encyclopedia Judaica,* 5:878.

19. B. Shabbat 32a.

20. *Shulhan 'Arukh,* Yoreh De'ah 338:1; M. Sanhedrin 6:2, B. Sanhedrin 43b; and see B. Yoma 36b.

21. Bonfil, *Jewish Life in Renaissance Italy,* 265–66, 273.

22. Aaron Berechia ben Moses of Modena, *Ma'avar Yabboq.*

23. Bonfil, *Jewish Life in Renaissance Italy,* 272; B. Pesahim 56a.

24. B. Berakhot 61b; Y. Sotah 5:5 20c, 930; Fishbane, *Kiss of God,* 66–71, who does not stress the difference between the midrash and the 1096 narratives. Neither does Boyarin, *Dying for God,* chap. 4, who reads the Talmudic accounts as already advocating by implication reciting the Shema at a time of martyrdom even if it is not, as in the stories, the required time of day to recite the liturgical Shema.

25. See *Jews and the Crusaders,* ed. and trans., Eidelberg, 23, 34, 83, and 88 and below.

26. See Marcus, *Piety and Society,* 151; and Judah ben Samuel, He-Hasid, *Sefer Hasidim,* ed. Wistinetzky, pars. 2 and 43 (end); Marcus, "Jewish-Christian Symbiosis."

27. *Shulhan 'Arukh,* Yoreh De'ah 339:1.

28. For the ancient Jewish practice of lighting a candle on the ground near the body, see T. Shabbat 6:2, 22, and Lieberman, *Tosefta Ki-Feshuta,* ad loc., 83, who quotes Rabbi Aaron ben Jacob ha-Kohen of Lunel, *Sefer Orhot Hayyim,* pt. 2, Hilekhot Evel, 576: "why do we place a candle on the ground in the house of mourning?" See, too, Ariès, *Hour,* 162.

29. B. Shabbat 114a.

30. Leon Modena, *History of the Rites,* 5.8.4, 241; Gaster, *Holy and Profane,* 154–55; Glick, *Or la-Aveil,* 123–26; Gagin, *Keter Shem Tov,* 706.

31. See, too, Jer. 16:1–8 on the house of mourning.

32. B. Mo'ed Qatan 22b and elsewhere.

33. *Shulhan 'Arukh,* Yoreh De'ah 380; 382:1.

34. *Masekhet Semahot* 1:2; 9:2; B. Mo'ed Qatan 24b ff.

35. As we saw in Chap. 3, there are dozens of parallel customs that are associated with weddings and funerals. See Glick, *Or Nagah 'Aleihem.*

36. And see Jer. 6:26 for an only child.

37. See Ezek. 32:16; 2 Chron. 35:25; Amos 5:16.

38. Jer. 19:19.

39. Goitein, *Mediterranean Society,* 5:163.

40. B. Berakhot 59b.

41. B. Shabbat 151a, M. Mo'ed Qatan 1:6; B. Mo'ed Qatan 27b.

42. B. Mo'ed Qatan 23b; B. Berakhot 17b; *Masekhet Semahot* 10:1.

43. See Isa. 14:9–11; Ezek. 32:17–32; and Job 26:5–6, cited in de Vaux, *Ancient Israel,* 1:56.

44. See Jer. 16:4; 22:19; Ezek. 29:5, cited in de Vaux, loc. cit.

45. B. Ketubbot 17a.

46. The most detailed description of this process is the personal and ethnographic account in Heilman, *When a Jew Dies,* 31–71; and see Klein, *Guide,* 276–79.

47. See 1 Sam. 28:14 ("wrapped in a robe") and Ezek. 32:27 ("went down to Sheol in their battle gear").

48. See the parallels in Mark 15:42–47; Luke 23:50–56.

49. See the detailed data collected and analyzed in Bloch-Smith, *Judahite Burial Practices and Beliefs,* summarized in Hallote, *Death, Burial, and Afterlife.*

50. Schwartz, *Imperialism,* 42, 148–49; Rubin, *Qeiz ha-Hayyim;* Kraemer, *Meanings of Death.*

51. See *Masekhet Semahot,* chap. 13. Cf. Orme, *Medieval Children,* 116–17 on charnel houses.

52. Schwartz, *Imperialism,* 153–58.

53. Bloch-Smith, *Judahite Burial Practices and Beliefs,* 113.

54. See de Vaux, *Ancient Israel,* 1:58.

55. Goitein, *Mediterranean Society,* 5:144–45, 165–66; 2: 285; *Jewish Encyclopedia* 12:183–95; *Encyclopedia Judaica* 15:1218–32.

56. See, too, 2 Sam. 3:33–34 and Ezek. 32:16. B. Mo'ed Qatan 27b.

57. B. Mo'ed Qatan 25b; Schauss, *Lifetime,* 235–36.

58. Gagin, *Keter Shem Tov,* 674.

59. B. Sanhedrin 19a.

60. Ibid. See, too, B. Mo'ed Qatan 24b and Rashi s.v. "ve-ein 'omedin 'alav be-shurah," where he says, "when people return from the cemetery,

they pass before the mourner and each one says to him, "be comforted" (titnahem).

61. B. Ketubbot 8b.

62. *Midrash Pirqei de-Rabbi Eliezer*, chap. 17, 41b; trans. Friedlander, 122, cited in *Arba'ah Turim*, Yoreh De'ah 393.

63. In *Arba'ah Turim*, n. 3 to "Perishah" on Yoreh De'ah 393.

64. Gagin, *Keter Shem Tov*, 707.

65. B. Sanhedrin 19a and B. Avodah Zarah 18a (twice); B. Yevamot 12b and 100b.

66. The quotation changes "ha-arez" (the land) to "ha-sadeh" (the field).

67. *Mahzor Vitry*, par. 289, 247 and n. 60; Wieseltier, *Kaddish*, 52; Nahon, "From the *rue aux juifs*," 327, where the passage is translated. Gagin, *Keter Shem Tov*, 674.

68. *Be'er Heiteiv*, par. 8, on *Shulhan 'Arukh*, Orah Hayyim 224:12, cited by Gelbard, *Rite and Reason*, 661–62; Shalom mi-Neustadt, *Halakhot u-Min-hagim*.

69. On flowers, see Gagin, *Keter Shem Tov*, 681. See, below, for a detailed description of a modern traditional funeral and burial.

70. *Ha-Hilluqim*, ed. Margaliot, no. 5, 76.

71. See, too, Hosea 9:4. On putting food into the graves in ancient Israel, see de Vaux, *Ancient Israel*, 1:60; and Bloch-Smith, *Judahite Burial Practices and Beliefs*, 122–26.

72. On covering mirrors, see Gagin, *Keter Shem Tov*, 704.

73. B. Mo'ed Qatan 27b.

74. B. Mo'ed Qatan 21a. *Masekhet Semahot*, chap. 6.

75. B. Mo'ed Qatan 15a–15b; and see Y. Mo'ed Qatan 3:5 83a, 818.

76. It is not clear if Bar Kappara means that death is the result of the sin of Adam, as in Ben Sira (Ecclus.) 25:28, or is the result of the sins by the person who died, as in Shabbat 55b ("there is no death without sin"). See Mo'ed Qatan 27a; and Glick, *Or la-Aveil*, 77n160 and discussion there.

77. Rabbi Meir ben Barukh of Rothenburg, *Sefer Hilekhot Semahot ha-Shalem*, par. 138, ed. Landa, who bases the suspension of the custom on Y. Mo'ed Qatan 3:5 that a mourner who lives in an inn, presumably among non-Jews, need not upset his bed. Rabbi Jacob ben Asher, *Arba'ah Turim*,

Yoreh De'ah, 387; bases it on the difference between beds then and in his own day.

78. *Shulhan 'Arukh,* Yoreh De'ah 387:1–2.

79. Y. Mo'ed Qatan 3:5 83a, 818.

80. B. Mo'ed Qatan 15a.

81. Y. Mo'ed Qatan 3:5 82d, 816 (bottom).

82. B. Mo'ed Qatan 24a. See Zimmer, "Wrapping the Head"; Sperber, "Wrapping the Neck."

83. Glick, *Or la-Aveil,* 80n176.

84. Tosafot to B. Mo'ed Qatan 21a s.v. "eilu devarim."

85. Moses ben Maimon (Maimonides), *Mishneh Torah,* Hilekhot Aveil, 5:19 and 4:9. See, too, Karo, *Beit Yosef* on *Arba'ah Turim,* Yoreh De'ah 386, and Isserles (Rema) on *Shulhan 'Arukh,* Yoreh De'ah 386:1.

86. *Ha-Hilluqim,* no. 14, 80 and 122–23; ed. Margaliot.

87. B. Mo'ed Qatan 23a; Y. Mo'ed Qatan 3:5 82b, 815; *Masekhet Semahot* 10:12.

88. Isaac ben Judah Ibn Ghayyat, *Halakhot Kelulot=Sha'arei Simhah= Me'ah She'arim,* 2:51–52, discussed in Freehof, "Home Rituals," 508–9.

89. Rabbi Moses ben Nahman, "Torat ha-Adam," 2:217; and see Freehof, loc. cit.

90. Rabbi Isaac bar Sheshet, *She'elot u-Teshuvot,* no. 158, 1:166–67.

91. *Shulhan 'Arukh,* Yoreh De'ah 393:2.

92. Isserles, loc cit.

93. Rabbi Isaac bar Sheshet, *She'elot u-Teshuvot,* no. 158, 1:166–67. Cf. *Masekhet Semahot* 8:1; Glick, *Or la-Aveil,* 114–15.

94. Heilman, *When a Jew Dies,* 119–54; Lamm, *Jewish Way,* 93–144; Diamant, *Saying Kaddish,* 112–35.

95. B. Mo'ed Qatan 19b.

96. B. Mo'ed Qatan 22b; Y. Mo'ed Qatan 3:8, 83d, 827; *Masekhet Semahot* 9:15.

97. See Elbogen, *Jewish Liturgy,* 82 (mourner's Kaddish and Yahrzeit), 163 (Yizkor).

98. B. Qiddushin 31b.

99. For an important study of Christian rites, see McLaughlin, *Consorting with Saints,* esp. chaps. 1 and 2. My thanks to Elisheva Baumgarten for calling this to my attention. No comprehensive book has been written on the history of the memory of the dead, let alone about the cult of the dead, in Judaism, but see Goldin, *'Alamot Aheivukha,* and Roos, *"God Wants It!".*

100. See Bloch-Smith, *Judahite Burial Practices and Beliefs,* 121–22. For references to a Jewish cult of the dead, including petitions to be addressed to the dead, see Horowitz, "Speaking to the Dead"; Marcus, "Jewish-Christian Symbiosis," 163; and the separate book by Rabbi Jacob ben Abraham Solomon, an early seventeenth-century Bohemian rabbi, *Ma'aneh Lashon* (Prov. 16:1), first published anonymously around 1615. On him, see *Encylopedia Judaica* 9:1213–14.

101. *Sifrei Be-Midbar,* Naso, pisqa 4, ed. Horowitz, 7 (end); Rashi on B. Me'ilah 10b: s.v. "velad hatat"; Glick, *Or la-Aveil,* 127n2.

102. *Sifrei Devarim,* sec. 210, ed. Finkelstein, 244; trans. Hammer, 210, with modifications.

103. E.g., B. Keritot 26a (not 6a, as in Ta-Shema, "Some Matters," 301n8); and see, too, B. Horayot 6a.

104. *Midrash Pesiqta Rabbati,* sec. 20, 95b, with extensive notes to other versions; trans. Braude, 1:401.

105. *Midrash Tanhuma,* preface to Ha'azinu [ed. Vilna], reprinted, Tel Aviv: Sefarim Pardes, n.d., 246, not in ed. Buber. The text quoted is not from *Sifra* [torat kohanim] but is in *Sifrei Devarim,* as noted by Shimon Horowitz in his edition of *Mahzor Vitry,* 173n1. See, too, Montefiore and Loewe, *Rabbinic Anthology,* 675–76, for translation of the *Tanhuma* passage. Davidson, *Ozar, yod* 2405, 370, corrects the passage. The first reference is really to *Sifrei Devarim,* Ha'azinu par. 1; second reference is to *Midrash Pesiqta Rabbati,* sec. 20, with some variants.

106. B. Ta'anit 27b.

107. B. Shabbat 152b–153a.

108. See *Midrash Tehillim,* Ps. 11, sec. 6, 51b and notes; trans. Braude, 165.

109. See *Mahzor Vitry,* par. 190, 173.

110. See Marcus, "Jewish-Christian Symbiosis."

111. See *Seder ha-Qinot* nos. 23, 26, 30, and 34; and for English translations, see *Authorized Kinot*, 127–28, 132–34, 139–42, and 148–49.

112. Of special interest is the anthology of past historical and religious narratives compiled by a father for his sons in Oxford, Bodleian, Hebrew Manuscript D 11 as *Sefer ha-Zikhronot*. Moses Gaster translated the author's comments as the "Compiler's Preface" in his translation of *The Chronicles of Jerahmeel*, 1–4. On collective memory and 1096, see Cohen, *Sanctifying*.

113. The translation is based on *Authorised Daily Prayerbook*, 510–15. For the German custom of reciting it only twice a year, see *Seder 'Avodat Yisrael*, 233.

114. *Martyrologium des Nürnberger Memorbuches*, 5–12 (Hebrew) and 101–19 (German). See McCulloh, "Martyrology," 161–62, and the literature cited there.

115. Translation from *Daily Prayers*, 703. In *Daily Prayer Book*, 603, the quid pro quo in the Hebrew of pledging charity for the father's or mother's eternal reward is toned down: "I pledge charity in his/her behalf and pray that his/her soul be kept among the immortal souls. . . ." The English "and pray" is not in the Hebrew original.

116. Rabbi Jacob ben Moses Ha-Levi Molin (Maharil), *Sefer Maharil, Minhagim*, end of Hoshanah Rabbah, 388.

117. Davidson, *Ozar*, alef no. 3808, 176.

118. Translation from *Daily Prayers*, 705–7. The version in *Daily Prayer Book*, 606, is significantly modified and omits the italicized reference to giving charity, as do many who chant the prayer today at funerals.

119. Weiser, *Handbook*, 307–16.

120. Rabbi Joseph ben Moses, *Sefer Leqet Yosher*, I, 32.

121. Glick *Or la-Aveil*, 134.

122. B. Berakhot 58b and cf. B. Mo'ed-Qatan 8b.

123. See *Teshuvot ha-Geonim Sha'arei Zedeq*, 3:4:12, 46 and the annotated version in *Ozar ha-Geonim*, Mashqin (Mo'ed Qatan), Teshuvot, 48. See the comments by Mann, *Texts and Studies*, 1:414n10 and references there.

124. Mann, *Texts and Studies*, 1:321.

125. Glick, *Or la-Avei*, 135–36.

126. See Gagin, *Keter Shem Tov,* 260–65 and the notes there.

127. Rabbi Moses ben Maimon (Maimonides), *Teshuvot ha-Rambam,* no. 329, 2:596–97.

128. *Ozar ha-Geonim,* Hagiga, Teshuvot, 27–28, cited in Ta-Shema, "Some Matters," 301n8.

129. See Rabbi Abraham bar Hiyya, *Sefer Hegyon ha-Nefesh ha-'Azuvah,* ed. Freimann, 32a (top) (not 33, as cited in Ta-Shema, "Some Matters," 301n8).

130. Rabbi Eleazar ben Judah of Worms, *Sefer ha-Roqeah,* par. 217.

131. For other references to remembering the dead on the Sabbath in medieval Europe, see Zidqiyah ben Rabbi Avraham ha-Rofe, *Sefer Shibbolei ha-Leqet,* par. 81, 30a–30b and notes; *Tanya Rabbati,* par. 16, among others.

132. B. Shevuot 20a; B. Nedarim 12a, 14a.

133. Judah ben Samuel, He-Hasid, *Sefer Hasidim,* ed. Wistinetzky, par. 68 (end); pars. 290, 291, and 1554.

134. Rabbi Moses ben Isaac Mintz, *Teshuvot Maharam Minz,* par. 80, 91c, referring to Bamberg and environs. For the term in Christian usage, see Grimm and Grimm, *Deutsches Wörterbuch,* IV/II (H-I-J), 2249–50; and *Germania Judaica* III/1, 73.

135. Jacob ben Moses Ha-Levi Molin, *Sefer Maharil, Minhagim,* Hilekhot Semahot, [3], 599.

136. Rabbi Joseph ben Moses, *Sefer Leqet Yosher,* 1:32, Orah Hayyim, 49.

137. That a son can affect a dead father for the better, see B. Sanhedrin 104a.

138. *Mahzor Vitry,* 112–13. For versions, see references in Ta-Shema, "Some Matters," 299n1, and the passages on the relations of the living and the dead in Judah ben Samuel, He-Hasid, *Sefer Hasidim,* Bologna ed., par. 1177, which in ed. Margaliot is par. 1171!

139. *Mahzor Vitry* par. 145, 113, discussed Ta-Shema, "Some Matters," 299. The following discussion is based mainly on that study and the references cited there. See, too, Sperber, "May His Great Name;" 71–77 and Lerner, "Story."

140. See *Encyclopedia Judaica* 10:660–62 for what follows up to the thirteenth century.

141. See *Sifrei Devarim,* Ha'azinu, par. 306, ed. Finkelstein, 342; trans. Hammer, 309.

142. B. Shabbat 119b (in Aramaic); and see *Midrash Mishlei,* chap. 10, 84; *Midrash on Proverbs,* 57; and *Sifrei Devarim,* par. 306, ed. Finkelstein, 342; trans. Hammer, 308.

143. B. Sota 49a, and see B. Berakhot 3a and Tosafot s.v. "ve-onin," as to why the Kaddish is in Aramaic.

144. See *Masekhet Soferim,* 10:6, 214.

145. Rabbi Joseph ben Moses, *Sefer Leqet Yosher,* 1:56.

146. Rabbi Jacob ben Moses Ha-Levi Molin, *She'eilot u-Teshuvot,* no. 28, 27–29.

147. In Rabbi Isaac ben Moses of Vienna, *Sefer Or Zaru'a* 2:89 (end); Ta-Shema, "Some Matters," 307.

148. Glueckel of Hameln, *Memoirs,* 131.

149. *Shulhan 'Arukh,* Yoreh De'ah 376:4.

150. Rabbi Jacob ben Moses Ha-Levi Molin, *Sefer Maharil, Minhagim,* 599. See M. 'Eiduyot 2:10. In the Rhineland, Jewish grooms also wore this garment.

151. Rabbi Moses ben Isaac Mintz, *Teshuvot,* par. 80, 91a–92a.

152. Ibid.

153. Form letter sent to members of the Young Israel of New Rochelle, N.Y. (Orthodox), January 5, 1998.

154. Notice sent to member for Yahrzeit by Rabbi Amiel Wohl, Temple Israel of New Rochelle, N.Y. (Reform), no date.

155. Letter sent by Beth El Synagogue Center, New Rochelle, N.Y. (Conservative), February 18, 1997.

156. See, too, Neusner, "Death in Jerusalem"; Heilman, *When a Jew Dies.*

Bibliography

PRIMARY SOURCES

In Manuscripts

Eleazar ben Judah of Worms. *Sefer ha-Roqeah.* Paris. Bibliothèque Nationale. Hebrew MS 363 [1452].

Kaplan, Mordecai. *Journals.* New York: JTS Library Archives. See Kaplan, Mordecai, under Published Sources.

Leipzig Mahzor. Leipzig, Universitätsbibliothek, Hebrew MS Vollers Katalog 1101. See Katz, Elias, under Published Sources.

Mahzor Vitry, "MS Reggio." New York, Library of the Jewish Theological Seminary of America. Mic. 8092.

Sefer ha-Asufot. London. Jews College 134 (Montefiore 115).

Sefer Minhagim. Paris, Bibliothèque Nationale, Hebrew Manuscript no. 586.

In Published Sources

Aaron ben Jacob Ha-Kohen of Lunel. *Sefer Orhot Hayyim.* Pt. 1.1751. Reprint. Jerusalem, 1957.

———. *Sefer Orhot Hayyim.* Pt. 2. Edited by M. Schlesinger. 4 pts. in 2 vols. 1902. Reprint. Jerusalem, n.d.

Aaron Berechia ben Moses of Modena. *Ma'avar Yabboq.* Venice, 1626.

Abraham bar Hiyya. *Sefer Hegyon ha-Nefesh ha-'Azuvah.* Edited by Yitzhak Freimann. Leipzig, 1860.

Abraham ben Azriel. *Sefer 'Arugat ha-Bosem.* Edited by Ephraim E. Urbach. 4 vols. Jerusalem: Meqizei Nirdamim, 1939–63.

Abraham Ibn Daud. *Sefer ha-Qabbalah (The Book of Tradition).* Edited by Gerson D. Cohen. Philadelphia: Jewish Publication Society, 1967.

Abraham Ibn Ezra. *Shirei ha-Qodesh.* Edited by Yisrael Levin. 2 vols. Jerusalem: Ha-Aqademiah ha-Le'umit ha-Yisraelit la-Mada'im, 1977.

Abramovitz, Moshe. *Sefer Zon Qodashim.* Benei Braq, n.d.

Abrams, Daniel, and Israel Ta-Shema, eds. *Sefer Gematriot of R. Judah the Pious.* Facsimile edition of a unique manuscript. Los Angeles: Cherub Press, 1998.

Addison, Lancelot. *The Present State of the Jews: (More Particularly Relating to those in Barbary) Wherein is Contained an Exact Account of their Customs, Secular and Religious: to which is Added, a Summary Discourse of the Misna, Talmud, and Gemara.* London, 1675.

Aha bar Shabha. *She'iltot de-Rav Ahai Gaon.* Edited by R. Shmuel Kalman Mirsky. 5 vols. Jerusalem: Mosad Ha-Rav Kook, 1960–77.

Ahad Ha-'Am. "Memories of Childhood." In *Memoirs of My People,* edited by Leo W. Schwarz, 248–53. New York: Schocken Books, 1963.

Alter, Robert, ed. and trans. *The David Story.* New York: Norton, 1999.

Ancient Near Eastern Texts Relating to the Old Testament. Edited by James B. Pritchard. 2nd ed. Princeton: Princeton University Press, 1955.

Anton, Carl. *Kurzer Entwurf der Erklaerung juedischer Gebraeuche . . . entworfen.* Braunswick, 1751.

Arba'ah Turim. By Rabbi Jacob ben Asher. New York: Friedman, n.d.

Asher ben Yehiel (Rosh). *She'elot u-Teshuvot le-Rabbeinu Asher ben Yehiel.* Edited by Yitzhaq Shelomo Yudlov. Jerusalem: Makhon Yerushalayim, 1994.

Assaf, Simha, ed. *Meqorot le-Toledot ha-Hinukh be-Yisrael.* 4 vols. Tel Aviv: Dvir, 1925–48.

Authorised Daily Prayerbook. Edited by Joseph H. Hertz. New York: Bloch, 1955.

Bibliography

Authorised Kinot for the Ninth of Av. Edited and translated by Abraham Rosen-
feld. New York: Judaica Press, 1979. See *Seder ha-Qinot.*

Avigdor ha-Zarfati. *Peirushim u-Pesaqim 'al ha-Torah.* Jerusalem, 1996.

Avot de-Rabbi Natan. Edited by Solomon Schechter. Vienna, 1887. See *The
Fathers according to Rabbi Nathan.*

B. =Babylonian Talmud. Vilna: Romm, 1886.

Bacharach, Yair Hayyim ben Moses Samson. *Sefer She'elot u-Teshuvot Havvat
Ya'ir.* 2 vols. Ramat Gan: Makhon Eiqed Sefarim, 1997.

Bar Mitsvah et Bath Mitsvah. [Paris]: Association Consistoriale Israélite de
Paris, n.d.

Baskin, Judith R., ed. and trans. "Dolce of Worms: The Lives and Deaths
of an Exemplary Medieval Jewish Woman and Her Daughters." In
Judaism in Practice: From the Middle Ages through the Early Modern Period,
edited by Lawrence Fine, 429–37. Princeton: Princeton University Press,
2001.

Bat Mitzvah: The Orthodox Jewish Woman and Ritual. Edited by Jennifer
Breger and Lisa Schlaff. New York: Jewish Orthodox Feminist Alliance,
n.d.

Bialik, Hayyim Nahman. "Before Thirty." In *Memoirs of My People,* edited
by Leo W. Schwarz, 254–68. New York: Schocken Books, 1963.

Bodenschatz, Johann Christoph Georg. *Kirchliche Verfassung der heutigen Juden.*
Frankfurt am Main and Leipzig, 1748–49.

The Book of Legends. Translated by William G. Braude. New York: Schocken
Books, 1992. References are to the English trans. See *Sefer ha-Aggadah.*

Brandwein, R. M. *Ich Bin Alt 3 Yahr/Kalaring Bookh* (Coloring Book). Monsey, N.Y., n.d.

Broner, E. M. *Mornings and Mourning: A Kaddish Journal.* New York:
HarperSanFrancisco/HarperCollins, 1994.

Buxtorf, Johann. *The Jewish Synagogue.* London, 1663.

———. *Juden Schül.* Basel, 1603 [German]; *Synagoga Judaica,* 1614 [Latin].

Carmi, T., ed. *The Penguin Book of Hebrew Verse.* Philadelphia: Jewish Publication Society, 1981.

The Chronicles of Jerahmeel. Translated by M[oses] Gaster. 1899. Reprint. New
York: KTAV, 1971.

Cole, Peter, trans. *Selected Poems of Shmuel HaNagid.* Princeton: Princeton University Press, 1996.

Conigliani, Emma Boghen. "Iniziazione religiosa delle fanciulle." In *dal Vessillo Israelitico del 1899,* 185ff.

Daily Prayer Book (Ha-Siddur ha-Shalem). Edited by Philip Birnbaum. New York: Hebrew Publishing Co., 1949.

Daily Prayers (Seder Tefillot mi-Kol ha-Shanah). Translated by A. Th. Phillip. New York: Hebrew Publishing Co., n.d.

David ben Joseph Abudarham. *Sefer Abudarham ha-Shalem.* 2 vols. Jerusalem, 1995.

David ben Samuel Halevi. *Turei Zahav.* Printed in editions of *Shulhan 'Arukh,* Orah Hayyim.

Davis, Nina. "The Ages of Man by an Unknown Author." *Jewish Quarterly Review* 11 (1899): 565–66.

Death and Mourning. New York: Jewish Orthodox Feminist Alliance, n.d.

Diqduqei Sofrim. Edited by Raphael Rabbinovicz. 1875. Reprint. 12 vols. Jerusalem: Ma'ayan ha-Hokhmah, 1960.

Eisenstein, Judith Kaplan. "'No Thunder Sounded, No Lightning Struck.'" In *Eyewitnesses to American Jewish History: A History of American Jewry: Part IV: The American Jew: 1915–1969.* Edited by Azriel Eisenberg, 30–32. New York: Union of American Hebrew Congregations, 1982.

Eleazar ben Judah. *Sefer ha-Roqeah.* Fano, 1505; Cremona, 1557; Jerusalem, 1960.

Eliezer ben Joel Halevi (Raviah). *Sefer Raviah.* Edited by Victor Aptowitzer. 4 vols. Reprint. Jerusalem: Harry Fischel Institute, 1964–65.

Eliezer ben Natan. *Even ha-'Ezer=Sefer Ravan.* Edited by Shalom Albeck. 1905. Reprint. Jerusalem, 1975.

Eliyahu ben Elqana Capsali. *Seder Eliyahu Zuta.* Edited by Aryeh Shmuelevitz, Shlomo Simonsohn, and Meir Benayahu. 3 vols. Tel Aviv: Tel Aviv University, 1976–83.

Emden, Jacob. *Megillat Sefer.* 1897. Reprint. New York: 1957. See *Memoires de Jacob Emden.*

The Fathers According to Rabbi Nathan. Translated by Judah Goldin. New Haven: Yale University Press, 1955.

Friedlander, Gerald, trans. *Pirke de Rabbi Eliezer.* 1916. 2nd edition. New York: Hermon Press, 1965.

Gagin, Shem Tov. *Keter Shem Tov.* 1934. Reprint. Jerusalem, n.d.

Geller, Beverly. *The Upsherin: Ephraim's First Haircut.* New York: CIS Publishers, 1991.

Glueckl of Hameln. See *The Memoirs of Gluekel of Hameln.*

Goldschmidt, Daniel. *Mahzor le-Yamim Nora'im,* vol. 2, Yom Kippur. 2 vols. Jerusalem: Koren, 1970.

Gottlieb, Yaffa Leba. *My Upsheren Book.* Brooklyn: Hachai Publishing, 1991.

Hahn (Nordlingen), Joseph Yuspa ben Phinehas Seligmann. *Yosif Omez.* 1723. 2nd ed. 1928. Reprint. Jerusalem, 1965.

Harkavy, Avraham. *Teshuvot ha-Geonim.* In *Zikaron la-Rishonim ve-gam la-Ahronim.* 1887. Reprint. Jerusalem, 1966.

Ha-Hilluqim she-Bein Anshei Mizrash u-Venei Erez-Yisrael. Edited by Mordecai Margaliot. Jerusalem: Rubin Mass, 1957.

Hebrew Ethical Wills. Edited by Israel Abrahams. 1926. Reprint. Philadelphia: Jewish Publication Society, 1976.

"Herman-Judah's Account." In *Conversion and Text,* ed. Karl F. Morrison, 39–113. Charlottesville: University Press of Virginia, 1992.

Holzer, Isaak. "Aus dem Leben der alten Judengemeinde zu Worms." *Zeitschrift für die Geschichte der Juden in Deutschland,* n.s. 5 (1934): 169–81.

"Hora'ot Mei-Rabbanei Zarfat z"l." In *Pisqei Rabbeinu Yehiel Mi-Paris,* edited by Eliahu Dov Pines. Jerusalem: Makhon Yerushalayim, 1973.

Isaac bar Sheshet. *She'elot u-Teshuvot.* Edited by David Metzger. Jerusalem: Makhon Yerushalayim, 1993.

Isaac ben Abba Mari of Marseilles. *Sefer ha-'Ittur.* [Vilna], 1874. Reprint. Jerusalem, 1987.

Isaac ben Judah Ibn Ghayyat, *Halakhot Kelulot,* published as *Sha'arei Simhah= Me'ah She'arim.* Edited by Simha Bamberger. 1861–62. 2 pts. Reprint. Jerusalem, 1961.

Isaac ben Moses of Vienna. *Sefer Or Zaru'a.* 2 pts in 1. Zhitomir, 1882.

Israel ben Petahiah Isserlein. *Sefer Terumat ha-Deshen.* Reprint. Benei Braq, 1971.

Itim. The Jewish-Life Cycle Information Center. *www.itim.org.il* [Hebrew, English, Russian Web site about Jewish life-cycle occasions in Israel. Accessed April 2004.]

Jacob ben Abraham Solomon. *Ma'aneh Lashon.* Prague, c. 1615.

Jacob ben Asher. See *Arba'ah Turim.*

Jacob ben Meir [Rabbeinu Tam]. *Sefer ha-Yashar le-Rabbeinu Tam.* Edited by Shraga Rosenthal. 1898. Reprint. n.p., n.d.

Jacob ben Moses Ha-Levi Molin (Maharil). *Sefer Maharil, Minhagim.* Edited by Shlomo Spitzer. Jerusalem: Makhon Yerushalayim, 1989.

———. *She'eilot u-Teshuvot Maharil ha-Hadashot.* Edited by Yizhaq Satz. Jerusalem: Makhon Yerushalayim, 1977.

Jacob Ha-Gozer. *Zikhron Brit Rishonim.* Edited by Jacob Glasberg. 2 vols. in 1. 1892. Reprint. Jerusalem, 1971.

The Jewish Catalogue: A Do-It-Yourself Kit. Edited by Richard Siegel, Michael Strassfeld, and Sharon Strassfeld. Philadelphia: Jewish Publication Society of America, n.d. [1973]. See *The Second Jewish Catalogue* and *The Third Jewish Catalogue.*

The Jews and the Crusaders. Edited and translated by Shlomo Eidelberg. 1977. Reprint. Hoboken, N.J.: KTAV, 1996.

Joseph ben Meir Teomim, *Mishbezot Zahav (Pri Megadim).* Frankfurt am Main, 1827.

Joseph ben Moses. *Sefer Leqet Yosher.* 2 vols. in 1. Edited by Jacob Freimann. 1903. Reprint. Jerusalem, 1964.

Joseph da Modena. "Trouble in the Sienna Ghetto." In *Memoirs of My People,* edited by Leo W. Schwarz, 95–102. New York: Schocken Books, 1963.

Joseph Hayyim ben Elijah al-Hakam. *Sefer Ben Ish Hai.* Jerusalem, 1986.

Judah ben Samuel, He-Hasid. *Sefer Hasidim.* Edited by Judah Wistinetzky. Frankfurt am Main: Wahrmann, 1924.

———. *Sefer Hasidim.* Bologna, 1538. The text and paragraph numbers of this edition are not the same as the following.

———. *Sefer Hasidim.* Edited by Reuven Margaliot. Jerusalem: Mosad ha-Rav Kook, 1957. This edition is based on but is *not* the same as the Bologna edition.

Juda Löw Kirchheim. *Minhagot Vermaiza* (Worms). Edited by Israel Mordecai Peles. Jerusalem: Makhon Yerushalayim, 1987.

Rabbi Juspa, Shammash of Warmaisa (Worms): Edited by Shlomo Eidelberg.
Jerusalem: Magnes, 1991. See Yuspa Shamash.

Kafka, Franz. "Before the Law." In *German Stories.* Edited by Harry Steinauer.
New York, 1984.

Kaplan, Mordecai. *Communings of the Spirit: The Journals of Mordecai M. Kaplan.*
Volume I, 1913–1934. Edited by Mel Scult. Detroit: Wayne State University Press, 2001.

Karo, Joseph ben Ephraim. See *Shulhan 'Arukh.*

Katz, Elias, ed. *Machsor Lipsiae.* Leipzig, 1964.

Kessler, Eve. "The Return of the Long-Lost Upsheren." *Forward,* vol. 3 (May
1996).

Kirchner, Paul Christian. *Ceremoniale Judaicum.* Erfurt, 1717; expanded edi-
tion with additions and revisions, including plates commissioned by
Sebastian Jugendres, as *Jüdisches Ceremoniel, 1724.* Reprint. New York:
Olms, 1974.

Klein, Michele, and Michal Harmelech, eds. *New Life: A Diary for Jewish
Parents.* New York, 1992.

Kol Bo. Naples, 1490.

Kotick, Ezekiel. "Love Found a Way." In *Memoirs of My People,* edited by Leo
W. Schwarz, 233–42. New York: Schocken Books, 1963.

Levin, Shmarya. *Childhood in Exile.* Translated by Maurice Samuel. New York:
Harcourt Brace and Co., 1929.

The Living Talmud. Edited and translated by Judah Goldin. 1955. New York:
New American Library of World Literature, 1957.

Luria, Shlomo ben Yehiel. *Yam shel Shlomo,* Bava Qama. Prague, 1616–18.

M. =Mishnah. *Shisha Sidrei Mishnah.* Edited by Hanokh Albeck. 6 vols.
Jerusalem: Mosad Bialik, 1958–59.

Machlin, Edda Servi. "Pitigliani: The Little Jerusalem." In her *The Classic
Cuisine of the Italian Jews,* 18–38. New York: Everest House, 1981.

Maharil. See Jacob ben Moses Ha-Levi Molin.

Mahzor Vitry. Edited by Shimon Horowitz. 2nd ed. Nuremberg, 1923.

Maimon, Solomon. "My Struggle with Amazons." In *Memoirs of My People,* edited by Leo W. Schwarz, 192–207. New York: Schocken Books, 1963.

Mann, Jacob, ed. *Texts and Studies in Jewish History and Literature.* 1931. Reprint. 2 vols. New York: KTAV, 1972.

Marcus, Jacob R., ed. *The Jew in the Medieval World—a Source Book: 315–1791.* 1938. Reprint. New York: Harper and Row, 1965 and since.

Das Martyrologium des Nürnberger Memorbuches. Edited by Siegmund Salfeld. Berlin: Leonhard Simion Verlag, 1898.

Masekhet Semahot [=Eivel Rabbati]. Edited by Michael Higger. 1931. Reprint. Jerusalem: Maqor, 1970. See *The Tractate Mourning.*

Masekhet Soferim. Edited by Michael Higger. 1937. Reprint. Jerusalem: Maqor, 1970.

Meir ben Barukh of Rothenburg. *Sefer Hilekhot Semahot ha-Shalem.* Edited by Akiva Landa. Jerusalem, 1976.

———. *Sefer She'eilot u-Teshuvot.* Edited by N. Rabinowitz. 1860 [Lemberg]. Reprint. Jerusalem, 1968.

Mekhilta de-Rabbi Shimon bar Yohai. Edited by J. N. Epstein and E. Z. Melamed. Jerusalem: Meqizei Nirdamim, 1955.

Mekhilta de-Rabbi Yishmael. Edited by H. S. Horowitz and I. A. Rabin. 1930. 2nd ed. Jerusalem, 1970.

Memoires de Jacob Emden. Translated by Maurice-Ruben Hayoun. Paris: Editions du Cerf, 1992.

The Memoirs of Gluekel of Hameln. Translated by Marvin Lowenstein. 1932. Reprint. New York: Schocken Books, 1977.

Memoirs of My People. Edited by Leo W. Schwarz. 1943. Reprint. New York: Random House, 1963.

Menahem ben Shlomo. *Midrash Sekhel Tov.* Edited by Shlomo Buber. 2 vols. 1900–1901. Reprint. Tel Aviv, n.d.

Midrash Bereishit Rabbah. Edited by J. Theodor and H. Albeck. 1903–36. Reprint. 3 vols. Jerusalem: Wahrmann, 1965.

Midrash Mishlei. Edited by Burton Visotzky. New York: Jewish Theological Seminary of America, 1990. See *The Midrash on Proverbs.*

The Midrash on Proverbs. Edited and translated by Burton Visotzky. New Haven: Yale University Press, 1992.

Midrash on Psalms. Translated by William Braude. New Haven: Yale University Press, 1959.

Midrash Pesiqta Rabbati. Edited by Meir Friedmann. Vienna, 1880.

———. Translated by William G. Braude. 2 vols. New Haven: Yale University Press, 1968.

Midrash Qohelet Rabbah. In *Midrash Rabbah,* vol. 2: *Midrash Rabbah.* Reprint. 2 vols. Jerusalem, 1961.

Midrash Rabbah. Reprint. 2 vols. Jerusalem, 1961.

Midrash Ruth Rabbah. In *Midrash Rabbah,* vol. 2.

Midrash Tanhuma. Reprint. [Vilna]. N.p., n.d.

Midrash Tanhuma. Edited by Solomon Buber. Vilna, 1885.

Midrash Tehillim. Edited by Solomon Buber. 1891. Reprint. Jerusalem, 1965–66

Midrash Vayyiqra Rabbah. Edited by Mordecai Margaliot. 1956–58. Reprint. New York: Jewish Theological Seminary of America, 1993.

Montefiore, C. G., and H. Loewe, eds. *A Rabbinic Anthology.* 1960. Reprint. Philadelphia: Jewish Publication Society, 1963.

Modena, Leon. *The Autobiography of a Seventeenth-Century Venetian Rabbi: Leon Modena's Life of Judah.* Translated and edited by Mark R. Cohen. Princeton: Princeton University Press, 1988.

———. *Historia de' riti hebraici.* Venice, 1638 [but written in 1616].

———. *History of the Rites, Customs, and Manner of Life of the Present Jews Throughout the World.* Translated by Edmund Chilmead. London, 1650.

———. *Lev Aryeh.* Venice, 1610.

Mordekhai ben Hillel. *Sefer ha-Mordekhai.* In Vilna edition of the Babylonian Talmud.

Morosini, Giulio. *Via della feda.* Rome, 1683.

Moses ben Isaac Mintz. *Teshuvot Maharam Mintz.* 1802. Reprint. Tel Aviv, 1969

Moses ben Jacob of Coucy. *Sefer Mizvot Gadol.* 1547. Reprint. Jerusalem, 1961.

Moses ben Maimon (Maimonides). *Mishnah Torah.* New York: Friedman, n.d.

———. *Peirush ha-Mishnah* (Commentary to the Mishnah). Edited by Joseph Kafih. 3 vols. Jerusalem: Mosad Ha-Rav Kook, 1965.

———. *Teshuvot ha-Rambam,* Edited by Joshua Blau. 3 vols. Jerusalem, 1958–61.

Moses ben Nahman (Nahmanides). *Torat ha-Adam.* In *Kitvei Rabbeinu Moshe ben Nahman,* edited by Charles Chavel, 2: 9–311. 2 vols. Jerusalem: Mosad Ha-Rav Kook, 1964.

Ner-David, Haviva. *Life on the Fringes: A Feminist Journey toward Traditional Rabbinic Ordination.* Needham, Mass.: JFL Books, 2000.

Neusner, Jacob. "Death in Jerusalem." In *Jewish Reflections on Death,* edited by Jack Riemer, 158–159. New York: Schocken Books, 1974.

The Old Testament Pseudoepigrapha. Edited by James H. Charlesworth. 2 vols. New York: Doubleday, 1985.

Ozar ha-Geonim. Edited by Benjamin M. Levin. 13 vols. Haifa, 1928; Jerusalem, 1929–n.d.

Pesiqta de-Rab Kahana. Translated by William G. (Gershon Zev) Braude and Israel J. Kapstein. Philadelphia: Jewish Publication Society, 1975.

Pesiqta de Rav Kahana. Edited by Bernard Mandelbaum. 2 vols. New York: Jewish Theological Seminary of America, 1962.

Picart, Bernard. *The Ceremonies and Religious Customs of the Various Nations of the Known World, with Historical Annotations, and Curious Discourses.* London, 1733.

————. *Cérémonies et coutumes religieuses de tous les peuples du monde.* 11 vols. Amsterdam, 1723–43.

Pirqei de-Rabbi Eliezer. 1852. Reprint. Jerusalem, 1970. See Friedlander.

Pisqei Rabbeinu Yehiel Mi-Paris ve-Hora'ot mei-Rabbanei Zarfat. Edited by Eliahu Dov Pines. Jerusalem: Makhon Yerushalayim, 1973.

Rigord. *Oeuvres de Rigord et de Guillaume le Breton.* Edited by H. François Delaborde. Paris, 1882.

Robinson, James Harvey, ed. *Readings in European History.* Boston: Ginn and Co., 1904.

Roth, Ernst. *Cod. hebr. 17 und 61. Hamburg.* [Facsimile edition of both manuscripts.] Jerusalem, 1980.

Roth, Norman. "The 'Ages of Man' in Two Medieval Hebrew Poems." *Hebrew Studies* 24 (1983): 41–44.

Sarna, Jonathan, ed. and trans. *People Walk on Their Heads.* New York: Holmes and Meier, 1982.

Bibliography

Scheindlin, Raymond P. *Wine, Women, and Death: Medieval Poems on the Good Life.* Philadelphia: Jewish Publication Society, 1986.

Schirmann, Haim, ed. *Ha-Shirah ha-'Ivrit bi-Sefarad u-ve-Provence.* 4 vols. Jerusalem: Mosad Bialik, 1961.

Schudt, Johann Jacob. *Jüdische Merckwürdigkeiten.* 4 vols. in 2. Frankfurt am Main, 1714–17.

Schwarz, Leo W., ed. *Memoirs of My People: Jewish Self-Portraits from the 11th to the 20th Centuries.* New York: Schocken Books, 1963.

The Second Jewish Catalogue. Edited by Sharon Strassfeld and Michael Strassfeld. Philadelphia: Jewish Publication Society, 1976.

Seder 'Avodat Yisrael. Edited by Seligmann Baer. Rödelheim, 1868.

Seder ha-Qinot le-Tish'ah be-Av. Edited by Daniel Goldschmidt. Jerusalem: Mosad Ha-Rav Kook, 1972. See *Authorised Kinot for the Ninth of Av.*

Seder Rav 'Amram Gaon. Edited by Daniel Goldschmidt. Jerusalem: Mosad Ha-Rav Kook, 1971.

Sefer Gezeirot Ashkenaz ve-Zarfat. Edited by A. M. Habermann. Jerusalem: Ofir, 1945.

Sefer ha-Aggadah. Edited by Hayim Nahman Bialik and Yehoshua Hana Ravnitzky. 1908. Reprint. Tel Aviv: Dvir, 1968.

Sefer ha-Razim. Edited by Mordecai Margaliot. Jerusalem, 1966.

Sefer Raziel. Amsterdam, 1701.

Sefer ha-Zikhronot. Edited by Eli Yassif. Ramat Gan: Tel Aviv University, 2001.

Segre, Dan Vittorio. *Memoirs of a Fortunate Jew: An Italian Story.* Northvale, N.J.: Jason Aronson, Inc., 1995.

Selig, Gottfried. *Der Jude, eine Wochenschrift.* 2nd abr. ed. Leipzig, 1768–72.

Shakespeare, William. *As You Like It.* In *The Riverside Shakespeare,* edited by G. Blackemore-Evans. 2nd ed. Boston: Houghton Mifflin, Co., 1997.

Shalom mi-Neustadt. *Halakhot u-Minhagim (Derashot Maharash).* Edited by Shlomo Spitzer. Jerusalem, 1977.

Shimshon ben Zadoq. *Sefer Tashbez.* Lemberg, 1858.

Shulhan 'Arukh. By Rabbi Joseph ben Ephraim Karo. New York: Friedman, 1961.

Siddur Nehamat Yisrael: The Complete Service for the Period of Bereavement. Edited by Jacob J. Schachter and David Weinberger. New York: Union of Orthodox Jewish Congregations of America, 1995.

Siddur R. Saadja Gaon. Edited by I. Davidson, S. Assaf, and B. I. Joel. Jerusalem: Meqizei Nirdamim, 1985.

Sifre: A Tannaitic Commentary on the Book of Deuteronomy. Translated by Reuven Hammer. New Haven: Yale University Press, 1986.

Sifrei Devarim. Edited by Louis Finkelstein. 1939. Reprint. New York: Jewish Theological Seminary of America, 1969. See *Sifre.*

Sifrei Be-Midbar. Edited by H. S. Horowitz. 1862. Reprint. New York, 1947.

Slonik, Benjamin Aaron ben Abraham. *Mas'at Benyamin.* Vilna, 1894.

Stern, Menahem, ed. *Greek and Latin Authors on Jews and Judaism.* 3 vols. Jerusalem: Israel Academy of Sciences and Humanities, 1976–84.

Strabo, Walafried. "The School Life of Walafried Strabo." Translated by James Davie Butler. *Bibliotheca Sacra* 40 (1883): 152–72.

T. = *Tosefta.* Edited by Saul Lieberman. New York: Jewish Theological Seminary of America, 1955–93 [Zeraim-Nesiqin]. Other tractates, edited by Moses Zuckermandel. 1877. Reprint. Jerusalem: Wahrmann, 1962.

Tanya Rabbati. 1879. Reprint. Jerusalem, 1978.

Teomim, Joseph ben Meir. *Mishbezot Zahav.* 1787. Reprint. In standard editions of the *Shulhan 'Arukh.*

Teshuvot ha-Geonim. Edited by Abraham Harkavy. Berlin, 1887.

Teshuvot ha-Geonim Sha'arei Zedeq. Jerusalem, 1966.

The Third Jewish Catalogue. Edited by Sharon Strassfeld and Michael Strassfeld. Philadelphia: Jewish Publication Society, 1980.

The Tractate Mourning. Translated by Dov Zlotnick. New Haven: Yale University Press, 1966.

Weinberger, Moses. *Sefer ha-Yehudim ve-ha-Yahadut be-Neyu Yorq (Jews and Judaism in New York).* Hebrew. New York, 1887. Edited and translated by Jonathan Sarna as *People Walk on Their Heads.* See Sarna.

Wengeroff, Pauline. *Memoiren Einer Grossmutter.* 2 vols. in 1. Berlin: M. Poppelauer, 1913.

Y. = Talmud Yerushalmi. Jerusalem: Academy of the Hebrew Language, 2001.

Ya'akov ha-Gozer im beno R. Gershom ha-Gozer. *Zikhron Brit Rishonim.* 1892. Reprint. Jerusalem, 1971.

Yuspa Shamash. *Minhagim de-Q" Q Vermaiza (Worms) le-Rabbi Yuspa Shamash.* Edited by Benjamin Salomon Hamburger and Eric Zimmer. Jerusalem: Makhon Yerushalayim, 1988.

Zidqiyah ben Rabbi Avraham ha-Rofe. *Sefer Shibbolei ha-Leqet.* Edited by Solomon Buber. Reprint. Jerusalem, 1962.

Zohar Hadash. Edited by Reuven Margaliot. Jerusalem: Mosad Ha-Rav Kook, 1957.

SECONDARY SOURCES

Abrahams, Israel. *Jewish Life in the Middle Ages.* 1896. Reprint. New York, 1975.

Abramovitch, Henry. "The Clash of Values in the Jewish Funeral: A Participant-Observer Study of a Hevra Kadisha." *Proceedings of the Ninth World Congress of Jewish Studies,* Division D, 2:127–34. Jerusalem, 1986.

Alexandre-Bidon, Danièle, and Monique Closson. *L'Enfant à l'ombre des cathédrales.* Lyon: Presses Universitaires de Lyon, 1985.

———. "La lettre volée. Apprendre à lire à l'enfant au moyen âge." *Annales ESC* (juillet–août 1989), 953–92.

Alexandre-Bidon, Danièle, and Didier Lett. *Children in the Middle Ages: Fifth–Fifteenth Centuries.* Translated by Jody Gladding. Notre Dame, Ind.: University of Notre Dame Press, 1999.

Amdor, Michal. "Wedding Customs in the Jewish Community of Aden." Hebrew. *Yeda' 'Am* 23 (1986): 53–54.

Ames, Lynne. "Burial Society's Sacred Task of Performing a Ritual for the Dead." *New York Times,* Sunday, March 9, 1997, sec. 13, 2.

Andree, Richard. "ABC Kuchen." *Zeitschrift für Volkskunde* 15 (1905): 94–96.

Apple, Raymond. "Marriage: The Concept." *Encyclopedia Judaica.* 16 vols. (1971), 11:1029–30.

Arend, Aaron. "The Bride's Circling the Groom at the Wedding." Hebrew. *Sidra* 7 (1991): 5–11.

Ariès, Philippe. *Centuries of Childhood: A Social History of Family Life.* Translated by Robert Baldick. New York: Vintage Books, 1962.

———. *The Hour of Our Death.* New York: Knopf, 1981.

Bibliography

Arnold, Klaus. *Kind und Gesellschaft in Mittelalter und Renaissance.* Munich: Lurz, 1980.

Assaf, David. *Sefer Ha-Qaddish: Meqoro, Mashma'uto ve-Dinav.* Haifa, 1966.

Atkinson, Clarissa W. *The Oldest Vocation: Christian Motherhood in the Middle Ages.* Ithaca: Cornell University Press, 1991.

Baker, Paula Eisenstein. "Eisenstein, Judith Kaplan (1909–1996)." In *Jewish Women in America: An Historical Encyclopedia,* edited by Paula E. Hyman and Deborah Dash Moore, 1:370-71. 2 vols. New York: Routledge, 1997.

Bar'am-Ben-Yosef, Noam, ed. *Bo'i Kallah.* Jerusalem: Israel Museum, 1998.

Bartlett, Robert. "Symbolic Meanings of Hair in the Middle Ages." *Transactions of the Royal Historical Society,* ser. 6, 4 (1994): 43–60.

Baumgarten, Elisheva, "Circumcision and Baptism: The Development of a Jewish Ritual in Christian Europe." In *The Covenant of Circumcision,* edited by Elizabeth Mark, 114–27. Hanover, N.H.: Brandeis University Press, 2003.

———. "Imahot Viladim ba-Hevrah ha-Yehudit bimei ha-Beinayim." Ph.D. diss., Hebrew University of Jerusalem, 2000.

———. *Mothers and Children.* Princeton: Princeton University Press, 2004.

———. "'So Say the Expert Midwives': Midwives and Midwifery in Thirteenth-Century Ashkenaz." Hebrew. *Zion* 65 (2000): 45–74.

Belmont, Nicole. "Levana: Or, How to Raise Up Children." 1972. Reprint. In *Family and Society: Selections from the Annales, Economies, Sociétiés, Civilisations,* edited by Robert Forster and Orest Ranum, 1–15, Baltimore: Johns Hopkins University Press, 1976.

Ben-Ami, Issacher. "Customs of Pregnancy and Childbirth among Sephardic and Oriental Jews." In *New Horizons in Sephardic Studies,* edited by Yedida Stillman and George K. Zucker, 253–67. Albany: SUNY Press, 1992.

Benayahu, Meir. "Customs of Safed Kabbalists in Meron." Hebrew. *Sefunot* 6 (1962): 11–40.

Bender, A. P. "Beliefs, Rites, and Customs of the Jews, Connected with Death," *Jewish Quarterly Review* (1894–95), 101–18, 259–69.

Ben-Yehudah, Eliezer. *Millon ha-Lashon ha-'Ivrit.* 8 vols. Reprint. New York: Thomas Yoseloff, 1980.

Bibliography

Bergmann, J[ehuda]. "Schebua ha-ben." *Monatsschrift für die Geschichte und Literatur der Juden* 76 (1932): 465–70.

Berkey, Jonathan P. "Circumcision Circumscribed: Female Excision and Cultural Accommodation in the Medieval Near East." *International Journal of Middle East Studies* 28 (1996): 19–38.

Bernstein, Elizabeth. "You Don't Have to Be Jewish to Want a Bar Mitzvah." *The Wall Street Journal,* January 14, 2004.

Bhabha, Homi K. *The Location of Culture.* New York: Routledge, 1994.

Biale, David. "Childhood, Marriage, and Family in the Eastern European Jewish Enlightenment." In *The Jewish Family: Myths and Reality,* edited by Steven M. Cohen and Paula E. Hyman, 45–61.

———. *Eros and the Jews: From Biblical Israel to Contemporary America.* New York: Basic Books, 1992.

Biale, Rachel. *Women and Jewish Law.* New York: Schocken Books, 1985.

Bilu, Yoram. "From Circumcision (mei-milah) to the Word (le-millah): Psychocultural Analysis of Male Identity Formation in Childhood Rites in Ultra-Orthodox Society." Hebrew. *Alpayyim* 19 (2000): 17–46.

Blank, Debra Reed. "Jewish Rites of Adolescence." In *Life Cycles in Jewish and Christian Worship,* edited by Paul F. Bradshaw and Lawrence A. Hoffman, 81–110.

Blau, Ludwig. *Das altjüdische Zauberwesen.* Budapest, 1898.

Bloch, Abraham P. *The Biblical and Historical Background of Jewish Customs and Ceremonies.* New York: KTAV, 1980.

Bloch-Smith, Elizabeth. *Judahite Burial Practices and Beliefs about the Dead.* Sheffield: JSOT Press, 1992.

Blumenfeld-Kosinski, Renate. *Not of Woman Born: Representations of Caesarean Birth in Medieval and Renaissance Culture.* Ithaca: Cornell University Press, 1990.

Blumenthal, David. "Observations and Reflections on the History and Meanings of the Kaddish." *Judaism* 50 (2001): 35–51.

Bonfil, Robert. *Jewish Life in Renaissance Italy.* Translated by Anthony Oldcorn. Berkeley: University of California Press, 1994.

———. "'What Is Hinuma?' An Early Jewish Marriage Custom." Hebrew.

In *Hagut 'Ivrit be-Eiropa,* edited by Menahem Zohari and Aryeh Tartakover, 57–70. Tel Aviv, 1969.

Bonner, Stanley F. *Education in Ancient Rome.* Berkeley: University of California Press, 1977.

Bornstein, Diane. "Betrothal." In *The Dictionary of the Middle Ages,* edited by Joseph R. Strayer, 2:207–8. New York: Scribners, 1983.

Boswell, John. *The Kindness of Strangers.* New York: Pantheon, 1988.

Boyarin, Daniel. *Dying for God: Martyrdom and the Making of Christianity and Judaism.* Stanford: Stanford University Press, 1999.

Boyarin, Jonathan, and Daniel Boyarin. "Self-Exposure as Theory: The Double Mark of the Male Jew." In *Rhetorics of Self-Making,* edited by Debbora Battaglia, 16–42. Berkeley: University of California Press, 1995.

Bradshaw, Paul F. "Christian Marriage Rituals." In *Life Cycles in Jewish and Christian Worship,* edited by Paul F. Bradshaw and Lawrence A. Hoffman, 111–28.

———. "Christian Rites related to Birth." In *Life Cycles in Jewish and Christian Worship,* edited by Paul F. Bradshaw and Lawrence A. Hoffman, 13–31.

Bradshaw, Paul F., and Lawrence A. Hoffman, eds., *Life Cycles in Jewish and Christian Worship.* Notre Dame, Ind.: University of Notre Dame Press, 1996.

Brauer, Erich. "Birth Customs of the Jews of Kurdistan." Hebrew. *'Edot* 1 (1946): 65–72.

———. "Circumcision and Childhood among the Jews of Kurdistan." Hebrew. *'Edot* 1 (1946): 129–38.

———. *The Jews of Kurdistan.* Translated by Raphael Patai. Detroit: Wayne State University Press, 1993.

———. *Yehudei Kurdistan.* Edited by Raphael Patai. Jerusalem, 1947.

Breuer, Mordecai. "Chapters in the History of Rabbi Samson Raphael Hirsch." Hebrew. *Ha-Ma'ayan* 12 (1972): 55–62.

Briggs, David. "Catholic Church Tests Combining Communion, Confirmation." Religion News Service, 2000, from http://www.beliefnet.com/story/44/story_4402.html.

Briggs, Lloyd Cabot, and Norina Lami Guède. *No More For Ever.* Papers of the Peabody Museum of Archeology and Ethnology, Harvard University, vol. 55, no. 1. Cambridge, Mass.: Harvard University Press, 1964.

Brill, Jacques. *Lilith ou la mère obscure.* Paris: Editions Payot, 1981.

Brill, Moshe. "The Age of the Child When He Enters School." Hebrew. *Tarbiz* 9 (1938): 350–74.

Brown, Erica S. "The Bat Mitzvah in Jewish Law and Contemporary Practiced." In *Jewish Legal Writings by Women,* edited by Micah D. Halpern and Chana Safrai, 232–58. Jerusalem: Urim Publications, 1998.

Büchler, Adolph. "The Induction of the Bride and Bridegroom into the Chuppah in the First and Second Centuries in Palestine." In *Sefer Zikaron le-Poznanski {=Livre d'hommage à la memoire du Dr. Samuel Poznanski},* 82–132. 2 vols. Warsaw, 1927.

———. "Das Jüdische Verlöbnis und die Stellung der verlobten priesters im ersten und zweiten Jahrhundert." *Festschrift zu Israel Lewy's Siebsigstem Geburtstag,* edited by M. Brann and J. Elbogen, i–xxxv. Breslau, 1911.

Burnett, Stephen G. *From Christian Hebraism to Jewish Studies.* Studies in the History of Christian Thought, vol. 68, edited by Heiko A. Oberman. Leiden: E. J. Brill, 1996.

Burrow, J. A. *The Ages of Man.* Oxford: Oxford University Press, 1986.

Butler, James Davie. "Medieval German Schools." *Bibliotheca Sacra* 39 (1882): 401–17. Berkeley: University of California Press, 1982.

Carlebach, Elisheva. *Divided Souls: Converts from Judaism in Germany, 1500–1750.* New Haven: Yale University Press, 2001.

Cassuto, Moshe David. "Avnayim." Hebrew. *Enziqlopedia Miqra'it,* 1:57–59. 8 vols. Jerusalem: Mosad Bialik, 1965–82.

Cohen, Aaron. *Zeved ha-Bat.* Jerusalem, 1990.

Cohen, Alfred S. "Celebration of the Bat Mitzvah." *Journal of Halacha and Contemporary Society* 12 (1986): 5–16.

Cohen, Aryeh. "'Do the Dead Know?' The Representation of the Dead in the Bavli." *AJS Review* 24 (1999): 45–71.

Cohen, Boaz. "On the Laws of a Minor in Jewish and Roman Law." Hebrew. *Ha-Doar,* 11 Nissan 1963. [Issue in Honor of Saul Lieberman's Sixty-Fifth Birthday.]

Cohen, Debra Nussbaum. *Celebrating Your New Jewish Daughter: Creating Jew-*

ish Ways to Welcome Baby Girls into the Covenant. Woodstock, Vt.: Jewish Lights Publishing, 2001.

Cohen, Esther, and Elliott Horowitz, "In Search of the Sacred: Jews, Christians, and Rituals of Marriage in the Later Middle Ages." *Journal of Medieval and Renaissance Studies* 20 (1990): 225–49.

Cohen, Gerson D. "The Blessing of Assimilation." 1966. Reprint. In Gerson D. Cohen, *Jewish History and Jewish Destiny,* 145–56, New York: Jewish Theological Seminary of America, 1997.

Cohen, Jeremy. *"Be Fertile and Increase, Fill the Earth and Master It."* Ithaca: Cornell University Press, 1989.

———. *Sanctifying the Name of God: Jewish Martyrs and Jewish Memories of the First Crusade.* Philadelphia: University of Pennsylvania Press, 2004.

Cohen, Mark R. "Leone da Modena's *Riti:* A Seventeenth-Century Plea for Toleration of the Jews." *Jewish Social Studies* 34 (1972): 287–321.

Cohen, Richard I. *Jewish Icons: Art and Society in Modern Europe.* Berkeley: University of California Press, 1998.

Cohen, Shaye J. D. *The Beginnings of Jewishness: Boundaries, Varieties, Uncertainties.* Berkeley: University of California Press, 1999.

———. "A Brief History of Jewish Circumcision Blood." In *The Covenant of Circumcision,* edited by Elizabeth Mark, 30–42. Hanover, N.H.: Brandeis University Press, 2003.

Cohen, Steven M., and Paula E. Hyman, eds. *The Jewish Family: Myths and Reality.* New York: Holmes and Meier, 1986.

Cooper, John. *The Child in Jewish History.* Northvale, N.J.: Jason Aronson, 1996.

Cooper, Samuel. "The Laws of Mixture: An Anthropological Study in Halakhah." In *Judaism Viewed from Within and from Without,* edited by Harvey E. Goldberg, 55–74.

Cramer, Peter. *Baptism and Change in the Early Middle Ages, c. 250–c. 1150.* Cambridge: Cambridge University Press, 1993.

Cressy, David. *Birth, Marriage and Death: Ritual, Religion, and the Life-Cycle in Tudor and Stuart England.* Oxford: Oxford University Press, 1997.

Cunningham, Hugh. "Review Essay: Histories of Childhood." *American Historical Review* 103 (1998): 1195–1208.

Dan, Joseph. "Samael, Lilith and the Concept of Evil in Early Kabbalah." *AJS Review* 5 (1980): 19–25.

———. "Ultra-Orthodoxy on Top: A Consequence of Secular Israel." Hebrew. *Alpayyim* 15 (1997): 234–53.

Davidson, Israel, ed. *Ozar ha-Shirah ve-ha-Piyyut.* 1924. Reprint. 4 vols. New York: KTAV, 1970.

Davis, Judith. "The Bar Mitzvah as a Multigenerational Ritual of Change and Continuity." In *Essays in the Social and Scientific Study of Judaism and Jewish Society,* edited by Simcha Fishbane and Jack N. Lightstone with Victor Levin, 231–50. Montréal: Department of Religion, Concordia University, 1990.

Davis, Natalie Zemon. *Fiction from the Archives.* Stanford: Stanford University Press, 1987.

———. "Glikl bas Judah Leib: Arguing with God." In *Women on the Margins: Three Seventeenth-Century Lives,* 5–62. Cambridge, Mass.: Harvard University Press, 1995.

Demaitre, Luke. "The Idea of Childhood and Child Care in Medieval Writings of the Middle Ages." *Journal of Psychohistory* 4 (1977): 461–90.

Demand, Nancy. *Birth, Death, and Motherhood in Classical Greece.* Baltimore: Johns Hopkins University Press, 1994.

Deutsch, Yaakov. "'A View of the Jewish Religion': Conceptions of Jewish Practice and Ritual in Early Modern Europe." *Archiv für Religionsgeschichte* 3 (2001): 273–95.

de Vaux, Roland. *Ancient Israel.* 2 vols. New York: McGraw-Hill, 1965.

Diamant, Anita. *The New Jewish Baby Book.* New York: Summit Books, 1985.

———. *The New Jewish Wedding.* New York: Simon and Schuster, 1985.

———. *Saying Kaddish: How to Comfort the Dying, Bury the Dead and Mourn as a Jew.* New York: Schocken Books, 1998.

Diemling, Maria. "'Christliche Ethnographien' über Juden und Judentum in der Frühen Neuzeit: Die Konvertiten Victor von Carben und Anthonius Margaritha und ihre Darstellung Jüdischen Lebens und jüdischer Religion." Dissertation zur Erlangung des Doktorgrades der Philosophie eingereicht an der Geisteswissenschaftlichen Fakultät der Universität Wien, 1999.

Diner, Hasia R., and Beryl Lieff Benderly, eds. *Her Works Praise Her: A History of Jewish Women in America from Colonial Times to the Present.* New York: Basic Books, 2002.

Dobrinsky, Herbert C. *A Treasury of Sephardic Laws and Customs.* New York: Yeshiva University Press, 1986.

Duby, Georges. *Love and Marriage in the Middle Ages.* Translated by Jane Dunnett. Chicago: University of Chicago Press, 1994.

——. *Medieval Marriage: Two Models from Twelfth-Century France.* Translated by Elborg Forster. Baltimore: Johns Hopkins University Press, 1978.

Ehrlich, Uri. *"Kol 'Azmotai Tomarna": Ha-Safah ha-Lo-Milulit shel ha-Tefillah.* Jerusalem: Magnes, 1999.

Elbogen, Ismar. *Jewish Liturgy: A Comprehensive History.* Translated by Raymond P. Scheindlin. Philadelphia: Jewish Publication Society; New York: Jewish Theological Seminary of America, 1993.

Eliade, Mircea. *Rites and Symbols of Initiation.* New York: Harper and Row, 1958.

Eliav, Mordecai. *Ha-Hinukh ha-Yehudi be-Germaniya bi-mei ha-Haskalah ve-ha-Imanzipaziah.* Jerusalem: Jewish Agency, 1961.

Eliav-Feldon, Miriam, and Yitzhak Hen, eds. *Nashim, Zeqeinim va-Taf.* Hebrew. Jerusalem: Merkaz Zalman Shazar, 2001.

Elper, Ora Wiskind, ed. *Traditions and Celebrations for the Bat Mitzvah.* Jerusalem: Urim Publications/Matan, 2003.

Epstein, Louis. *The Jewish Marriage Contract: A Study in the Status of the Woman in Jewish Law.* New York: Jewish Theological Seminary of America, 1927.

——. *Sex Laws and Customs in Judaism.* 1948. Reprint. New York: KTAV, 1967.

Epstein, Y. N. *Mavo le-Nusah ha-Mishnah.* Jerusalem: Magnes; Tel Aviv: Dvir, 1948.

Erikson, Erik H. *Childhood and Society.* 1950. 2nd ed., rev. and enl. New York: Norton, 1963.

——. *Identity and the Life Cycle.* New York: Norton, 1980.

——. *Identity, Youth and Crisis.* New York: Norton, 1968.

Falk, Ze'ev W. *Jewish Matrimonial Law in the Middle Ages.* Oxford: Oxford University Press, 1966.

Feldman, David. *Marital Relations, Birth Control and Abortion in Jewish Law.* New York: Schocken Books, 1968.

Feldman, W. M. *The Jewish Child: Its History, Folklore, Biology, and Sociology.* London, 1917.

Fernandez, James W. "The Performance of Ritual Metaphors." In *The Social Use of Metaphor,* edited by J. David Sapir and J. Christopher Crocker, 100–131. Philadelphia: University of Pennsylvania Press, 1977.

Feuchtwanger, Naomi. "The Coronation of the Virgin and of the Bride." *Jewish Art* 12–13 (1986/87): 213–24.

———. "Interrelations between the Jewish and Christian Wedding in Medieval Ashkenaz." *Proceedings of the Ninth World Congress of Jewish Studies,* Division D, 2:31–36. Jerusalem, 1986.

Feuchtwanger-Sarig, Naomi. "'May He Grow to Torah': The Iconography of Torah Reading and *Bar Mitzvah* on Ashkenazi Torah Binders." In *Liturgy in the Life of the Synagogue: Studies in the History of Jewish Prayer,* edited by Ruth Langer and Steven Fine. Winona Lake, Wis.: Eisenbrauns, in press.

———. "Torah Binder from Denmark." Hebrew. Ph.D. diss., Hebrew University of Jerusalem, 1999.

Fildes, Valerie. *Breasts, Bottles and Babies: A History of Infant Feeding.* Edinburgh: Edinburgh University Press, 1986.

Fine, Lawrence, ed. *Judaism in Practice: From the Middle Ages through the Early Modern Period.* Princeton: Princeton University Press, 2001.

Fishbane, Michael. *The Kiss of God: Spiritual and Mystical Death in Judaism.* Seattle: University of Washington Press, 1994.

Fisher, J. D. C. *Christian Initiation: Baptism in the Medieval West.* London: S.P.C.K., 1965.

Fleishman, Joseph. *Horim Viladim be-Mishpetei ha-Mizrah ha-Qadum u-ve-Mishpat ha-Miqra.* Jerusalem: Magnes, 1999.

Flusser, David. "Tuvia, Sefer Tuvia." Hebrew. In *Encyclopaedia Miqra'it,* 3:367–75. 8 vols. Jerusalem, 1965–82.

Fossier, Robert. *La petite enfance dans l'Europe médiévale et moderne.* Toulouse: Presses Universitaires du Mirail, 1997.

Freehof, Solomon B. "Ceremonial Creativity among the Ashkenazim." 1967. Reprint. In *Beauty and Holiness,* edited by Joseph Gutmann, 486–500.

―――. "Hazkarat Neshamot." *Hebrew Union College Annual* 36 (1965):

―――. "Home Rituals and the Spanish Synagogue." 1962. Reprint. In *Beauty and Holiness,* edited by Joseph Gutmann, 501–13.

―――. "The Chuppah." In *In the Time of Harvest: Essays in Honor of Abba Hillel Silver on the Occasion of His 70th Birthday,* edited by Daniel Jeremy Silver, 186–93. New York: Macmillan, 1963.

Freeze, ChaeRan Y. *Jewish Marriage and Divorce in Imperial Russia.* Hanover, N.H.: University Press of New England, 2002.

Freimann, Abraham Haim. *Seder Qiddushin ve-Nissu'in.* Jerusalem: Mosad Ha-Rav Kook, 1964.

Friedland Ben Arza, Sara, ed. *Bat-Mitzvah.* Hebrew. Jerusalem: Matan, 2002.

Friedman, Menahem. *Ha-Hevrah ha-Hareidit: Meqorot, Megamot, ve-Tahalikhim.* Jerusalem: Mehqerei Yerushalayim le-Heqer Yisrael, 41, 1991.

Friedman, Mordecai A. *Jewish Marriage in Palestine: A Cairo Geniza Study.* 2 vol. Tel Aviv: Tel Aviv University; New York: Jewish Theological Seminary of America, 1980.

―――. "Marriage as an Institution: Jewry under Islam." In *The Jewish Family: Metaphor and Memory,* edited by David Kraemer, 31–46. New York: Oxford University Press, 1989.

From This World to the Next: Jewish Approaches to Illness, Death and the Afterlife. New York: Library of the Jewish Theological Seminary of America, 1999.

Gafni, Isaiah. "The Institution of Marriage in Rabbinic Times." In *The Jewish Family: Metaphor and Memory,* edited by David Kraemer, 13–30. New York: Oxford University Press, 1989.

Gaster, Theodor H. *The Holy and the Profane: Evolution of Jewish Folkways.* Rev. ed. New York: William Morrow, 1980.

Gaudin, A. "Colybes." In *Dictionnaire d'archéologie chrétienne et de liturgies,* edited by Fernand Cabrol and Henri Leclercq, 3.2 (1914), 2342–46. 15 vols. Paris, 1907–50.

Geffen, Rela M., ed. *Celebration and Renewal: Rites of Passage in Judaism.* Philadelphia: Jewish Publication Society, 1993.

Gelbard, Shmuel Pinchas. *Rite and Reason: 1050 Jewish Customs and Their Sources.* Translated by R. Nachman Bulman. 2 vols. Petach Tikvah, Israel: Mifal Rashi Publishing, 1998.

Gélis, Jacques. *History of Childbirth: Fertility, Pregnancy and Birth in Early Modern Europe.* Translated by Rosemary Morris. Oxford: Polity Press, Blackwell Publishers, 1991.

Gendler, Mary. "Sarah's Seed: A New Ritual for Women." *Response: A Contemporary Jewish Review* 24 (1974–75): 65–75.

Germania Judaica. Edited by Ismar Elbegan, et al. 3 pts. in 6 vols. Tübingen: J. C. B. Mohr (Paul Siebeck), 1963–2003.

Gibson, Gail McMurray. "Scene and Obscene: Seeing and Performing Late Medieval Childbirth." *Journal of Medieval and Early Modern Studies* 29 (1999): 7–24.

Gies, Frances, and Joseph Gies. *Marriage and the Family in the Middle Ages.* New York: Harper and Row, 1987.

Gil'adi, Avner. *Children of Islam: Concepts of Childhood in Medieval Muslim Society.* London: MacMillan, 1992.

———. "Concepts of Childhood and Attitudes towards Children in Medieval Islam." *Journal of the Economic and Social History of the Orient* 32 (1989): 121–51.

Gilat, Yitzhaq. "Age Thirteen for the Commandments?" Hebrew. In *Mehqarei Talmud,* [I]. Edited by Yaakov Zussman and David Rosenthal. Jerusalem, 1992.

Gilman, Sandor L. "The Indelibility of Circumcision." *Qorot* 9, nos. 11–12 (1991): 806*–817*.

Glasberg, Jacob. *Zikhron Brit la-Rishonim.* Cracow, 1892.

Glick, Shmuel. *Or la-Aveil: le-Hitpathutan shel 'Iqarei Minhagei Aveilut be-Masoret Yisrael.* Ephrat, 1997.

———. *Or Nagah 'Aleihem: Ha-Ziqah she-Bein Minhagei Nissuin le-Minhagei Aveilut be-Masoret Yisrael.* Ephrat, 1997.

Goetz, Hans-Werner. *Life in the Middle Ages: From the Seventh to the Thirteenth Century.* Translated by Albert Wimmer. Edited by Steven Rowan. Notre Dame: University of Notre Dame Press, 1993.

Goitein, S. D. "Jewish Education in Yemen as an Archetype of Traditional Jewish Education." Hebrew. In S. D. Goitein, *Ha-Teimanim,* 241–68.

———. *A Mediterranean Society.* 6 vols. Berkeley: University of California Press, 1967–93.

————. *Sidrei Hinukh.* Jerusalem, 1962.

————. *Ha-Teimanim: Historiah, Sidrei Hevrah, Hayyei ha-Ruah.* Edited by Menahem Ben-Sasson. Jerusalem: Makhon Ben-Zvi, 1983.

————. "Three Trousseaux of Jewish Brides from the Fatimid Period." *AJS Review* 2 (1977): 77–105.

Goldberg, Harvey E. "Anthropology and the Study of Traditional Jewish Societies." *AJS Review* 15 (1990): 1–22.

————. *Jewish Passages: Cycles of Jewish Life.* Berkeley: University of California Press, 2003.

————. "A Jewish Wedding in Tripolitania: A Study in Cultural Sources." *Maghreb Review* 3 (1978): 1–6.

————. "Torah and Children: Symbolic Aspects of the Reproduction of Jews and Judaism." In *Judaism Viewed from Within,* edited by Harvey Goldberg, 107–30.

————, ed. *Judaism Viewed from Within and from Without.* Albany: SUNY Press, 1987.

————, ed., *The Life of Judaism.* Berkeley: University of California Press, 2001.

Goldberg, Jacob. "Jewish Marriage in Eighteenth-Century Poland." *Polin: Studies in Polish Jewry* 10 (1997): 3–39 [=*Jews in Early Modern Poland.* Edited by Gershon Hundert. London: Littman Library, 1997].

Goldberg, Sylvie-Anne. *Crossing the Jabbok: Illness and Death in Ashkenazi Judaism in Sixteenth- through Nineteenth-Century Prague.* Translated by Carol Cosman. Berkeley: University of California Press, 1996.

Golden, Mark. *Children and Childhood in Classical Athens.* Baltimore: Johns Hopkins University Press, 1990.

Goldin, Simha. *'Alamot Aheivukha—'Al Mavet Aheivukha.* Lod: Dvir, 2002.

————. "Die Beziehung der jüdischen Familie im Mittelalter zu Kind und Kindheit." *Jahrbuch der Kindheit* 6 (1989): 211–33; 251–56.

————. "A Rite as a Research Text." Hebrew. Review of Ivan G. Marcus, *Tiqsei Yaldut. Zemanim* 70 (1998): 123–24.

————. *Ha-Yihud ve-ha-Yahad.* Tel Aviv: University of Tel Aviv Press, 1997.

Goldman, Ari. *Living a Year of Kaddish: A Memoir.* New York: Schocken Books, 2003.

Goodich, Michael. *From Birth to Old Age: The Human Life Cycle in Medieval Thought, 1250–1350.* Lanham, Md.: University Press of America, 1989.

Goodman, Philip, and Hanna Goodman. *The Jewish Marriage Anthology.* Philadelphia: Jewish Publication Society, 1965.

Gottleib, Nathan. *A Jewish Child Is Born: Laws and Rites of Circumcision, Naming Boys and Girls.* New York: Bloch Publishing Co., 1960.

Grimes, Ronald L. *Beginnings in Ritual Studies.* 1982. Rev. ed. Columbia: University of South Carolina Press, 1995.

———. *Deeply into the Bone: Re-Inventing Rites of Passage.* Berkeley: University of California Press, 2001.

Grimm, Jacob, and Wilhelm Grimm, eds., *Deutsches Wörterbuch.* Leipzig, 1877.

Gross, Abraham. "The Blood Libel and the Blood of Circumcision: An Ashkenazic Custom That Disappeared in the Middle Ages." *Jewish Quarterly Review* 86 (1995): 171–74.

Grossman, Avraham. *Hakhmei Ashkenaz ha-Rishonim.* Jerusalem: Magnes, 1981.

———. *Hasidot u-Moredot.* Jerusalem: Magnes, 2000.

———. "The Historical Background to the Ordinances on Family Affairs Attributed to Rabbenu Gershom Me'or ha-Golah ('The Light of the Exile')." In *Jewish History,* edited by Ada Rapoport-Albert, 3–24. London: Halban, 1988.

———. "Young Marriage in Jewish Society in the Middle Ages to the Thirteenth Century." Hebrew. *Pe'amim* 45 (1991): 108–25.

Gruzman, Meir. "The Development of Virginal Blood from Pure to Impure." Hebrew. *Sidra* 5 (1989): 47–62.

Güdemann, Moritz. *Geschichte des Erziehungswesens und der Cultur der abendländischen Juden.* 3 vols. 1880–88. Reprint. Amsterdam: Philo Press, 1969.

Gutmann, Joseph. "Christian Influences on Jewish Customs." In *Spirituality and Prayer: Jewish and Christian Understandings,* edited by Leon Klenicki and Gabe Huck, 128–38. New York: Paulist Press, 1983.

———. *The Jewish Life Cycle.* Leiden: E. J. Brill, 1987.

———. "Jewish Medieval Marriage Customs in Art: Creativity and Adap-

tation." In *The Jewish Family: Metaphor and Memory,* edited by David Kraemer, 47–62. New York: Oxford University Press, 1989.

———. "Die Mappe Schuletragen: An Unusual Judeo-German Custom."
Visible Religion 2 (1983): 167–73.

———. "The Strange History of the *Kapporot* Ritual." *Zeitschrift für die alt-
testamentliche Wissenschaft und die Kunde des nachbiblischen Judentums* 112
(2000): 624–26.

———. "Wedding Customs and Ceremonies in Art." In *Beauty and Holiness,* edited by Joseph Gutmann, 313–39.

———, ed. *Beauty and Holiness: Studies in Jewish Customs and Ceremonial Art.*
New York: KTAV, 1970.

Hallo, William W. "Isaiah 28:9–13 and the Ugaritic Abecedaries." *Journal of Biblical Literature* 77 (1958): 324–28.

Hallote, Rachel. *Death, Burial, and Afterlife in the Biblical World.* Chicago:
Ivan R. Dee, 2001.

Halpern (Halperin), Israel. "The 'Rush' into Early Marriages among Eastern European Jews." Hebrew. *Zion* 17 (1962): 36–58.

Hamburger, Binyamin Shlomo. *Shorashei Minhag Ashkenaz.* 2 vols. Benei
Brak: Makhon Moreshet Ashkenaz, 1995.

Hanawalt, Barbara. "Medievalists and the Study of Childhood." *Speculum*
77 (2002): 440–60.

Hazan, Ephraim. *Ha-Shirah ha-'Ivrit bi-Zefon Afriqa.* Jerusalem: Magnes,
1995.

Heilman, Samuel C. *Defenders of the Faith: Inside Ultra-Orthodox Jewry.* New
York: Schocken Books, 1992.

———. *When a Jew Dies: The Ethnography of a Bereaved Son.* Berkeley: University of California Press, 2001.

Higger, Michael. "Circling (the Bride)." Hebrew. *Horev* 1 (1934): 207–16.

Hildesheimer, Azriel. "The History of the Betrothal and Marriage Blessings." Hebrew. *Sinai* 10 (1942): 107–18.

Hoffman, Lawrence A. *Covenant of Blood: Circumcision and Gender in Rabbinic
Judaism.* Chicago: University of Chicago Press, 1996.

———. "The Jewish Wedding Ceremony." In *Life Cycles in Jewish and Chris-*

tian Worship, edited by Paul F. Bradshaw and Lawrence A. Hoffman, 129–53.

———. "Life Cycle as Religious Metaphor." In *Life Cycles in Jewish and Christian Worship,* edited by Paul F. Bradshaw and Lawrence A. Hoffman, 1–12.

———. "Life Cycle Liturgy as Status Transformation." In *Eulogema: Studies in Honor of Robert Taft, S. J.,* edited by E. Carr et al., 161–77. Rome: Centro Studi S. Anselmo, 1993.

———. "Rites of Death and Mourning in Judaism." In *Life Cycles in Jewish and Christian Worship,* edited by Paul F. Bradshaw and Lawrence A. Hoffman, 214–39.

———. "Rituals of Birth in Judaism." In *Life Cycles in Jewish and Christian Worship,* edited by Paul F. Bradshaw and Lawrence A. Hoffman, 32–54.

———. "The Role of Women at Rituals of Their Infant Children." In *Judaism in Practice,* edited by Lawrence Fine, 105–14.

Horowitz, Elliott. "'Bringing in the Bride' in the Venetian Ghetto: Tradition and Innovation, Ideal and Reality." Hebrew. *Tarbiz* 56 (1987): 347–71.

———. "'A Different Mode of Civility': Lancelot Addison on the Jews of Barbary." In *Christianity and Judaism,* edited by Diane Wood, 309–25. [Studies in Church History 29]. Cambridge: Cambridge University Press, 1992.

———. "Enlightening Letters: On Ritual and Cultural History of the Jews." Hebrew. Review of Ivan G. Marcus, *Tiqsei Yaldut. Pe'amim* 85 (2001): 194–200.

———. "The Eve of Circumcision: A Chapter in the History of Jewish Nightlife." *Journal of Social History* 23 (1989): 45–70.

———. "Giotto in Avignon, Adler in London, Panefsky in Princeton: On the Odyssey of an Illustrated Hebrew Manuscript from Italy and on Its Meaning." *Jewish Art* 19/20 (1993/4):98–111.

———. "Membership and Its Rewards: The Emergence and Decline of Ferrara's Gemilut Hasadim Society (1515–1603)." In *The Mediterranean and the Jews: Society, Culture and Economy in Early Modern Times,* edited by

Elliott Horowitz and Moise Orfali, 27–66. Ramat Gan: Bar-Ilan University Press, 2002.

———. "Speaking to the Dead: Cemetery Prayer in Medieval and Early Modern Jewry." *Journal of Jewish Thought and Philosophy* 8 (1999): 303–17.

Hsia, R. Po-chia. "Christian Ethnography of Jews in Early Modern Germany." In *The Expulsion of the Jews: 1492 and After,* edited by R. B. Waddington and A. H. Williamson, 223–35. New York: Garland, 1994.

Hunt, David. *Parents and Children in History: The Psychology of Family Life in Early Modern France.* New York: Basic Books, 1970.

Hurwitz, Siegmund. *Lilith — The First Eve: Historical and Psychological Aspects of the Dark Feminine.* Translated by Gela Jacobson. Einsiedeln: Daimon Verlag, 1992.

Hyams, Helge-Ulrike. *Jüdische Kindheit in Deutschland: Eine Kulturgeschichte.* Munich, 1995.

Hyman, Paula. "Bat Mitzvah." In *Jewish Women in America: An Historical Encyclopedia,* edited by Paula E. Hyman and Debra Dash Moore, 126–28. 2 vols. New York: Routledge, 1997.

———. "The Introduction of Bat Mitzvah in Conservative Judaism in Postwar America." *YIVO Annual* 19 (1990): 133–46.

Isaacs, Ronald H. *Rites of Passage: A Guide to the Jewish Life Cycle.* Hoboken, N.J.: KTAV, 1992.

Jacoby, Ruth. "The Relation between Elijah's Chair and the Sandak's (Godfather) Chair." Hebrew. In *Birth, Childhood, and Bar-Mitzvah,* edited by Shalom Sabar, 43–53.

Jacquart, Danielle, and Claude Thomasset. *Sexuality and Medicine in the Middle Ages.* Princeton: Princeton University Press, 1988.

Jordan, William Chester. "A travers le regard des enfants." *Provence Historique* 150 (1987): 531–43.

Joselit, Jenna Weissman. *The Wonders of America, Reinventing Jewish Culture, 1880–1950.* New York: Hill and Wang, 1994.

Juynboll, Th. W., and J. Pedersen. "'Akika." In *Encyclopedia of Islam.* 2nd ed. 1:337.

Kafih, Joseph. *Halikhot Teiman.* Jerusalem: Makhon Ben-Zvi, 1963.

Kafih, Joseph, and Avivah Lanze. "Wedding Costumes of Jews in the Yemenite Capital San'a." Hebrew. *Yeda' 'Am* 8 (1963): 20–26.

Kahn, Nancy E. "The Adult Bar Mitzvah: Its Use in Female Development." Ph.D. diss., Smith College School for Social Work, Northampton, Mass., 1992.

Kanarfogel, Ephraim. "Attitudes toward Childhood and Children in Medieval Jewish Society." In *Approaches to Judaism in Medieval Times,* edited by David Blumenthal, 2:1–34. Chico, Calif.: Scholars Press, 1985.

―――. *Jewish Education and Society in the High Middle Ages.* Detroit: Wayne State University Press, 1992.

Karel, Zvi. "The Kaddish." Hebrew. *Ha-Shiloah* 35 (1918): 36–49; 426–30; 521–27.

Katz, Ernst. "Torah Study on the Mountain and by the Water." Hebrew. *Yeda' 'Am* 11 (1966): 4–8.

Katz, Jacob. *Exclusiveness and Tolerance.* New York: Schocken Books, 1961.

―――. "Family, Kinship, and Marriage among Ashkenazim in the Sixteenth to Eighteenth Centuries." *Jewish Journal of Sociology* 1 (1959): 4–22.

―――. "Marriage and Family Life in the Late Middle Ages." Hebrew. *Zion* 10 (1945): 21–54.

Kaufmann, David. "Le chant nuptual *mi adir.*" *Revue des études juives* 24 (1892): 288–90.

Keefe, Susan Ann. "Baptism." In *The Dictionary of the Middle Ages,* edited by Joseph R. Strayer, 2:83–86. New York: MacMillan, 1985.

Kirshenblatt-Gimblett. "The Cut That Binds: The Western Ashkenazic Torah Binder as Nexus between Circumcision and Torah." In *Celebration: Studies in Festivity and Ritual,* edited by Victor Turner, 136–46. Washington, D.C.: Smithsonian Institution, 1982.

Klein, Isaac. *A Guide to Jewish Religious Practice.* New York: Jewish Theological Seminary of America, 1979.

Klein, Michele. *A Time to Be Born: Customs and Folklore of Jewish Birth.* Philadelphia: Jewish Publications Society, 1998.

Kotek, S. "On the Period of Childhood in *Sefer Hasidim:* Medicine, Psychology and Education in the Middle Ages." Hebrew. *Qorot* 8 (1984): 297–318.

Kraemer, David. "Images of Jewish Childhood in Talmudic Literature." In *The Jewish Family: Metaphor and Memory,* edited by David Kraemer, 65–80. New York: Oxford University Press, 1989.

———. *The Meanings of Death in Rabbinic Judaism.* London and New York: Routledge, 2000.

———. "What Does Bar/Bat Mitzvah *Really* Signify?" *Conservative Judaism* 53 (2001): 3–8.

Kraemer, Joel. "The Life of Moses ben Maimon." In *Judaism in Practice,* edited by Lawrence Fine, 413–28.

Kriegk, G. L. "Das Schulwesen." In *Deutsches Bürgerthum im Mittelalter,* edited by G. L. Kriegk, 2:64–127; 357–65. 1871. Reprint. 2 vols. Frankfurt am Main, 1969.

Kroll, J. "The Concept of Childhood in the Middle Ages." *Journal of the History of Behavioral Sciences* 13 (1977): 384–96.

Kugel, James. *The Great Poems of the Bible: A Reader's Companion with New Translations.* New York: Free Press, 1999.

Kummer, Bernhard. "Frau Holle." In *Handwörterbuch des deutschen Aberglaubens,* edited by Hanns Bächtold-Stäubli. 10 vols. Berlin, 1927–41.

Künzl, Hannelore. "Symbolism in the Art of Jewish Gravestones in Europe." *Proceedings of the Ninth World Congress of Jewish Studies* (Jerusalem, August 4–12, 1985), Division D, vol. 2, Art, Folklore, Theatre, Music, 53–57. Jerusalem: World Union of Jewish Studies, 1986.

Krygier, Rivon. "The Multiple Meanings of the Mourner's Kaddish." *Conservative Judaism* 54 (2002): 67–77.

Lamm, Maurice. *The Jewish Way in Death and Mourning.* New York: Jonathan David, 1969.

———. *The Jewish Way in Love and Marriage.* Rev. ed. Middle Village, N.Y.: Jonathan David, 1991.

Landsberger, Franz. "Illuminated Marriage Contracts with Special Reference to the Cincinnati Ketubahs." 1965. Reprint. In *Beauty and Holiness,* edited by Joseph Gutmann, 370–413.

Langer, Ruth. "The Birkat Betulim: A Study of the Jewish Celebration of Bridal Virginity." *Proceedings of the American Academy for Jewish Research* 61 (1995): 53–94.

Lasareff, V. "Studies in the Iconography of the Virgin." *Art Bulletin* 20 (1938): 42–65.

Lasker, Daniel J. "Transubstantiation, Elijah's Chair, Plato, and the Jewish-Christian Debate." *Revue des études juives* 143 (1984): 31–58.

Lauers, Michel L. *La mémoire des ancêtres, le souci des morts.* Paris: Beauchesne, 1997.

Lauterbach, Jacob Z. "The Ceremony of Breaking a Glass at Weddings." 1925. Reprint. In *Beauty and Holiness,* edited by Joseph Gutmann, 340–69.

———. "The Naming of Children." 1932. Reprint. In *Studies in Jewish Law, Custom and Folklore,* by Jacob Lauterbach, 30–74.

———. "The Ritual for the Kapparot Ceremony." 1935. Reprint. In *Studies in Jewish Law, Custom and Folklore,* by Jacob Lauterbach, 133–42.

———. *Studies in Jewish Law, Custom and Folklore.* [New York]: KTAV, 1970.

Lehnhart, Andreas. *Qaddish: Untersuchungen zur Entstehung und Rezeption eines rabbinischen Gebetes.* Tübingen: J. C. B. Mohr [Paul Siebeck], 2002.

Lerner, Miron Bialik. "The Story of the Rabbi and the Dead Man." Hebrew. *Asufot* 2 (1988): 29–70.

Levi, Giovanni, and Jean-Claude Schmitt, eds. *A History of Young People.* Translated by Carol Volk. 2 vols. Cambridge, Mass.: Harvard University Press, 1997.

Levi, Yosef. "Bar Mitzvah and the Development of the Individual." Hebrew. *'Eit La'asot* 3 (1991): 101–19.

Lewy, Yosef. *Sefer Minhag Yisrael Torah.* 5 vols. in 4. N. p., 1999.

Lieberman, Dale. *Witness to the Covenant of Circumcision: Bris Milah.* Northvale, N.J.: Jason Aronson, 1997.

Lieberman, Saul. Review of *Masekhet Soferim,* edited by Michael Higger. In *Qiryat Sefer* 15 (1939): 56–57.

———. *Tosefta Ki-Feshuta.* 10 vols. New York: Jewish Theological Seminary of America, 1955–88.

———. *Yevanit vivanut be-Erez Yisrael.* Jerusalem: Mosad Bialik, 1962.

Liebes, Yehuda. "The *Zohar* as a Book of Jewish Law." Hebrew. *Tarbiz* 64 (1995): 581–605.

Lilienthal, Regina. "Das Kind bei den Juden." *Monatsschrift für die Geschichte und Literatur des Judenthums* 25 (1908): 1–18; 26 (1908): 1–55; also in *Mitteilungen zur jüdischen Volkskunde* 25, no. 1 (1908): 1–24; 26, no. 2 (1908): 41–55.

Löw, Leopold. *Die Lebensalter in der jüdischen Literatur.* Szegedin, 1875.

Lynch, Joseph H. *Godparents and Kinship in Early Medieval Europe.* Princeton: Princeton University Press, 1986.

Macrides, R. "The Byzantine Godfather." *Byzantine and Modern Greek Studies* 11 (1987): 139–62.

Mann, Jacob. "Rabbinic Studies in the Synoptic Gospels." *Hebrew Union College Annual,* n.s., 1 (1924): 323–55.

Mann, Vivian B. and Emily D. Bilski, *The Jewish Museum New York.* London: Scala Publications, 1993.

Marcus, Ivan G. "Circumcision, Jewish." In *The Dictionary of the Middle Ages,* edited by Joseph R. Strayer, 3:410–12. New York: Scribners, 1983.

———. "The Dynamics of Jewish Renaissance and Renewal in the Twelfth Century." In *Jews and Christians in Twelfth-Century Europe,* edited by Michael Signer and John Van Engen, 27–45. Notre Dame: University of Notre Dame Press, 2001.

———. "Exegesis for the Few and for the Many: Judah he-Hasid's Biblical Commentaries." In *The Age of the Zohar,* edited by Joseph Dan, 1–24. [=*Mehqarei Yerushalayim be-Mahshevet Yisrael* 8 (1989)].

———. "Honey Cakes and Torah: A Jewish Boy Learns His Letters." In *Judaism in Practice,* edited by Lawrence Fine, 115–30.

———. "A Jewish-Christian Symbiosis: The Culture of Early Ashkenaz." In *Cultures of the Jews: A New History,* edited by David Biale, 449–516. New York: Schocken Books, 2002.

———. "Mothers, Martyrs, and Moneymakers: Some Jewish Women in Medieval Ashkenaz." *Conservative Judaism* 38 (1986): 34–45.

———. *Piety and Society: The Jewish Pietists of Medieval Germany.* Leiden: E. J. Brill, 1981.

———. *Rituals of Childhood: Jewish Acculturation in Medieval Europe.* New Haven: Yale University Press, 1996; 1998 [paperback]; revised Hebrew edition, *Tiqsei Yaldut,* Jerusalem: Merkaz Zalman Shazar, 1998.

Marcus, Jacob R. *Communal Sick-Care in the German Ghetto.* Cincinnati: Hebrew Union College Press, 1947.

Margalit, D. "On Memory." Hebrew. *Qorot* 5 (1972): 759–72.

Mark, Elizabeth Wyner, ed. *The Covenant of Circumcision: New Perspectives on an Ancient Rite.* Lebenon, N.H.: University Press of New England, 2003.

Markon, I. "The Kitl." Hebrew, *Ha-Melilah* 1 (1944): 121–28.

Markowitz, Fran. "A Bat Mitzvah among Russian Jews in America." In *The Life of Judaism,* edited by Harvey E. Goldberg, 121–35.

Mason, Ruth. "Adult Bat Mitzvah: Changing Women, Changing Synagogues." *Lilith* 14 (1989): 21–24.

Matras, Hagit. "Contemporary Amulets for Mother and Child." Hebrew. In *Birth, Childhood,* edited by Sabar, 15–27.

May, Miranda. "The Practice of Covering the Bridal Pair in Jewish and Christian Marriage Rituals: Its Development and Metaphorical Associations in the Medieval Period." Senior Essay in the Humanities Major, Yale University, Spring 1999.

McCulloh, John M. "Martyrology." In *The Dictionary of the Middle Ages,* edited by Joseph R. Strayer, 8:161–62. New York: Scribners, 1985.

McLaughlin, Mary Martin. "Survivors and Surrogates: Children and Parents from the Ninth to the Thirteenth Centuries." In *The History of Childhood,* edited by Lloyd deMause, 101–81. New York: Harper and Row, 1974.

McLaughlin, Megan. *Consorting with Saints: Prayer for the Dead in Early Medieval France.* Ithaca: Cornell University Press, 1994.

Meek, Theophile James. *Hebrew Origins.* New York: Harper and Row, 1936.

Melammed, Renee Levine. "Life Cycle Rituals of Spanish Crypto-Jewish Women." In *Judaism in Practice,* edited by Lawrence Fine, 143–54.

Metzger, Thérèse, and Mendel Metzger, eds. *Jewish Life in the Middle Ages.* New York: Alpine, 1982.

Meyer, Michael A. *Response to Modernity: A History of the Reform Movement in Judaism.* New York: Oxford University Press, 1988.

Meyers, Eric M. "The Theological Implications of an Ancient Jewish Burial Custom." *Jewish Quarterly Review* 62 (1971): 95–119.

Bibliography

Meyers, Ruth A. "Christian Rites of Adolescence." In *Life Cycles in Jewish and Christian Worship*, edited by Paul F. Bradshaw and Lawrence A. Hoffman, 55–80.

Mielziner, M. *The Jewish Law of Marriage and Divorce.* New York, 1901.

Mitchell, Leonel L. "Confirmation." In *The Dictionary of the Middle Ages,* edited by Joseph R. Strayer, 3:535–36. New York: Scribners, 1983.

Modrzejewski, Joseph Mélèze. *The Jews of Egypt.* Translated by Robert Cornman. Philadelphia: Jewish Publication Society, 1995.

Momigliano, Arnoldo. "A Medieval Jewish Autobiography." 1981. Reprint. In Arnoldo Momigliano, *On Pagans, Jews, and Christians,* 222–30; 319–20. Middletown, Conn.: Wesleyan University Press, 1987.

Morgenstern, Julian. *Rites of Birth, Marriage, Death and Kindred Occasions among the Semites.* Cincinnati: Hebrew Union College Press, 1966.

Morrison, Karl F., ed. *Conversion and Text.* Charlottesville: University Press of Virginia, 1992.

Moser, Hans. "Maibaum und Maienbrauch." 1961. Reprint. In *Volksbräuche im geschichtlichen Wandel,* by Hans Moser, 199–268. Munich: Bayerischen Nationalmuseum, 1985.

Moskovitz, Patti. *The Complete Bar/Bat Mitzvah Book: Everything You Need to Plan a Meaningful Celebration.* Franklin Lakes, N.J.: Career Press, 2000.

Motzki, Harold. "Das Kind und seine Sozialisation in der islamischen Familie." In *Zur Sozialgeschichte der Kindheit,* edited by Jochen Martin and August Nitschke, 391–441. Freiburg, 1986.

Muchawsky-Schnapper, Ester. *The Jews of Yemen.* Jerusalem: Israel Museum, 1994.

Nahon, Gerard. "From the *rue aux juifs* to the *Chemin du Roy:* The Classical Age of French Jewry, 1108–1223." In *Jews and Christians in Twelfth-Century Europe,* edited by Michael A. Signer and John Van Engen, 311–39. Notre Dame, Ind.: University of Notre Dame Press, 2001.

Narkiss. Bezalel. "Illuminated Hebrew Children's Books from Medieval Egypt." In *Studies in Jewish Art.* [Scripta Hierosolymitana 24], edited by Moshe Barasch, 58–79. Jerusalem, 1972.

———. "Introduction" to *Machsor Lipsiae.* Edited by Elias Katz. Leipzig, 1964.

Nelson, Janet L. "Parents, Children, and the Church in the Earlier Middle Ages." In *The Church and Childhood,* edited by Diana Wood, 81–114.

Neubauer, Jacob. *Toledot Dinei ha-Nisu'in ba-Miqra u-va-Talmud.* Jerusalem: Magnes, 1994.

Neusner, Jacob. *The Enchantments of Judaism: Rites of Transformation from Birth through Death.* New York: Basic Books, 1987.

Noth, Martin. *Die Israelitischen Personennamen im Rahmen der Gemeinsemitischen Namengebung.* Stuttgart: Verlag von W. Kohlhammer, 1928.

Orenstein, Debra. *Lifecycles,* Volume 1: *Jewish Women on Life Passages and Personal Milestones.* Woodstock, Vt.: Jewish Lights, 1994.

Orme, Nicholas. *Medieval Children.* New Haven: Yale University Press, 2001.

Orsborn, Carol Matzkin. "The Initiation of Confirmation in Judaism: A Psychohistorical Study of a Jewish Ritual Innovation." Ph.D. diss., Vanderbilt University, 2002.

Pardes, Ilana. *The Biography of Ancient Israel.* Berkeley: University of California Press, 2000.

Patterson, Lee. *Negotiating the Past: The Historical Understanding of Medieval Literature.* Madison: University of Wisconsin Press, 1987.

Paxton, Frederick. *Christianizing Death.* Ithaca: Cornell University Press, 1990.

Perdue, Leo G., Joseph Blenkinsopp, John J. Collins, and Carol Meyers, *Families in Ancient Israel.* Louisville, Ky: Westminster John Knox Press, 1997.

Perez, Danielle Storper, and Harvey E. Goldberg. "Meanings of the Western Wall." In *The Life of Judaism,* edited by Harvey E. Goldberg, 173–94.

Petuchowski, Jakob J. "Manuals and Catechisms of the Jewish Religion in the Early Period of Emancipation." In *Studies in Nineteenth-Century Jewish Intellectual History,* edited by Alexander Altmann, 47–64. Cambridge, Mass.: Harvard University Press, 1964.

Pollack, Herman. "An Historical Explanation of the Origin and Development of Jewish Books of Customs (*Sifre Minhagim*): 1100–1300." *Jewish Social Studies* 49, nos. 3–4 (1987): 195–216.

———. *Jewish Folkways in Germanic Lands* (1648–1806): *Studies in Aspects of Daily Life.* Cambridge, Mass.: Harvard University Press, 1971.

Pool, David da Sola. *The Old Jewish-Aramaic Prayer the Kaddish.* Leipzig: Rudolf Haupt, 1909.

Porten, Bezalel. *Archives from Elephantine: The Life of a Jewish Military Colony.* Berkeley: University of California Press, 1968.

Propp, William H. "The Origins of Infant Circumcision in Israel." *Hebrew Annual Review* 11 (1987): 355–70.

———. "That Bloody Bridegroom (Exodus IV 24-6)." *Vetus Testamentum* 43 (1993): 495–518.

Qoret, Zevulun. "Betrothal and Marriage Customs in Herat, Afganistan." Hebrew. *Yeda' 'Am* 15 (1971): 15–22.

Quinn, Patricia A. "Benedictine Oblation: A Study of the Rearing of Boys in Monasteries in the Early Middle Ages." Ph.D. diss., SUNY, Binghamton, 1985.

Rappoport, Shabtai A. "Differences between the Bat Mitzvah Ceremony and Confirmation Ceremonies." Hebrew. In *Bat-Mitzvah,* edited by Sara Friedland Ben Arza, 31–39.

Ratzhabi, Yehudah. *Bo'i Teiman.* Tel Aviv: Afiqim, 1967.

Ravid, Benjamin, "*Contra Judaeos* in Seventeenth-Century Italy: Two Responses to the *Discorso* of Simone Luzzatto by Melchiore Palontrotti and Giulio Morosini." *AJS Review* 7–8 (1982–83): 301–51.

Riché, Pierre, and Danièle Alexandre-Bidon, eds. *L'enfance au moyen âge.* Paris: Editions de Seuil/Bibliothèque Nationale de France, 1994.

Ritzer, Korbinian. *Formen, Riten und religiöses Brauchtum des Eheschliessung in den christlichen Kirchen des ersten Jahrtausend.* 2nd ed., edited by Ulrich Hermann and Willibrord Heckenbach. Münster Westfalen: Aschendorffsche Verlagsbuchhandlung, 1981.

Rivkind, Yitzhak. "From Cradle to Wedding Canopy." Hebrew. *Yeda' 'Am* 6 (1960): 3–6.

———. *Le-Ot u-le-Zikkaron.* New York, 1942.

Roos, Lena. "*'God Wants It!'*" *The Ideology of Martyrdom of the Hebrew Crusade Chronicles and its Jewish and Christian Background.* Uppsala: Uppsala University 2003.

Roqeah, Zefirah Entin. "Unnatural Child Death among Christians and Jews in Medieval England." *Journal of Psychohistory* 18, no. 2 (fall 1990): 201–26.

Roskies, Diane. "Alphabet Instruction in the East European Heder: Some Comparative and Historical Notes." *Yivo Annual of Jewish Social Science* 17 (1978): 21–53.

Rosman, Moshe. *Founder of Hasidism: A Quest for the Historical Ba'al Shem Tov.* Berkeley: University of California Press, 1996.

Roth, Cecil. "Bar Mitzvah—Its History and Its Association." In *Bar Mitzvah,* edited by Abraham Katsh, Introduction: New York: Shengold, 1955.

Roth, Ernst. "Azkarah, Haftarah, ve-Qaddish Yatom," *Talpiyot* 7 nos. 2–4 (1961): 369–81.

———. "Educating Jewish Children on Shavuot." Hebrew. *Yeda' Am* 11 (1966): 9–12.

Rozen, Minna. "The Life Cycle and the Significance of Old Age During the Ottoman Period." In *Daniel Carpi: Jubilee Volume,* edited by [Anita Shapira, et al.], 109–78. Tel Aviv: Tel Aviv University, 1996.

Rubin, Nissan. "*Brit Milah:* A Study of Change in Custom." In *The Covenant of Circumcision,* edited by Elizabeth Mark, 87–97.

———. "The Price of Redemption: Jewish First Born and Social Change." In *Essays in the Social and Scientific Study of Judaism and Jewish Society,* edited by Simcha Fishbane and Stuart Schoenfeld with Alain Goldschlaeger, 3–12. Hoboken, N.J.: KTAV, 1992.

———. *Qeiz ha-Hayyim: Tiqsei Qevurah ve-Eivel bi-Meqorot Hazal.* Tel Aviv: Ha-Kibbutz Ha-Me'uhad. 1997.

———. *Reishit ha-Hayyim: Tiqsei Leidah, Milah, u-Fidyon ha-Ben bi-Meqorot Hazal.* Tel Aviv: Ha-Kibbutz Ha-Me'uhad 1995.

Ruderman, David. *The World of a Renaissance Jew.* Cincinnati: Hebrew Union College Press, 1981.

Russo-Katz, Miriam. "Childbirth." In *Sephardi Jews in the Ottoman Empire: Aspects of Material Culture,* edited by Esther Juhasz, 254–70. Jerusalem: Israel Museum, 1990.

Sabar, Shalom. "The Bar-Mizvah Ceremony in the Traditions and Art of Jewish Communities, East and West." Hebrew. *Rimonim* 5 (1997): 61–78.

———. "The Beginnings of *Ketubbah* Decoration in Italy: Venice in the Late Sixteenth to the Early Seventeenth Centuries." *Jewish Art* 12–13 (1986–87): 96–110.

————. "Childbirth and Magic: Jewish Folklore and Material Culture." In *Cultures of the Jews, a New History,* edited by David Biale, 671–722. New York: Schocken Books, 2002.

————. *Ketubbah: Jewish Marriage Contracts of the Hebrew Union College Skirball Museum and Klau Library.* Philadelphia: Jewish Publication Society, 1990.

————. "The Use and Meaning of Christian Motifs in Illustrations of Jewish Marriage Contracts in Italy." *Journal of Jewish Art* 10 (1984): 47–63.

————, ed. *Birth, Childhood, and Bar-Mitzvah in the Art and Traditions of Jewish Communities.* Hebrew. *Rimonim,* vol. 5 (1997).

Sadan, Dov. "Bat Mitzvah." Hebrew. *Dat u-Medinah* (1949), 59–60.

Salkin, Jeffrey K. *Putting God on the Guest List: How to Reclaim the Spiritual Meaning of Your Child's Bar or Bat Mitzvah.* 2nd ed. Woodstock, Vt.: Jewish Lights, 1996.

Saperstein, Marc. *Decoding the Rabbis: A Thirteenth-Century Commentary on the Aggadah.* Cambridge, Mass.: Harvard University Press, 1980.

Satlow, Michael L. *Jewish Marriage in Antiquity.* Princeton: Princeton University Press, 2001.

Scannell, T. B. "Confirmation." In *The Catholic Encyclopedia.* 1908. Online edition, 1999.

Schäfer, Peter. "The Ideal of Piety of the Ashkenazi Hasidim and Its Roots in Jewish Tradition." *Jewish History* 4, no. 2 (fall 1990): 9–23.

Schauss, Hayyim. *The Lifetime of a Jew throughout the Ages of Jewish History.* New York: Union of American Hebrew Congregations, 1950.

Schechter, Solomon. "The Child in Jewish Literature." 1889. Reprint. In Solomon Schechter, *Studies in Judaism,* 1st ser., 282–312. Philadelphia: Jewish Publication Society, 1920.

————. "The Memoirs of a Jewess of the Seventeenth Century." In Solomon Schechter, *Studies in Judaism.* 2nd ser. 1908. Reprint. Philadelphia: Jewish Publication Society, 1945, 126–47.

Schmelzer, Menachem. "Wedding Poems by the Early Sages of Ashkenaz." Hebrew. In *Memorial Volume for Aron Mirsky,* edited by Joseph Yahalom and Ephraim Hazan. Tel Aviv: Bar Ilan University Press, in press.

Schneider, Michael. "'Joseph and Osnat' and Early Jewish Mysticism." Hebrew. *Kabbalah* 3 (1998): 303–44.

Schoenfeld, Stuart. "Folk Judaism, Elite Judaism and the Role of Bar Mitzvah in the Development of the Synagogue and Jewish School in America." *Contemporary Jewry* 9 (1988): 67–85.

———. "Integration into the Group and Sacred Uniqueness: An Analysis of Adult Bat Mitzvah." In *Persistence and Flexibility: Anthropological Perspectives on the American Jewish Experience,* edited by Walter Zenner, 117–35. Albany: SUNY Press, 1985.

———. "Some Aspects of the Social Significance of Bar/Bat Mitzvah Celebrations." In *Essays in the Social and Scientific Study of Judaism and Jewish Society,* edited by Simcha Fishbane and Jack N. Lightstone with Victor Levin, 277–304. Montréal: Department of Religion, Concordia University, 1990.

———. "Theoretical Approaches to the Study of Bar and Bat Mitzvah." *Proceedings of the Ninth World Congress of Jewish Studies,* Division D, 2:119–26. Jerusalem, 1986.

Scholem, Gershom. "Lilith." In *Encyclopedia Judaica,* 11:245–49. Jerusalem: Keter, 1971.

Schremer, Adiel. "Nisu'in ve-Haqamat Mishpahah be-Yahadut Bavel bi-Tequfat ha-Talmud." Ph.D. diss., Hebrew University of Jerusalem, 1996.

Schultz, James A. *The Knowledge of Childhood in the German Middle Ages, 1100–1350.* Philadelphia: University of Pennsylvania Press, 1995.

Schwartz, Seth. *Imperialism and Jewish Society, 200 B.C.E. to 640 C.E.* Princeton: Princeton University Press, 2001.

Scult, Mel. *Judaism Faces the Twentieth Century: A Biography of Mordecai M. Kaplan.* Detroit: Wayne State University Press, 1993.

Sears, Elizabeth. *The Ages of Man: Medieval Interpretations of the Life Cycle.* Princeton: Princeton University Press, 1986.

Shahar, Shulamith. *Childhood in the Middle Ages.* London: Routledge, 1990.

———. *Growing Old in the Middle Ages: "Winter Clothes Us in Shadow and Pain."* Translated by Yael Lotan. London: Routledge, 1997.

———. "Infants, Infant Care, and Attitudes toward Infancy in the Medieval Lives of Saints." *Journal of Psychohistory* 10 (1982–83): 281–309

Shamgar-Handelman, Lea, and Don Handelman. "Celebrations of Bureaucracy: Birthday Parties in Israeli Kindergartens." *Ethnology* 30, no. 4 (1991): 293–312.

Shapiro, Mendel [Rabbi]. "Qeri'at ha-Torah by Women: A Halakhic Analysis," *Edah Journal* 1, no. 2 (Sivan 5761): 2–52. [The journal is available on line at www.edah.org.]

Shatzky, Yaakov. *Geshikhte fun Yidn in Varsha.* 2 vols. New York: YIVO, 1948.

Shatzmiller, Joseph. "Desecrating the Cross: A Rare Medieval Accusation." Hebrew. In *Mehqarim be-Toledot 'Am Yisrael ve-Erez Yisrael,* vol. 5, edited by B. Oded, 159–73. Haifa: University of Haifa, 1980.

———. "'Tumultus et Rumor in Synagoga.'" *AJS Review* 2 (1977): 227–55.

Sheehan, Michael M. *Marriage, Family, and Law in Medieval Europe: Collected Studies.* Toronto: University of Toronto Press, 1996.

———. ed. *Aging and the Aged in Medieval Europe.* Toronto: University of Toronto Press, 1990.

Shulman, Nisson E. *Authority and Community: Polish Jewry in the Sixteenth Century.* Hoboken, N.J.: KTAV, 1986.

Siegel, Richard. "Adult Bar Mitzvah." *Moment* 1, no. 4 (October 1975): 66–67.

Signer, Michael A. "Honour the Hoary Head: The Aged in the Medieval European Jewish Community." In *Aging,* edited by Michael M. Sheehan, 39–62.

Silber, Michael K. "The Emergence of Ultra-Orthodoxy: The Invention of a Tradition." In *The Uses of Tradition,* edited by Jack Wertheimer, 23–84. New York: Jewish Theological Seminary of America, 1992.

Soloveitchik, Haym. "Rupture and Reconstruction: The Transformation of Contemporary Jewry." *Tradition* 28, no. 4 (1994): 63–131.

Sperber, Daniel. "Customs of Mourning during the Counting of the Omer." In Daniel Sperber, *Why Jews Do What They Do: The History of Jewish Customs throughout the Cycle of the Jewish Year,* translated by Yaakov Elman, 86–101. Hoboken, N.J.: KTAV, 1999.

———. "Going to the Cemetery during the First Seven Days of Mourning." Hebrew. In Daniel Sperber, *Minhagei Yisrael,* 4:30–32.

———. "Lighting Candles after the Wedding." Hebrew. In Daniel Sperber, *Minhagei Yisrael,* 4:157–60.

———. "'May His Great Name.'" Hebrew. In Daniel Sperber, *Minhagei Yisrael,* 2:71–77.

———. *Minhagei Yisrael.* 6 vols. Jerusalem: Mosad Bialik, 1989–98.

———. "On Death, Burial and the Cemetery." Hebrew. In Daniel Sperber, *Minhagei Yisrael,* 6:81–119.

———. "Social Influence on Custom: Use of Wine during Circumcision and the Stratus of Women in Society." Hebrew. In Daniel Sperber, *Minhagei Yisrael,* [1]:60–66.

———. "Throwing Wheat near the Huppah." Hebrew. In Daniel Sperber, *Minhagei Yisrael,* 4:150–56.

———. "Wedding Rings That Are Not Wedding Rings." Hebrew. In Daniel Sperber, *Minhagei Yisrael,* 4:143–149.

———. "Wrapping the Neck of the Mourner and the Custom of Wrapping the Head." Hebrew. In Daniel Sperber, *Minhagei Yisreael,* 4:65–68.

Sperber, David. "The Huppah in Legal and Artistic Sources." Hebrew. In Daniel Sperber, *Minhagei Yisrael,* 4:78–148.

Spiegel, Yaakov. "The Woman as Circumciser—the Law and Its Development in the Semag." Hebrew. *Sidra* 5 (1989): 149–57.

Stein, Regina. "The Road to Bat Mitzvah in America." In *Women and American Judaism: Historical Perspectives,* edited by Pamela S. Nadell and Jonathan D. Sarna, 223–34. Hanover, N.H.: Brandeis University Press, 2001.

Stern, Shmuel Eliezer. *Sefer Hilekhot ve-Halikhot Eirusin ve-Nesu'in ha-Shalem: Pisqei Halakhot u-Minhagim be-'inyanei Tena'im, Eirusin, Hupah, Nesu'in, ve-Sheva' Berakhot.* Benei Beraq: Makhon Sha'arei Hora'ah. 1999.

———. "The Torah Education Rite among German Rabbis." Hebrew. *Zefunot* 1, no. 1 (fall 1988): 15–21.

Taglia, Kathryn Ann. "The Cultural Construction of Childhood: Baptism, Communion, and Confirmation." In *Women, Marriage, and Family in Medieval Christendom: Essays in Memory of Michael M. Sheehan, C. S. B.,* edited by Constance M. Rousseau and Joel T. Rosenthal [Studies in Medieval Culture 37], 255–87. Kalamazoo: Western Michigan University, 1998.

Tal, Uriel. "Mourners Kaddish." Hebrew. 1970. Reprint, In Uriel Tal, *Mythos u-Tevunah be-Yahadut Yameinu,* 221–32. Tel Aviv: Sifriyat Po'alim, 1987.

Talmage, Frank. "So Teach Us to Number Our Days: A Theology of

Longevity in Jewish Exegetical Literature." In *Aging,* edited by Michael M. Sheehan, 49–62.

Talmon, Sh[emaryahu]. "Bridegroom of Blood." Hebrew. *Eretz-Israel* 3 (1954): 93–96.

Ta-Shema/Ta-Shma, Israel. "Blessing on Circumcision." Hebrew. In Ta-Shema, *Minhag Ashkenaz ha-Qadmon.*

———. "By the Power of the Name (of God): On the History of a Forgotten Custom." Hebrew. *Bar-Ilan, Sefer ha-Shanah* 26–27 [Yitzhaq Gilat Festschrift] (1995), 389–99.

———. "Children in Medieval Germanic Jewry: A Perspective on Ariès from Jewish Sources." In *Studies in Medieval and Renaissance History* 12 (o.s. 22), edited by J. A. S. Evans and R. W. Unger, 263–80. New York: AMS Press, 1991.

———. "The Jewish Birthday." Hebrew. *Zion* 67 (2002): 19–24.

———. *Minhag Ashkenaz ha-Qadmon.* Jerusalem: Magnes, 1992.

———. "More on the Ashkenazi Origins of the Zohar." Hebrew. *Kabbalah* 3 (1998): 259–63.

———. *Ha-Nigleh she-ba-Nistar.* Exp. 2nd ed. N.p.: Ha-Kibbutz Ha-Me'uhad, 2001.

———. Review of Ivan G. Marcus, *Rituals of Childhood. Jewish Quarterly Review* 87, nos. 1–2 July–October 1996): 233–39.

———. "A Rite of Initiation: Its Sources, History, Symbolism, and Developments." Hebrew. *Tarbiz* 68, no. 4 (1999): 587–98.

———. "Some Matters concerning Mourner's Qaddish and Its Customs." Hebrew. In Ta-Shema, *Minhag Ashkenaz ha-Qadmon,* 299–310.

Trachtenberg, Joshua. *Jewish Magic and Superstition.* 1939. Reprint. Philadelphia: University of Pennsylvania Press, 2004.

Treggiari, Susan. *Roman Marriage: Iusti Coniuges from the Time of Cicero to the Time of Ulpian.* Oxford: Oxford University Press, 1991.

Trexler, Charles C. *The Christian at Prayer.* Binghamton: Medieval and Renaissance Texts and Studies, 1987.

Urbach, Ephraim E. "The Homiletical Interpretations of the Sages and the Expositions of Origen on Canticles, and the Jewish-Christian Disputa-

tion." In *Studies in Aggadah and Folk-Literature.* [Scripta Hierosolymitana, 22], edited by Joseph Heinemann and Dov Noy, 247–75. Jerusalem:
Magnes, 1971.

———. "On Accidentally Killing in a Crib." Hebrew. *Asufot* 1 [=Sefer ha-
Shanah le-Mada'ei ha-Yahadut], edited by Meir Benayahu, 319–32.
Jerusalem, 1987.

Valensi, Lucette. "Religious Orthodoxy or Local Tradition: Marriage Celebration in Southern Tunisia." In *Jews among Arabs: Contacts and Boundaries,* edited by Mark R. Cohen and Abraham L. Udovitch, 65–84.
Princeton: Darwin Press, 1989.

van Gennep, Arnold. *Rites of Passage.* Chicago: University of Chicago Press,
1960.

Warshaw, Mal. *Tradition: Orthodox Jewish Life in America.* New York:
Schocken Books, 1976.

Wasserteil, David. *Yalqut Minhagim.* Jerusalem, 1980.

Weber, Vicki L., ed. *The Rhythm of Jewish Time: An Introduction to Holidays
and Life-Cycle Events.* West Orange, N.J.: Behrman House, 1999.

Weckman, George. "Understanding Initiation." *History of Religions* 10
(1970–71): 62–79.

Weill, Shalva. "The Language and Ritual of Socialization: Birthday Parties
in a Kindergarten Context." *Man* 21 (1986): 329–41.

Weinstein, Roni. "'Ad Ya'avor Za'am ha-Na'arut': Yaldut, Na'arut, ve-
Hitbagrut ba-Hevrah ha-Yehudit be-Italiyah ba-Me'ah ha-16." Master's
thesis, Hebrew University of Jerusalem, 1989.

———. *Marriage Rituals Italian Style: A Historical Anthropological Perspective on Early Modern Italian Jews.* Leiden: E. J. Brill, 2004.

———. Review of Ivan G. Marcus, *Tiqsei Yaldut.* Hebrew. *Zion* 66 (2001):
389–95.

Weiser, Francis X. *Handbook of Christian Feasts and Customs.* New York: Harcourt Brace and Co., 1958.

Weissler, Chava. "Coming of Age in the Havurah Movement: Bar Mitzvah
in the Havurah Family." In *The Jewish Family: Myths and Reality,* edited
by Steven M. Cohen and Paula E. Hyman, 200–17.

————. "Measuring Graves and Laying Wicks." In *Judaism in Practice*, edited by Lawrence Fine, 61–73.

Weitzman, Michael. "The Origin of the Qaddish." In *Hebrew Scholarship and the Medieval World*, edited by Nicholas de Lange, 131–37. Cambridge: Cambridge University Press, 2001.

Wensinck, A. J. "Khitan" (Circumcision), 5:20–22. In *Encyclopedia of Islam*. 2nd ed. Edited by C. E. Bosworth et al. 10 vols. Leiden: E. J. Brill, 1960–2000.

Wieseltier, Leon. *Kaddish*. New York: Knopf, 1998.

Wolfson, Elliot R. "Circumcision and the Divine Name: A Study in the Transmission of Esoteric Doctrine." *Jewish Quarterly Review* 78, nos. 1–2 (July–October 1987): 77–112.

————. "Circumcision, Vision of God, and Textual Interpretation: From Midrashic Trope to Mystical Symbol." *History of Religions* 27, no. 2 (November 1987): 189–215.

Wolfthal, Diane, "Imaging the Self: Representations of Jewish Ritual in Yildish Books of Customs." In *Imagining the Self, Imagining the Other*, edited by Eva Frojnovic, 189–211. Leiden: E. J. Brill, 2002.

Wolowelsky, Joel B. *Women, Jewish Law and Modernity: New Opportunities in a Post-Feminist Age*. Hoboken, N.J.: KTAV, 1997.

Wood, Diana, ed. *The Church and Childhood* [Studies in Church History 31]. Oxford: Blackwell Publishers, 1994.

Ya'ari, Avraham. "The History of the Festival in Meron." Hebrew. *Tarbiz* 31 (1962): 72–101.

Yaron, Reuven. "Aramaic Marriage Contracts from Elephantine." *Journal of Semitic Studies* 3, no. 1 (1958).

Yaskowitz, Herbert A., ed. *The Kaddish Minyan: The Impact on Ten Lives*. Austin: Eakin Press, 2001.

Young, Robert J. C. *Colonial Desire: Hybridity in Theory, Culture and Race*. London: Routledge, 1995.

Yudlov, Yizhaq. "Italian Alphabet Charts." Hebrew. *Qiryat Sefer* 62, nos. 3–4 (1987): 930–32.

Zafrani, Haim. "Traditional Jewish Education in Morocco." Hebrew. In

Zakhur le-Avraham {Studies in Memory of Abraham Elameliach}, edited by H. Z. Hirschberg, 123–39. Jerusalem, 1972.

Zhao, Yilu. "Episcopal Church Offers Rite of Its Own." *New York Times,* Sunday, February 9, 2003, sec. 14, 6.

———. "New Age for an Ancient Rite." *New York Times,* Sunday, February 9, 2003, sec. 14, 1 and 6.

Zimmels, H. J. *Ashkenazim and Sephardim.* London: Oxford University Press, 1958.

Zimmer, Eric. "Body Gestures during Prayer." Hebrew. 1989. Reprint. In *'Olam ke-Minhago Noheg,* edited by Eric Zimmer, 72–113. Jerusalem: Merkaz Zalman Shazar, 1996.

———. "The Days of Impurity of a Parturient." Hebrew. In *'Olam ke-Minhago Noheg,* edited by Eric Zimmer, 220–39. Jerusalem: Merkaz Zalman Shazar, 1996.

———. "A Mourner's Wrapping the Head." Hebrew. 1985. Reprint. In *'Olam ke-Minhago Noheg,* edited by Eric Zimmer, 191–210. Jerusalem: Merkaz Zalman Shazar, 1996.

Zinner, Gavriel. *Sefer Nit'ei Gavriel.* Hilekhot Nesu'in. 2 vols. Jerusalem: Shemesh, 1998.

Zlotnick, Dov. *The Iron Pillar—Mishnah.* Jerusalem: Mosad Bialik, 1988.

[Zotenberg, H.]. *Catalogues des manuscrits hébreux et samaritains de la Bibliothèque impériale.* Paris, 1866.

Index

Aaron (biblical), 66, 221

Aaron ben Jacob Ha-Kohen of Lunel, R., 88–89, 92, 99, 168

Aaron Berechia ben Moses of Modena, R., 199

Abner ben Ner (biblical), 204, 205, 210

Abraham (biblical), 30, 37–38, 208; Abram becomes, 46; aging of, 196; and circumcision of Isaac, 43; covenant of, 166; marriage of Isaac and, 128–30, 136; mourning for Sarah, 202; weaning of Isaac and, 62, 63

Abraham bar Hiyya, R., 234

Abraham Ibn Ezra, R., 16

Abram (biblical), 46, 59, 127

Absalom (biblical), 194, 204–5

acculturation: inward, 4–6, 27, 124, 191; outward, 5, 9

Adam (biblical), 125, 127, 128, 131, 141, 295n76

Addison, Lancelot, 153, 156

adultery, 139, 141

adulthood, 13, 18, 82, 84

Africa, 45

afterlife, 223, 224–25, 238

age of majority. See boys, age of majority; girls, age of majority

"ages of man," 11–18, 44, 194

aging, 196–97

Ahab, King, 197

Aha bar Shabha of Sura, Gaon R., 147

Ahasuarus, King, 159–60

Akiva, R., 77, 197–98, 200, 237–38

Akkadians, 4

Albert, Prince, 183

Alfasi, 100

'aliyah/'aliyot, 64, 65, 84, 120; bar mitzvah and, 91, 116, 119; wedding ceremonies and, 118; women and, 115; Yahrzeit and, 235

347